A quartet of Hunters which appeared at one of the many Farnborough air displays.

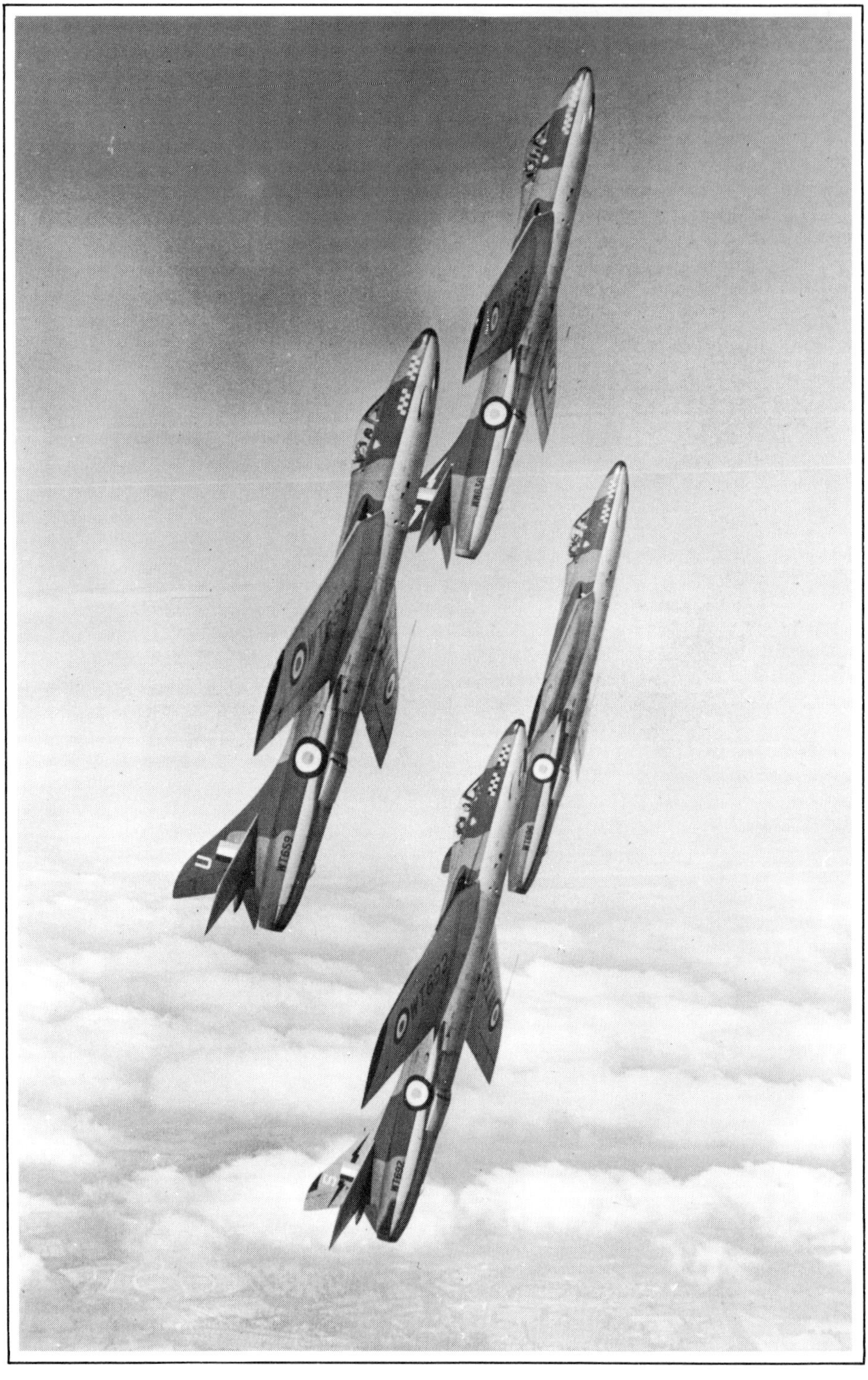

HAWKER HUNTER
Biography of a thoroughbred

Francis K. Mason
Foreword by Bill Bedford

PSL Patrick Stephens, Cambridge

© Francis K. Mason 1981

All rights reserved. No part of this publication may be reproduced, stored in a retrieval system or transmitted, in any form or by any means, electronic, mechanical, photocopying, recording or otherwise, without prior permission in writing from Patrick Stephens Limited.

First published in 1981

British Library Cataloguing in Publication Data
Mason, Francis Kenneth
  Hawker Hunter.
  1. Hunter (Turbojet fighter planes)
  I. Title
  623.74'64   TL686.H32

ISBN 0 85059 476 6

Frontispiece *Early formation aerobatics by Hunter 1s of No 54 (F) Squadron.*

Text photoset in 10 on 11 pt Plantin by Manuset Limited, Baldock, Herts. Printed and bound in Great Britain, on 120 gsm Huntsman Velvet coated cartridge by The Garden City Press, Letchworth, Herts, for the publishers Patrick Stephens Limited, Bar Hill, Cambridge, CB3 8EL, England.

Contents

Foreword by A.W. Bedford, OBE		4
Introduction		5
Chapter 1	Concept and design	7
Chapter 2	Early flight test and development	18
Chapter 3	Into service and into trouble	29
Chapter 4	The Hunter transformed	39
Chapter 5	The big engine	50
Chapter 6	Two-seaters for the RAF	69
Chapter 7	Ground support	82
Chapter 8	The Naval Hunters	87
Chapter 9	Exports—a lesson in orthodoxy	91
Chapter 10	Hunters overseas—the second phase	103
Chapter 11	The Hunter described	115
Chapter 12	In the cockpit	130
Chapter 13	The future	133
Appendices		134
Appendix 1	Hunter prototypes	135
Appendix 2	Hunter production	137
Appendix 3	Export and licence-built orders (new-build)	189
Appendix 4	Conversion of Hunters for export	206
Index		214

Foreword

Neville Duke made the Hunter's maiden flight on July 20 1951 and he played a vital part in the flight development programme. He deservedly hit the headlines with his stimulating Hunter demonstrations in the early 1950s, and by gaining the world speed record. Thus Neville and the Hunter became almost as synonymous as Sydney Camm and Hawker Aircraft Ltd were.

It was my privilege to join Hawker as an Experimental Test Pilot under Neville in 1951 sharing the Hunter programme and taking over from him as Chief Test Pilot from 1956 to 1967; thus the Hunter became an essential part of my life and one that I always reflect on with some pride and pleasure.

If ever there was a real pilot's aeroplane it was the Hunter but, like any worthwhile project, it had its fair share of teething troubles before it emerged as a winner. Problems were experienced with buffeting at high speed, longitudinal control, radio reliability, demisting, pitch-up, gun-firing, airbrakes, engine surge and the like. Their solution extended the ingenuity of the Hawker team but they were to be the making of an outstanding multi-purpose combat aircraft. It excelled in the roles of interceptor fighter, ground attack, reconnaissance, research vehicle and two-seater trainer, not forgetting the dramatic formation aerobatic performances. Not content to sit back on its laurels the T Mk 8M two-seat Hunter entered service in 1980 with the Royal Navy as the weapons system trainer for their V/STOL Sea Harrier FRS Mark 1.

For three decades pilots have enthused about the beautiful Hunter with its smooth aerodynamic lines, 4 × 30 mm cannon, the Rolls Royce Avon engine, outstandingly honest handling characteristics combined with a lively performance.

It was undoubtedly a classic thoroughbred of its time from the stables of one of the finest fighter manufacturers in the world.

A typical example of the Hunter's success was during a highly professional evaluation carried out in Switzerland in 1957 with intense competition from the Swedish Saab Draken, the Canadair Sabre 6, the French Mystère, the indigenous Swiss P16 and the North American F86. As a result Hawker received a contract for 100 aircraft to be followed in the early 1970s by a further order for 60 refurbished aircraft. Small wonder that 1,972 Hunters were manufactured and nearly 400 were refurbished to serve in 18 different countries throughout the world.

Thirty years after its first flight, hundreds of Hunters remain in active service, spread out over the world from the UK, Europe, the Middle East, India and South East Asia, still loved by pilots and highly respected by the potential opposition.

It is therefore most appropriate for the Hunter history to be put on record at this time by Frank Mason, who worked in the Project Office of Hawker during an important period of the aircraft's life and under that genius of fighter aircraft design, Sir Sydney Camm.

The story of the Hunter is a book well and interestingly written and one which will provide a valuable addition internationally to aeronautical libraries and to the book collections of aviation enthusiasts.

In conclusion and on behalf of the test pilots, may I take this opportunity to pay a tribute to the Hawker design and development teams for the outstanding aircraft they produced, in particular the Hunter, and to thank them for the close understanding that existed between pilot and engineer.

A.W. (Bill) Bedford, OBE, AFC, FRAeS
Hawker Experimental Test Pilot then Chief Test Pilot 1951-67

Introduction

I count myself fortunate in having worked in the Project Office of Hawker Aircraft Limited, both at the old Canbury Park Road works and in Richmond Road at Kingston-upon-Thames for eight years at a time when the Hunter fighter was entering service with the Royal Air Force and with many air forces overseas. Although much of our time was employed on later projects there were always constant demands for new variations of the basic Hunter design. Thus I was privileged to work under the late Sir Sydney Camm, a veritable Winston Churchill among the aviation fraternity, and a man to whom this nation owes an enormous debt. He had, after all, led the Hawker design team since 1925 and had produced the immortal Hurricane fighter that effectively won the Battle of Britain.

Camm was more than a genius; he was a wonderful character, possessed of shy charm, yet ruthless and uncompromising when so inclined. He demanded and obtained extraordinary loyalty among his staff, and in return always supported its members in the presence of outsiders. Many of its seniors had joined him twenty years previously and had come to know and respect his whims; maybe the strength of this team stemmed from an unparalleled continuity of service and experience. Around such a man as this it was inevitable that anecdote flourished.

No single member of a design team imposes his will upon the overall concept of an aeroplane more than the Chief Designer, and it was within Sydney Camm's character to impose his will. Being somewhat detached from the detailed work of the office, I was perhaps in an excellent position to watch and to listen to the Great Man, and many were the occasions when he would stroll up and 'pass the time of day'. In this unique situation I was able to appreciate some of his memorable remarks and, as these provide an insight to his technical philosophies, I have taken this opportunity to punctuate this book with these deathless saws.

As to the Hunter itself—for this is a biography of an aeroplane and not a man—there has been a tendency to bestow a personality upon the machine; this is only really credible when bestowed by the men who built and flew it. The Hunter has been a long-serving and faithful workhorse, a beast admired and respected by most, and perhaps hated by a few. It certainly had its tribulations in its early days, now almost forgotten, but these were overcome—they *had* to be, for after the disastrous eclipse of the Supermarine Swift, the Hunter was the only British fighter on the horizon.

Certainly as time passed this very beautiful aeroplane began to acquire a kind of charisma. It was as if the meticulous design treatment by the dedicated team, led by a man who possessed a unique appreciation of beauty and grace in the flying machine, was being reflected in the behaviour of the Hunter. The pilots quickly learned how to get the best from their aeroplanes and became their staunch advocates. And long after individual aircraft had passed their predicted fatigue life (the 'three-score years and ten' of the aeroplane), Hunters were being painstakingly refurbished and sent into the air again. There are numerous instances, as told in this book, in which individual Hunters have flown with three or four different air forces of the world, and at least one has flown with no fewer than seven! Little wonder that something of a mystique can be detected in the 'character' of the Hunter. It is said that in at least one air force Hunters will have served for almost fifty years before they are finally retired. Unquestionably this will not be matched by any other front-line aeroplane in history.

'I'm only interested in designing fighters; there's no finesse, no skill in designing anything else.'
(Sir Sydney Camm, to the author, September 1959.)

Photograph credits (Unless otherwise stated, all photographs are from the author's collection.) R.C.B. Ashworth 185; British Aerospace 80, 110, 129; *Fotodienst,* Emmen 197; Hawker Aircraft Ltd Endpapers, 7, 9, 10, 13, 16, 19, 20, 23, 27, 28, 29, 31, 35, 36, 37, 38, 40, 44, 46, 49, 51, 53, 56, 59, 60, 71, 73, 83, 84, 97, 100, 118, 119, 124, 166; Hawker Siddeley Aviation Ltd 80, 83, 86, 89, 96, 104, 107, 111, 112; Eric Hayward 100, 104, 112, 132; *Koninklijke Luchtmacht* 100; *Luchtmachtvoorlichtdienst* 92; Ministry of Defence 49, 66; Cyril Peckham 73, 78; Rolls-Royce Ltd 53; Sir W.G. Armstrong Whitworth Aircraft Ltd 35.

Chapter 1

Concept and design

'There can be no economy where there is no efficiency.'
(Benjamin Disraeli to his constituents, October 3 1868.)

When the Second World War ended in September 1945, Great Britain emerged from the holocaust as the third most powerful nation on earth, after the United States and the Soviet Union. In the sphere of technology—other than the application of nuclear physics to warfare—Britain still led the world, particularly in aeronautical sciences. Evidence of this leadership was provided by the progress already achieved in the development of the gas turbine and its associated advanced metallurgy. Britain alone among the wartime Allies had fielded jet-propelled fighters in operational service, while her jet engines had provided the basis on which American technology in this sphere came to be based. Already she was preparing plans for jet-powered commercial air travel—plans that would mature one day in the magnificent Comet airliner.

Britain's technological lead, however, was to be shortlived, just as it had been after the 1918 Armistice. The war had impoverished the nation, and post-war austerity, combining with governmental vacillation, dictated a policy of military cutback and research deceleration. In truth the path of aviation progress had reached a crossroads: the advent of the jet engine had, at this very moment, brought the aeroplane to the threshold of the

Hawker's first essay in jet propulsion; the beautiful P.1040, VP401, with Sqn Ldr T.S. Wade at the controls.

speed of sound—an area of aviation science which demanded highly complex and costly research programmes.

On previous occasions the British aircraft industry had been capable of financing most of its own research, and many of the courageous 'private ventures' of the pre-war era had brought their own rewards through substantial government and export orders. Indeed, some of the war-winning aeroplanes had been conceived and launched with privately subscribed finance.

Post-war Britain was deemed no place to canvass support for expensive technological innovation. The end of the war brought widespread cancellation of military orders, and many factories and workforces were working to meet the demands of peace.

Nevertheless, by adopting the simple, doctrinaire policy of military neglect, the Attlee government closed its eyes to reality; instead it chose to bequeath the fruits of world leadership, first by default, to America; and soon afterwards, by premeditated export of jet engines, to the Soviet Union. Without careful study of the consequence of this neglect, the British socialist administration in 1945-46 created a technological wilderness that was to remain relatively fallow for close on twenty years, while other nations reaped the benefits of carefully planned continuity of effort.

Perhaps it was too much to expect post-war Britain to arm herself against a Third World War so soon, yet the division between military necessity and research continuity quickly became blurred in the scramble for political capital. It was as if the lesson of the old 'ten year rule' of the 1930s had never been learned.

In the field of military aviation Britain, supposedly secure in the belief that the momentum of wartime research and development programmes would carry her through the convalescent years ahead, made no provision to introduce new equipment into service, and only half-heartedly sponsored a pitifully austere research investigation into the problems of high-speed flight. In front line service the Meteor, Vampire, Tempest, Hornet, Mosquito, Lancaster and Lincoln—all of which had flown during the war—were to provide the backbone of the RAF for a further ten years. In America the F-84 and F-86 jet fighters and B-45 four-jet bomber (all unquestionably second-generation aircraft) would enter service well within five years, and provide a lead over Britain that would never be eliminated.

The lack of research funding between 1945 and 1948 deprived the RAF of an up-to-date jet fighter with which to play its part in the Korean War, and it was only with the return of the Churchill administration to office in 1951 that remedies were put in hand. But a further three years passed before Britain could field a jet fighter capable of matching American in-service equipment. This was Sydney Camm's superb Hawker Hunter.

Alas, much damage had already been done. The apathy and prevarication by government and Treasury alike in the late 1940s prevented the Hunter from entering service in step with the technology it represented, with the inevitable result that the natural development towards advanced technology came to be slowed disastrously. And history has demonstrated time and again the folly of leapfrogging essential research.

It was nevertheless in this troubled environment that the Hunter was conceived, was given life and survived to pursue a distinguished career the world over. Its record of longevity in the Royal Air Force is unequalled.

* * *

Leaving aside the strategic situation that faced Britain after the Second World War, the Royal Air Force was in 1946 engaged on the one hand in adjusting to the substantially reduced appropriations voted by Parliament, and on the other in introducing into service

The Hawker P.1081 'all-swept' research aircraft, VX279, shown here at the 1950 Royal Air Force Display at Farnborough, in company with the prototype English Electric Canberra, Supermarine 510 and (scarcely visible) de Havilland Venom prototype.

those aircraft the bulk of whose development costs had already been absorbed. To achieve the former the RAF had to contract swiftly as squadron after squadron was disbanded, and many second line and obsolete aircraft were scrapped and wartime aircrews demobilised. The fighter aircraft to be retained or introduced into service were the Meteor and Vampire jet day fighters, the Hornet and Tempest propeller day fighters and the Mosquito propeller night fighter.

These five aircraft had two characteristics in common. All were armed with four 20 mm Hispano cannon, and all were effectively at the end of their development potential. In other words, there was no immediate prospect of phasing into RAF Fighter Command progressively improved aircraft without either radical design evolution or expensive research in the fields of engines, armament or aerodynamics—or a combination of all three.

The trouble was that no one at the Air Ministry or the Ministry of Supply was prepared to suggest with any authority in what direction the development of military aviation should be pointed. To demand higher speed would be to authorise huge expenditure on engine development, bearing in mind the disproportionate increase in power required to

The P.1081, VX279, after addition of wing fences early in 1951, shortly before its loss with the death of 'Wimpey' Wade, seen here at the controls.

achieve relatively small increases in aircraft speed. Who was to suggest that the age-old four-cannon armament was inadequate? And who was the RAF likely to be called on to fight in 1946?

If not to answer these questions, the solution seemed straightforward, to introduce the Meteor and Vampire into service and leave them there as long as it took to discover where military aviation was moving, and only then try to produce new designs accordingly. This expedient, however, took no account of the development time scale needed by a modern military aircraft in peacetime. The Meteor had progressed from design to operational service in four years during the war; in peacetime this could be expected to increase by about 50 per cent.

Faced by an almost total lack of public money to support research, the responsibility for this now fell upon the British aircraft industry. And imaginative though the immediate fruits of this private research were, they could not compare with the benefits of a centrally co-ordinated, publicly funded research programme. It is therefore interesting to examine the trains of thought that existed in the Operational Requirements Branch at the Air Ministry for, whether or not money could be provided to humour these deliberations, the views expressed were those of professional airmen whose job it was to look into the future.

To start with, when it became clear that any significant performance beyond that of the Meteor (which, let it be said, established a new World Absolute Speed Record of 606 mph in November 1945) would be out of the question, resort was made to the age-old formula of increased armament. The belief persisted that, deprived of substantial speed advantage over an adversary, only one firing pass would be possible for an interceptor fighter, so that the weapon fired on that occasion must be lethal. Unfortunately the old 20 mm Hispano cannon was the only reliable gun available, and recourse was sought from a number of very large calibre weapons—including the 57 mm Molins gun that had been used by the Mosquito XVIII on anti-shipping strikes during the war. Several fighter specifications were drafted around such armament proposals, but it soon became clear that the unwieldy bulk of these guns—even assuming they could be aimed—wholly compromised the performance of any realistic fighter design. Among these Specifications were F.43/46 and F.44/46, issued to the aircraft industry in the hope that someone would come up with an efficient general-purpose fighter that could, with a minimum of adaptation, be used both by day and by night. Several companies tendered proposals, among them Gloster, de Havilland and Hawker (the latter proposing a design, the P.1054, with twin Armstrong-Siddeley Sapphire turbojets mounted close to the fuselage). As in an examination,

Left *Original nose intake ducting mock-up of the P.1067 showing the centrebody fairing for the radar ranging and the extremely confined space for the cockpit between the ducts.*

Above right *Full-size installation mock-up of the P.1067; by this time, 1949, the engine air intakes have been moved to the wing roots, but the tailplane is still shown in the high position.*

wherein neither examiner nor student understands the question fully, so these specifications failed to produce any satisfactory answers.

To discover why Hawker in particular failed to come up with a satisfactory solution, one must go back once more to 1944 to examine the work being done by Sydney Camm's design team at that time. Hawker Aircraft Limited was very nearly a non-starter in the race to initiate jet aircraft designs in those early years. Throughout the war the design staff had been fully occupied with the Hurricane, Typhoon and Tempest fighters, all produced in large numbers which had filled the factories. Terminating the piston-engine era were the excellent Fury and Sea Fury fighters, and these carried the company through the lean years when so many other aeroplanes and designs were discarded as 'surplus to requirements'.

However, towards the end of 1944, at the moment that the Meteor was beginning to demonstrate the feasibility of jet aircraft in service, Hawker submitted a scheme employing the proposed Rolls-Royce B.41 turbojet (later to become the Nene) mounted amidships in the Fury. In this design, the P.1035, the jet engine exhausted through the tail, but soon afterwards a more detailed proposal introduced bifurcated tail pipes exhausting on either side of the fuselage aft of the wings.

During 1945 the Project Office staff developed this design further and in October that year the management decided to go ahead with the manufacture of an unarmed prototype at private expense under the designation P.1040. At this point the Air Ministry declined further interest in the project on the grounds that it promised no improvement beyond the Meteor Mark IV. The Admiralty on the other hand encouraged Camm to draw up proposals for a naval interceptor, based on the P.1040, which might in due course supersede the Sea Fury—then about to enter production. This in turn led the Admiralty to issue Specification N.7/46, and in due course to the beautiful and successful Sea Hawk naval fighter. 'Thank God for the Navy', as Sydney Camm said in a letter dated August 21 1946.

Whereas the Sea Hawk followed a separate course, its development and production being ultimately taken off Hawker's hands by Sir W.G. Armstrong Whitworth Aircraft Limited, the prototype P.1040 had a direct bearing on the early concept of the Hunter.

The first prototype P.1067 in the course of hand-built construction at Richmond Road.

The P.1040 prototype, eventually supported by public funding, first flew at Boscombe Down on September 2 1947 and, with the limited power—4,500 lb thrust—of the Nene I turbojet, returned a modest speed of about Mach 0.77 (510 mph) in spite of a relatively thin wing of 0.095 thickness/chord ratio. However, perhaps stung by the Air Ministry's lack of interest in the project, Camm had in 1946 proposed to fit swept wings to the P.1040 (under the designation P.1047) and this attracted the attention of the Royal Aircraft Establishment at Farnborough. It must be remembered that little of a practical nature was known in Britain at this time about the detailed aerodynamic characteristics of swept wings, almost all the fruits of German research having been sequestrated by America at the end of the war. Discussions dragged on throughout 1946 about the design of the P.1047's proposed wing form and in November that year Specification E.38/46 was agreed between Hawker and the Ministry of Supply, and two examples of the swept-wing P.1040 (designated P.1052) were ordered. These were to embody a sweepback of 35 degrees on the quarter-chord and a thickness/chord ratio of 0.10. With a 5,000 lb thrust Nene 2, a maximum speed in excess of Mach 0.86 (560 mph at 36,000 ft) was expected.

In the event the two P.1052s turned out to be extremely useful aeroplanes and were popular with everyone who flew them. They proved capable of speeds up to Mach 0.90 (595 mph at 36,000 ft) and possessed some pleasant flying characteristics. They did, however, introduce the phenomenon known as Dutch rolling, and when flown in mock combat against a Meteor 4 were found to possess inadequate elevator control probably owing to the fact that while the mainplane was swept, the tailplane was not. While Hawker busied itself to redesign one of the P.1052s to incorporate all-swept tail surfaces and a straight-through tail jetpipe, Supermarine were already flying the Type 510 research aircraft to Specification E.41/46 which was capable of exceeding the performance of the P.1052 without its tendency to Dutch roll. It may thus be said that Hawker in 1948 was lagging behind its competitors in practical experience of trouble-free high-subsonic flight.

In the Hawker design office Camm had been forcing the pace. Model tests had already confirmed the limitations of the P.1052, and towards the end of 1947 his project designers

Concept and design

schemed up an aircraft employing the new Rolls-Royce A.J.65, soon to become the Avon axial-flow turbojet which was expected to produce around 6,500 lb installed thrust.

Several design conferences, centred on this proposal, were held at the Ministry of Supply between September and November 1947, and early the following year Specification F.3/48 was issued to Hawker. This called for a single-seat interceptor fighter, capable of Mach 0.94 (620 mph at 36,000 ft, 724 mph at sea level), to be armed with either four 20 mm Hispano or two of the new 30 mm Aden guns, to possess a normal sortie endurance of 60 minutes, and to be powered by either an Avon or Armstrong-Siddeley Sapphire engine. An ejector seat was mandatory and provision was required for a yet-unfinalised radar-ranging gunsight.

Camm's design staff produced a total of twelve alternative design studies to F.3/48 over a period of about six months under the designations P.1067, 1069, 1070 and 1071; some of these are shown in the accompanying drawings. The basic design, referred to as the P.1067/1, was a mid-wing aircraft with an Avon engine mounted in the fuselage amidships with annular nose air intake and exhausting through a long jet pipe in the extreme tail. The wing, of 0.095 thickness/chord ratio, was swept back 42½ degrees on the quarter-chord and a straight-tapered tailplane was mounted on top of the fin. The mainwheels of a wide-track tricycle undercarriage retracted inwards into the wings and the nosewheel forward into a well between the split nose intake ducts. Four 20 mm Hispano guns were proposed, all of them mounted in the underside of the fuselage nose. Fuel was to be carried in the wings and in the fuselage immediately aft of the Martin-Baker ejector seat. The small scanner for the radar-ranging gunsight was to be located in a cone set in the centre of the nose intake.

A general view of the Richmond Road experimental shops. In the background the second prototype P.1067, WB195, takes shape, its Avon engine awaiting installation alongside. Immediately following it can be seen the centre and front fuselage of the third prototype, WB202; in the foreground is the centre fuselage mock-up for WB202 with a manufacturer's mock-up of the Sapphire engine. A photograph taken at about the time of the first prototype's maiden flight.

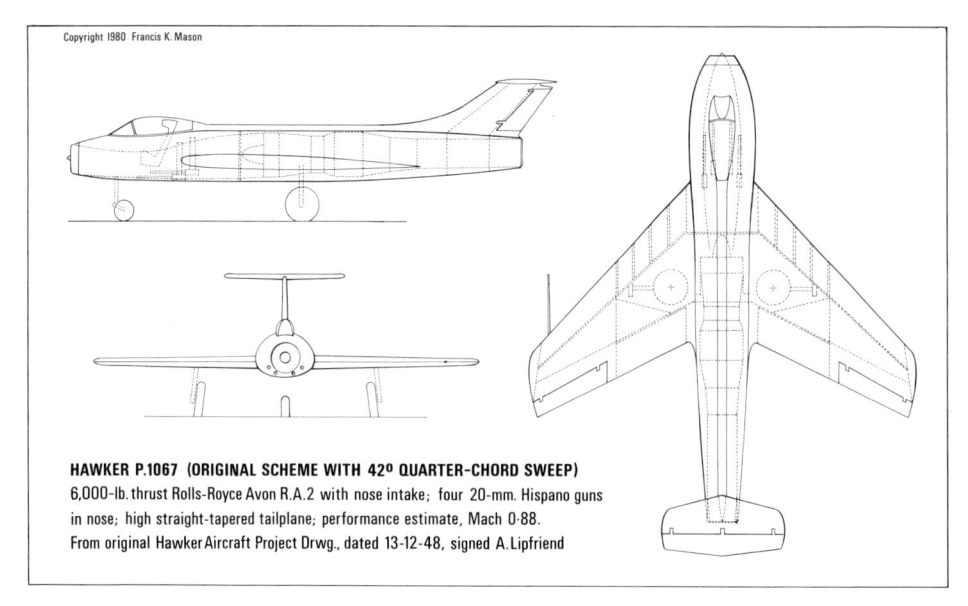

HAWKER P.1067 (ORIGINAL SCHEME WITH 42° QUARTER-CHORD SWEEP)
6,000-lb. thrust Rolls-Royce Avon R.A.2 with nose intake; four 20-mm. Hispano guns in nose; high straight-tapered tailplane; performance estimate, Mach 0·88.
From original Hawker Aircraft Project Drwg., dated 13-12-48, signed A. Lipfriend

As originally designed, the aircraft would carry a total of 300 gallons of fuel—according to initial drag and thrust figures sufficient to meet range and endurance demands—and would take off at around 15,100 lb all-up. Design figures suggested a maximum level speed of Mach 0.94 and transonic speed in a shallow dive at altitude.

Encouraged by these figures, which exceeded those of the North American XP-86 Sabre, which had just flown in prototype form, the P.1067 secured Air Ministry approval, and in June 1948 Hawker was notified that a contract would be drawn up for the manufacture of three prototypes. Thus was the Hunter conceived.

There can be no denying the value derived by the Americans from the fruits of German experience in high speed flight, for this contributed directly to the design of the Sabre's wing. Without that start Britain had been groping for first-hand data, and although it has been fairly authoritatively suggested that de Havilland's small DH 108 swept-wing, tailless research aircraft was the first aeroplane to achieve transonic flight in a dive in September 1946 (before it disintegrated, killing Geoffrey de Havilland, Jr), Britain was still about four years from achieving transonic flight by a military prototype.

In the Soviet Union the early examples of the MiG-15 were probably flying or nearing the flight stage, following the ill-advised sale of Rolls-Royce Tay centrifugal-flow turbojet engines in 1947 to that country by the British government; there is now little doubt but that this 'gift' of modern technology provided the Russians with the impetus required to accelerate their indigenous engine technology.

Without doubt, however, the fighter which at this moment led the world in performance and was closest to operational status was the excellent F-86. Its sole criticism was to be its puny armament of six 0.5-in guns.

With agreement reached on the design parameters of Specification F.3/48, F.43/46 was temporarily withdrawn, an interim night fighter requirement being formulated in F.24/48, this being met by adaptation of the Meteor (in the Meteor NF Mark 11), while F.44/46 was replaced by F.4/48 which in turn brought forth the DH 110—ultimately to join the Royal Navy as the Sea Vixen. An amalgam of F.43/46 and F.4/48 produced the Gloster Javelin. Thus, in this self-generated confusion, can be detected the slow

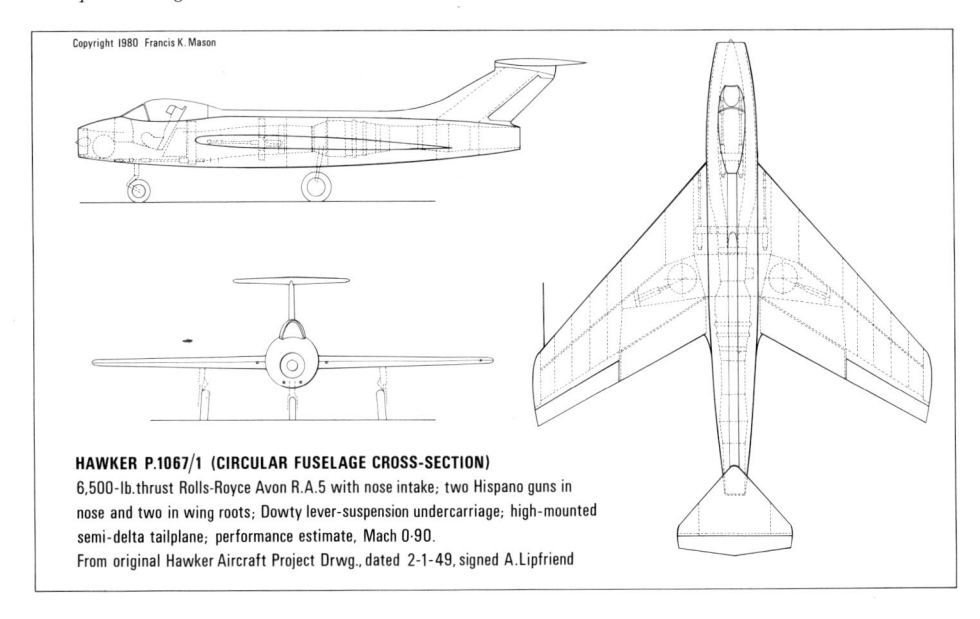

HAWKER P.1067/1 (CIRCULAR FUSELAGE CROSS-SECTION)
6,500-lb.thrust Rolls-Royce Avon R.A.5 with nose intake; two Hispano guns in nose and two in wing roots; Dowty lever-suspension undercarriage; high-mounted semi-delta tailplane; performance estimate, Mach 0·90.
From original Hawker Aircraft Project Drwg., dated 2-1-49, signed A. Lipfriend

realisation that development of day and night/all weather fighters in Britain must, at least for the time being, follow different paths, and that there was still a place for the relatively nimble single-seat interceptor, while the extensively-equipped radar-carrying night fighter demanded two crew members in a much larger airframe.

At the end of 1948 work started on installation mock-ups of the P.1067 in the Richmond Road experimental shops, while wind tunnel work was initiated to determine optimum wing and tail planforms. By the time detail design commenced, however, fundamental alterations were being undertaken. Initial experience with the P.1052 suggested the advisability of increasing the tailplane sweepback, and its planform was

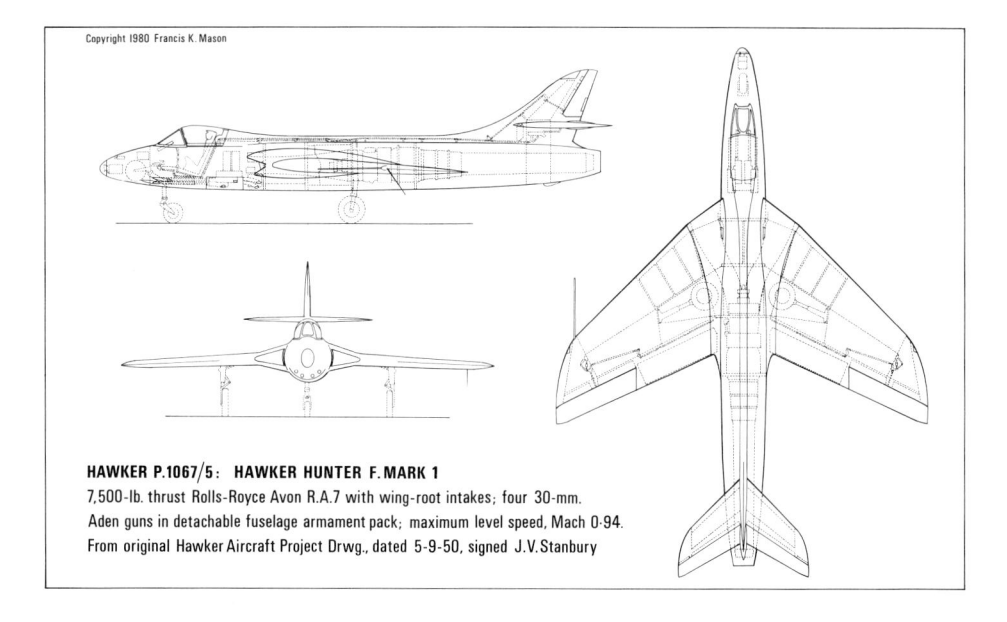

HAWKER P.1067/5: HAWKER HUNTER F.MARK 1
7,500-lb. thrust Rolls-Royce Avon R.A.7 with wing-root intakes; four 30-mm. Aden guns in detachable fuselage armament pack; maximum level speed, Mach 0·94.
From original Hawker Aircraft Project Drwg., dated 5-9-50, signed J.V. Stanbury

Above *An early flight Rolls-Royce Avon R.A.7 engine.* **Above right** *First flight Armstrong Siddeley Sapphire engine for WB202 about to be installed in the airframe; note annular combustion chamber, compared with the early Avon's individual 'cans'.*

altered to semi-delta. The ungainly nose contours were radically slimmed, thus causing two of the 20 mm guns to be moved to the wing roots. Next, Rolls-Royce raised doubts as to the efficiency of the long intake ducts, and asked if shorter, wing-root intakes (similar to those on the Sea Hawk) could be incorporated. Faced with the alternative of reducing the armament by discarding the wing root guns, Camm resisted this argument until told that the centrebody location for the radar-ranging scanner was too restricted and inaccessible. It is also only fair to point out that Camm had been expressing concern at the increasingly cramped nature of the cockpit as more and more equipment was demanded by the Air Ministry.

Thus, faced with something of a *fait accompli*, the Hawker designers altered the P.1067 to include wing root intakes and produced new, slim nose contours which incorporated a scanner radome in the extreme tip, yet at the same time managed to increase the cockpit volume by some 50 per cent.

In due course the tunnel tests also foreshadowed control problems with the high-mounted tailplane (possibly confirmed by trouble later experienced by the Gloster Javelin), and this was accordingly moved down to a position at roughly one-third of the height of the fin, whose tip was now given a graceful tapering curve.

The P.1067 had by April 1949 arrived at its finalised aerodynamic shape, but the matter of armament continued unresolved. Camm had remained unconvinced by the arguments for heavier gun armament until confronted by evidence of the very substantially increased firepower of the compact 30 mm Aden gun, and it was quite possible that he might have remained satisfied with an armament of two nose-mounted 30 mm guns; this was, after all, the armament adopted by the contemporary Supermarine Swift. However when one of his installation design staff, Mr. C.F.G. Cray, suggested that the gun bodies of four such weapons together with their magazines could be accommodated in a removable pack located behind the cockpit, Camm quickly realised the value and ingenuity of such a scheme, adopted a complete *volte face* and henceforth became its staunch advocate. Such a devastating gun armament was not, of course, unprecedented (the German Messerschmitt Me 262 jet fighter had been similarly armed more than four years previously), and both Javelin and DH 110 were being developed to mount four Aden guns; but the Hawker P.1067 was at that time the only single-seat, single-engine fighter in the world to feature this battery.

For a day interceptor, in which rapid turnround times between sorties was deemed of paramount importance, the detachable gunpack could be replaced quickly by a pre-loaded unit and this, together with the inclusion of a single refuelling point, found quick approval in the Operational Requirements Branch of the Air Ministry. Nevertheless, by the time final sanction for the four-Aden pack was received from the Ministry of Supply, construction of the first prototype P.1067 had got underway and it was agreed that this aircraft would feature ballast in lieu of armament.

Meanwhile the matter of engine availability cast doubt on the wisdom of a single choice of powerplant. Not only was the Swift destined to use the Rolls-Royce Avon, but the English Electric Canberra would soon be flying with two such engines, as would several other aircraft destined for quantity production. The decision was therefore taken for one of the three P.1067 prototypes to be powered by a Sapphire engine, the other two retaining the Avon. If successful, both versions would be ordered into quantity production for the RAF.

In common with normal practice at that time the prototypes were 'hand-built'; that is to say the aircraft were produced in *ad hoc* jigs from drawings prepared in the experimental design offices, a process later generally acknowledged as being both costly and time-consuming. It should, however, be recalled that many now-seemingly outdated practices and circumstances still persisted. One manufacturer could well be producing several different aircraft in quantity simultaneously, and most British aircraft companies retained fully autonomous experimental departments so as not to disrupt the smooth flow of quantity production. So it was at Kingston with Sea Fury production tailing off to make way for Sea Hawks. The factory itself was one of the oldest in the country (having originated as Aircraft Factory No 1 early in the Kaiser's War for the production of Sopwith aircraft).

The P.1067 prototype jigs commenced assembly in December 1949 and by the following April much of the first fuselage structure was complete, and a start was made on the second. As might be expected, some dismay was evoked when the following month the Ministry of Supply announced its intention of abandoning the 30 mm Aden gun on the grounds of cost, a step stoutly condemned by Camm and others. A period of confusion and indecision followed, but six weeks later it was revoked and manufacture of the three P.1067s went ahead smoothly. ☐

'I may not suffer fools gladly, but Heaven save me from the accountants and economists of this world.'

(Sir Sydney Camm, on numerous occasions.)

Chapter 2

Early flight test and development

'All my aeroplanes are "pilots' aeroplanes"; but then all my pilots are "designers' pilots".'
(Sir Sydney Camm, circa 1959.)

Hawker has always been fortunate to employ outstanding test pilots, men whose application and skill have placed them right at the top of their profession. There has moreover existed what can perhaps best be described as a benevolent rapport at Hawker between those in the cockpit and those at the drawing board, and this has probably been more evident at Hawker than elsewhere in the aircraft industry. That is not to suggest that downright friction necessarily existed elsewhere, but the common desire 'to get things right from the start' that flourished at Kingston, Brooklands, Langley and Dunsfold was reflected in the pride which Camm always professed in his pilots, and vice versa. Just as Camm himself rose to the pinnacle of his profession, men like 'George' Bulman, 'Gerry' Sayer, Philip Lucas, Hubert Broad, 'Roly' Beamont, Frank Murphy, Neville Duke, Bill Bedford, 'Wimpey' Wade, Hugh Merewether and Duncan Simpson must share the accolades for the fact that from 1925 up to the present day there has never been a moment when Britain's air forces have been without a Kingston-designed aeroplane in first line service, and that these aeroplanes 'have been got right'. These pilots not only became famous among the public at large through their achievements but were widely respected among the whole flying fraternity.

As the first P.1067 prototype, WB188, neared completion the company's Chief Test Pilot was Squadron Leader T.S. ('Wimpey') Wade, and his assistant Squadron Leader Neville Duke. Wade had been a distinguished fighter pilot during the Second World War and was a well-known member of No 54 (Fighter) Squadron, flying Spitfires during the Battle of Britain. Neville Duke had also been a very successful fighter pilot and was the highest-scoring Allied pilot in the Middle East and Mediterranean theatres with 28 air combat victories to his credit. It thus fell to these pilots to keep abreast of the design characteristics of the new fighter prototypes, and to discuss with the design team such features as cockpit layout, control response, and handling and performance parameters.

Then a tragic setback occurred. Wade, who had gained considerable experience while flying the P.1040, Sea Hawk and P.1052, lost his life in an accident to the P.1081—the 'all-swept' development of the P.1052—on April 3 1951; the cause of the accident was never fully established. Neville Duke, who would in any case have shared with Wade much of the early flight testing of the P.1067, was now appointed Chief Test Pilot. In many respects the tall, slim Duke was the antithesis of the stocky, ebullient Wade, yet both shared a characteristic finesse in their flying. Duke possessed a rare degree of tact when it came to a discussion of a matter with the design office, although for all his inherent shyness and reserve there were seldom instances of prolonged disagreement, and if a compromise was found to be the only solution, the remedy tended to favour the pilot.

Squadron Leader Neville Duke in the cockpit of the first prototype prior to its first flight at Boscombe Down.

That Duke was a magnificent, analytical pilot was unquestioned—probably one of the greatest of all British pilots.

By the standards of the day, the P.1067 was a long time coming to the flight stage, more than three years elapsing between project design and first flight. The reasons for this delay have been explained, and the prototype emerged a very different aeroplane from that first envisaged early in 1948. It emerged as a surpassingly beautiful aeroplane in a world already becoming increasingly accustomed to stark angularity in high speed aeroplanes.

Towards the end of June 1951 the finishing touches were being put to the first prototype, WB188, and the whole aircraft was given a glossy pale green paint finish. It was then dismantled and loaded on to a lorry, starting out from Kingston in the early hours of the 27th, and arriving at the Aeroplane and Armament Experimental Establishment at Boscombe Down, Wiltshire, later the same day. The next day the Hawker Resident Technical Officer (RTO) endorsed the flutter clearance, and on the 29th WB188 was given full design clearance for flight.

The choice of Boscombe Down for the P.1067's first flight was made on account of the lack of adequate facilities yet installed at Hawker's new test field at Dunsfold, Surrey. The old airfield at Langley, Buckinghamshire, which had proved entirely adequate during the war, and had sufficed for aircraft like the Sea Fury, was unsuitable for jet aircraft (owing mainly to its proximity to London-Heathrow airport) with the result that much of the Sea Hawk flying was carried out from the airfield at Farnborough, Hampshire, until Dunsfold could be made ready.

Even before WB188 was ready to fly, Hawker had received an Instruction to Proceed on preparations for production (on October 20 1950), and on March 14 1951 Contract No 5910 was raised by the Ministry of Supply to cover the production of 198 aircraft at Kingston at a unit cost initially estimated at £172,000 including powerplant. With the certainty of further production orders in the offing, the Hawker Siddeley Group Board of Directors decided to close down production of the Sea Hawk at Kingston and transfer all future development of this aircraft to Sir W.G. Armstrong Whitworth Aircraft Ltd, at Coventry. In the event only 35 production Sea Hawks were completed at Kingston.

Returning to WB188 at Boscombe Down, the aircraft was reassembled during June 28-

30, the first flight engine being received and installed at the same time. The first engine run was carried out on July 1, and weighing to check all-up weight and centre of gravity position was completed two days later. Thus far progress towards the first flight had been trouble-free, but on the 8th, during the initial taxiing runs, Duke experienced trouble with the differential wheel braking system, a problem that occupied Dunlop for ten days before the snag was rectified.

On July 20, however, Duke expressed himself satisfied with the feel of the aircraft after a number of fast runs along the runway and, after checking the fuel state at 220 gallons, flew WB188 off the ground for a 47-minute flight over Wiltshire, Hampshire and Dorset. During this first flight he took the aircraft up to about 32,000 feet and performed a series of fairly gentle manoeuvres before descending to 10,000 feet to carry out stalls at various flap settings and with undercarriage up and down. At no time did he attempt transonic flight, but kept his speed below Mach 0.88. On landing Duke reported that he was delighted with the new aeroplane and remarked that it handled beautifully. At first, on checking the fuel consumption during the flight, doubt was cast on the consumption figures provided by Rolls-Royce, until it was discovered after several further flights that the rear fuselage fuel tank has been leaking a significant quantity of fuel in flight. Duke also gave his opinion that the centre of pressure seemed slightly far aft for comfort and, following confirmation by wind tunnel tests, it was found possible to move this forward.

Flying by WB188 continued during August and early the following month Duke flew it at the Society of British Aircraft Constructors' display at Farnborough. For all the disruption caused by the attendance at this show to the flight schedule, Duke nevertheless managed to combine useful development work with his characteristically polished flying displays.

Much of October was spent on performance measurement, Duke doing about nine hours' flying in WB188 before the aircraft was completely dismantled for inspection, to carry out a number of minor modifications and to instal a production R.A.7 Avon engine (No 244) with variable swirl. The first prototype did not fly again until the end of April 1952 by which time an extensive programme of strength testing of a structural specimen had been completed. During this programme the specimen had failed at 57 per cent on November 28 1951 in the c.p. back condition, but had comfortably exceeded proof loading in the c.p. forward condition. However, after local strengthening (achieved at a mere 4 lb weight penalty) the strength tests were successfully passed when the specimen achieved 112 per cent before failure in the c.p. back condition.

On May 5 Duke first flew the second P.1067 (now officially named the Hunter), WB195, from Dunsfold. From the start this aeroplane was powered by a production R.A. 7 Avon and featured full military equipment, including four Aden guns and radar ranging gunsight. However, it had not all been plain sailing hitherto, and prior to the dismantling of WB188 Duke had remarked on two flying characteristics of the aircraft which would probably meet with Service disapproval. The first was a high frequency vibration apparently emanating at the rear of the aircraft at high subsonic speed (the P.1067 had still to achieve transonic speed); and the second was the aircraft's very poor deceleration capabilities—of as vital importance in combat as high speed and manoeuvr-

Top right *Resplendent in its pale green finish, WB188, ready for starting up at Boscombe Down. Note the anti-spin parachute fairing over the tailpipe.* **Centre right** *Airborne at last, WB188 takes off on its first flight.* **Right** *A magnificent in-flight study made by the famous air photographer, Cyril Peckham, of WB188 and Neville Duke. The beautiful shape of the Hunter is never more apparent than in this picture of the aeroplane before its acquisiton of wing leading-edge extensions, airbrake, ammunition link collectors and wing pylons.*

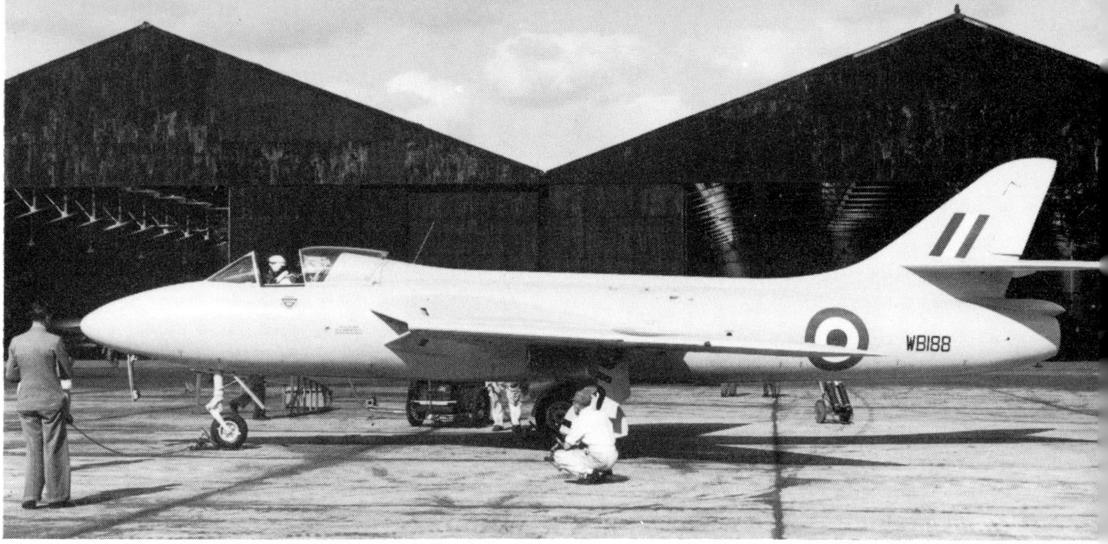
WB188

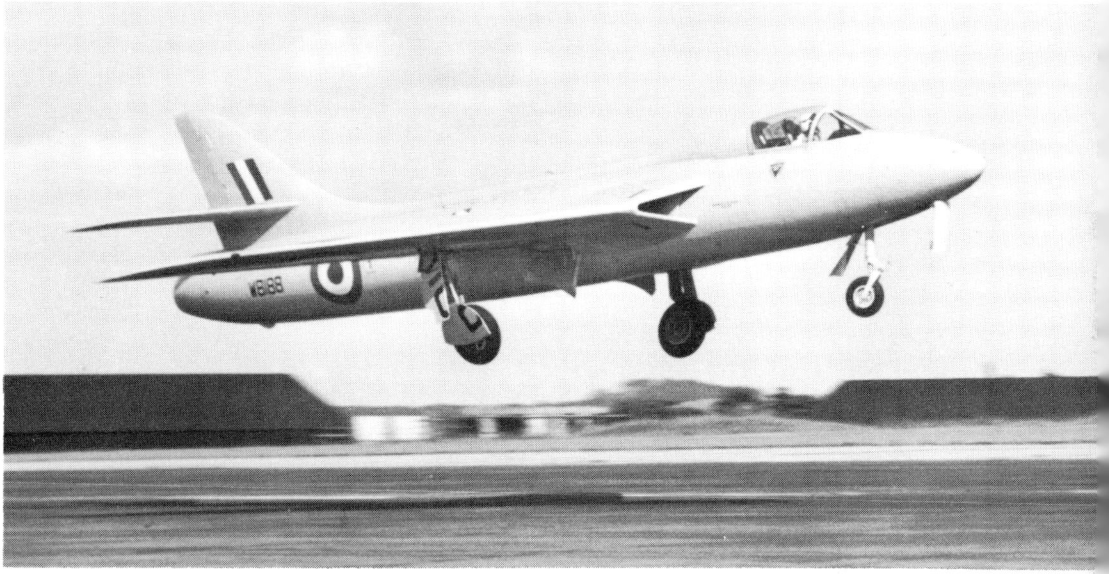
WB188

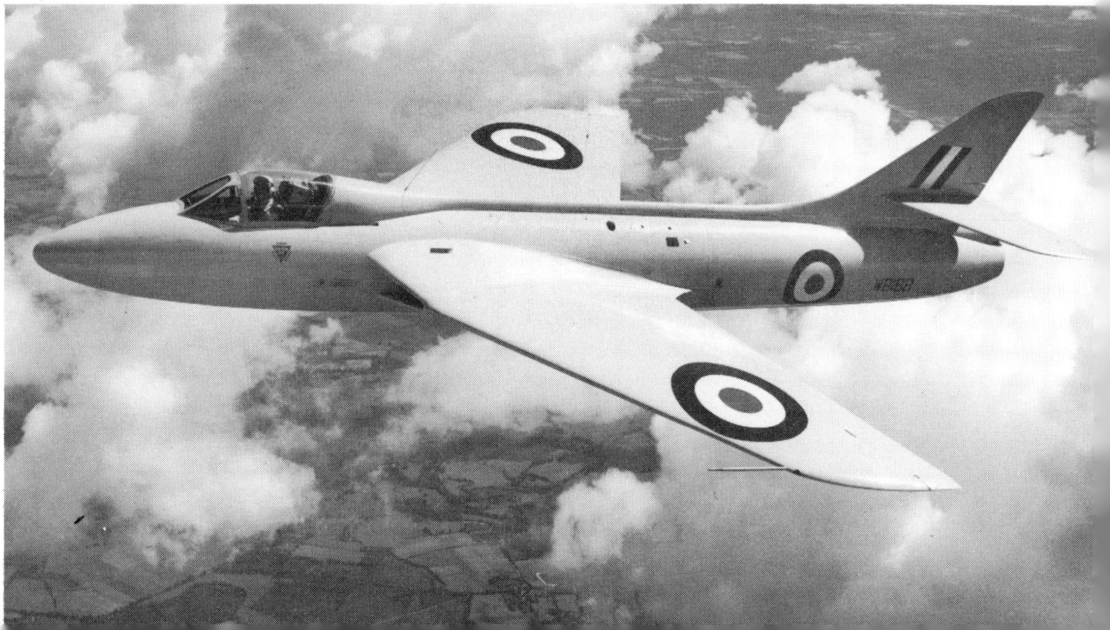
WB188

ability. The first phenomenon was traced to airflow breakdown at the base of the rudder and was cured by the addition of a conical fairing aft of the fin/tailplane junction. The other shortcoming was far less straightforward to remedy, and it was perhaps surprising that standard deceleration requirements had never been formulated by the Service to be included in mandatory fighter manoeuvrability parameters. For example, the Gloster Meteor had for almost eight years possessed very effective airbrakes, yet it does not seem to have occurred to anyone to 'write into' future requirements the provision of such brakes. The truth was that the Hunter was such a very clean aerodynamic shape that to achieve the necessary deceleration considerable drag would have to be generated; just how to achieve this, quickly and without a massive pitching moment in the aircraft, was to occupy Hawker for well over a year.

Soon after WB195 first flew the aircraft embarked on a series of flight trials aimed at developing a satisfactory airbrake. First a small flap was fitted to the upper surface of the wing, and this was followed by employing the landing flaps as airbrakes, the flaps being perforated along their hinged edge; neither scheme succeeded in producing the required deceleration without substantial trim change.

Meanwhile, on June 4 WB195 was flown to West Raynham, Norfolk, where Duke gave a flying demonstration for the benefit of the RAF's Central Fighter Establishment, the unit that would be the first to receive production Hunters prior to their entry into squadron service. At about this time a Ministry of Supply party of test pilots from Boscombe Down visited Dunsfold—where all Hawker flight test work was now conducted—to fly WB188, and they expressed satisfaction that no 'tail end' vibration existed. Thus encouraged, Duke took the aircraft up on the 24th and for the first time achieved supersonic speed in a shallow dive from about 30,000 feet; he reported no sensation was evident as the aircraft accelerated through Mach 1.0 and that, provided recovery was initiated not lower than about 15,000 feet, control response was smooth and positive. On July 10 Duke took WB188 to the Brussels Air Show where it attracted considerable attention and much favourable comment.

Once again the Hunter was displayed at the SBAC show at Farnborough, this time

In-flight photo of the second prototype P.1067, WB195, showing the perforated landing flaps-cum-airbrakes. The idea of using the flaps as airbrakes was discarded owing to the pitching moment imposed at high speed.

Early flight test and development

WB195 being flown each day while WB188 was held in reserve. It was on September 6 that, following its supersonic arrival at Farnborough, the de Havilland DH 110 prototype broke up in the air as it turned towards the crowds, killing 30 and injuring 63 people. The de Havilland test crew, John Derry and Anthony Richards, were among those who lost their lives. It speaks volumes for the courage of Neville Duke, who had just witnessed the death of his close friend, John Derry, that he taxied out in WB195 and took off to give a magnificent flying display (including a transonic dive) as if nothing had occurred.

★   ★   ★

It is important here to take a brief glance at events elsewhere in the world, for they were to have an inevitable bearing on the course of the Hunter's approach towards production. The war in Korea had been in progress for about a year when the Hunter first flew, and the appearance in that theatre of the Communist-flown MiG-15 transonic fighter had accelerated the Americans' decision to deploy a Wing of F-86A Sabres in South Korea to meet the threat. Owing to the absence of suitable RAF fighter equipment the British contribution to the United Nations' air forces had been confined to the Fleet Air Arm whose Sea Furies were regarded as adequate to perform fighter-bombing tasks in coastal areas under the protection of American jet aircraft. A small number of RAF fighter pilots were sent to Korea on exchange postings with the American Sabre squadrons, but the only other RAF pilots to serve in the theatre were a few who served on No 77 Squadron of the Royal Australian Air Force, flying the markedly subsonic Meteor 8. Casualties among these RAF pilots were nevertheless distressingly high.

This was the situation that existed when the Attlee administration was defeated in Britain in favour of a government headed by Winston Churchill in October 1951, and at once the status of the armed forces was afforded public scrutiny, and not least the delay in introducing modern aircraft into RAF service. To remedy the situation realistically was, however, almost impossible for, such had been the parsimony in funds for research and development over a period of six years, there existed no industrial or technical capacity available to accelerate the development of prototype aircraft scheduled for RAF service.

Neville Duke in the cockpit of the Sapphire-prototype P.1067, WB202, at Dunsfold. Note the Sea Hawk and Sea Fury trainer in the background.

No panacea existed, and in its absence a political expedient was invented. Five key aircraft types, regarded as of vital importance, were selected for special attention—the Hawker Hunter, Hawker Sea Hawk, Supermarine Swift, English Electric Canberra and Fairey Gannet—these being afforded 'Super Priority' in the acquisition of production materials and components, of rig time at Government test establishments, and so on. At Hawker the quotation of the contract number, now prefixed by 'Super Priority', was intended to achieve swift action where previously it had been assumed there existed administrative lethargy.

Whether indeed the Super Priority programme achieved any worthwhile acceleration is open to doubt; if it did so, one must wonder when the Hunter would have entered service without it. What is certain is that, after the conclusion of the emergency procedure, it took many years to rectify the administrative chaos created by preferential precedents, particularly in the Civil Service and at the Ministry test establishments. Whether in fact the origins of the various setbacks that later occurred—particularly in the Supermarine Swift—can realistically be traced to the artificial remedies of Super Priority is debatable, but history has certainly shown all too frequently the risks attendant upon accelerated research and development.

In the instance of the Hunter it can now be seen that, for an aircraft which was to be so vital in the re-equipment of the RAF, the original order for only three prototypes was wholly inadequate, and that had provision been made for twice that number, or at least a dozen pre-production development aircraft, the means would have existed to introduce the Hunter into service at least a year earlier.

The lesson was thankfully learned and, despite substantially inflated costs, aircraft such as the Lightning and Buccaneer subsequently benefitted enormously from increased prototype and pre-production aircraft purchase.

* * *

As it was, the Hunter's initial development rested upon flight trials by just three prototypes, the last of which, WB202 with Sapphire engine, was first flown by Duke

Third prototype, WB202, shown with the four de Havilland Firestreak missile dummies. Although advocated for a number of years, the Hunter never entered service with these weapons.

Early flight test and development

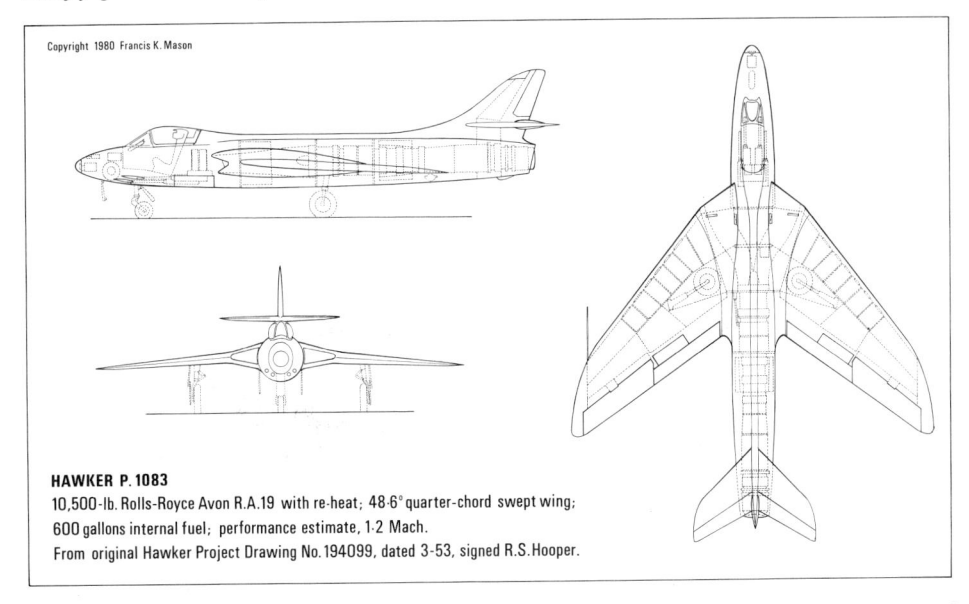

HAWKER P.1083
10,500-lb. Rolls-Royce Avon R.A.19 with re-heat; 48·6° quarter-chord swept wing; 600 gallons internal fuel; performance estimate, 1·2 Mach.
From original Hawker Project Drawing No. 194099, dated 3-53, signed R.S. Hooper.

from Dunsfold on Sunday November 30 1952. And it was now that the shortage of prototype aircraft became fully apparent.

Now that the Hunter was firmly established as future RAF equipment, both Hawker and the Operational Requirements Branch at the Air Ministry were investigating the aircraft's future development. Already the call was for more speed and greater range and endurance, and Camm's project team was at work on the P.1083, a genuinely supersonic version of the Hunter with an afterburning R.A.14 Avon engine and 50-degree swept wing. In October 1952 manufacture of the wings for this aircraft was started in the Kingston experimental shops.

In preparation for the 're-heated' P.1083 it was decided to withdraw WB188 from the flight programme for the installation of a re-heated Avon and the inclusion of wing fuel tanks, and this was effected on December 3. Two days later WB195 was delivered to the A&AEE at Boscombe Down for initial operational trials.

At about this time a survey of the results afforded by the various wing-mounted airbrakes on WB195, together with preliminary wind tunnel tests, prompted the decision to abandon wing brakes and to evolve a brake or brakes on the rear fuselage. The opportunity was thus taken to fit WB188 with twin 'clam-shell' brakes on the sides of the rear fuselage, operated by powerful hydraulic rams, at the same time as it was being adapted to take the Avon's afterburning tailpipe.

Thus by the beginning of 1953, as the first production aircraft components began to take shape in their jigs at Kingston, a number of important matters still remained to be resolved and, ideally to be tested on the prototypes now effectively reduced to two by the considerable divergence from standard by WB188.

To begin with, no in-flight gun firing had been carried out by WB202 owing to the fact that preliminary trials with an Aden gun in a Bristol Beaufighter suggested that the discharge of spent cartridge cases and links might cause damage to the airframe, giving rise to the question whether to discharge or collect cases and/or links; moreover ground firing tests had to be carried out with the Hunter to ensure that discharged links did not enter the engine air intakes. In the event the ground firing trials with WB202, which started on February 16 1953, indicated no such hazard, and air firing trials got underway at Boscombe Down on March 9.

No sooner had WB202 completed its initial gun trials than it was returned to Dunsfold to join the airbrake development programme; by now tunnel tests confirmed that a single large ventral airbrake would give the best results. Accordingly a pair of vernier rails was mounted under the rear fuselage and flight trials carried out to discover the best position for the brake to be located. The first flight with the single ventral airbrake was made on April 25.

On May 16 the first production Hunter Mark 1, WT555, made its first flight, flown by Frank Murphy from Dunsfold. However, much remained to be done on the prototypes before a final production standard of preparation could be achieved. By the middle of June WB202 had completed 30 flying hours and was returned to the factory for inspection, and for the installation of a 'flying tail' and two dummy drop tanks under the wings (work on a Meteor-type slipper tank having been abandoned the previous October). Design work was now also started in collaboration with de Havilland for the installation of the Firestreak air-to-air missile (Blue Jay) in the Hunter, and in due course four such dummy weapons were mounted under the wings of WB202.

Perhaps Hawker's biggest setback to occur at this time was the cancellation of the P.1083. The final conclusion of the Korean War seemed to presage yet another repetition of post-war cutback when Air Vice-Marshal Geoffrey Tuttle (Comptroller of Supplies, Air) and Air Commodores Glynn Silyn-Roberts and Wallace Kyle from DOR and DMARD visited Hawker to discuss current Air Ministry policies. It seemed that once more long term aerodynamic research was to be discarded in the interests of pursuing short term economies. No longer was the increased swept wing to be developed in the Hunter, so the *raison d'être* for the P.1083 disappeared at a stroke. Yet while the DOR (Directorate of Operational Requirements) seemed to favour continuation of the re-heated Avon, DMARD (Directorate of Military Aircraft Research and Development) wanted to explore the potentialities of larger 'dry' Avons being proposed by Rolls-Royce. Assembly of the prototype, WN470, thus stopped when official cancellation of its contract was received on July 13. Although more will be told of this aircraft in due course, its premature abandoning can now be seen to have created yet another alarming situation for the RAF some six years hence. Doubt has been expressed as to whether the P.1083 would, in its R.A.14-powered version, have been truly supersonic in level flight, yet the continuation of the advanced wing would have brought other associated development in its wake, such as the 'slab' tailplane, all of which withered and died.

Above left *Close-up of the dummy Firestreak installation showing the missile pylons and shoes on WB202.*

Above *WB188, now referred to as the Hunter Mark 3, in its coat of bright red paint at Tangmere for the successful attack on the World Absolute Air Speed Record in September 1953. Note the rear nozzle profile (concealing the 'racing' Avon's afterburner), the side-mounted airbrakes and the modified nose section.*

Right *Modified side-mounted airbrakes fitted to WB188 after the speed record flights.*

This all left future design policy at Hawker suspended in mid-air and, in the absence as yet of the new, enlarged Avon engines, it was decided to press ahead with work on re-heated engines. As a working preliminary, WB188 which, it will be recalled, was being re-worked to incorporate wing fuel tanks, side-mounted airbrakes and re-heated Avon, was in August 1953 adapted to take an R.A.7R—in effect a 'racing' Avon—for an attack on the World Absolute Air Speed Record. At the time this stood at 715.75 mph to the credit of a North American F-86D Sabre flown by Lieutenant-Colonel William F. Barnes on July 16 1953.

Developing 7,130 lb thrust 'dry' and 9,600 lb with re-heat lit, the new Avon exhausted through a two-position final nozzle. WB188 was ready for flight at the end of August and flown to Tangmere in Sussex where preparations were in hand for the record attempts. Several practice flights were made over the three-kilometre course off the coast of Rustington (during which Duke suffered a slight taxiing accident which necessitated repairs to WB188's undercarriage doors) during the first week in September. On the 7th conditions seemed ideal and Duke flew the bright red Hunter, now designated the Mark 3, along the course to return an average speed of 727.63 mph which, in the temperature

Hunter wings in production at Richmond Road. The wings, built side-by-side in pairs, were rigidly attached to vertical stanchions by their spar root bolts and at the mainwheel hinge-point.

and humidity prevailing, represented Mach 0.92 at sea level. For record purposes a sharply pointed nose cone fairing was fitted to the Hunter, but a windscreen fairing of increased rake, originally fitted, was discarded just prior to the record flight.

On September 19 Duke flew WB188 round a 100-kilometre closed circuit to establish a new world record for this course at 709.2 mph. (Not to be outdone, Supermarine took their Swift fighter to Libya in North Africa soon afterwards to benefit from higher ambient temperature and set up a new world record of 735.70 mph.)

After this Hawker was advised to discontinue work on re-heated engines, and WB188 came to the end of its useful life. It passed into the hands of the RAF and, after a period spent as a ground instruction machine, it languished outside the main gates at RAF Melksham in Wiltshire before being rescued for eventual preservation.

'High speed has always been my aim.'

(Sir Sydney Camm, on numerous occasions.)

Chapter 3

Into service and into trouble

While considerable work still remained to be done with the second and third prototypes, production was getting underway with the Avon-powered Hunter Mark 1 at Kingston, and the Sapphire-powered Mark 2 at Coventry. As already mentioned, Frank Murphy flew WT555 at Dunsfold on May 16 1953, but it was to be more than a year before deliveries could be made to the RAF.

In effect the first twenty production aircraft now had to be regarded as development machines, so critical had the shortage of prototypes been found to be. The second production Hunter to fly, WT556, took to the air in June and most of its early life was spent giving demonstrations to NATO air forces in preparation for likely service on the Continent. By the end of the year sixteen Mark 1s had flown and these underwent all manner of trials, ranging from preliminary spinning to gun firing, under Service conditions. At Boscombe Down the job of compiling Pilots' Notes started. WT558 underwent trials with wing fences; WT559 was used for canopy jettisoning trials; WT562 featured one-third-span landing flaps, and WT570 was the first Hunter to include full-power ailerons.

Work on WB202 eventually confirmed the best position for the ventral airbrake and efforts now started to incorporate this and its operating jack in Hunters now beginning to crowd the production lines at Kingston, Coventry and Blackpool. Until this could be flown and accepted by the Service pilots at Boscombe Down the Hunter's CA Release continued to be withheld.

Meanwhile, as unmodified production aircraft continued to stockpile at Dunsfold early in 1954, further problems were being encountered at Boscombe Down. Doubts were being expressed about the Hunter's endurance, several aircraft, flown by very experienced Service pilots of the Aircraft and Armament Experimental Establishment, landing with

The first production Hawker Hunter F Mark 1, WT555.

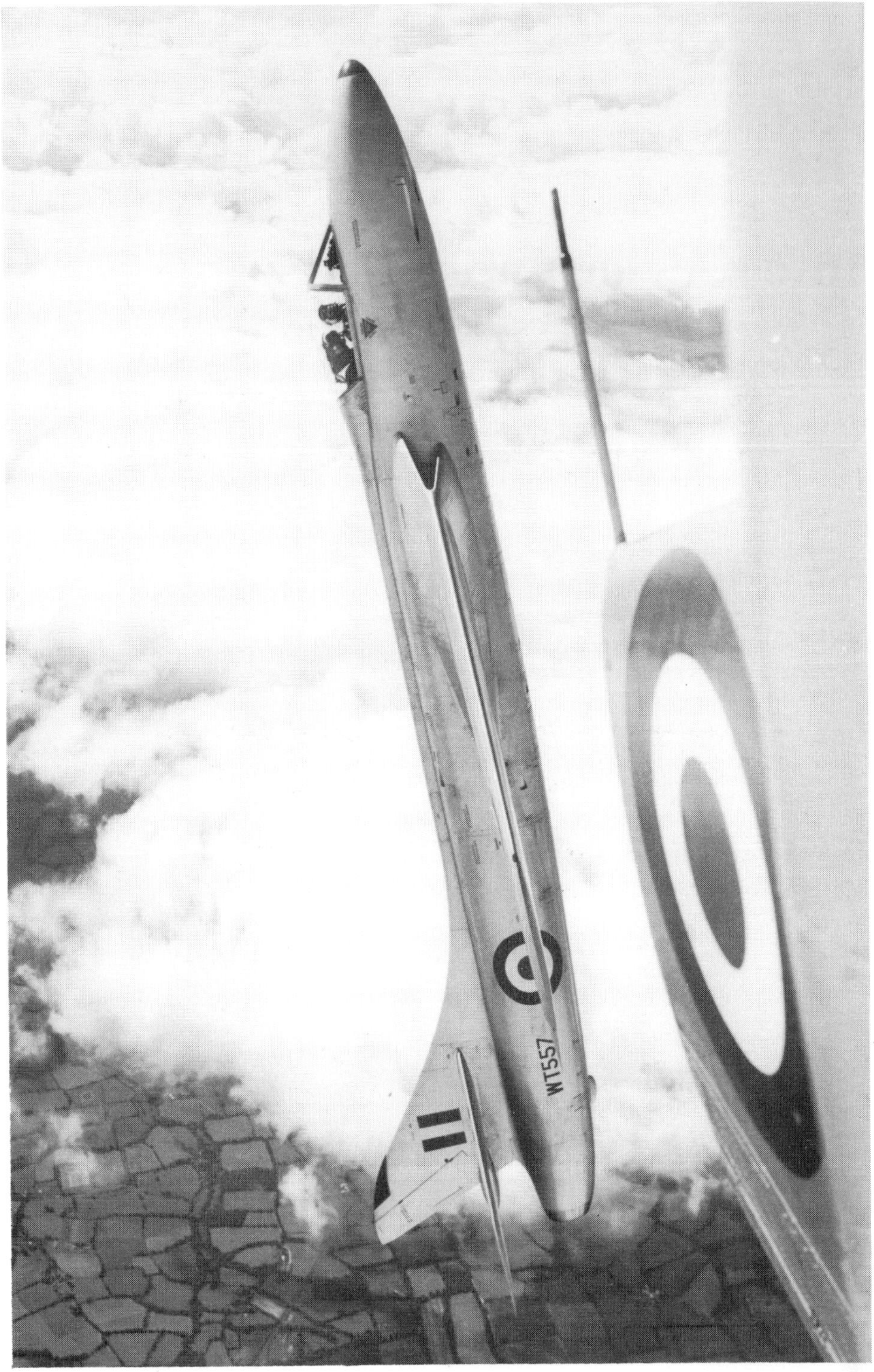
WT557

insufficient fuel remaining to taxi away from the runway; complaints were voiced about severe canopy misting after descending from high altitude, and there were four instances of engines flaming-out during gun-firing—although the reasons for the latter were not yet fully understood.

To overcome the endurance criticisms Hawker at once embarked on the design of auxiliary tanks, two alternative schemes being studied. An initial approach employing detachable 85-gallon integral tanks was discarded in favour of 100-gallon underwing drop tanks, and a pair of such tanks was flown, first on WB202 on January 7 1954 and later on a modified CA's Mark 1.

The first production airbrake-equipped Hunter was tested at Boscombe Down between April and June and, after increasing the angular travel, this was pronounced acceptable by the Service. (Meanwhile an airbrake fitted under the front fuselage of WT566 had been found to be unsatisfactory.)

It was now decided to issue the Hunter F Mark 1 with a limited CA Release on July 1 so that it could be flown by the experienced pilots of the Central Fighter Establishment at West Raynham, and also by a single RAF squadron under strictly supervised Service conditions. Accordingly a dozen newly modified Mark 1s were delivered to the CFE during the following week, and four of these participated in the major annual air defence exercises. Some value was gained, and the Hunter showed its paces (particularly when a high-flying Canberra crew was astonished to be 'attacked' from *above* by a pair of Hunters), although almost all the successful interceptions achieved by the new fighters took place less than 80 miles from base owing to exaggerated fuel limitations. A new criticism was also now expressed at West Raynham: that following nights spent on the exposed Operational Readiness Platform at the end of the runway, condensation rendered the Hunters' radio and radar unserviceable the next morning.

The same month No 43 (Fighter) Squadron at Leuchars, commanded by Squadron Leader R. Lelong, was selected to become the first RAF Hunter squadron. Four aircraft arrived in July and within two months the established strength had been reached. By October the squadron was beginning to undertake full operational flying.

Meanwhile, investigations into the flame-out problems that had been reported at Boscombe Down (and confirmed at West Raynham), disclosed that gun firing at high altitude was almost invariably accompanied by severe compressor surging—heralded by a loud bang—owing to local pressure disturbance around the engine intakes. (Although this phenomenon was new and entirely unforeseen at the time, it was to be encountered during the following ten years by numerous other British, French and American aircraft.) Little could be done to alter the Hunter airframe—other than by a major redesign—to overcome the engine surging, and it was thus left to Rolls-Royce to seek a remedy in the powerplant.

This was an unhappy time for RAF Fighter Command. The Supermarine Swift, which had preceded the Hunter into service by a few weeks with its issue to No 56 (Fighter) Squadron at Waterbeach, had run into serious control problems (and there were hints of engine surging during gun firing); there were several instances in which the electrically actuated tailplane had 'run away' soon after take-off, with fatal results. After two such accidents the Swifts were grounded pending system checks; several weeks later they were cleared for limited flying which was again suspended after two more fatal crashes. The Swift Mark 2 was then issued to No 56 Squadron, but returned a dismal serviceability rate (possibly due to exaggerated caution following the squadron's recent unhappy experiences). The CA Release was effectively withdrawn and the Swift was quickly

Left *Third production Hunter 1, WT557, accompanies a Meteor 7 into a loop.*

phased out of service as a fighter. (Much later it re-appeared to give limited service as an acceptable reconnaissance fighter.)

Nor were matters yet going well for the Hunter. It soon became clear that engine surging could not be overcome without the introduction of a new Avon, and No 43 (Fighter) Squadron suffered two accidents (neither fatal) following flame-out. The gun-firing limitations were severely restricted to the point at which the Hunter Mark 1 could scarcely be regarded as a combat-ready interceptor—at least for the time being.

The other equally fundamental shortcoming of the Hunter lay in its critically short endurance, this being dramatically illustrated at West Raynham. Eight pilots of the Day Fighter Leaders' School, on returning to base, found their airfield shrouded by a sudden sea mist and were diverted to Marham, less than a dozen miles away. Six pilots ejected when their aircraft ran out of fuel and the other two bellied down beside the runway. The Hunters had been airborne for just under 40 minutes!

Nevertheless, remedies to overcome this daunting list of shortcomings, were, as shown above, in hand. It was indeed the acceleration into production and service—one should probably say the *premature* entry into service—that accentuated a situation which would probably never have arisen without the parsimonious attitudes towards military procurement and research funding of the late 1940s.

It was the knowledge that remedies were being found and introduced into the Hunter production lines that prompted the decision to go ahead with further deliveries to the Service of the existing Mark 1s and 2s with their known deficiencies. In matters so politically delicate as national defence capabilities it was not possible to disclose to the public just how serious Fighter Command's problems were at this time, despite some searching questions being asked in the House of Commons.

Thus it was that the first Hunter F Mark 2s to enter service were delivered to No 257 (Fighter) Squadron at Wattisham, their Sapphire engines being immune to surging so that gun firing was cleared up to 47,000 ft. Two months later the other Wattisham Squadron, No 263, commanded by Squadron Leader R. Aytoun, also took deliveries of Hunter 2s.

Meanwhile, with around 150 Mark 1s completed by the end of 1954 (the first Blackpool-built aircraft, WW599, had flown on July 7), three further squadrons discarded their Meteor 8s in favour of the Hunter. The second Leuchars-based Squadron, No 222, commanded by Squadron Leader K.F.W. Tapper, received its new fighters in December 1954, and the following February Odiham became the third operational Hunter base when No 54 (Fighter) Squadron, commanded by Squadron Leader W.M. Sizer, DFC and Bar, was re-equipped. No 247 (Fighter) Squadron, also at Odiham, received its Hunter 1s in July 1955.

Such was the importance attached to the introduction of later versions of the Hunter into service throughout RAF Fighter Command, and the dire necessity to overcome its seemingly sinister problems, it was decided to retain the Mark 1s and 2s in the United Kingdom within convenient reach of manufacturers' working parties, Maintenance Units and so on.

Apart from such establishments as the Empire Test Pilots' School at Farnborough and the Fighter Weapons School at Leconfield, the only other RAF units to receive the Hunter 1 and 2 were the two Operational Conversion Units, No 229 at Chivenor and No 233 at Pembrey in South Wales. The task of these two units was not only to provide a flow of young pilots for the new Hunter squadrons but also 'convert' the erstwhile Meteor pilots to the new single-engine fighter.

With all the difficulties imposed by the operational restrictions on the early Hunters, it was inevitable that accidents would occur, and these received considerable notoriety in the media of the day; yet it must be emphasised that the very high accident rate was far

Above *Changing the gun pack on a Hunter Mark 1 at the Empire Test Pilots' School.* **Below** *A Blackpool-built Hunter F Mark 1, WW604, of No 233 OCU, Pembrey.*

from wholly attributable to the aeroplane itself. Now that the RAF could boast possession of a transonic fighter it was natural and commendable that a policy of flying the aeroplane to its utmost limits—such as they were—should be advocated throughout Fighter Command; this philosophy, emphasised for the benefit of all young pilots passing through the Flying Training Schools and Operational Conversion Units, had perhaps become tempered with caution on the squadrons now just giving up their five- and six-year-old Meteors and Vampires.

Formation aerobatics, undertaken by several Meteor squadrons in the past, now became 'all the rage' on the Hunter units, beginning with No 54 (Fighter) Squadron, which quickly formed a four-man team. One of the pilots of this team flew too close to his leader and on landing found that his canopy and tail had been very badly distorted by the other aircraft's exhaust heat.

At the Day Fighter Leaders' School of the CFE, a pilot flew through a tree while examining his map on a low level cross-country flight, but landed safely. Also at the CFE, a Hunter Mark 1 collided with a Mark 2 during a dogfight; the former made a safe belly landing and the latter, flown by Major Beck of the USAF, made a good wheels-down landing at base despite the loss of its starboard tailplane and elevator, and with the tail cone torn off.

The OCUs naturally had their share of accidents but almost all these were attributable to the inexperience of their pilots. On one occasion a young pilot, who forgot to lower his wheels before landing, was forcibly reminded of his omission when he bounced heavily on the runway threshold, but managed to open up to go round again to make a more orthodox landing. Another pilot, engaged in a mock dogfight at 41,000 ft, was suddenly and unexpectedly ejected when his ejector seat fired under negative-G.

It must be said that the Sapphire-powered Hunter 2 was normally preferred to the Mark 1 in service, although generally speaking the only pilots who had the opportunity to make comparisons were those at West Raynham. Not only was the Sapphire virtually surge-free, thereby allowing a greater flight envelope to be exploited, but it also developed slightly more thrust at a lower specific fuel consumption. It is also perhaps of interest to note that of the 139 production Hunter Mark 1s built, 37 suffered serious flying accidents (of which 15 were fatal), whereas of the 45 Hunter 2s built only five suffered flying accidents—comparable rates of 26.6 and 11.1 per cent respectively.

If the Service career of the Hunter 1 and 2 was inauspicious, the various CA aircraft retained at Dunsfold and elsewhere continued to contribute interesting and valuable research information. On the purely experimental side two aircraft were particularly noteworthy. The first, WT571, was modified to incorporate the principles of 'area rule', which were subsequently designed integrally from the outset in high performance aircraft. The principle embraces the theory that by maintaining the overall cross-sectional area of an aircraft as far aft as possible airflow separation will be delayed thereby reducing drag. However, despite the addition of smoothly faired bulges to the sides of the Hunter's rear fuselage, the increase in speed was found to be only very marginal, and it was generally agreed that at 0.93 Mach (the Hunter 1's level flight maximum speed) the drag rise so near the speed of sound was so great in any case that area-ruling the rear fuselage would have little effect, while severe flow separation around the tail gave rise to marked control deterioration.

The other experiment carried out on a Hunter Mark 1, WT656, was instigated by the Royal Aircraft Establishment in furtherance of the current preoccupation with 'blown flaps', employing the circulation of air tapped from the engine compressor over the landing flaps to increase lift, thereby reducing the stalling speed of the aircraft, and hence the landing speed and ground run. Like the area-ruled Hunter, WT656 featured a long nose boom.

CA Hunter 1s were also the first to fly with wing leading-edge extensions (as part of the pitch-up investigation, referred to in the following chapters), and cartridge link collector tanks and underwing store pylons. The CA Hunters assigned to Rolls-Royce flew with a wide assortment of Avons (both of R.A.7 and R.A.14 ratings) as part of the continuing programme to overcome the worrying problem of surging. (Details of all these aircraft are given in the Appendix.) □

'I could have told Farnborough it wouldn't improve the Hunter. When you've designed aeroplanes as long as I have, you can see the airflow . . .'
(Sir Sydney Camm, 1956, on the subject of area rule.)

Top *The first production Hunter F Mark 2 built at Coventry, WN888.*

Above *Perforated split landing flaps were flown on an early production Hunter 1 as part of the airbrake development programme.*

Right *Vernier-mounted twin-jack ventral airbrake.*

Above *Frank Bullen (right) discusses the production-type airbrake with Hugh Merewether.* **Below** *In-flight photograph of Hunter F Mark 1, WT594, showing the production-type airbrake extended.*

Bottom left and above *Two ground views of the 'area rule' Hunter 1, WT571.* **Below and bottom** *Two views of the 'blown-flap' Hunter 1, WT656.*

Top *The first Hunter to carry drop tanks, WT569.*

Above *A production Hunter F Mark 2 seen at Halton.*

Left *Major Beck's Hunter 2 which survived the mid-air collision, showing the loss of its starboard tailplane and fuselage tail cone.*

Chapter 4

The Hunter transformed

The opinion used to be voiced that Hawker, for all its fine reputation for continuity of design and sound aeroplanes, never embarked upon a radical step. The authors of such views would point to aeroplanes such as the Hart, Hurricane and Sea Fury, all of which gave long service, yet represented no brilliant advance in technology. While this is superficially true it can surely be argued that such aircraft represented an amalgam of the latest technology with sound, proven principles of design practice. The combination was achieved through the experience gained in adaptability, so that Camm's designs were capable of meeting a much greater range of demands made upon them than were the products of other companies; this was the strength of the Hawker philosophy which gave birth to the Hunter. Just as the Hurricane had been the RAF's first monoplane fighter, so the Hunter was to become its first successful transonic interceptor. True, its introduction into service was accompanied by all manner of problems—it has been remarked about the Hunter 1 that the RAF was called upon to fly 139 prototypes—but the low level of research funding during the post-war era had been inadequate to ensure the aircraft's uncomplicated entry to service. And it is again emphasised that there had been no possible means whereby the engine surging during gun firing could have been predicted, particularly during the design stages. The outstanding characteristic of the basic Hunter design was its inherent capacity to accommodate technological advances as well as ever-increasing demands for adaptability without recourse to radical alteration of its overall airframe envelope.

With the evolution and introduction by Rolls-Royce of the surge-free Avon R.A.21, the Hunter was transformed as at a stroke the gun-firing limitations were removed. Production of the Hunter continued unchecked as most of the modifications, which had been evolved to overcome the various shortcomings already described, were introduced into the 114th airframe at Kingston and the 27th at Blackpool. The new aircraft were designated Hunter F Mark 4s.

To meet the chronic endurance criticism the internal fuel capacity was increased from 337 gallons in the Hunter Mark 1 to 414 gallons in the Mark 4, while provision was made to carry two 100-gallon drop tanks on inboard wing pylons; later, with the introduction of 'Mod.228', the fuel system was revised to allow carriage of two further drop tanks on outboard pylons—thus enabling the Hunter to accommodate 814 gallons of fuel. (In November 1956 No 93 (Fighter) Squadron at Jever in Germany carried out an experiment to discover how long a 'clean' Hunter 4 could remain airborne. A duration of one hour 47 minutes was achieved before the aircraft landed with 45 gallons of fuel remaining).

Also introduced in the Hunter 4 was a 'full flying tail' (replacing the interim type in the earlier versions), an addition much appreciated by the Service pilot in its alleviation of stick loads during high-G manoeuvres.

Not all the early Mark 4s were powered by the fully-modified Avon 115 (R.A.14) from

The first production Hunter F Mark 4, WT701, shown here fitted with 36 three-in rocket projectiles. This was not a standard RAF armament requirement for the Mark 4.

the outset, but those aircraft employing the older engine were initially delivered into storage at Maintenance Units to await retrospective modification when adequate Avon 115s (and later Avon 120s) became available.

The first Hunter Mark 4, WT701, was flown by Frank Murphy on October 20 1954 (although a dozen Mark 1s had yet to fly), and before the end of the year this was joined by the following five aircraft in a routine programme of flight trials. It was in the next aircraft, WT707, that Murphy experienced a tragic accident. During a test flight on January 25 1955 he was forced to make an emergency belly landing at the Naval Air Station at Ford; the Hunter skidded wildly on the wet grass and ploughed through the boundary fence into a caravan park, killing three people. Frank Murphy escaped without serious injury.

The first Blackpool-built Hunter 4, WW646, was flown on January 20 1955, and by the end of March 28 aircraft from Kingston and 11 from Blackpool had been delivered to the Maintenance Units at Kemble and Lyneham. An unlimited CA Release was given and the aircraft commenced delivery to the RAF.

First to receive the Hunter Mark 4 was No 98 (Fighter) Squadron, commanded by Squadron Leader J.H. Smith-Carington, AFC, and No 118 (Fighter) Squadron, both of 2nd Tactical Air Force based at Jever in Germany; each squadron received 12 aircraft during April 1955. The decision to equip these German-based squadrons with the new Hunter—although regarded by the pilots themselves as long overdue—was not, however, without its complications. Being early aircraft from the production lines, the Hunters were far from being of a common standard of preparation and modification, and a source of some amusement were the roughly scribbled notices attached to the instrument panels announcing 'Caution. This aircraft is not fitted with a full flying tail.'

The same month Hunter 4s started to arrive at West Raynham although the AFDS and DFLS continued to employ Mark 1s and 2s for more than a further year so as not to disrupt their training syllabus, the new aircraft being used simply to provide end-of-course experience prior to the departure of newly appointed flight and squadron commanders to their squadrons.

May 1955 brought deliveries of Hunter 4s to No 14 (Fighter) Squadron, commanded by Squadron Leader C.W. Beasley at Oldenburg, and No 247 (Fighter) Squadron at Odiham—the latter expressing itself thankful to be rid of its Mark 1s. The following month a second Oldenburg Squadron, No 26, commanded by Squadron Leader J.A.G. Jackson, received Hunter 4s in place of its Sabres, while that most famous of all RAF

The Hunter transformed 41

fighter squadrons, No 111 at North Weald, commanded by Squadron Leader Roger Topp, AFC, gave up its Meteor 8s for Hunter 4s. In July No 54 (Fighter) Squadron at Odiham also discarded its Hunter 1s in favour of Mark 4s, and the first few Mark 4s also now reached No 229 OCU at Chivenor. Two more squadrons received Hunter 4s during 1955, No 20 (Fighter) Squadron at Oldenburg, and No 222 (Fighter) Squadron at Leuchars, their new aircraft being delivered in November; and the next month Hunter 4s began arriving at the Royal Air Force Flying College at Manby.

Thus within a year the RAF had undergone considerable invigoration with the re-equipping of ten fighter squadrons—six in Germany and four in Britain. The Swift was by now no more than a bad dream and the days of the Meteor day fighter were clearly numbered.

Re-equipment continued without interruption into 1956 and within the next five

Below *Hunter F Mark 4, WT775, of No 247 (F) Squadron; an early Mark 4 prior to fitting of ammunition link collector tanks.* **Bottom** *Another No 247 Squadron Hunter 4, WV317, showing the addition of link collector tanks.*

months eight further squadrons, five in Germany and three at home, gave up Hunter 1s and Sabres for the Hunter 4. These were No 67 (Fighter) Squadron at Bruggen and No 93 (Fighter) Squadron at Jever, which re-equipped in January; No 43 (Fighter) Squadron at Leuchars in February; No 92 (Fighter) Squadron, commanded by Squadron Leader R.W.G. Freer and No 66 (Fighter) Squadron, commanded by Squadron Leader A.F. Osborne, DFC, both at Linton-on-Ouse, and No 130 (Fighter) Squadron at Bruggen in March; No 112 (Fighter) Squadron, commanded by Squadron Leader F.M. Hegarty, also at Bruggen, in April; and No 234 (Fighter) Squadron, commanded by Squadron Leader R. Emmett, at Geilenkirchen in May.

This completed the first phase of re-equipment of RAF fighter squadrons with the Hunter 4. Two other squadrons had been scheduled for re-equipment in 1956, namely Nos 74 and 245 which had both been based at Horsham St Faith just outside Norwich, Norfolk. However, events at this airfield were to disrupt these plans; early in 1956 a modification centre for Hunter 4s and 6s was established at Horsham St Faith (see below) and it soon became clear that space did not exist to accommodate the large number of Hunters undergoing modification, as well as two line squadrons—not to mention a growing unrest among local residents over the increasing noise of jet fighters taking off so close to a fast-growing city. No 245 Squadron was therefore moved to Stradishall in Suffolk where it received its Hunter 4s in April 1957. No 74 (Fighter) Squadron—the famous 'Tigers'—gave up Meteor 8s in February that year to fly Hunter 4s, although these in turn gave place to Hunter 6s only eight months later.

Despite some inconvenience caused on RAF squadrons by an initial disparity of modification standard among the first hundred or so Hunter 4s, this version became extremely popular among Service pilots who spoke of it as a true 'pilot's aeroplane'. Its controls were light and positive, and serviceability rates quickly increased to previously unaccustomed levels. Once more formation aerobatic teams proliferated, led in Germany by that of No 93 Squadron, and at home by No 111 Squadron.

It was, however, the low modification standard of many squadron aircraft, combined with the need to re-engine the early aircraft in storage at Maintenance Units, that led to the setting up of the CWP (Contractor's Working Party) at Horsham St Faith. This 'unit's' most pressing task was to fit the full flying tail to all unmodified Hunters, and later to incorporate Modification 228 to allow carriage of 100-gallon drop tanks outboard; in the event few of the RAF squadrons ever required to fly with four drop tanks, and most of these aircraft were earmarked for sale overseas (in particular to Peru, see Chapter 9). As pressure of work increased with the arrival of Hunter 6s later on, the CWP expanded to sites at North Weald and Leconfield, while modification of most German-based Hunters was carried out at Bückeberg by RAF personnel.

In all a total of 191 Mark 4 Hunters was produced at Kingston and 177 at Blackpool. Of these, two (WT770 and WW991) never carried RAF markings but were despatched to Sweden and Denmark respectively.

Meanwhile, a similar transformation had been undergone by the Sapphire-powered Hunter. It will be recalled that only the two Wattisham-based squadrons, Nos 257 and 263, had been equipped with the Mark 2 in late 1954 and early 1955. These squadrons had been relatively untroubled by engine surge and it was only the very short endurance of their Hunters that prompted some urgency in their re-equipment. Thus it was that after only 45 Hunter Mark 2s had been completed at Coventry similar fuel system modifications to those of the Hunter 4 were introduced into subsequent airframes, to produce the Hunter Mark 5. Indeed the first production Mark 5 was flown one day sooner than the first Mark 4—on October 19 1954.

Reluctance to support Sapphire engine maintenance in Germany resulted in the

The Hunter transformed

Modification 228 made provision to carry drop tanks on outboard pylons in addition to those fitted inboard.

decision being taken to equip only home-based Fighter Command squadrons with the Hunter 5, the first being No 263 at Wattisham in March 1955 (again just beating the Hunter 4 into service). No 56 (Fighter) Squadron, whose Swift Mark 2s were now withdrawn, followed in May at Waterbeach. No 1 (Fighter) Squadron, commanded by Squadron Leader F.W. Lister, discarded its Meteor 8s and received Hunter 5s in June, the same month in which No 41 (Fighter) Squadron took deliveries at Biggin Hill. No 257 (Fighter) Squadron exchanged its Mark 2s for Mark 5s in July, and just before the end of the year No 34 (Fighter) Squadron at Tangmere became the last to equip with Hunter 5s. Production of the Sapphire-engined Hunter 5 ran out in August 1955, completion of the 105 aircraft at Coventry having occupied less than a year; henceforth Sir W.G. Armstrong Whitworth Aircraft Limited would embark on production of the Hunter 6.

Hitherto the rôle of the Hunter had been entirely confined to the air-to-air combat function, and it was in this capacity that it was first called upon to participate in a fighting campaign. With the breaking of the Suez Crisis late in 1956, and Egypt's seizure of the Canal, Britain and France sailed an assault fleet eastwards through the Mediterranean and deployed bomber forces in Cyprus and Malta to support the amphibious landings on the Egyptian coast. At the same time 16 Hunter F Mark 5s of No 34 (Fighter) Squadron were flown out to Cyprus to provide top cover for naval aircraft operating over the beach-head area. The Hunters, painted with distinctive black and yellow stripes on wings and rear fuselages for ease of identification, each carried a pair of 100-gallon drop tanks but while flying from Cyprus their pilots found difficulty in operating from the 2,000-yard runways in the high ambient temperatures at the increased weights imposed. When landing with any quantity of fuel remaining they had difficulty in braking, and two aircraft ran on into the overshoot area. Owing to the lack of replacement tanks immediately available, the pilots were ordered not to jettison them unless faced with active air combat or in extreme emergency. However, no air combat ensued involving the Hunters and in due course No 34 Squadron brought all its aircraft home to Tangmere. Nevertheless, this brief foray had spotlighted a number of interesting facets of potential Hunter operations in the Middle East, and these were carefully studied when the Central Fighter Establishment embarked on tropical trials with the Hunter 6 several months later.

While Hunter 4s and 5s continued to give excellent service in the RAF, Hawker was able to concentrate upon extending the aircraft's capabilities, and while the emphasis of this effort had already shifted to the development of the Hunter 6, considerable work continued to be done on the Hunter 4—and to a lesser extent the Hunter 5.

Led by Frank Murphy, the production test pilots, Frank Bullen, Duncan Simpson, David Lockspeiser and Don Lucey had their hands full through 1955 and 1956 with upwards of eight new aircraft emerging from the final assembly shed every week. Neville Duke had suffered an aggravating spinal injury as the result of a forced landing in a Hunter and was absent from active test flying for almost all of 1956, so that responsibility for the experimental flying now rested largely upon Bill Bedford (shortly to be formally appointed Hawker's Chief Test Pilot), assisted by Hugh Merewether. In addition some of the routine test flying of production aircraft was undertaken by several RAF pilots seconded temporarily to the company.

Undoubtedly the most intertesting of the trial Hunter Mark 4s was XF310, an aircraft delivered to Fairey Aviation Limited in June 1956 for installation of that company's beam-riding air-to-air missile, the Fireflash (or Blue Jay, to give its code name). Two of these weapons were carried on special pylons under the wings and featured large booster rockets above and below the missile's body. Although the missile and its application to various experimental aircraft attracted polite interest in the RAF and Ministry of Supply, preference was already being shown for the infra-red-seeking Firestreak being developed by de Havilland. Indeed, the Ministry of Supply forbade XF310 from appearing at the Farnborough Show wearing RAF markings lest it should infer that it was the subject of Government backing! Several Fireflash rounds were fired over the Aberporth range, but

The Fireflash Hunter, XF310, with early nose configuration.

A standard Hunter 4 with Mod. 228 outboard drop tanks and 1,000-lb bombs inboard about to take off at Farnborough.

by 1958 all interest in the missile had flagged and XF310 was converted to a two-seat Hunter.

Despite the popularity and success of the Hunter 4 in RAF service, it was already implicit in the demands being made to accelerate development of the Mark 6 that the life of the Hunter as an interceptor would be relatively shortlived. Yet it was initially no more than customary company practice to investigate possible diversification of the aircraft's rôles, particularly as it was clear that the Service would shortly require a replacement for the Venom in the ground attack rôle.

Carriage of 100-gallon drop tanks on the Hunter 4's inboard wing pylons suggested the feasibility of substituting 1,000-lb bombs, and work started late in 1955 to produce modifications to permit the mounting of four rocket tiers under each outer wing, so that up to 24 3-in rocket projectiles could be carried in addition to the inboard bombs or drop tanks. Considerable work was carried out on the Mark 4, WT703, and the Mark 5, WN958 (both of which spent much time at Boscombe Down on armament trials), and although no ground attack capability was ever demanded of the Marks 4 and 5 during their Service currency, these aircraft contributed valuable information and experience for the later development of the Marks 6 and 9 in the ground attack rôles.

In the same vein another Mark 4, WT780 (the company's Trial Installation aircraft), was modified at private expense to feature a fan of no fewer than five cameras in the nose to suit the Hunter for the fighter reconnaissance rôle. Four of the cameras were mounted obliquely and the fifth 'looked' forward through the extreme tip of the nose, the camera lens being protected from dirt by eyelid shutters which opened during operation of the camera. All manner of trials were undertaken by the company pilots to eliminate misting of the lenses after descent from high altitude, and gun firing was carried out to confirm that muzzle-blast caused no damage to the cameras. This time the Government agencies sat up and took notice, and although the Swift was already being considered as a contender for the fighter-reconnaissance rôle in the RAF, work started at the Operational Requirements Branch at the Air Ministry to formulate a new FR specification.

In the meantime, its immediate job done, WT780 was stripped of its Service cameras, equipped for movie filming and leased to Warwick Films to provide the flying sequences of an excellent film, *High Flight*, which was to include many dramatic low-level sequences filmed at high speed.

WT780 had a long and varied life. Among its numerous trial installations was an experimental ram-air turbine incorporated in the rear fuselage to provide emergency power for a proposed slab tailplane being developed for the Hunter. Work on the latter was abandoned in 1957, but experience with the ram-air turbine proved valuable when a similar installation was incorporated in the P.1127 V/STOL aircraft three years later. WT780 was also used in the development of the landing parachute fairing for the Hunter two-seater, and the airfield arrestor hook for the naval Hunters.

With the introduction of the 'large-Avon' Hunter 6, interest in the Hunter 4 waned early in the 1960s, and although service aircraft seldom reached 1,000 flying hours it was thought unlikely that redundant Hunter 4s would find potential customers overseas. The Hunter was still widely regarded as an inexpensive aircraft in a world becoming increasingly resigned to multi-million pound unit costs. No one at this stage, least of all in the Hawker design offices, contemplated the adaptation of redundant Mark 4 Hunters to accommodate the more powerful Avon 200-series engine. It was assumed that to replace almost every frame in the centre fuselage to take the larger engine would require extensive re-jigging and involve astronomical costs, not to mention the inclusion of countless other modifications introduced in the meantime.

Without the gift of prescience therefore, both Hawker and the RAF authorised the scrapping of numerous redundant Hunter 4s and 5s between 1960 and 1963. Only when it was realised that such airframes could contribute numerous components in the big refurbishing programme which got underway in 1963 was the order revoked, and the surviving Hunter 4s were saved. Furthermore, much later it was discovered to be sufficiently cost-effective to re-build entire Hunter 4s to accommodate the Avon 200-series engine. □

'Why do people use the word "sophistication" in aircraft design? To me the word means "complication", and "complication" means "ruination".'

(Sir Sydney Camm, 1960.)

Top right *The Fireflash Hunter as displayed at Farnborough; note the deletion of RAF markings.*
Centre right and right *The Hunter 4, WT798, was the first aircraft used by Hawker to fly dummy 230-gallon drop tanks; this was a particularly successful enterprise undertaken by the company at private expense.*

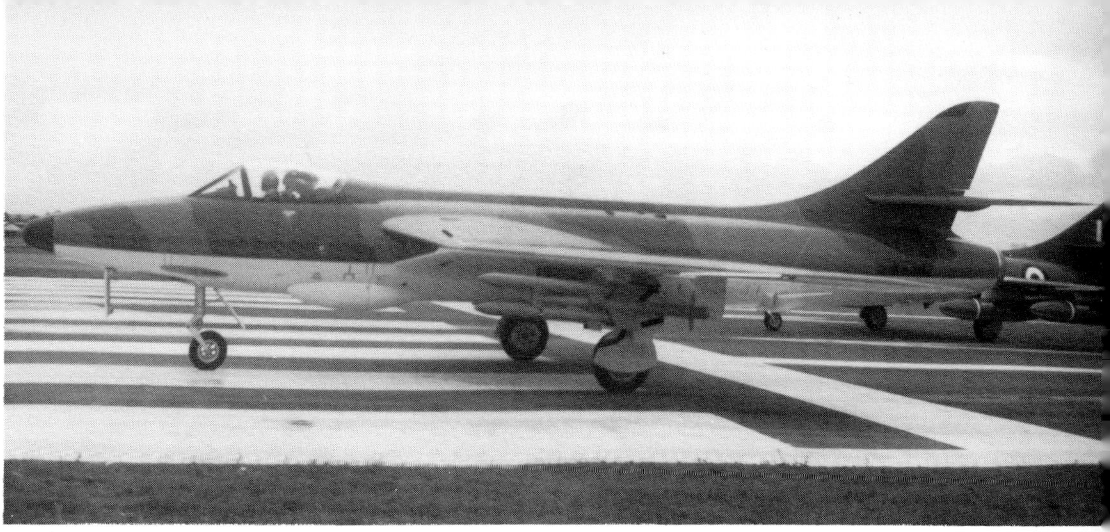

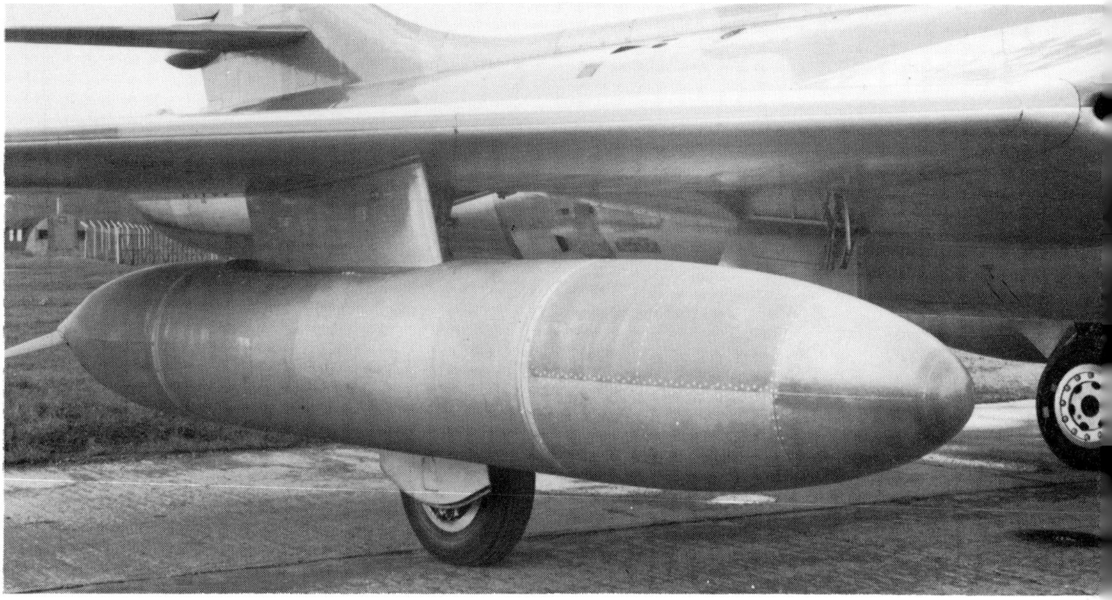

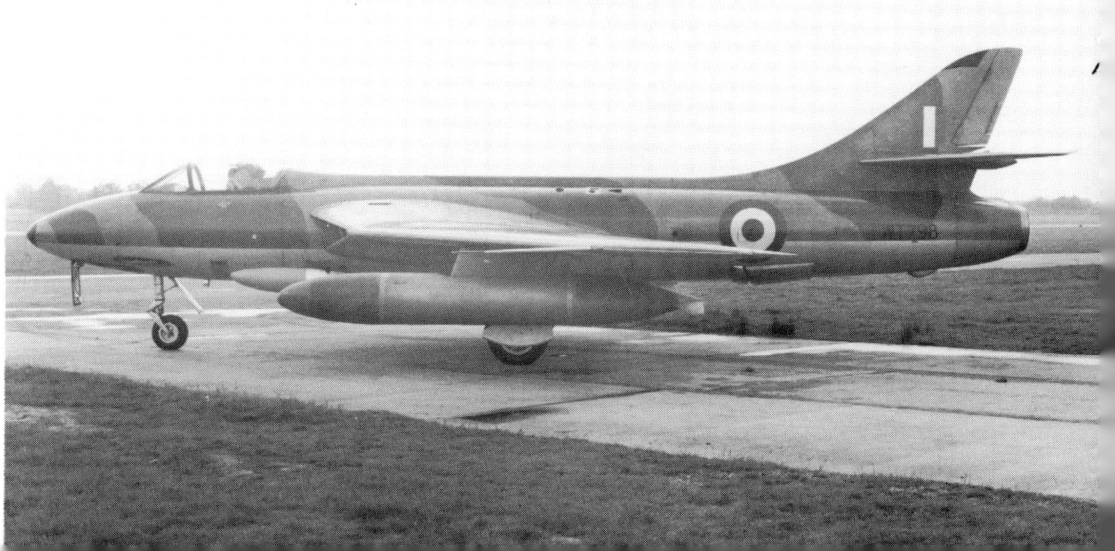

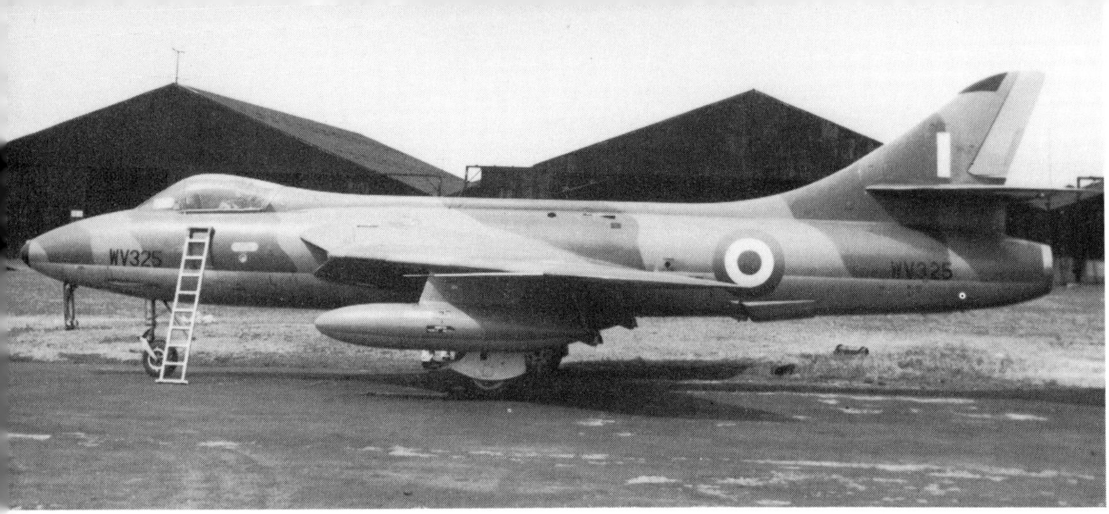
WV325
WV325

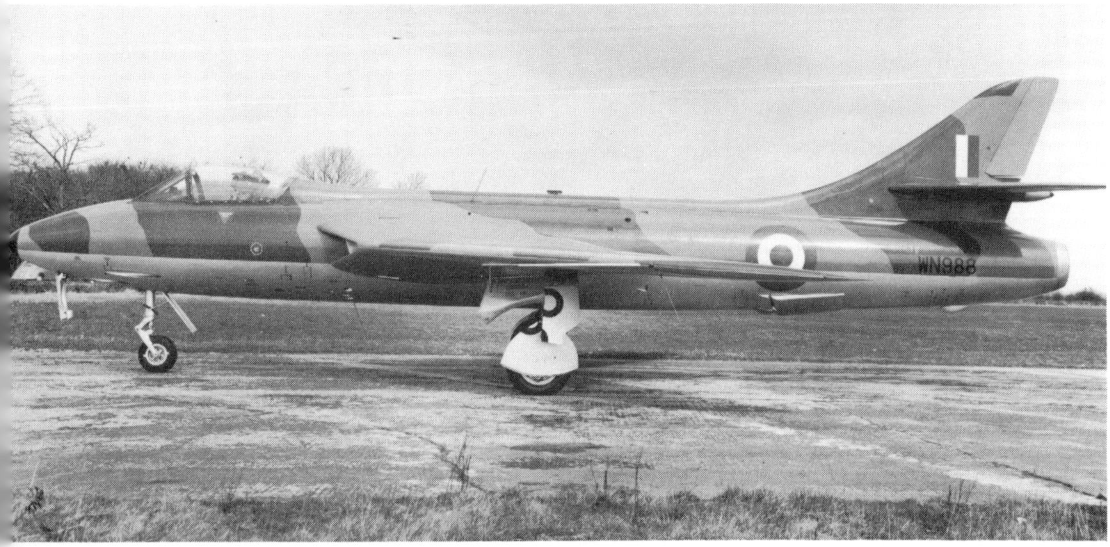
WN988

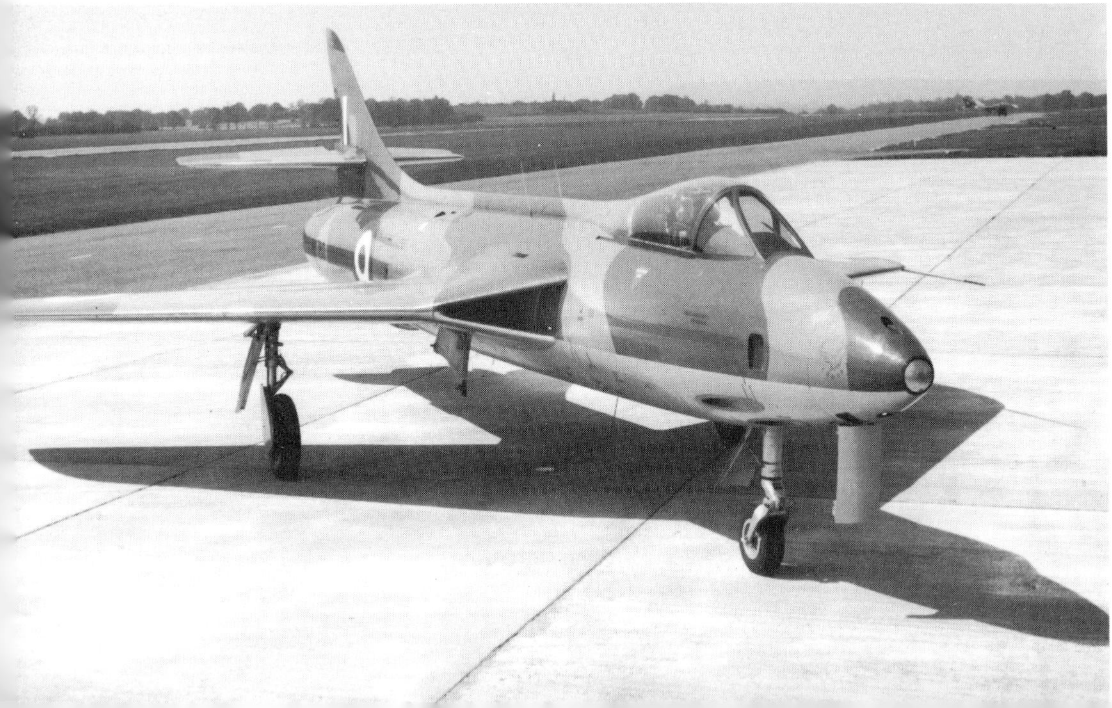

Left *Hunter 4, WV325, displays an unusual practice of repeating the serial number on the nose of the aircraft.*

Below left *A standard production Hunter F Mark 5, WN988.*

Bottom left *The fighter-reconnaissance Hunter Mark 4, WT780, with five-camera nose; this was another privately initiated project which later led directly to the development of the RAF's Hunter FR Mark 10.*

Above right and right *The ram-air turbine experimentally fitted in the rear fuselage of WT780, showing open and closed positions.*

Below *This Hunter 5, WN958, with Mod. 228 wings, was employed by Hawker to carry out trials with various external store combinations; the white patches under the wings were for camera definition during fuel tank jettisoning tests.*

Chapter 5

The big engine

Long before even the first P.1067 prototype flew on July 20 1951, Camm's project designers were investigating means of projecting the basic design forward both in weapon development and in its aerodynamics. We have already seen, at least by implication, that neither the British aircraft industry nor the Royal Air Force was yet ready to embark on a realistic air-to-air guided missile system, and that the trial installations of Fairey Fireflash and de Havilland Firestreak (Blue Jay and Blue Sky) had only been pursued for trials and feasibility purposes. Indeed the whole concept of a 'weapons system' lay in the future with the eventual introduction into service of the English Electric Lightning fighter seven years hence.

As was perhaps natural, Hawker's preoccupation was in the development of the airframe to extend the performance of the Hunter, and in response to enquiries by the DMARD on March 7 1951 Camm and his senior designers discussed with the RAE at Farnborough on May 31 of that year the likelihood of producing a truly supersonic version of the F.3/48. Wind tunnel models were constructed with a 50-degree swept wing on which preliminary tests were sufficiently encouraging to prompt Hawker to start detailed design and stress work the following November, and on February 14 1952 design studies were initiated to compare the relative merits of the Sapphire Sa.4 and Avon R.A.14R engines, now being canvassed among fighter manufacturers.

In the event the Rolls-Royce engine was selected for the P.1083, as the new design was termed. It is worthwhile to comment here on Camm's choice, made in April. For almost thirty years Camm had enjoyed a unique rapport with the Rolls-Royce engineers and it is quite plausible to conjecture that his faith in the Avon, both now and in the next three years—when so much trouble was being experienced with engine surge—was more intuitive than logical. After all, the Sapphire was designed and produced by a fellow member of the Hawker Siddeley Group; it had produced higher thrust figures (and sooner) than the Avon; it was marginally less costly to manufacture; and it eventually proved far less prone to surge. No surviving records give evidence of Camm's reasoning for his choice, and one is left with an impression that he personally canvassed the reputation of Rolls-Royce, and carried the decision.

In October 1952 work started in the Richmond Road Experimental Department on manufacture of the new 50-degree swept wings of the P.1083 prototype, WN470, covered by Contract No 6296, and went ahead for several months. A wooden mock-up was built and in February 1953 a mock-up of the Avon R.A.14R assembled into it. By June the prototype was about 80 per cent complete when the blow fell. The end of the Korean War once more heralded cutbacks in the funding of military equipment, and Hawker was warned to expect cancellation of the P.1083. On the 22nd Air Marshal Geoffrey Tuttle and Air Commodore Kyle met Camm to tell him that the official preference would now

The big engine

rest on less radical alterations to the basic Hunter, and suggested that future work should be concentrated on larger, un-reheated Avons in the existing airframe.

Despite it being made perfectly clear to the Ministry of Supply that the existing Hunter wing was incapable of true supersonic speed in level flight, the P.1083 was officially cancelled on July 13, but the following month Tuttle agreed that the fuselage and tail of WN470 could be employed in the preparation of a new Hunter prototype, the P.1099, with un-reheated Avon R.A.14 and standard wings. A new contract was raised (No 10032) to cover this prototype, XF833, and, by extensive recourse to overtime working throughout the company, the aircraft was ready for its first flight by Neville Duke on January 23 1954. Thus flew the prototype Hunter Mark 6 several months before even the Mark 1 was cleared for service.

The early trials of XF833 were, however, to be dogged by a succession of engine failures. The aircraft was delivered to Boscombe Down for flight observation by Ministry of Supply pilots on February 8, but suffered a forced landing twelve days later. It was returned to Dunsfold by road for repair, and resumed flying on April 23 with a new engine; this, however, failed on the 28th. During the course of extensive ground running by Rolls-Royce engineers which lasted throughout May, it was discovered that failure of the new Avons had occurred following fatigue fracture of the compressor blades. The remedy was to de-rate the engine from 10,500 to 10,000 lb thrust, and to fit steel stator and rear rotor blades. XF833 once more resumed its flying programme on July 20.

While production of the Mark 1 and 4 gathered momentum at Kingston and Blackpool during 1954, steps were taken to agree a standard of preparation for the production version of the 'big-engined' Hunter, now designated the F Mark 6, at the same time introducing into the prototype the progressive modifications found necessary in the earlier production aircraft, such as wing-store strongpoints, wing leading-edge extensions and link-collector tanks. Moreover, so as to avoid the same chronic shortage of pre-production aeroplanes that had been such a significant feature of the early Hunter development, the Hawker Board decided to set aside seven Mark 1 airframes to be completed quickly at 'interim Mark 6' standard to serve as pre-production aircraft. Indeed the first of these, WW592, was first flown by Bill Bedford on March 25 1955, three months before the Final Conference on the Service Standard of Preparation (June

The 10,000-lb thrust Rolls-Royce Avon 200-series engine which characterised the Hunter Mark 6.

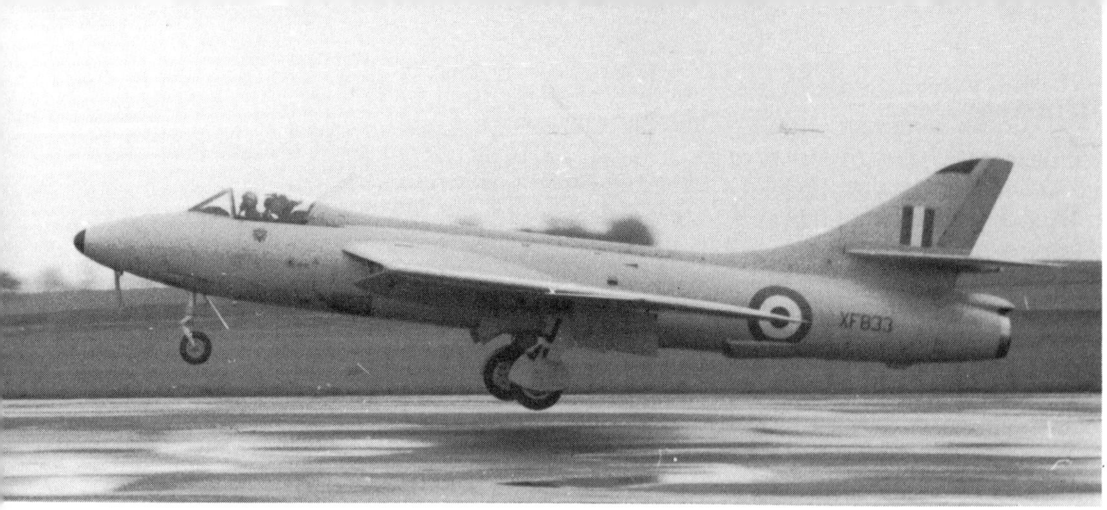
XF833

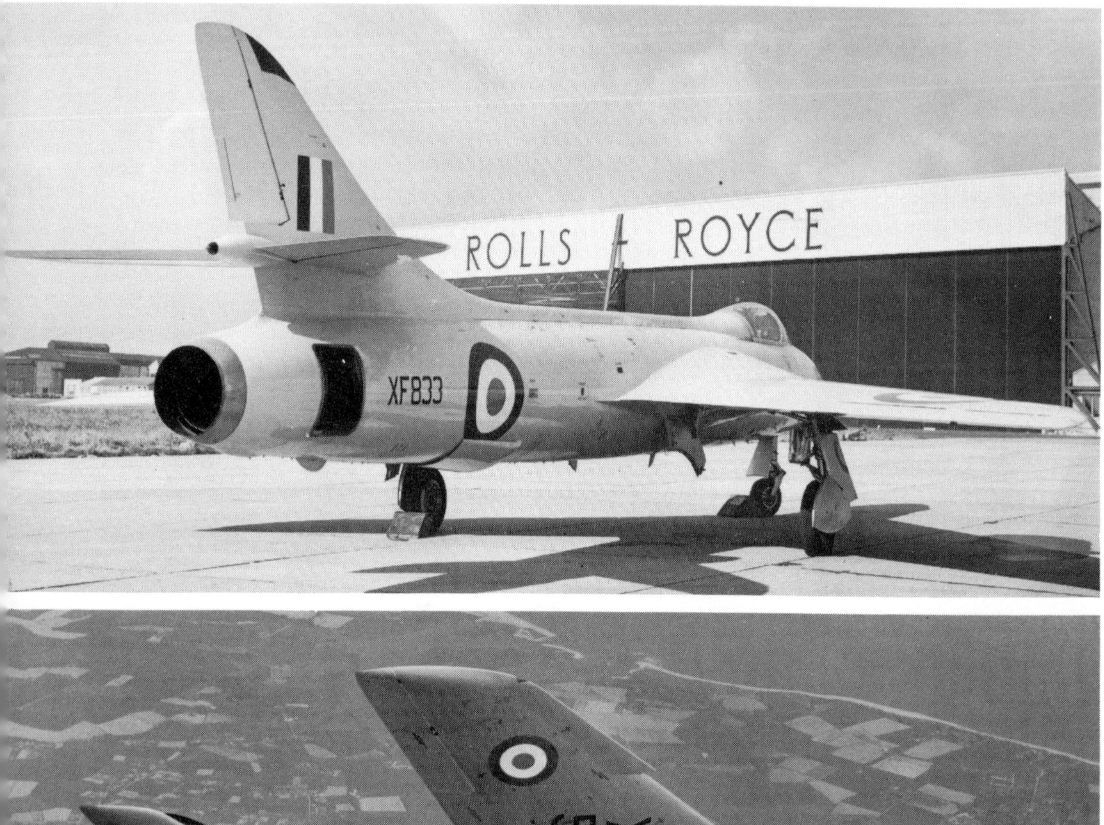
ROLLS ROYCE
XF833

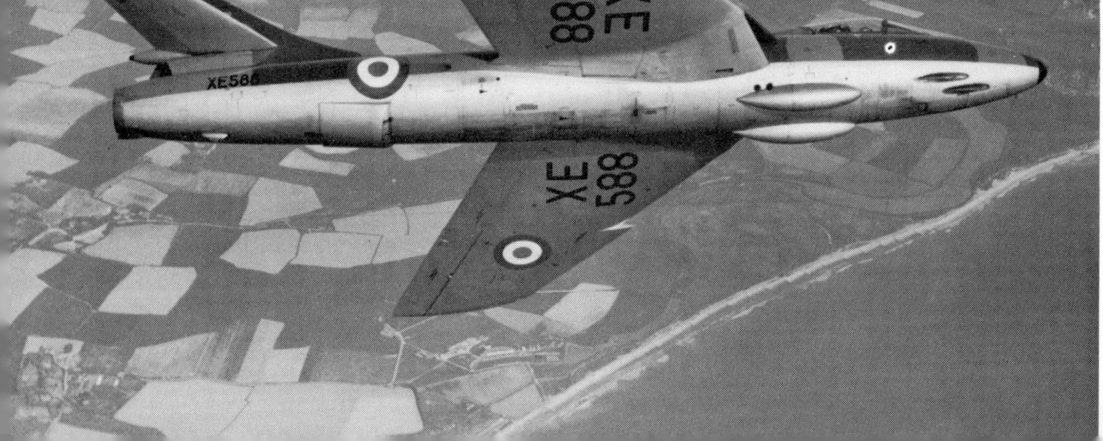
XE
588
XE588

The big engine

21). (The speed with which this aircraft and the following six Hunter 6s, WW593-WW598, were completed was due to the fact that the airframes had been partly completed as Mark 1s at Kingston in 1954 prior to the remainder of that contract (No 8435) being transferred to Blackpool. Indeed, so non-standard were these 'interim Mark 6s' that none of them were initially delivered to the RAF, but were retained for all manner of trial installations. Only when there existed a desperate shortage of Hunters during the 1960s, and airframes were being scavenged from all over the world, were the survivors of this small batch returned to Hawker and brought up to full production standard and distributed as such.)

The Mark 6 Hunter, with its 10,000-lb thrust engine, came to be regarded as virtually a new aircraft and not simply as an extension of the Mark 4. Indeed, most RAF pilots asserted that it felt 'quite different'. Yet nothing could disguise the fact that the Hunter's chance of ever being capable of level-flight supersonic speed had gone forever. Although the Mark 6 initially entered service as an interceptor fighter, pending the arrival of the first supersonic Lightnings still some years hence, it was never realistically considered as such either by Hawker or the Royal Air Force, despite possessing a very good rate of climb. Instead almost all the development flying was to be devoted to clearing the aircraft in the ground attack rôle.

By the end of 1955 production of the RAF's 368 Hunter 4s had been completed at Kingston and Blackpool, as had the last Mark 5 at Coventry. While the new Mark 6 production lines were being prepared at Kingston and Coventry, production of the 120 Swedish and 30 Danish Hunters (Marks 50 and 51 respectively, both based on the Mark 4) was being conducted at Dunsfold and Blackpool.

Mark 6s now emerged from the production lines at an increasing rate, and by mid-1956 just over one hundred aircraft had been completed, most of which were awaiting the CA Release at the Maintenance Units. The delay was occasioned partly as a result of further engine surge problems as well as a new 'pitch-down' phenomenon, both of which occurred during gun firing. Intensive trials had been undertaken at all altitudes using Mark 6s at Dunsfold and Boscombe Down, while Nos 1 and 34 (Fighter) Squadrons at Tangmere joined in with their Mark 5s (with surge-free Sapphire engines), firing their guns at maximum airspeed. During the course of these tests at least one aircraft fired more than 40,000 rounds at maximum speed to examine the pitch-down characteristics of the Hunter.

It was now decided to attempt to cure both the Avon surging and the pitch-down due to gun-firing by developing blast deflectors fitted to the gun muzzles and, after a number of alternative designs had been tried out, a suitable remedy was found. The Mark 6's CA Release was eventually promulgated on May 29 1956, and the first aircraft were delivered to No 19 (Fighter) Squadron commanded by Squadron Leader D.J. Fowler at Church Fenton (replacing Meteor 8s), followed by No 63 at Waterbeach commanded by Squadron Leader S. Walker (also replacing Meteor 8s), No 111 at North Weald commanded by Squadron Leader R.L. Topp (replacing Hunter 4s) and No 43 at Leuchars commanded by Major R.O. Roberts, USAF (also replacing Hunter 4s). All these squadrons were employed in the interception rôle.

★ ★ ★

Top left *The prototype Hunter 6, XF833, in its original configuration with the early tail parachute fairing, but without link collector tanks or wing leading edge extensions.* **Centre left** *XF833, after conclusion of its prototype trials, was experimentally fitted with thrust reversal, as shown here by the exhaust louvres in the rear fuselage.* **Left** *Fine air-to-air study of the Hunter 6, XE588, over the English South Coast, showing the link collector tanks and wing leading-edge extensions.*

Before going on to describe the fortunes of the Hunter 6 in RAF service it is worth while here to mention some of the numerous projects and trials associated with this version that were being examined by Hawker during 1956-57.

At this time the Hawker designers were still toying with applications of the DH Firestreak infra-red sensing air-to-air missiles, despite the lack of official interest shown in the original Sapphire-Hunter prototype trial installation. This missile was, after all, the only such British weapon—with its Red Top development—to reach operational service (in the Javelin and Lightning) and there seemed to be scope for the Hunter to be employed similarly armed. Following encouragement given by the Directorate of Guided Weapons at the Ministry of Supply, Hawker accordingly embarked on the preparation of two aircraft, WW594 and XF378, to be equipped with AI Mark 20 radar and a pair of Firestreak weapons. This project, the P.1109, was undertaken as a private venture. Although the aircraft performed entirely satisfactorily during trials with de Havilland Propellers Limited (the Firestreak's manufacturers), there was never anything but academic interest by Government agencies which reiterated the fact that the Hunter's days as an interceptor were numbered. One of the P.1109s was later stripped of its radar and missile equipment and flown in the Middle East on a series of intensive flight investigations into the effects of severe gusts on aircraft flying at high speed at low altitude as part of the preliminary approach to the tactical requirements being formulated for the Blackburn Buccaneer and BAC TSR-2 strike bombers.

Associated with these Firestreak proposals was a parallel suggestion tendered by Hawker for two-seat all-weather fighters (the P.1114 and P.1115 with Avon and Sapphire engines respectively). Because it was felt that extra fuel would be required for the all-weather rôle, and that Firestreaks and underwing drop tanks would severely reduce the aircraft's performance, it was proposed to develop fixed wingtip fuel tanks, and these were flown as a trial installation in a Mark 6, XG131, in August 1956. Severe buffet was, however, encountered and, as no support for the experiment was forthcoming from the Ministry of Supply, the project was abandoned; after a brief static appearance at the

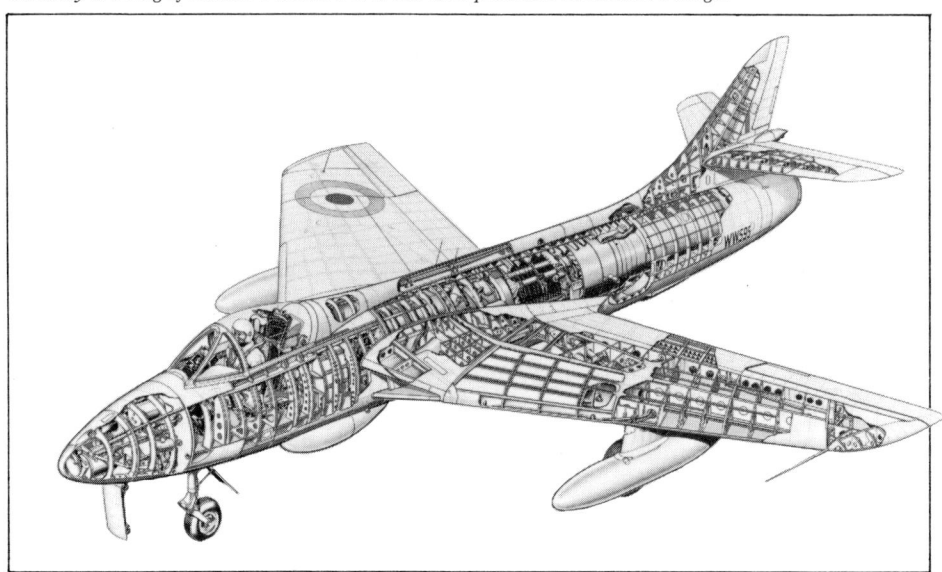

Cutaway drawing of Hunter F Mark 6 WW595 with pre-Mod. 228 Mark 4 wings.

Late production Hunter 6, XK161, with two 1,000-lb bombs and 24 three-in rocket projectiles.

SBAC Display the following month, the tanks were removed and the Hunter returned to standard.

More important—some would say more realistic—was the prolonged series of clearance trials carried out to enable the Hunter to carry a very wide range of external stores, an ability that is commonplace today but which in the 1950s was still something of an innovation which demanded extensive trials owing to the unaccustomed speeds at which these stores might be carried, discharged or jettisoned. Both the Hunter 4 and 5 had entered service cleared to carry a pair of 100-gallon drop tanks, and more often than not did so in the interceptor rôle. Trial installation of stores on a pair of outboard pylons and the carriage of up to 24 3-in rocket projectiles (unguided) had been satisfactorily completed by the company on these versions, but the need for this facility did not arise in service.

Tests on the Mark 6, however, were far more rigorous and the aircraft had to be cleared to carry and discharge a much greater range of stores at all speeds and altitudes. These preliminary store combinations included:

(a) Two 100-gallon drop tanks or napalm bombs (the latter in effect employed the same containers as the former but were fitted with phosphorous igniters);

(b) Four 100-gallon drop tanks, or napalm bombs;

(c) Two 100-gallon drop tanks outboard and two 1,000-lb bombs inboard;

(d) Two 100-gallon drop tanks or two 1,000-lb bombs inboard, and up to 24 3-in rocket projectiles under the outer wings;

(e) Up to 36 3-in rocket projectiles;

(f) Two 100-gallon drop tanks or two 1,000-lb bombs inboard, and two rocket-launcher pods outboard, each carrying 24 or 36 2-in rockets; and

(g) Four rocket launcher pods, each with 24 or 36 2-in rockets.

Very soon fresh demands were being made to increase yet further the range of the Hunter and the company decided to develop a 230-gallon drop tank, flying a pair of dummies on a Mark 4 prior to seeking contract cover for a full trial installation on a Mark 6. The first pair was flown on November 26 1956 with complete success (although shortly afterwards they were accidentally jettisoned over Hampshire by Hugh Merewether). The background to this activity was an increase in political tension in the Middle East, of which the Suez Crisis was a serious manifestation for Britain. Mark 5 Hunters were operating from Cyprus with the Tangmere squadrons with limited success, although not actively engaged in air combat. British interests in the area were to some extent protected by the presence of RAF squadrons at Aden and in East Africa, but it soon became obvious that only by swift reinforcement of these forces from the United Kingdom could British

Mark 6 Hunter with two two-in rocket batteries inboard and 24 three-in rocket projectiles outboard.

armed presence in the Middle East be effective. Doubtful political alignments (again displayed during the Suez adventure) might seriously restrict the staging of these air reinforcements so that, in order to reduce the dependence upon refuelling stops en route, much greater range was needed from the Hunter 6. On May 4 1957 a Hunter 6 with two 230-gallon tanks was flown from Dunsfold to Turin and back, this achievement being followed immediately by an official request by Tuttle (by now Deputy Chief of the Air Staff) to clear the Hunter for a ferry range of 1,700 nautical miles. This would involve carrying about 900 gallons of fuel in external tanks, representing a take-off weight of around 27,000 lb; at that time the Hunter was cleared for take-off at up to about 23,000 lb.

Then, on June 19, a Hunter 6 flew from Dunsfold to Elba and back, fitted with two 230- and two 100-gallon drop tanks, a total distance of 1,300 nautical miles; take-off weight was over 24,000 lb. In order to meet Tuttle's requirements, the next stage would have been to clear the Hunter to carry four 230-gallon tanks, but as the Elba flight had shown the Hunter to be capable of reaching Cyprus non-stop, this capability was deemed acceptable so that the four 230-gallon tank configuration was never pursued.

It is also interesting that, in this context, no attempt was ever made to adapt the Hunter for in-flight refuelling—unusual though not unique among post-war British fighters. Nevertheless the manufacturer continued to carry out long-distance 'proving' flights, culminating in a 1,500-nautical mile trip by Hugh Merewether from Dunsfold to El Adem in Libya on October 2.

Turning now to the Hunter Mark 6 in RAF service, it will be recalled that by the end of 1956 four UK-based interceptor squadrons had been re-equipped, and with the issue of clearance to carry weapons and other stores on all four pylons nine further squadrons (two of them in Germany and the remainder home-based) were scheduled to receive Hunter 6s in 1957 and six in 1958. By the beginning of 1957 a total of 515 Mark 6s had been ordered for the RAF, of which roughly half had been completed.

Already investigations were underway to develop specialist ground support versions of the Mark 6 and it seemed likely that further production orders would be forthcoming later that year. Instead there occurred—quite unexpectedly—an event that was to have far reaching effects not only upon the Hunter but on British military aviation affairs for the next dozen years. Exactly who was responsible for tendering advice that led to the publication of the 1957 White Paper on Defence, now generally referred to as the Sandys' Defence White Paper, was never divulged but its immediate effect upon Hawker was the

Above left *25-lb practice bomb-carrier on the inboard wing pylon.* **Above right** *Two T.10 rocket projectiles and nine three-in rockets under the starboard outer wing of a Hunter 6.*

summary *cancellation* of the last one hundred Hunter 6s, effectively emptying the production lines by the late summer of that year. As will be shown in due course this death sentence was to 'concentrate the mind wonderfully', and may indeed have rescued Hawker from a hazardous stagnation with outdated technology while others were free to exploit new concepts.*

At the time it seemed that the Defence White Paper had been carefully reasoned, although it became evident later that some politicians had not been accurately informed as to the true in-service 'state of the art'. In a world fast becoming accustomed to the threat of the intercontinental ballistic missile (indeed, its use had been threatened during the Suez Crisis), it was argued that the days of the manned interceptor fighter were numbered and that, as far as Britain was concerned, the English Electric Lightning would, when it eventually materialised, be the last such aircraft produced for the Royal Air Force. No one seems to have pointed out to the Government that the Hunter was already being prepared for the ground attack rôle, a function of manned military aircraft that would remain in vogue for many years, particularly in limited conflicts, of which the operations at Suez provided the latest example. Of course no one could foresee the frequency and scope of such campaigns during the next twenty years, yet within one year the Royal Air Force was calling on the Hunter to compete in trials to decide how best to provide substantial ground support capabilities in Europe, Africa, the Middle East, the Far East and East Indies. That the Hunter emerged superior to all comers on every occasion was ample vindication of all the hard work had had been done on store carrying, gun firing, range improvement and so on.

In terms of lost revenue the cancellation of those last hundred Hunters was to have no immediate, adverse effect upon Hawker. The production lines existed, so that first the Indians and then the Swiss immediately availed themselves of the quick delivery of upwards of 200 new Hunters now made possible by the cancellation. It is, moreover, a

---

* *Although outside the scope of this book, it may be explained here that beside the development of the Hunter in 1957, Camm's designers had for two years been engaged in work on an air superiority fighter, the P.1103, a very large de Havilland Gyron-powered aircraft intended for Mach 2 performance. A prototype had commenced building at private expense but, in harmony with attitudes explicit in the 1957 White Paper, this was developed into a strike fighter, the P.1121, which in turn was abandoned in 1958 when the Government stated its intention to back what was to become the ill-fated TSR-2. Thus, faced with a vacuum in the Hawker Project Office, Camm needed little encouragement to pursue ideas put forward, particularly by Ralph Hooper, to exploit the 'new' concept of vertical take-off; these were to reap rich harvest in the superb P.1127, Kestrel and Harrier.*

Flight view of Hunter 6, XK148, carrying 36 three-in rocket projectiles.

fact of modern military aircraft dealings that for every overseas sale of aircraft that can be negotiated, two more come up for discussion. And so it proved with the Hunter.

The cancellation, however, proved infinitely more embarrassing for the RAF itself. The demand for the FGA Mark 9s and FR Mark 10s half a dozen years hence could in the first instance only be satisfied by extensive—and expensive—modification of ageing Mark 6s of which there came to exist an extraordinary famine, while Hawker itself was able to conduct a very lucrative business in the purchase and re-export of surplus Belgian- and Dutch-built Mark 6s!

The RAF squadrons which received Hunter 6s in 1957 were Nos 54 and 247 at Odiham, No 65 at Duxford, No 66 at Acklington, No 74 at Horsham St Faith, No 92 at Linton-on-Ouse and No 263 at Stradishall; the two 2nd Tactical Air Force Squadrons to fly Hunter 6s first were Nos 14 at Oldenburg and 118 at Jever. As was to be expected, the German-based squadrons at first reported very unfavourably on the serviceability rates achieved with their new aircraft, this being due to a somewhat confused modification state evident in their machines, some of which were delivered from the UK Maintenance Units lacking the latest modifications such as wing leading-edge extensions, outboard wing pylon strongpoints and gun-blast deflectors. Utilisation rates were consequently low while the Contractor's Working Parties struggled to incorporate these improvements and in due course serviceability rates came to compare with those achieved with the popular Mark 4, now gradually being phased out of service.

Continuing the traditional aerobatic displays that spearheaded the RAF's attendance at the annual SBAC Displays at Farnborough, Squadron Leader Roger Topp brought No 111 (Fighter) Squadron, the famous 'Treble-One', to the show. A formation of nine black-painted Hunter 6s—a team christened the Black Arrows—performed a programme of scintillating aerobatics that was to become a favourite with the public during the next three years; their appearance was to set a pattern that was to be emulated but never surpassed by many other air forces the world over, yet no aircraft were so ideally suited to such flying as the Hunter 6s with their natural subsonic speed limitation with ample reserve of power and capacity for absolutely precise control.

Meanwhile, No 34 (Fighter) Squadron returned to Tangmere from Cyprus having discovered that the range limitation of its Hunter 5s compromised any real value in the theatre. At the end of the year the Sapphire aircraft were delivered into storage at Maintenance Units and the squadron was disbanded; most of its personnel remained at

The big engine

Tangmere to provide the nucleus of a new Hunter squadron, No 208, which was formed with Hunter 6s in January 1958 under Squadron Leader John Granville White. Three months later the squadron flew out to Cyprus, now with a long-range ground attack capability, where it remained for a year—although during that time it provided detachments for deployment throughout the Middle East.

Throughout 1958 work continued to extend the operating parameters of the Hunter for ground attack work, employing combinations of drop tanks, rockets, bombs and napalm. Of course, much had already been accomplished with the post-Mod.228 Mark 4s, and the Hunter 6 had been convincingly demonstrated to the Swiss in their own country during 1957 in the ground attack rôle. Yet it should be emphasised that hitherto most of the effort had been applied to demonstrating the feasibility of weapon carriage and delivery. It now remained to extend this operation to the limits of the aircraft's performance.

For example, there had always existed a limitation on the speed at which drop tanks could be jettisoned, and at which outboard drop tanks could be carried. It was soon found

Below *The 100-gallon napalm bomb shown here being carried by one of the Swiss evaluation Hunter 6s.*
Bottom *An unusual picture showing a Hunter 6 carrying 230-gallon drop tanks on the outboard wing pylons.*

Above *One of the earliest 'load combination' pictures ever taken. This illustrates the Hunter's ability to carry 230-gallon, 100-gallon drop tanks, 1,000- and 500-lb bombs, practice bombs, HVAR, three-in and two-in rockets, Fireflash and Firestreak air-to-air missiles in addition to its four 30 mm Aden guns.*
Above right *Shown here in its highest all-up weight configuration, with four 230-gallon drop tanks, the Hunter was never cleared for combat with such a load.* **Right** *The Hawker P.1109A, WW594—to many eyes the most beautiful of all Hunter shapes.* **Below right** *Air view of the Hawker P.1109B, XF378. Fully equipped with the Firestreak installation, this was a neat design but failed to excite real interest. Note the removal of two of the Hunter's Aden guns.*

that when jettisoning the 100-gallon tanks at high speed there was a tendency for the tanks to ride into the aircraft, striking the wings, so that before the speed limitation could be relaxed tail fins were added to the tanks to ensure their falling away cleanly.

A much more serious problem arose at high speeds when carrying 100-gallon tanks on the outboard pylons. Airflow separation at the rear of the tanks gave rise to severe aileron buffet, resulting in local skin damage. Numerous remedies were tried to delay the flow separation, including the use of inboard pylons in the outboard position (thus canting the tank down, so delaying the point of airflow separation); extending the pylon aft in an attempt to reduce airflow instability; introducing vortex generators around the drop tank itself; extension aft of the drop tank with large cylindrical fairings (this led to a privately-sponsored development of 150-gallon drop tanks which were later abandoned when the 230-gallon tanks were adopted as standard); and the evolution by Bristol of 'banana' tanks, so shaped as to maintain a smooth airflow between tank and aileron. The problem was never entirely solved and it was decided simply to reinforce the aileron skin; when, however, the 230-gallon drop tank came to be carried on the outboard pylon the trouble no longer arose.

Notwithstanding all this work, it was becoming more and more obvious that, in the light of the deteriorating political situation in the Middle East, this would be the theatre in which the RAF's use of the Hunter would centre. Carriage of large drop tanks, operation at high ambient temperatures and unrestricted operation in the ground attack mode would inevitably demand evolution of a new, specialised version of the Hunter 6. How this was to be achieved in view of the British Government's decision to end production of the Hunter for the RAF will be described in Chapter 7.

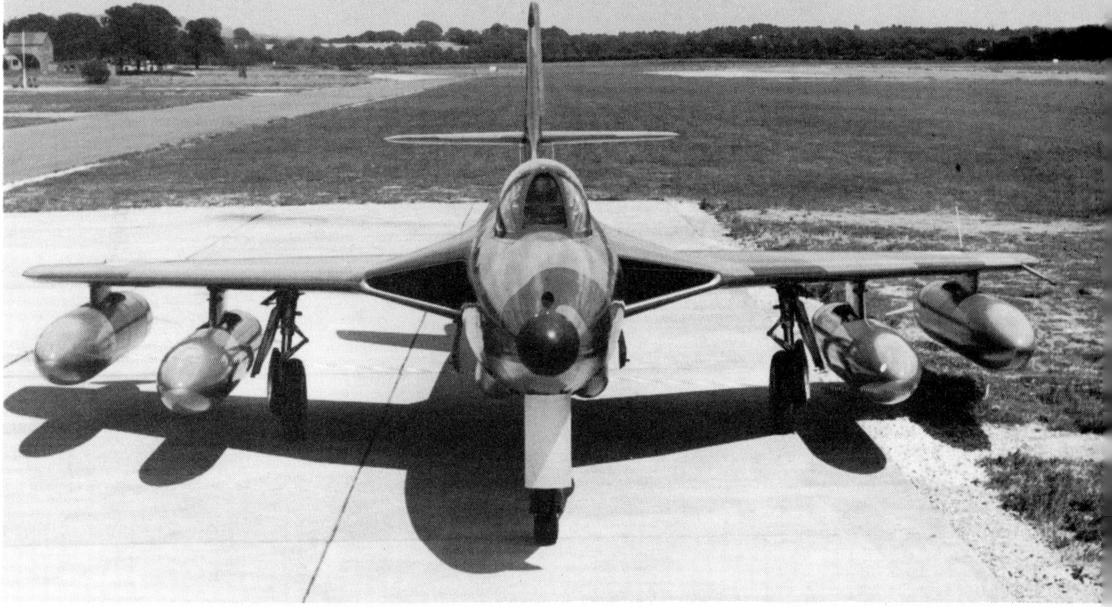

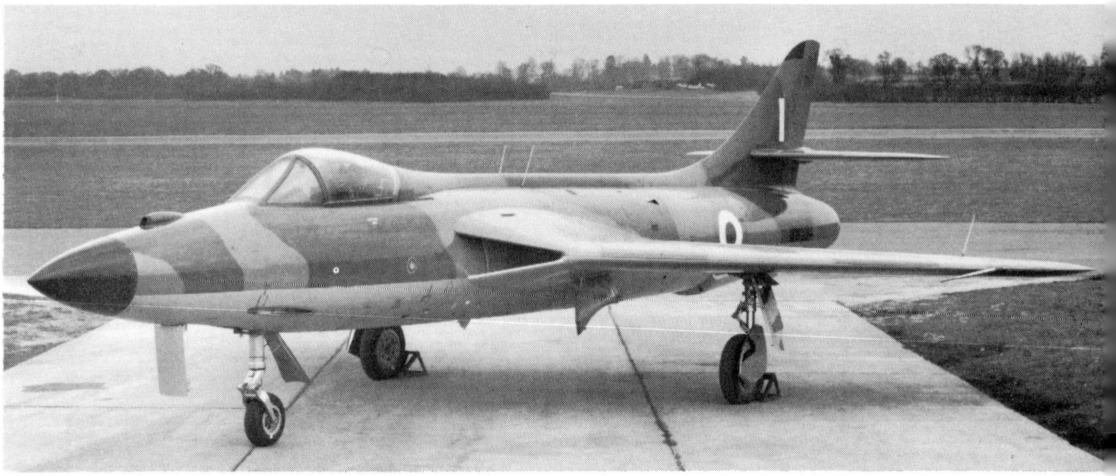

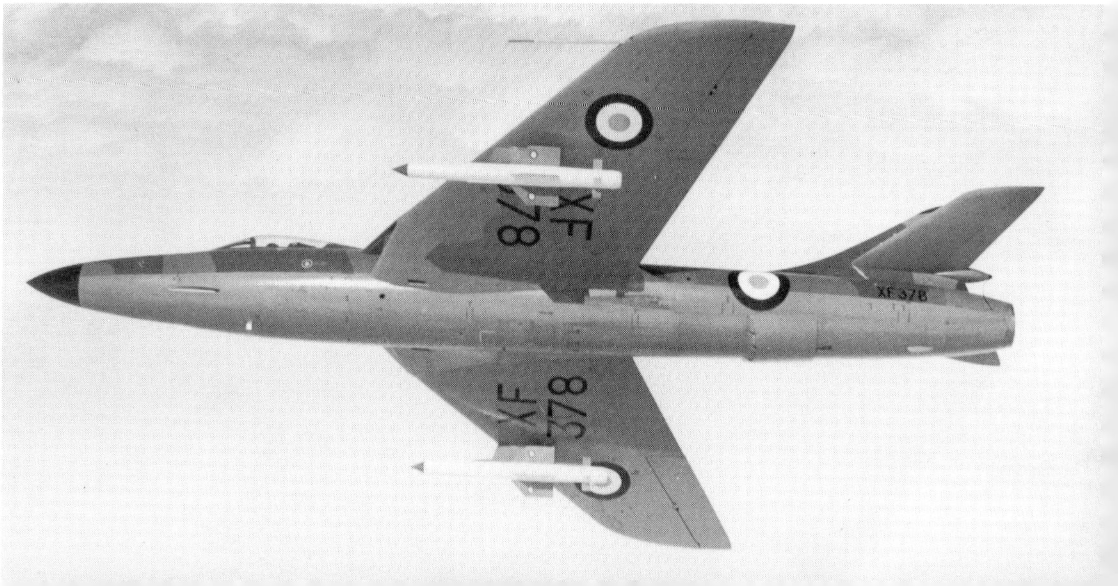
XF 378
XF 378
XF 378

Above *Close-up view of the ammunition link collector tank. The wire guard over the air intake was only employed during development of the cartridge case chutes, shown here in the original (short) form.*

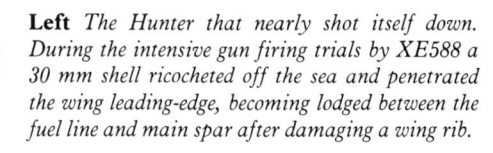

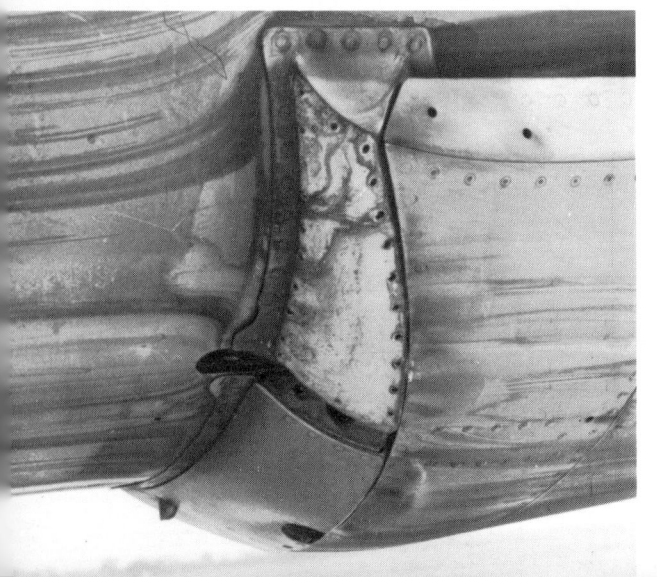

Left *The Hunter that nearly shot itself down. During the intensive gun firing trials by XE588 a 30 mm shell ricocheted off the sea and penetrated the wing leading-edge, becoming lodged between the fuel line and main spar after damaging a wing rib.*

Left and opposite page *Damage caused to air-brake fairing and drop tank by spent cartridge cases during the intensive gun firing trials. Lengthening the case chute cured the trouble.*

SE 662

This page *Various gun-blast deflector variations fitted to the Aden guns during trials to eliminate pitch-down.*

Right *Probably the most famous aerobatic displays of all time were those presented by 'treble-one'— No 111 (F) Squadron in their glossy all-black Hunter 6s at the Farnborough Air Displays. There is no doubt that these displays set a standard that many nations tried hard to emulate, but never succeeded in surpassing.*

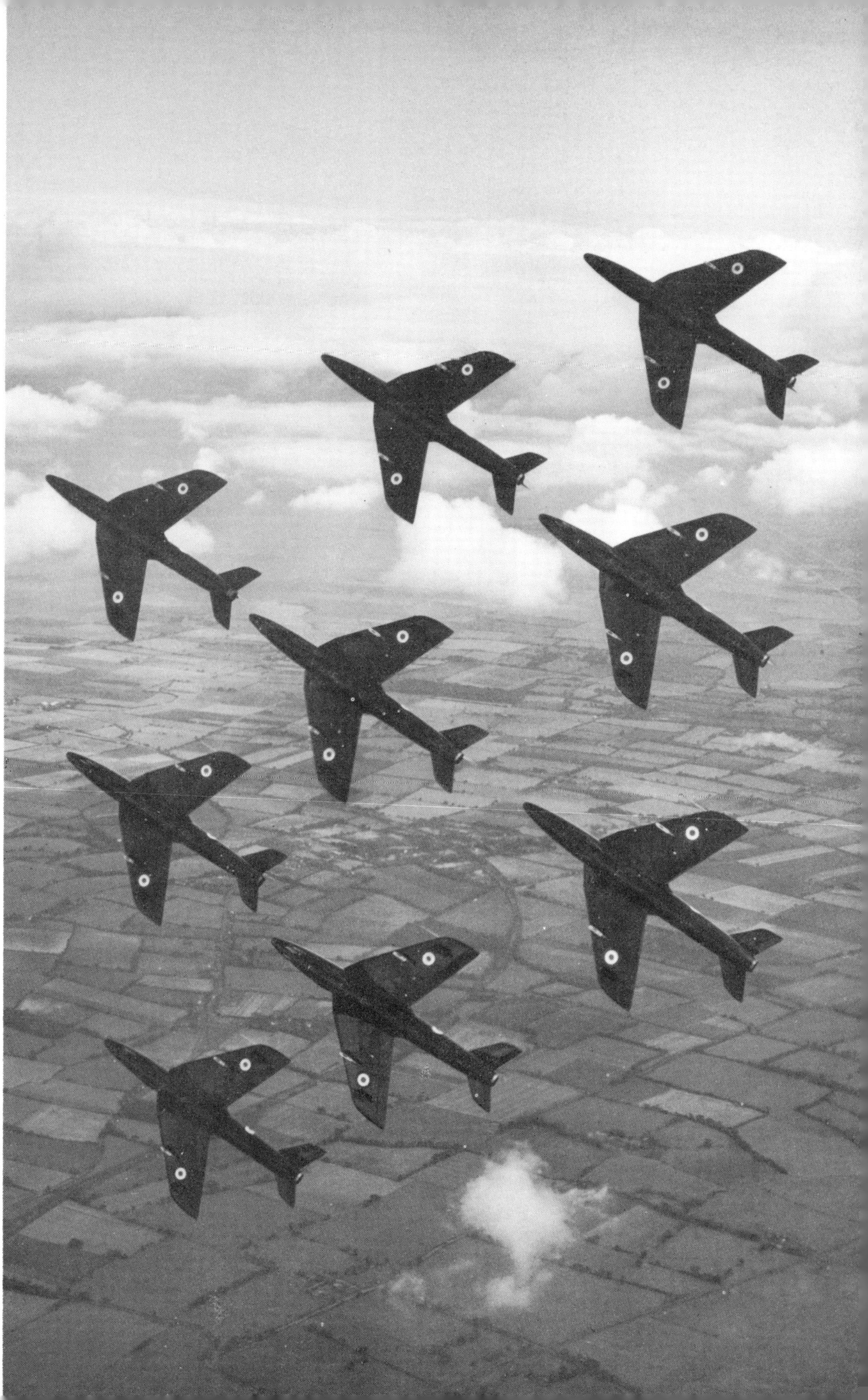

Hawker Hunter

Left *After the 'Black Arrows' came the 'Blue Diamonds', here seen flying Hunter 6s with leading-edge extensions.*

Below left *The unsuccessful tip-tank installation on XG131.*

Below *An experimental side airbrake installation. This should not be confused with the early airbrake development, but was associated with increased deceleration requirements of the all-weather Hunter fighter project.*

Opposite page top *Damage caused by buffeting while carrying outboard drop tanks.* **Centre** *Extended outboard wing pylon.* **Bottom** *Vortex generators added to outboard tank and pylon.*

OVERLEAF
Top *Cylindrical fairing added to outboard drop tank.* **Centre** *Inboard pylon fitted in the outboard position.* **Bottom** *The Bristol plastic 'banana' drop tank in the outboard position.*

The big engine

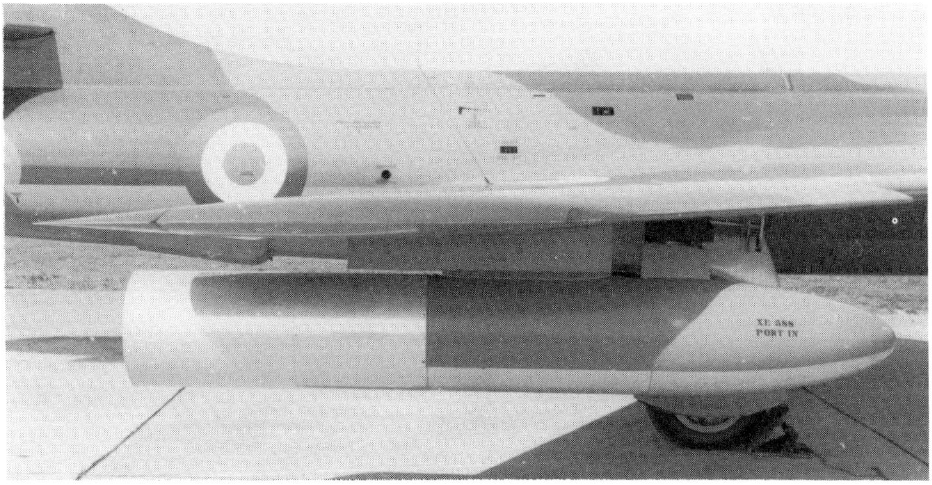
PORT IN

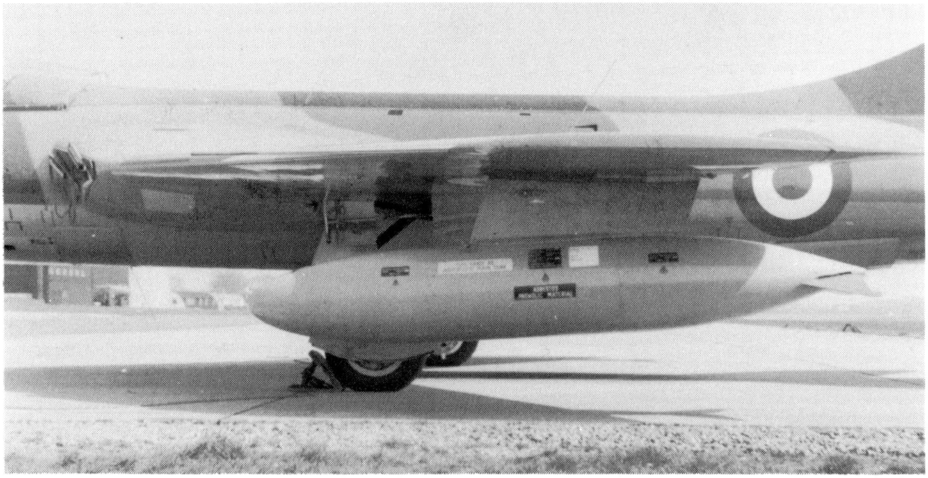

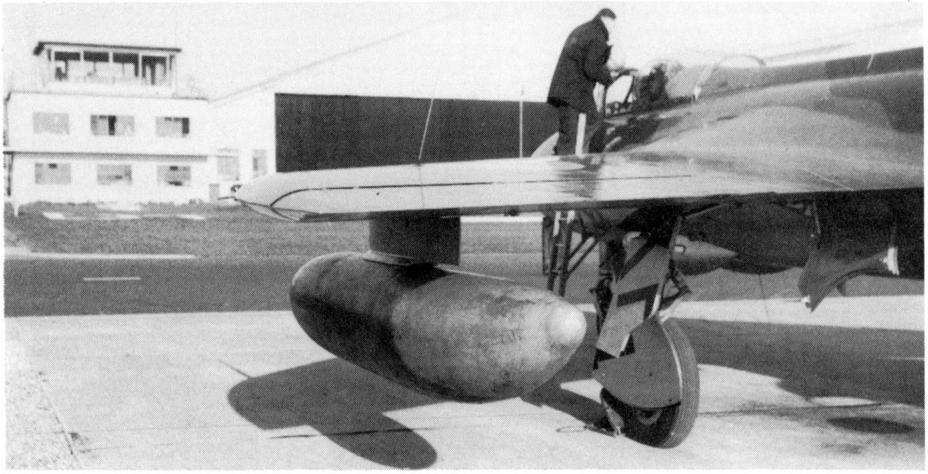

Chapter 6

Two-seaters for the RAF

The practice of adapting first-line single-seat interceptor fighters as two-seat trainers is almost as old as the military aeroplane itself. Such adaptations were fairly commonplace during the Second World War, particularly among German designs. The first generation of operational British and American jet fighters, the Gloster Meteor and Lockheed P-80 Shooting Star, both underwent evolution that produced two-seat layouts in which student pilot and instructor were accommodated in tandem, these training versions being employed both in the conversion and operational training rôles for their respective combat counterparts.

With such a long-established precedent, and the training requirement implicit in the evolution of Meteor and Shooting Star trainers, it is certainly strange that in neither of the RAF's second generation of interceptors, the Hunter and Swift, was any potential two-seat requirement foreshadowed in the original specifications. It has been said—perhaps a trifle unkindly—that had any mention been made of two-seat adaptability at the time of the initial project work on the F.3/48 design, Camm might well have refused to countenance such an implied compromise.

As it was, all three P.1067 prototypes had flown, and production of the Hunter Mark 1 was underway before any thoughts turned towards the evolution of a two-seater. Indeed, the Meteor T Mark 7 was considered wholly adequate for conversion training, while the Vampire trainer was entering service, these aircraft complementing each other for twin- and single-jet operational training respectively.

Although the transonic performance of the new Hunter fighter did not itself pose complications in the RAF training syllabus, it was recognised that in due course the range, endurance and weapon-delivery characteristics of the Hunter could only be realistically experienced by young trainee pilots in a two-seat equivalent. What had not yet been established was whether the RAF favoured tandem or side-by-side accommodation, and while no official preference was voiced, nor guidance offered to the Hawker designers, RAF pilots waxed eloquent in both camps. It is now clear in retrospect that those who favoured the tandem layout were considering mainly the pure flying training aspect, whereas those who advocated side-by-side seating were concerned with applied flying training, such as instrument flying and weapon delivery.

The initiative thus rested upon Camm's design team to scheme up alternative proposals, and in June 1953 the first calculations were undertaken in an attempt to support Camm's own preference for the tandem layout. It was not until August 21 that year, however, that the first formal proposals, under the designation P.1101, were presented in brochure form to Air Vice-Marshal Tuttle. By now the side-by-side seating had gained official preference, and henceforth all thoughts of tandem seating were abandoned, the principal difficulty facing the designers being in the matter of weapon aiming.

These privately sponsored proposals came in for ponderous discussion at the Ministry of Supply during the remainder of 1953. It should be recalled that at this time the only single-seat Hunter which existed was the 'small Avon' Mark 1 fighter, and it was around this engine that a specification was prepared. An entirely new nose section forward of the transport joint was envisaged, and one which precluded the use of the four-gun pack—it being assumed that fast re-arming in the training rôle would be of no importance. Alternative proposals were, however, considered for single- and twin-Aden gun armament.

Specification T.157D was issued early in 1954, and in July that year contract cover was secured for the manufacture of two prototype P.1101s. As a compromise, the first aircraft, XJ615, was to be powered by an Avon R.A.14 and armed with two Adens.

Owing to the delays in issuing the Mark 1's CA Release, design of the two-seat nose went ahead only slowly in 1954 and it was not until September that year that the cockpit layout was agreed by DDOR4 (Director, Department of Operational Requirements, Section 4) at the Ministry of Supply, although at this time an unusual feature was the location of the instructor's throttle quadrant on the *right-hand* side of the cockpit.

In March 1955 a wooden mock-up of the nose had been completed featuring a 'double-bubble' hood, but initial wind-tunnel tests showed this to be unsatisfactory, and the lateral hood contours were smoothed out. The twin ejector seats were delivered in June and on the 8th of the following month XJ615 made its first flight at Dunsfold in the hands of Neville Duke.

Early flights by XJ615 showed up a number of disagreeable characteristics, the worst of which was manifest with the onset of severe buffet, apparently emanating from airflow breakdown around the hood, causing a good deal of noise inside the cockpit, and some directional snaking. It soon became evident that the hood fairing contours aft of the canopy contracted too sharply to allow for smooth airflow, and recourse was initially made to that popular remedy, the vortex generator, to energise the airflow over the canopy itself. Various combinations of generators were applied to the top of the windscreen arch before it was realised that only a whole new canopy and hood fairing profile would suffice to cure the trouble, and it fell to a young project engineer, Cliff Bore, to apply the principles of area rule to evolve the new profile. In the meantime, to limit costs, XJ615 was flown with metal canopy panels until the final shape of the fairing and transparent canopy could be lofted. XJ615 was flown at the 1955 SBAC Show, but it was not until February the following year that the hood buffetting was finally cured.

The same month work started on the development of a landing (drag) parachute, a design exercise which proved relatively straightforward. Following a trial installation of a

Two-seaters for the RAF

Left It took some time to get used to the new shape of the Hunter which acquired a beauty of line all its own. A fine in-flight study of a production Hunter 7.

Right Wooden mock-up of the two-seat nose section showing the 'double-bubble' hood shape, discarded before construction of the prototypes started

Below The first two-seater prototype, XJ615, early in its life. Already trouble had been experienced with the canopy and in this picture are just visible the vortex generators added around the windscreen frame. Note also the twin-gun armament.

dummy parachute fairing over the tailpipe of Hunter 4 WT780, a suitable fairing was designed and flew on XJ615 in April.

Meanwhile Hawker Aircraft (Blackpool) Limited received a production contract (No 7353) for 55 production trainers, designated Hunter T Mark 7s. These were to be powered by the Avon R.A.21-rated engines, more specifically Avon Mark 121A and 122.

It now only remained to settle the matter of the gun armament of the trainer, and it may be recalled that XJ615 had been produced with twin Adens. Early in 1956 the RAF questioned the need for two guns, and in due course Hawker was instructed to proceed with routine gun-firing trials with the left-hand gun removed. Gun-firing at high altitude was carried out during May 1956 and the results were entirely predictable. Engine surging occurred (owing to XJ615 being powered by an old Avon 115) but this would not be present in the production aircraft with surge-free Avon 121As and 122s. Some pitch-down was experienced and in due course a blast-deflector was added to the gun muzzle to overcome this.

* * *

Before moving on to describe the fortunes of the production Hunter 7s, whose standard of preparation was closely allied to the evolution of the first prototype P.1101 (including the re-location of the instructor's throttle quadrant from the right-hand side of the cockpit to a more conventional console on the aircraft's centreline), mention should now be made of the second P.1101, XJ627, whose go-ahead by Hawker was sanctioned on May 31 1956. This aircraft was to be based upon the Hunter F Mark 6—by then moving off the production lines—with the 10,000-lb thrust Avon 200-series engines.

To many people, not least the line pilots of the RAF, it has always seemed illogical to have proceeded with the Hunter 4-based two-seater. After all, by the time the first production trainers appeared in service the Mark 4 fighter would have almost disappeared from the squadrons to be replaced by the Mark 6. This was to be highlighted during the next twenty years when maintenance responsibilities on Service units was complicated by the need to accommodate spares for both engines, to say nothing of the handicap imposed by the markedly different climb performance when carrying out mixed formation flying.

The reason for the Ministry of Supply's perseverance with the Avon 121A/122-powered trainer almost certainly lay in the very fact that many Mark 4 Hunters would soon become surplus in the interceptor rôle, it being mandatory in the original T.157D specification that conversion from fighter to trainer be a relatively straightforward modification process (albeit a factory undertaking). How efficiently Hawker was to satisfy this demand was to become increasingly evident as the years passed. (As will be shown in due course there were to be numerous instances in which Hunter 4s would not only be converted to two-seat trainers but also to Mark 6s with 'large Avon' engines—a process which during the 1950s even the Hawker designers proclaimed far too costly to contemplate!)

XJ627 first flew on November 17 1956 and initially produced no surprises. However, it soon transpired that on recovery from a supersonic dive both prototypes experienced fairly severe rudder buzz, this being attributed to the increased inertia at the input end of the rudder control circuit owing to the extra rudder pedals. Several remedies to overcome the buzz were tried, including a spring-loaded damper in the rudder circuit, but the most effective cure was found to be the simplest—an almost insignificant spoiler attached to the rudder surface at 25 per cent chord.

The 1957 Defence White Paper was in all likelihood partly responsible for confirming the Ministry of Supply's determination not to support the large-Avon two-seater, foreshadowing as that ill-conceived document did the imminent demise of the Hunter. Yet although XJ627 was itself soon relegated to ejector-seat tests at high speed at low level by the Martin-Baker company in October 1958, the limited work already done on the aircraft was to stand Hawker in excellent stead in the export field for many years to come. Indeed, XJ627 was to be 're-discovered' a dozen years hence, re-purchased by the manufacturers, refurbished and sold to Chile as a standard Service trainer (a Hunter T Mark 72).

It is convenient here to mention an interesting aspect of the efforts made by Hawker to cultivate support for the Avon 200-series two-seat Hunter. During 1956-57 members of the Project Office had been working on a two-seat all-weather fighter version of the Hunter, designated the P.1130, armed with two de Havilland Firestreak missiles, with AI Mark 23 radar. Owing to the use of inboard pylons by the missiles, development work had also been undertaken to fit wing-tip fuel tanks on a Hunter 6 (XG131), but when this installation was found to give rise to unacceptable buffet (a feature of almost all tip-tanks on swept-wing aircraft) the experiment was dropped. After the Ministry of Supply averred that the RAF's all-weather interceptor rôle would be satisfactorily accommodated by the Javelin until the eventual arrival of the Lightning (both armed with Firestreak missiles), Hawker obtained permission to approach foreign air forces with their proposal, in which the Indians seemed most interested. A brochure was prepared and in January 1958 taken out to India by Frank Murphy (who had by now retired from active test flying). Alas, the cost and complexity of the weapons system concept*—only then just being introduced to the RAF—surprised the Indian Government and, although polite

---

Stated in its simplest terms, the 'overall weapons system concept' was—and still is—an integrated air defence system employing co-ordinated early warning ground radar, manned missile-armed interceptor fighters and ground-to-air unmanned missiles. This was in effect the defence system foreshadowed by the 1957 Defence White Paper which excluded the gun-armed Hunter from the concept in favour of the forthcoming missile-armed Lightning.

Above *Realisation that the trouble with the canopy stemmed from the shape of the hood fairing is evidenced by the increased cross-section of the fairing aft of the cockpit. A photo of XJ615 at Dunsfold taken in August 1955.* **Below** *Cost-saving expedient was the use of metal panels in the canopy during the development of the hood fairing profile. XJ615 at Dunsfold early in 1956.* **Bottom** *The fruits of Mr. Bore's calculations. XJ615 with the final hood fairing shape.*

interest continued to be shown in the P.1130, it was obvious that to integrate a Firestreak-armed Hunter into a sophisticated air defence system in the sub-continent would be a relatively long-term and expensive process; in the meantime new interceptors would become available (and did so, in the form of MiG-21s a dozen years hence).

★ ★ ★

Returning now to the RAF's direct involvement with the Hunter two-seater, the first production T Mark 7 (XL563) was flown on October 11 1957 by Hawker's newly appointed Chief Production Test Pilot, Frank Bullen (production having been switched from Blackpool to Kingston as a result of the defence cuts earlier that year), followed by the remainder of the order at the rate of about three per month. It should be mentioned in passing that Hawker was also producing other Hunters, notably those for India and Switzerland at the rate of about 22 per month at the time, as well as embarking on a substantial programme of Hunter conversions.

The contract for Hunter Mark 7s had been complicated, not only by the 1957 Defence White Paper but by interest shown by the Admiralty in the Hunter from mid-1956 onwards, and further by the availability of Hunter 4s for conversion to two-seaters. The original order, discussed with Hawker in 1955, had envisaged 65 production Mark 7s; when issued, however, this had been reduced to 55 (ten aircraft having been diverted to the Dutch Air Force following Government negotiations; Hawker was also negotiating a commercial order for ten more two-seaters for Holland).

The RAF order was further eroded with the transfer of ten two-seaters to the Admiralty, re-designated T Mark 8s, these aircraft being selected at random along the production line. This reduction was, however, partly made up by the conversion of six redundant Hunter 4s to full T Mark 7 two-seat standard (among them the Mark 4 previously armed experimentally with Fairey Fireflash missiles, XF310). Few people, least of all the authors of the 1957 White Paper, could have foreseen that many of these two-seaters would still be flying twenty years hence and would have exceeded their forecast fatigue life by factors of three or four.

The principal planned employment of the RAF's Hunter trainer was by No 229 Operational Conversion Unit at Chivenor in North Devon, and in August 1958, immediately following the issue of the CA Release, the first aircraft were accordingly delivered; by the end of the year fourteen trainers had been flown in, and these continued

Tail parachutes. **Below left** *The anti-spin parachute fitted in XJ615 early in its flight trials.* **Below right** *Drag parachute dummy fairing as a trial installation in Hunter Mark 4, WT780.* **Above right** *Dummy drag chute fairing fitted to XJ615.* **Above far right** *Final fairing shape with parachute installed in XJ615.*

to give excellent service for the next dozen years. Single aircraft had also been issued to Nos 1, 54, 65 and 66 (Fighter) Squadrons for instrument and other routine training work, and several others were flying with the newly constituted Day Fighter Conversion Squadron with the Central Fighter Establishment at West Raynham.

In 1959 deliveries continued to the fighter squadrons, Nos 19, 43, 74 and 92 each being given one aircraft apiece. No 111 (Fighter) Squadron also 'borrowed' a two-seater which was given a glossy black coat of paint for participation in the squadron's memorable formation aerobatic displays by the famous 'Black Arrows' (the lesser-powered two-seater certainly showed no perceptible reluctance to 'keep up' with the beefier Hunter 6s). Several two-seaters were delivered to Sylt for use by No 402 (Weapon Training) Squadron, and others joined the Instrument Rating Squadron at West Raynham. The following year Nos 56 and 208 (Fighter) Squadrons received two-seaters, to be joined by several Station Flights, among them those at Jever and Gutersloh in Germany. Further afield, No 8 (Fighter) Squadron at Khormaksar, Aden, flew Hunter T Mark 7s (although one of the first to be delivered to this unit was destroyed soon after delivery when it flew into a hill at night killing both occupants). No 28 (Fighter) Squadron also flew a Hunter two-seater at Kai Tak, Hong Kong, during the 1960s.

Reference to service by Hunter two-seaters in the tropics should be qualified by mentioning that an early production Mark 7, XL566, had undergone tropical trials at Bahrein during the summer of 1958. This aircraft was of standard form save for the introduction of cockpit refrigeration to cope with the greatly increased cabin temperatures experienced. This modification was included in all two-seaters destined for service in the tropics.

Meanwhile, the training of young RAF fighter pilots was continuing at Chivenor. The Operational Conversion Unit's job was to provide the final training of new fighter pilots who had passed through *ab initio* training units and the RAF College, Cranwell, and successfully negotiated a Flying Training School where they would have flown about 60 hours on Meteor and Vampire trainers before coming face to face with the fighter they would fly with their first operational squadron. As well as the Hunter T Mark 7, on which they would be given instrument training, there were also about thirty Hunter 4s for solo gunnery and other weapon training, as well as 'pure flying' experience.

It was at Chivenor that a couple of flying accidents occurred in which student pilots evidently failed to recover from spins in two-seaters, and which initiated a series of spinning trials both at Dunsfold and Boscombe Down during 1959. In the event it was decided that the Hunter displayed no particular vice in the spin, although mismanagement of the controls could cause it to become inverted. As Bill Bedford was to demonstrate so convincingly and memorably at Farnborough, recovery from both erect

FRANCIS K. MASON © 1980

HAWKER HUNTER F. MARK 6
Rolls-Royce Avon 203

HAWKER HUNTER T. MARK 7
Rolls-Royce Avon 121

R.A.F. HUNTER F. MARK 6.
Shown carrying two finned
230-gallon drop tanks

R.A.F. HUNTER T. MARK 7.
Shown carrying two finned
100-gallon drop tanks

OUTBOARD PYLON STATION

INBOARD PYLON STATION

230-GALLON DROP TANKS

MATERIAL MILD STEEL
DTD189A
C

DTD189A
C

PP/41H/678686
DTD900/4288
C

STENCIL ON AILERONS AT MID-SPAN (LETTERS 1-INCH HIGH)

STENCILS ON STARBOARD SIDE OF FUSELAGE FORE AND AFT OF REAR TRANSPORT JOINT ABOVE CENTRELINE

PSCS/41H/679181
DTD900/APROV
C

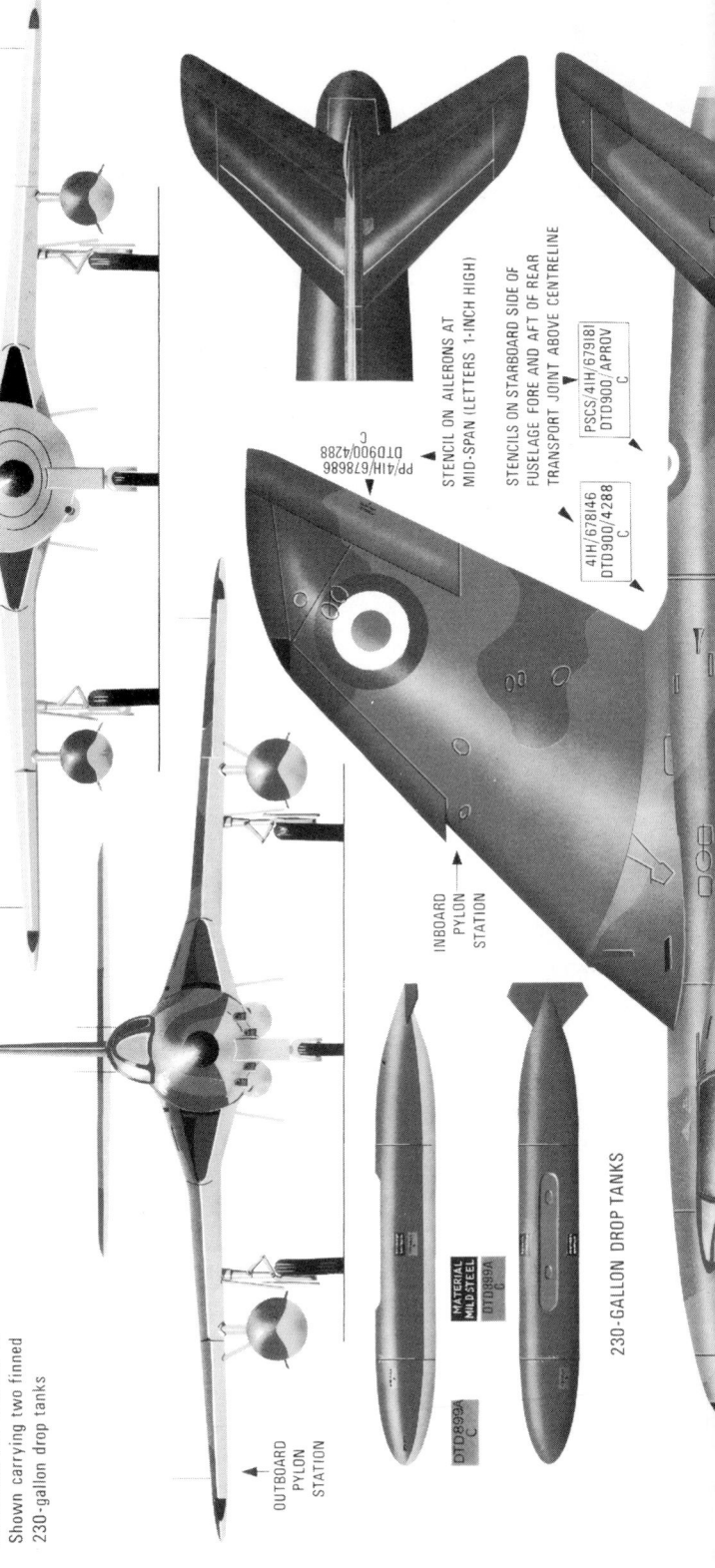

41H/678146
DTD900/4288
C

77

OUTER WING RIB STATIONS

ALL-BLUE HUNTER T.7 OF NO. 92 (FIGHTER) SQUADRON
(SHOWING RAKED FLASH AND SMALL SERIAL NUMBER)

XL571

XG253

BLOCK SECTION AT FRAME 38

TAIL CONE JOINT

REAR TRANSPORT JOINT

FRONT TRANSPORT JOINT

HUNTER F. MARK 6

FRONT TRANSPORT JOINT

HUNTER T. MARK 7

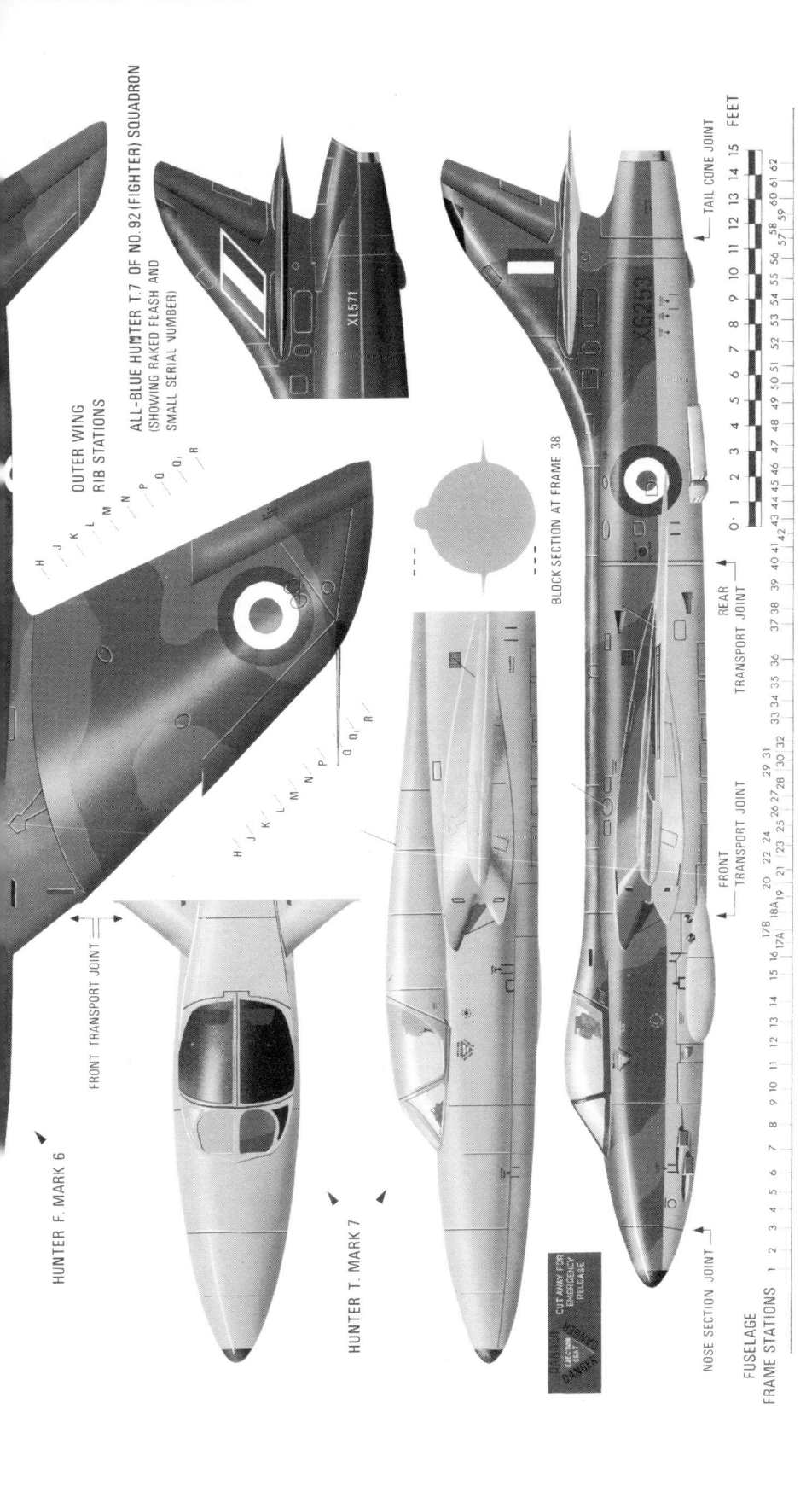

DANGER CUT AWAY FOR EMERGENCY RELEASE

NOSE SECTION JOINT

FUSELAGE FRAME STATIONS 1 2 3 4 5 6 7 8 9 10 11 12 13 14 15 16 17A 17B 18A 19 20 21 22 23 24 25 26 27 28 29 30 31 32 33 34 35 36 37 38 39 40 41 42 43 44 45 46 47 48 49 50 51 52 53 54 55 56 57 58 59 60 61 62

FEET 0 1 2 3 4 5 6 7 8 9 10 11 12 13 14 15

See also page 108/109

Fine landing study of XJ615 at Dunsfold in its 1956 Farnborough livery.

and inverted spinning was both straightforward and positive, and it was assumed that the student pilots—possibly distracted by the larger 'volume' of their cockpit surroundings—had not taken correct and positive recovery action.

Incidentally, it was at this time that the British Government decided to supply a number of ex-RAF Hunter 6s to the air forces of Iraq, Jordan and Lebanon (these aircraft being supplied direct from stocks held at Maintenance Units in Britain and paid for out of American funds). Simultaneously these air forces sent about fifty pilots to Chivenor where they underwent the standard conversion training course for operational use of the Hunter. By and large these pilots showed themselves to be no less capable of handling the Hunter than their RAF counterparts, although one distinguished himself by forgetting to lower his wheels for landing. A fortnight later the same pilot unaccountably opted to land his Hunter on the river bed alongside the more conventional runway at Chivenor—his aeroplane continuing to cover about half a mile as it progressively disintegrated around him. He escaped with little more than bruised feelings, but it is not known whether he was subsequently permitted to fly Hunters with the Iraqi Air Force!

The years passed and Hunters gradually disappeared from RAF front-line squadrons; two-seaters released from the squadrons were issued to No 4 Flying Training School at Valley in Anglesey as part of the RAF's policy of introducing more advanced training aircraft to the student pilot earlier in his flying training. As far back as 1958 Hawker had proposed introducing an advanced trainer version of the Hunter two-seater (the P.1120) to succeed the Meteor and Vampire trainers, but this had come to nothing owing to preference for the Folland Gnat. The wheel turned full circle when, in the early 1970s, the Gnat was retired from RAF service and its place taken by Hunter two-seaters in the advanced training rôle. Most of the Hunter two-seaters involved had been built and had given service before the Gnat had even entered production!

Two of the RAF's Hunter T Mark 7s (XL605 and XL620) were supplied to Saudi Arabia in 1966 as part of the 'Magic Carpet' defence deal with that country (which also included single-seat Hunters, Jet Provosts and Lightnings as part of a 'package' undertaking). These two trainers had already served on Nos 66, 74 and 92 Squadrons before joining the Royal Saudi Air Force, with which they took part in retaliatory strikes against the Egyptian Air Force early in 1967 alongside the single-seaters. When eventually they were declared redundant by the Saudis in 1974 they were re-purchased by Hawker, refurbished and sent back into RAF service at Chivenor!

Today the score or so of Hunter two-seaters which remain in RAF service also include a

Above left *The gun blast deflector developed for the two-seater to alleviate pitch-down.* **Above right** *XJ615 firing at the butts at Dunsfold; note the gun flash being deflected downwards.*

number of aeroplanes flown as instrument trainers with Buccaneer bomber squadrons, with No 337 (Buccaneer) OCU at Honington and with No 1 Tactical Weapons Unit at Brawdy alongside the Hawker Siddeley Hawk—the Gnat's 'official' successor. In 1976 it was calculated that the 51 two-seaters originally produced for the RAF had flown a total of 81,800 flying hours and performed just over 100,000 landings—far surpassing the record of any other RAF training aircraft of similar production quantity.

One final variation of the Hunter two-seater for the RAF remains to be mentioned. This was the T Mark 7A, for which an order to convert eight standard Mark 7s was received by Hawker in 1965. Work involved the installation of a TACAN navigation system. All eight aeroplanes were returned to the factory during 1966 and work got underway, but the contract was cancelled after only four conversions (XF289, XL568, XL611 and XL616) had been completed.

The Hunter Mark 12

This designation was applied to a two-seat Hunter, converted from a Mark 6, XE531, during the latter part of 1962 and delivered to the Royal Aircraft Establishment, Farnborough, on February 8 1963. At this time the Ministry of Supply was heavily preoccupied with the British Aircraft Corporation's forthcoming TSR-2 Mach-2 strike aircraft, a far-sighted and highly sophisticated twin Olympus-powered bomber whose design had emerged from a NATO-inspired requirement of some five years earlier.

The Hunter 12 itself had originated in a draft proposal for the Hunter 6 to be converted to a two-seat trainer for the TSR-2, and XE531 had been intended not only as a trial installation aircraft but also prototype for further likely conversions.

Powered by an Avon 208 engine, XE531 was equipped with a Ferranti head-up display preparatory to the future development of a terrain-following radar; it also featured a large vertical camera in the nose. Painted in an attractive green and white colour scheme, the aircraft continued to fly for many years at Farnborough long after the TSR-2 project was abandoned by the Wilson administration in 1964.

The Hunter Mark 66A

In terms of sheer variety of service no other Hunter can possibly compare with this famous aeroplane. The idea of a company-owned and sponsored demonstration two-seat

Avon 203-powered aircraft was formulated at a meeting of the Hawker management on May 15 1959. At this meeting it was decided to create a 'new' aeroplane by using such major components as could be purchased or salvaged from damaged and derelict Hunters. In due course a Belgian Mark 6 was selected to provide the basis of the new aircraft; this Mark 6, IF-19, had suffered a serious landing accident after completing only 24.05 flying hours, but its centre and rear fuselage with tailplane and elevators had escaped damage and these were contributed to the new aeroplane. The engine and gearbox from a redundant AWA-built Mark 6, XF378, was acquired, while the wings, fin and rudder were previously components of another Belgian Mark 6, IF-67. The newly-built two-seat nose had been produced as a ground display unit for the 1959 Paris Air Show and, being entirely representative of an Indian Hunter Mark 66, was thus suitable for flight purposes.

The new aeroplane, decked out in a dramatic glossy red and white livery and registered G-APUX (and henceforth universally referred to as 'Gappucks'), was first flown by Bill Bedford on August 12 1959. It then underwent a series of searching flights during which Hawker's chief pilot painstakingly—by asking for minute adjustments here and there—brought the aeroplane to the utmost edge of perfection. In it Bedford flew numerous demonstrations at home and abroad, frequently taking British and foreign dignitaries aloft to savour the experience of flight in a Hunter.

G-APUX flew with all manner of stores, including the 'private venture' 350-gallon ferry tanks, and it was in this aeroplane that Bedford performed his unique inverted spinning demonstrations—trailing smoke for display purposes—before the spellbound Farnborough crowds in 1959 and 1960.

In 1963, when it seemed possible that immediate overseas sales prospects for the Hunter had dried up, G-APUX was painted in service livery and leased for training purposes to the air forces of Iraq, Lebanon and Jordan in turn over a period of two years. When the leases expired, G-APUX was repossessed and returned to Dunsfold where it came under scrutiny as a candidate for refurbishing and further resale. In due course it was selected to join an order placed by Chile and in 1967 left Britain once more, this time as a Chilean Hunter T Mark 72 (re-registered J-718); when last heard of in the mid-1970s it had flown a total of 2,498 hours. □

Top right *The tropical trials Hunter T Mark 7, XL574. It is identifiable by the small exit louvre fairing above the trailing edge of the wing on the side of the fuselage. This aeroplane was later tested to destruction in the fatigue rig.* **Centre right** *Cockpit view of a Hunter T Mark 7, angled towards the left-hand side.* **Right** *The famous Hunter T66A two-seat demonstrator, G-APUX.*

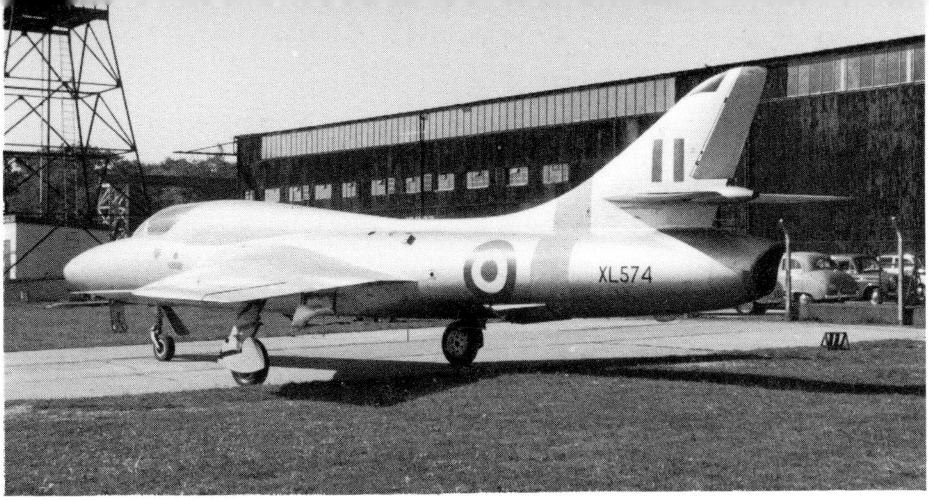
XL574

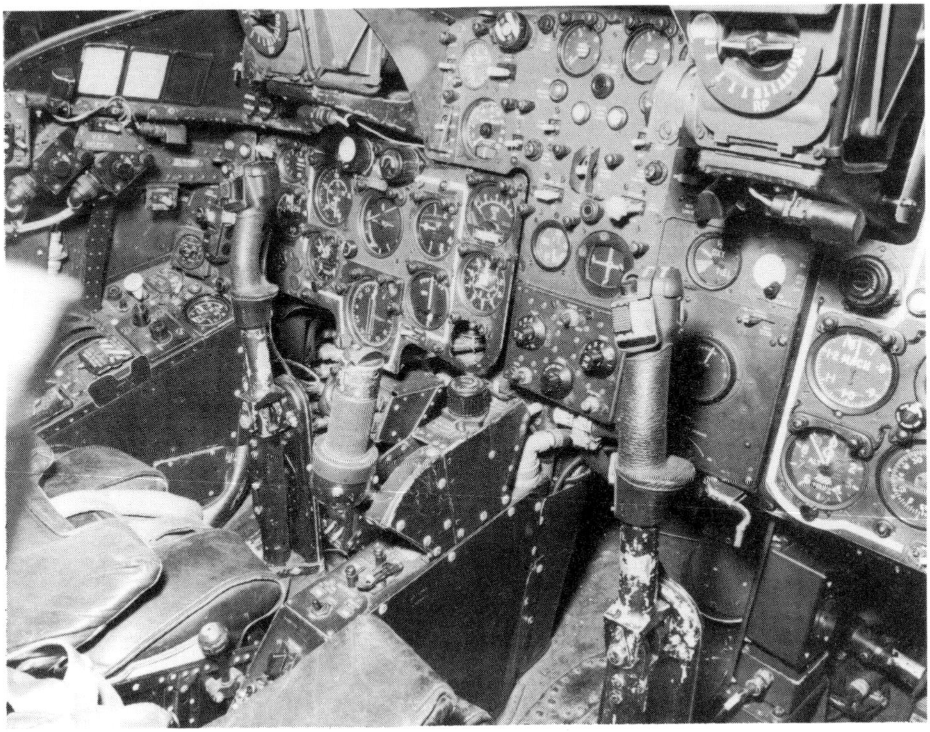

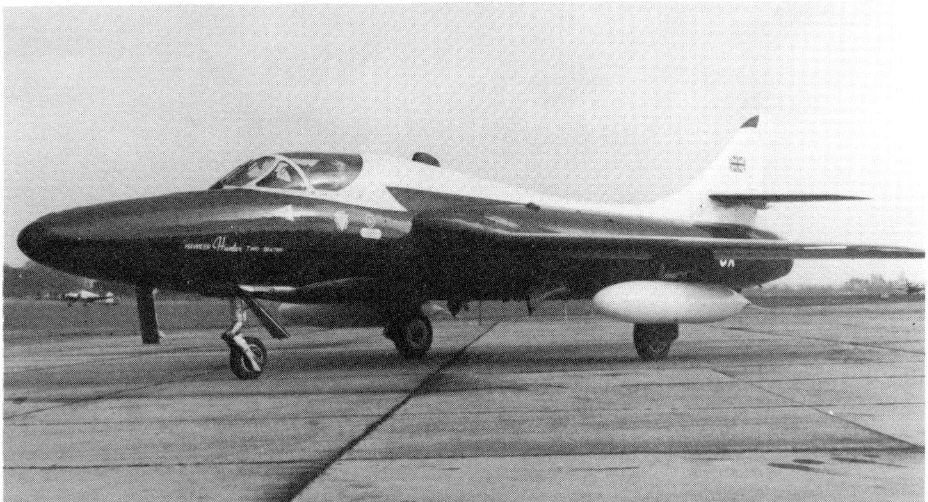

Chapter 7

Ground support

Returning once more to the Hunter single-seater, it will be recalled that work was in 1958 being concentrated on evolving the Mark 6 purely as a ground attack fighter. That this was to be a far-sighted decision has been confirmed by more recent events the world over. In passing, it is worth mentioning that land campaigns involving protracted activity by conventional military forces, instanced by the various Arab-Israeli wars and by the war in Vietnam, have all focused employment of subsonic strike aircraft operating beneath a top cover provided by advanced supersonic aircraft. Furthermore, the philosophy has been further extended by the development of subsonic 'counter-insurgency' aircraft in America.

The value of the Hunter in these limited, localised campaigns was clearly demonstrated in the disturbances immediately prior to the formal British withdrawal from Aden and the Persian Gulf areas. In much the same manner in which the Royal Air Force had assumed the policing function in Iraq after the First World War using limited numbers of aeroplanes, Nos 208 and 8 (Fighter) Squadrons, flying Hunters, discovered that 'lobbing a three-inch rocket through a fractious tribesman's bedroom window' imposed a far more 'cost-effective' discipline than all-out antagonism using bombs, napalm and the like.

No 208 Squadron, which had flown Hunter 6s in East Africa and the Aden Protectorate during 1958, returned home and was temporarily disbanded. The Central Fighter Establishment's AFDS now embarked on comparative trials at Aden to decide whether the Hunter, Gnat or Jet Provost was the most effective fighter in operations from 'hot and high' airfields. Equipped with tail parachutes (following experience gained with the Swiss Hunters), the two Hunter 6s, XK150 and XK151, were universally acclaimed superior in all aspects of the operational trials.

Forthwith a new standard of preparation for the Hunter was formulated calling for 40 Hunter 6s to be withdrawn from Maintenance Units and modified to the 'Aden' standard with the inclusion of tail parachutes, increased cockpit ventilation and refrigeration, 230-gallon drop tank capability and increased pilot's oxygen supply. Pending the availability of non-surge Avon 207 engines, a number of these aircraft were termed 'Interim Mark 9' while still powered by the Avon 203, but by the end of 1959 all Hunters were being converted to full 'Fighter, Ground Attack' Mark 9s.

Meanwhile, the arrival of the first English Electric Lightnings in service with RAF interceptor squadrons was, in 1959, beginning to release more Hunter 6s for conversion, and the preparation of the next 36 Hunter FGA Mark 9s was undertaken by the RAF at Maintenance Units and by the CWP at Horsham St Faith. 52 further conversions followed between 1961 and 1965.

The creation of RAF Strike Command in place of the old Fighter Command, and the deployment of ground attack Hunter squadrons at bases in the United Kingdom, coincided with the introduction of the Hunter FGA Mark 9 into service. In furtherance of

Above *A Hunter Interim FGA Mark 9, XF442, with SNEB-Matra rocket batteries and 230-gallon drop tanks. Note the outboard pylon strut and the jettison-gun blister above the outboard pylons.* **Below** *Interim FGA Mark 9, XE624, of No 1 (F) Squadron, showing the mounting of three rocket attachments in addition to the outboard wing pylons.* **Bottom** *The prototype Hunter FR Mark 10, XF429.*

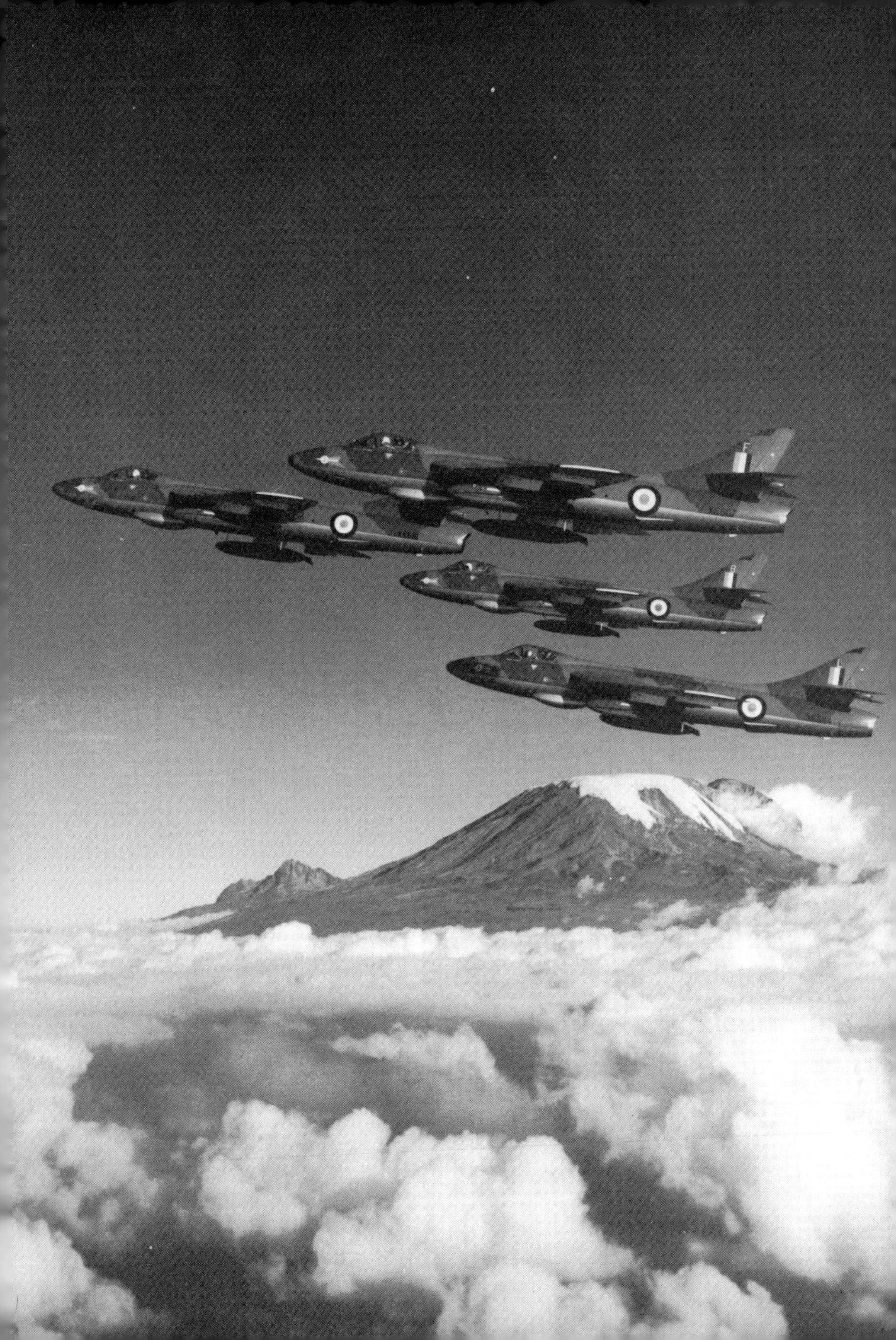

Left *Hunters of No 208 (F) Squadron engaged in formation aerobatics near Mount Kilimanjaro in East Africa.* **Above** *A standard Hunter FR Mark 10 showing the UHF blade aerials.*

Strike Command's 're-force' responsibilities—that is to say the capacity to reinforce distant campaign theatres by air direct—it soon became commonplace for RAF Hunters to carry the 230-gallon drop tank and, before long, the necessity arose to clear the carriage of these big tanks under limited combat conditions, resulting in the addition of a strut to give lateral strength to the inboard pylons. To ensure positive jettisoning of stores carried on the outboard pylons (which now included SNEB-Matra rocket batteries), jettison guns were added in the outer wings—distinguishable by a small 'blister' fairing on their upper surface above the pylon. It also became a familiar sight to see Hunter 9s carrying bombs on the inboard pylons, tanks on the outboard pylons and three of the four available wing mountings loaded with rockets; in this configuration the Hunter was operating at an all-up weight in excess of 25,000 lb—an extraordinary achievement in the high temperatures prevailing.

Hunter 9s served with RAF Strike Command for almost nine years, first joining Nos 1, 8 and 54 (Fighter) Squadrons in 1960-61. No 8 Squadron was deployed for operations around Aden in 1961, while Nos 43 and 208 (Fighter) Squadrons (the latter newly re-formed) commenced a programme of reinforcement training detachments from Britain to the Mediterranean and the Middle East. In 1962 Nos 20 and 28 (Fighter) Squadrons re-equipped with Mark 9s, the former being sent to the Far East for service at Kai Tak, Hong Kong, and taking part in operations over Borneo in 1964. During a detachment to Aden that year, No 43 (Fighter) Squadron was ordered to hand over its aircraft to Jordan as part of the British government's military assistance to that country, but No 8 Squadron retained its Mark 9s until 1968.

There is no doubt that the troublefree use by the RAF of the Hunter 9 in the fairly harsh environment of the Middle and Far East during these years greatly impressed many of the world's smaller air forces, and this as much as any 'sales talk' continued to lend support to the lively trade in export Hunters.

*　　*　　*

The other principal rôle in which the RAF Hunter was to operate was that of reconnaissance fighter. As long ago as 1956 work had been initiated at private expense to prepare a version of the Hunter 4 to include five nose cameras (qv) and Service interest in this aeroplane, WT780, had been manifest in the preparation of an Air Ministry Specification, FR.164D, issued to Hawker in 1957, calling for the development of the

Full drop tank load on a standard Hunter FR Mark 10, XG168.

Hunter 6 as a reconnaissance fighter. (With recent experience of the Swift in mind, it was by no means certain that this aeroplane would meet the Service FR requirements.)

A Coventry-built Hunter 6, XF429, which had been retained by Hawker for experimental work at Dunsfold in 1957, was set aside for a trial installation of the three nose cameras now called for, and was first flown in its FR guise on November 7 1958. In due course the aircraft completed its initial Service trials—assisted of course by all the valuable experience accumulated during the early work with WT780—and a production standard of preparation, embodying all the relevant modifications (such as tail parachute and 230-gallon drop tank capability) of the FGA Mark 9. In addition, the VHF radio was replaced by UHF, and a sub-miniature radio compass fitted beside the customary G4F and E2B compasses. Aircraft destined for service in the Middle East were finished in high-gloss Epoxy paint (DTD5555), while others retained the standard cellulose (DTD899).

Once more recourse was made to the conversion of ex-Service Hunter 6s to meet the order for 32 further aircraft, now designated the Hunter FR Mark 10. Deliveries started in September 1960 with the despatch of XE621 for trials at Boscombe Down following which, with the CA Release issued the following month, aircraft were delivered to the Maintenance Units at the rate of about four per month.

The only RAF squadrons to take delivery of full complements of Hunter 10s were Nos 2 and 4 in Germany, the latter at Gutersloh reverting to its traditional fighter reconnaissance rôle after flying Hunter 4s for nearly five years. Several other squadrons were issued with one or two aircraft each, including No 8 (Fighter) Squadron, at the time based at Khormaksar, Aden, to provide a reconnaissance service for local forces. One such aircraft was passed to Jordan in 1964—and in 1976 this was presented by Jordan to the Sultan of Oman.

With the appearance of such new aircraft as the Phantom and the introduction of its sophisticated reconnaissance packs, the Hunter 10 was phased out of RAF service towards the end of the 1960s; many such aircraft were then purchased by Hawker Siddeley Aviation for refurbishing and resale overseas. □

Chapter 8

The Naval Hunters

At the time when Hunters were entering service with the Royal Air Force, the Royal Navy's Fleet Air Arm was equipped with a wide range of fighters and strike aircraft, including such aeroplanes as the Sea Hawk, Sea Venom, Attacker and Wyvern, for which adequate pilot training could be provided by the Sea Fury and Vampire two-seaters. With the approach of the transonic Sea Vixen and Scimitar fighters, of which no training variant existed, it was not unnatural that the Hunter two-seater should attract the Admiralty's attention.

As already mentioned in Chapter 6, this interest found expression with the diversion of a number of the Ministry of Supply new-build Hunter T Mark 7s from the RAF to the Fleet Air Arm. A total of ten such aircraft were selected at random from the Mark 7 production line in 1957 and equipped with an airfield arrestor hook (previously developed on the Hunter Mark 4, WT780). The limited prototype work was carried out on a converted Hunter 4, WW664, this aircraft having suffered an accident in RAF service and been returned to Dunsfold for repair.

Delivered to Boscombe Down on May 9 1958, WW664 underwent brief trials following which the Service Release was issued and deliveries of new-build Mark 8s started. XL581 was issued to No 736 (Training) Squadron at Lossiemouth on July 3, and XL580 to No 764 (Training) Squadron later the same month. (Unfortunately XL581 was to be lost within a month in a crash following low level aerobatics over Lossiemouth; the

A conversion from a Hunter Mark 4, WW664 was employed by Hawker as the prototype Hunter T Mark 8 two-seat trainer for the Fleet Air Arm. Clearly visible in this picture is the airfield arrestor hook under the rear fuselage; at the time it was taken Hawker was flying underwing tanks without tail fins.

naval pilot, who was flying solo, was killed.) The remaining eight new-build Mark 8s had all been delivered to Lossiemouth by the end of January 1959, and these were then joined by seventeen further Mark 8s converted from Mark 4 single-seaters, the majority of these aircraft joining No 764 Squadron.

The training rôle assumed by No 764 Squadron was akin to that of its RAF counterpart, the Operational Conversion Unit, with the emphasis on applied flying and navigation. With such a limited availability of aircraft, it might have been expected that attrition would severely restrict operations, yet Lossiemouth achieved extraordinarily high utilisation of its Hunter 8s, and serious accidents were rare; apart from the early accident involving XL581, only three other aircraft were lost in ten years; XL582 suffered engine failure during take-off from Yeovilton in January 1968 (the pilot escaping unhurt), and XL599 collided with WT701 in August 1961.

A second phase of conversions of single- to two-seaters for the Fleet Air Arm commenced in 1963 with the issue of a requirement for operational training on TACAN, the navigation system now widely equipping Service aircraft. XL604, a Mark 8 which had been returned to Hawker for repair after being overstressed during aerobatics, was set aside for conversion with the installation of an interim TACAN navigator, this aeroplane being regarded as the prototype T Mark 8C. After brief trials, XL604 was delivered to No 759 (Training) Squadron at Brawdy on November 22 1963, followed by ten further aircraft, all converted to two-seaters from Mark 4s.

Some measure of the very high utilisation being achieved by the Fleet Air Arm may be judged from the fact that within six years these eleven trainers flew more than 22,500 hours—this despite the loss of four aircraft in flying accidents. Three further aircraft, XF967, XF978 and XF995, were also converted from Mark 4 to Mark 8 standard, this time being equipped with the complete TACAN system, these Hunters being designated T Mark 8Bs.

Among the most attractively finished of all Service Hunters were the three T Mark 8s assigned for use by the Flag Officer (Flying Training) at Yeovilton, Rear-Admiral P.D. Gick*. The Hunters, XE665, XL580 and XL584, were prepared by Hawker in high-

---

* Admiral Gick was a distinguished naval airman who, more than twenty years earlier as a young Lieutenant flying a Swordfish, had scored the vital torpedo hit on the German battleship Bismarck at large in the Atlantic.

The Naval Hunters

Left *An in-service Hunter T Mark 8, XF358—again a conversion from a Hunter 4.*

Right *Unusual picture of Lossiemouth's Hunter T Mark 8s in formation.*

OVERLEAF
Top *One of three specially finished Hunter T Mark 8s in a smart blue and white epoxy paint scheme, this aeroplane, XL580, was allotted to Flag Officer (Flying Training) at Yeovilton. Note the Admiral's flag painted on the nose.* **Centre** *The sun catches the highlights on the epoxy paint finish of this Hunter GA Mark 11, WV380.* **Bottom** *Hunter GA Mark 11, WV380, displays its white undersurfaces. Note the absence of guns and the addition of airfield arrestor hook.*

gloss epoxy paint, the upper surfaces being painted dark grey-blue and the lower surfaces white; the 100-gallon drop tanks were similarly finished and, widely referred to as 'the Admiral's barges', the aircraft carried the Admiral's flag painted on their nose.

★ ★ ★

In concert with the need to provide the Fleet Air Arm with a two-seat trainer was issued an Admiralty requirement for a single-seat weapons trainer, and once more the Hunter Mark 4 was selected as the basis for conversion. An order for forty such conversions was placed with Hawker in 1961, and in view of the nature of the weapon delivery training envisaged the Mark 4s recovered from the RAF were those with the lowest airframe hours.

The aircraft were delivered to Kingston-upon-Thames by road where they were dismantled and re-jigged; the Aden guns and gun pack were removed, a TACAN navigation system installed and an airfield arrestor hook added under the rear fuselage. The aircraft were finished in high gloss epoxy paint, the upper surfaces being dark grey and the lower surfaces white.

The first Hunter GA Mark 11, XE712—as the new aircraft was designated—underwent brief trials at Dunsfold and Boscombe Down in April and May 1962, and delivery of the remaining aircraft to No 739 (Training) Squadron at Lossiemouth started in June. A small number of aircraft, termed PR Mark 11s, were delivered to Short Bros at Belfast to be equipped with reconnaissance cameras, although these aircraft still remained strictly training aircraft.

In service with Nos 738 and 764 Squadrons, the Mark 11s flew with a very wide assortment of underwing stores, including HE and practice bombs, and rocket batteries of various sorts. At one time aircraft were experimentally modified to carry Martin Bullpup missiles and Philco Sidewinders.

Much later on it was intended to increase the number of Hunter single-seaters in use with the Fleet Air Arm in the weapons training rôle, but in line with the then-current policy of limiting expenditure on naval aviation further conversions to Mark 11 were refused. Instead a small number of standard Hunter 4s was temporarily transferred to Admiralty charge. ☐

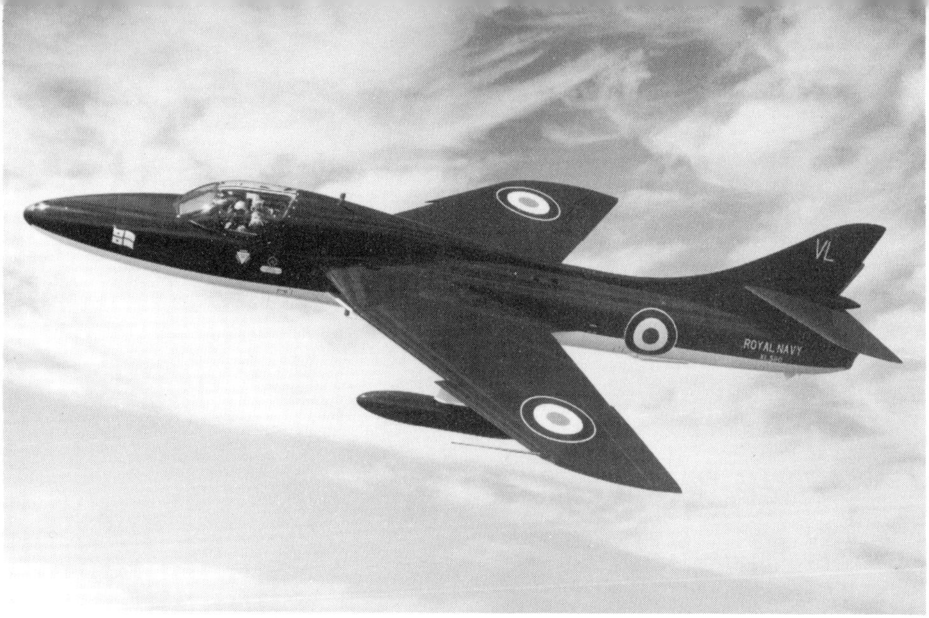
VL
ROYAL NAVY

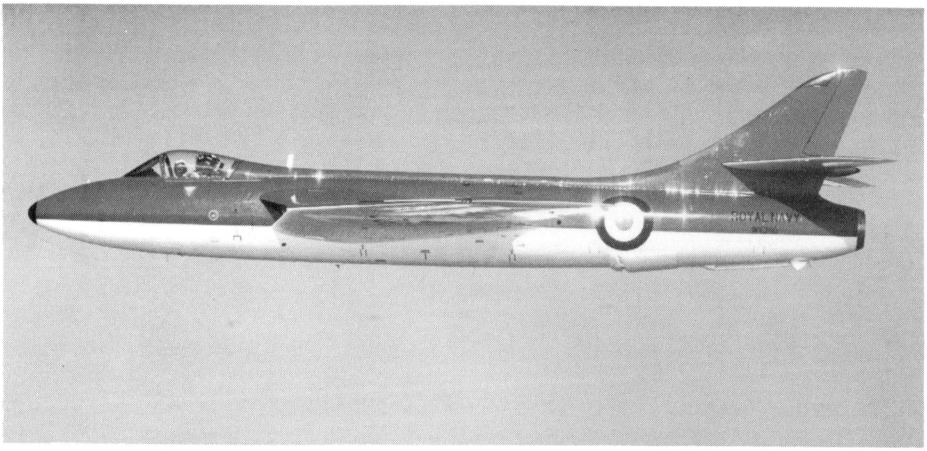
ROYAL NAVY

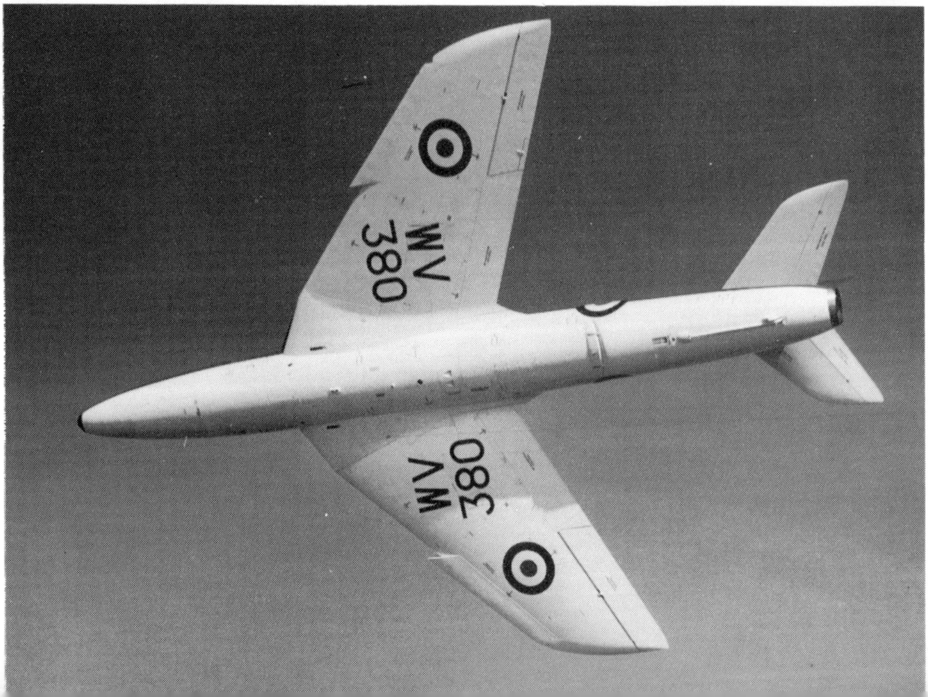
WV
380
WV
380

Chapter 9

Exports—a lesson in orthodoxy

The quite extraordinary volume and diversity of Hunter sales to foreign governments fall into two distinct categories, and to understand fully the nature of the division it is simplest to deal with them quite separately. However, it must always be remembered that, with few exceptions, these sales were the outcome of enterprising commercial effort by a dedicated sales organisation backed by an enthusiastic design term. And it must be added that for every instance wherein Government-sponsored sales were undertaken there was probably another private sale being frustrated by unwarrantable Government interference.

This in turn provokes two observations. First, one is prompted to reflect whether the same outstanding sales successes would or could have been achieved by a State-owned manufacturer with all the ponderous machinery designed to equate politics with economics. Secondly, one has become aware of the self-inflicted penalties imposed by ideological interference with the commercial sales of military aeroplanes. This is not to suggest that *national* susceptibilities may not dictate the rectitude of arms sales to potential enemies, but that to permit superficial dogma to interfere with commercial business—particularly in a capitalist democracy—is tantamount to economic suicide. To be specific, for every arms deal frustrated by ideological embarrassment there will be a queue of other Western democracies eager to capitalise on misplaced holier-than-thou sentiments. Behind this statement of fact lies the very reason for the decline of the British aircraft industry during the period 1958-1980, while in direct contrast the French industry has grown to flourish out of a state of almost total impotence in exactly the same period. (One is also prompted to recall that it was the vigour with which the old Hawker Company pursued its foreign sales during the early 1930s that enabled the whole British aircraft industry to survive the Depression and accommodate the radical Expansion Programme prior to the Second World War.)

★ ★ ★

Overseas interest in the Hunter fighter was first evident on November 14 1950 when the Australian Government, which had for some time been pursuing plans to build the Hawker P.1081 under licence, changed its mind in favour of the P.1067. These plans were overtaken by events in Korea where, in due course, the Royal Australian Air Force flew the F-86 Sabre, and this aircraft was put into production at Fishermen's Bend, near Melbourne, albeit powered by the Rolls-Royce Avon engine.

Much nearer home the NATO alliance had emerged intact after the lifting of the Berlin blockade by the Russians. However, the appearance in Communist-bloc air forces of the Russian MiG-15 jet fighter had spotlighted attention on the inadequacy of European air force fighter equipment, dependent as it was upon such obsolescent aircraft as the

First of the Hunter Mark 50s, 34001, destined for Sweden. Note the absence of wing extensions, link collector tanks and gun-blast deflectors.

Meteor, Vampire, Venom and Republic F-84 Thunderjet. American and Canadian air forces flew the F-86 in some numbers in Europe, but it was soon felt by European governments that dependence upon transatlantic reinforcement in time of crisis was unacceptable, especially in view of the fragile East-West relationships.

Following an impressive display by Neville Duke in WB188 at the Brussels Air Show on July 10 1952, NATO interest in the Hunter gained momentum and on October 22 that year two American NATO pilots, Colonel Johnson and Major Davis, visited Hawker to fly the prototypes. Further demonstrations followed in the next six months, a diversion that did nothing to alleviate the already overstrained flight test programme imposed on the meagre number of prototypes.

Nevertheless, these efforts quickly bore fruit and following decisions by the Dutch and Belgian governments to adopt the Hunter as their air forces' standard fighters, licence contracts were negotiated with Fokker of Holland and Avions Fairey and SABCA of Belgium for the manufacture of the Hunter in those countries. These negotiations were completed in May 1954, but owing to the impoverished state of these nations only eight years after the Second World War, 'off-shore' funding for the manufacture of the Hunters was to be provided by the United States of America.

Henceforth throughout all the trials and tribulations undergone by the Hunter during 1954 and 1955, the NATO countries and licence manufacturers were kept fully informed of the remedies adopted by the parent company. One may conjecture that there must have been numerous occasions whereon the decision to adopt the Hunter came in for painful recrimination, and it was not long before the choice for licence production in Holland and Belgium fell naturally upon the Mark 4 rather than the Mark 1, a decision finalised in November 1954.

Sweden

Meanwhile, a non-aligned nation had expressed interest in purchasing the Hunter. Sweden, whose air force, the *Flygvapnet*, had for many years flown aircraft manufactured abroad—as well as some excellent indigenous designs—now sought to standardise its choice of fighter, and on June 29 1954 signed an order with Hawker Aircraft (Blackpool) Limited for the delivery of no fewer than 120 Hunters, a contract valued at more than £25m.

Exports—a lesson in orthodoxy 93

Several *Flygvapnet* pilots visited Dunsfold during 1954 and 1955 to keep abreast of the Hunter's progress and, although the first 24 aircraft built at Blackpool were delivered with surge-prone Avon 113 and 115 engines, they were all brought up to Mark 4 standard eventually, and the remainder were produced at Kingston as Mark 4s. Prior to delivery of the first Swedish aircraft, a Hunter 4, WT770, was sold for evaluation and familiarisation in Sweden in February 1955.

The first Swedish Hunter Mark 50 made its maiden flight on June 24 1955, flown by Frank Murphy, and delivered by air to Sweden by Major D. Stenbeck of the *Flygvapnet* on August 26. (Stenbeck, as a Colonel, was later to command *Flygflottilj 18* at Tullinge from 1963 until 1966.)

Referred to as the J 34 in Sweden, the Hunter 50 (numbered 34001-34120) remained in front-line service until 1966, flying with four Wings; these were *F.8* at Barkarby, commanded by Colonel S. Uggla; *F.9* at Säve, commanded by Colonel A. Mangard; *F.10* at Ängelholm, commanded by Colonel W. Wagner; and *F.18*, originally commanded by Colonel E. Raab, and then by Stenbeck. It was *F.18* which produced a Hunter formation aerobatic team, the 'Acro-Hunters', in 1962.

Production of the Hunter 50 continued until 1958, the first 24 aircraft being flown by Murphy, Simpson, Bullen, Lockspeiser and Merewether by mid-1956. The Swedish Hunters were unusual in not being fitted with wing-leading edge extensions, and it was perhaps surprising that no two-seat trainers were purchased to accompany so large an order. On the other hand, the Swedes undertook conversion of their Hunters to carry Sidewinder air-to-air missiles—a facility that greatly increased the aircraft's combat potential.

Nevertheless Sweden, ever mindful of her exposed strategic location, situated in the no man's land between Russia and NATO's northern flank, was quick to appreciate the Hunter's short-term value as an interceptor, and by the late 1950s had already introduced the SAAB-32 Lansen all-weather fighter, and followed this with excellent indigenous fighters, beginning in the early 1960s with the SAAB-35 Draken.

Some efforts were made to improve the Hunter 50's performance with the withdrawal from service of several aircraft for installation of the Flygmotor re-heat system but, as already stated, no matter what additional power was provided, the Hunter's basic wing design was the limiting factor in the quest for speed.

Denmark

Not possessed of her own aircraft manufacturing industry, Denmark alone among the NATO nations ordered Hunters to be imported, signing a contract for thirty aircraft on July 3 1954. Once more these were of Mark 4 standard, designated Mark 51s, and they also lacked the leading edge extensions.

No 401 was first flown by David Lockspeiser on December 15 1955, this and the second aircraft being delivered to Denmark on Janury 30 1956. The final deliveries were made on September 10 that year, some Danish pilots undergoing conversion training at Dunsfold.

The Hunter 51s (401-430) gave magnificent service with the *Kongelige Dansk Flyvevåben,* and were flown continuously for eighteen years by *ESK 724* at Skrydstrup. The aircraft were immensely popular among the Danish pilots who flew their Hunters in more than sixty NATO exercises, and their accident record was extremely low.

Very early in their period of service a Danish Hunter suffered a flame-out while approaching to land at Skrydstrup. The pilot ejected safely some three miles from the airfield, and the aircraft continued down the flightpath and executed a perfect wheels-up

The sole Peruvian Hunter T Mark 62, 681; this aircraft was distinguishable by the radio compass fairing on the fuselage aft of the cockpit canopy.

landing on the runway! So little damage resulted that this aircraft was back in service within a month.

Denmark also ordered two Hunter trainers, T Mark 53s, in 1955 and these, 35-271 and 35-272, were delivered at the end of 1958. Like the Mark 51s, they did not feature wing leading-edge extensions. Two Mark 51s were also later converted to Mark 7 standard.

ESK 724 was eventually disbanded on March 31 1974 at Skrydstrup. The seventeen surviving Mark 51s, the two T 53s and two T 7s were flown away to Aalborg for their last rites. The majority were repurchased by the manufacturers during the following five years for superficial 'tidying-up' and presentation to museums in Britain. One aircraft, whose engine was restored by Rolls Royce to zero flying time, has been registered G-HUNT and is owned by Spencer Flack and flown by Stefan Karwowski.

Peru

The age-old political tensions in South America persisted after the Second Word War, and the continent provided a fertile market for the disposal of American war-surplus aircraft. This would have been a logical and acceptable state of affairs had not the Korean War focused American attention elsewhere. The outcome was that after-sales service and the supply of spare parts for these veteran aircraft fell far short of the level required to maintain serviceability. Against this background the Peruvian government approached Britain for the supply of modern aircraft, and the British Conservative government sanctioned the transfer of sixteen ex-RAF Hunter Mark 4s to the *Fuerza Aerea Peruana*.

The first RAF Mark 4, WT717, to be returned to Dunsfold had been withdrawn from North Weald Station Flight; three weeks later it emerged in Peruvian colours, renumbered 630, and flown by Frank Bullen on December 1 1955. Meanwhile a dozen or so *FAP* pilots arrived at the Hawker airfield for conversion training.

Preparation of the sixteen Peruvian Hunter Mark 52s was completed by February 13 1956 and delivery by sea made two months later. Flying from Limatambo and Talara, they entered service with *Escuadron Caza 14* before the end of the year. Two aircraft, 638 and 644, suffered a mid-air collision, but the pilots managed to set them down with only minor damage and they were subsequently repaired in Peru.

In 1959 a further approach to Britain was made for the supply of a two-seat Hunter, and once more an RAF Mark 4, WT706, was withdrawn from a Maintenance Unit, refurbished and given a two-seat nose at Dunsfold. Numbered 681, this Hunter Mark 62 entered service in Peru in March 1960.

These Hunters gave long service with the *FAP*, and in 1979 the ten surviving Mark 52s and the single T Mark 62 were flying with *Grupo de Caza 12* at Limatambo.

The NATO 'off-shore' Hunters

Following the conclusion of licence negotiations with the Dutch and Belgian manufacturers, two Hunter 4s were sold as pattern aircraft to Holland—the first, N-1, being delivered by Major Sonderman on March 3 1955—and one to Belgium, ID-1, flown over by Mr Anderson of Avions Fairey on March 16.

Dutch-built Hunter 4s (they were not afforded 'foreign' Marks) started to emerge from the Fokker factory before the end of 1955, numbered from N.101 onwards, and in due course equipped Nos 324 and 325 Squadrons of the *Koninklijke Luchtmacht* based at Leeuwarden, and No 327 at Soesterberg. Production continued with the Mark 4 until 1957 when a changeover to Mark 6s was undertaken, commencing with N.201. Like the Swedish Hunter 50s, the Dutch Mark 6s were modified to carry Sidewinder missiles on outboard wing stations, retaining the inboard pylons for the customary 100-gallon drop tanks.

Below *Danish Hunter Mark 51, 415, awaiting delivery at Dunsfold.* **Bottom** *The same aircraft a few weeks later! This was the Hunter which landed itself on its own airfield after its pilot had ejected some miles away.*

Fine air-to-air study of a licence-built Dutch Hunter F Mark 4, N-176, of No 323 Squadron, Royal Netherlands Air Force, complete with wing leading-edge extensions, drop tanks and gun-blast deflectors.

The development of the Hunter trainer also attracted Dutch attention and twenty such aircraft were ordered in 1955. Ten of these were ordered through the British Ministry of Supply and resulted in aircraft previously destined for the RAF being diverted (XM117-XM126 becoming N.311-N.320), and the remainder being a commercial contract placed direct with Hawker (N.301-N.310). Roughly half these aircraft were also afforded the Sidewinder capability. One of the two-seaters was flown by the Dutch Flight Research Establishment *(Nationaal Lucht-en Ruintevaartlaboratorium)*, painted in an attractive glossy blue, white and orange livery and given a civil registration, PH-NLH. Other Dutch Hunters were employed on high-altitude nuclear radiation research for a short time, equipped with samplers carried on the inboard wing pylons.

The Hunter in Belgium also served with front-line units for about ten years, the licence-built Mark 4s (numbered from ID-2 onwards) beginning to appear in 1955 and entering service with Nos 1, 7 and 9 Wings of the *Force Aérienne Belge/Belgische Luchtmacht* based at Beauvechaine, Chièvres and Bierset respectively, forming part of NATO's 2nd Allied Tactical Air Force. In 1958 these Mark 4s began to be replaced by licence-built Mark 6s which remained in service until gradually replaced by Lockheed F-104 Starfighters in the early 1960s. Belgium did not acquire any two-seat Hunters.

Total licence production amounted to 96 Dutch Mark 4s, 93 Dutch Mark 6s, 111 Belgian Mark 4s and 144 Belgian Mark 6s, and it is evident in retrospect that, if anything, they were underemployed. Certainly their airframe hours, on average, were considerably lower than any other Hunters in service between 1955 and 1966. Indeed, some of the Belgian aircraft spent almost all their lives in storage.

Thus it was that when world demand for Hunters increased during the mid- and late 1960s, the choice of Dutch and Belgian aircraft for purchase by the parent company was logical, and the fortunes of these 'second-hand' Hunters will be described in the following chapter.

India

It is perhaps interesting to reflect that, aside from Britain herself, India has employed the Hunter more than any other nation in the world, and was one of the first customers to start sales negotiations with Hawker.

The first indication that the Indian Air Force was looking at the Hunter with which to re-equip its fighter squadrons was apparent with the receipt by Hawkers in November

A Belgian-built Hunter F Mark 6, IF-61.

1954 of a request for outline specification, costs and delivery dates for 100 aircraft.

Clearly this was not the best of times for the company to commit itself, owing to the multitude of problems besetting the early Mark 1s and the uncertainty surrounding the production standard of preparation. Nevertheless, the fact that the RAF was persevering with its plans to acquire large numbers of Hunters was adequate spur to the Indians to maintain their interest, and on April 27 1956 an Indian Air Force Mission, headed by Air Vice-Marshal Engineer, arrived at Dunsfold and spent ten days assessing the Hunter 4 and 6 in the air and on the ground. The pilots were clearly impressed by the Mark 6 (and by the two-seater which they were also shown), and a follow-up assessment by Group Captain Dutt and Squadron Leader Dass in July the following year resulted in a contract being signed for the purchase of 160 Hunters at Mark 6 standard.

This order, the first by an overseas customer for the 'big-Avon' Hunter, could not have come at a better time for Hawker, for the 1957 Defence White Paper had just been published, considerably reducing the RAF's requirement for Hunters, and the supposed loss of so much production revenue would severely strain the company's ability to underwrite new projects, such as the P.1121 and P.1127, not to mention the necessity to retain its skilled labour force.

So as to embark on deliveries of the Indian Hunters (designated the Mark 56) as quickly as possible, the first 32 aircraft would be completed from the cancelled Ministry of

Early Indian Hunter Mark 56s awaiting delivery at Dunsfold. When delivered these aircraft lacked tail parachutes and gun-blast deflectors.

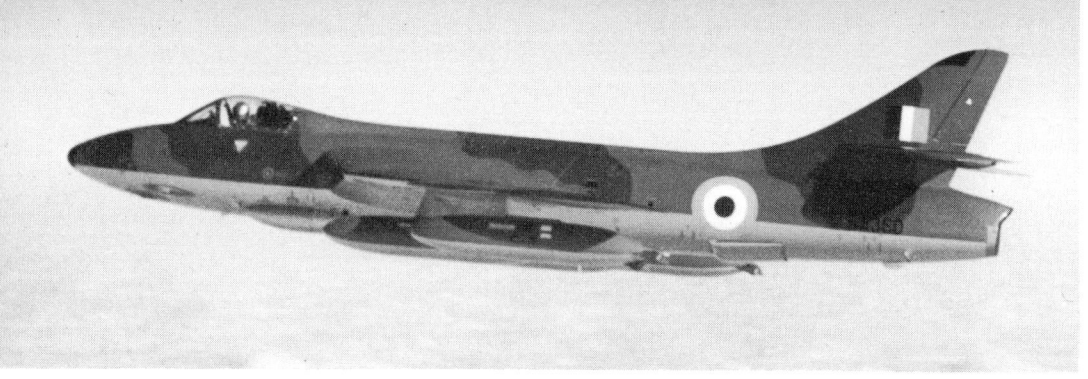

An Indian Hunter Mark 56, BA360, in fully modified state, with tail parachute and gun-blast deflectors.

Supply order (XK157-XK176 and XK213-XK224 becoming BA201-BA232) while the next sixteen aircraft would be withdrawn from RAF service, refurbished at Dunsfold and Kingston, and re-sold. These plans worked smoothly and by the end of 1957 the first 32 Mark 56s had been delivered. In most instances delivery was undertaken by pilots of the Indian Air Force, some of whom were given conversion training with the RAF, while others, including Flight Lieutenants Carson, Chopra, Mohlah and Tilak, and Flying Officers Dey and Karnik, joined the Hawker pilots in the routine test and clearance flying at Dunsfold before returning in their new aircraft to India. (The first deliveries were made by Hugh Merewether and Flying Officer Karnik in BA205 and BA206 respectively, leaving Dunsfold on October 25 1957.)

By the end of 1960 the entire order for Mark 56s had been completed according to the terms of the contract (although one ex-RAF Hunter, XE600, re-numbered BA239, which had evidently suffered some overstressing at Boscombe Down in its early life, began to exhibit 'premature fatigue' in the IAF and was returned to Hawker on April 15 1959, being replaced by a newly built BA239 in January 1961. XE600 was returned to its former identity, was re-built and re-emerged as an FGA Mark 9). In the Indian Air Force the Hunter 56 joined Nos 5 and 17 Squadrons at Poona, and Nos 7, 20 and 27 Squadrons at Ambala.

India was also the first overseas customer to purchase the 'big-Avon' two-seater. Indeed, so little work had been done on this version in 1956 in the absence of Ministry of Supply interest in the second P.1101 prototype that, when India requested very early delivery of the first two-seater (designated T Mark 66), Hawker had to resort to some ingenuity to meet the demand. The wings, engine and rear fuselage were assembled from spares while the nose section was hand-built in special jigs. This left a production Indian two-seat nose as surplus at the end of the contract and this became Hawker's property; it was later used as a static exhibit at the 1959 Paris Air Show and subsequently assembled on to the company demonstrator, G-APUX.

The initial order, placed in 1957, was for sixteen new-build Indian Hunter T 66s (BS361-BS376) and these, together with a follow-on order for six more (BS485-BS490) were all delivered by the end of 1960. One of them, BS366, was flown at the 1959 Paris Air Show and in the following month took part in the Paris-London Air Race. In the Indian Air Force they were allocated to the five operational squadrons.

Switzerland

Because of her unique political, economic and physical characteristics, Switzerland's *Flugwaffe* has come to be regarded as a very special potential customer among military

The first Swiss Hunter Mark 58, J-4001.

exporting nations. Her military funding is not only strictly limited but fluctuates much more than elsewhere, making it relatively difficult to support an indigenous aircraft industry capable of pursuing the sophisticated research necessary to produce modern combat aircraft of her own.

With a first-line aircraft strength of about 400 aircraft, distributed between some twenty *Fliegerstaffeln*, Switzerland has, since the Second World War, tended to standardise its fighter equipment with two or three aircraft types and retain these aircraft for very long periods, simply updating their armament and equipment from time to time from her own resources.

Thus, when in 1957, as the result of many months of canvassing interest in the Hunter by Hawker's sales team led by Mr George Anderson, Switzerland invited the company to participate in comparative evaluation trials during February and March 1957, Hawker went to considerable lengths to show off the Hunter in its best light. Competing against such aircraft as the F-86 and Gnat, the demonstration Hunters, XE587 and XE588, emerged triumphant after all manner of flying and weapon delivery trials in the rugged Swiss environment. By way of confirmation, the Swiss then asked for two Hunters—together with a supply of bombs and rockets—to spend a month's trial period with the *Flugwaffe*. By the end of 1958 a purchase contract for one hundred Hunters, of Mark 6 standard, had been signed.

To speed initial deliveries the first dozen Swiss Hunter Mark 58s were aircraft re-purchased from the Ministry of Supply, all being ex-RAF Mark 6s, and the first such aircraft (previously XE536 and re-numbered J-4001) was delivered to Emmen on April 3 1958. All twelve had reached Switzerland by the end of the year, and the last of the contract by April 1960.

Early on, the Swiss had shown interest in the braking parachute fitted in the Hunter 7 and requested that their Mark 58s be so equipped to assist landings on their mountain air bases. In due course the Swiss Hunters were adapted to carry Sidewinder missiles, thereby meeting the air interception rôle of the *Flugwaffe*, and flew initially with *Fliegerstaffeln 1, 4, 5, 7, 8, 11, 18, 19* and *21*.

The Middle East

The recurring upheavals in the Middle East have since the Second World War involved British interests threefold: the establishment of the Israeli nation, the protection of the vast oil resources and the freedom of access through the Suez Canal. That all three circumstances have periodically become interrelated has been evidenced by four bitter war campaigns, in two of which Britain has been directly involved.

Despite Britain's direct support for Israel in the Suez campaign of 1956, her tacit recognition that the vital oil interests have been directly controlled by Arab nations has been supported by repeated supply of weapons—and in particular of aircraft—to these nations during the past thirty years.

No doubt to some extent impressed by the presence of RAF Hunters in the Middle East theatre in 1956-57, Iraq sought from Britain a small number of Hunters early in 1957 and received six ex-RAF Hunter 6s in April that year, and ten more the following December. The revolution in Iraq brought to a temporary close this association, so that immediate follow-up spares were interrupted for several years.

Lebanon's Air Force *(Force Aérienne Libanaise/Al Quwwat Aljawwiya Alubnamiya)* also received six ex-RAF Hunter 6s in 1958-59, as did Jordan's *Al Quwwat Aljawwiya Almalakiya Alurduniya* at the same time.

These token arms packages, puny by comparison with the later avalanche of aircraft supplies from America and the Soviet Union, were nevertheless significant in that the Hunters in particular proved reliable and popular among their pilots, with the result that they paved the way for a lucrative resumption of commercial sales contracts some years later.

* * *

The foregoing constituted the first phase of Hunter sales referred to at the beginning of this chapter. By 1961 it seemed likely that, with the production of new Hunters at a end, the end of the Hunter's useful life was in sight when it reached the limits dictated by fatigue. In the RAF the Hunter FGA 9 and FR 10 were being employed in the most testing of all rôles, and with the oldest aircraft approaching the end of their forecast fatigue life, there seemed little prospect of further sales of ex-RAF Hunters to foreign customers. Indeed, because of the extraordinary squandering of RAF Hunters over the previous four years through cancellations, premature scrapping and philanthropic gestures to foreign air forces, a real shortage of Hunter airframes was about to occur. □

Top right *A Dutch Hunter F Mark 6, N-255, equipped with Sidewinder air-to-air missiles on the outboard pylons.* **Centre right** *Dutch Hunter F Mark 4 N-113 employed to collect radioactive particles from the upper atmosphere in a container on the port wing pylon. The picture shows Leeuwarden's met officer changing the filter in the container. (This was one of several Dutch Hunters nicknamed Sophia Loren; elsewhere the cartridge link collector tanks were dubbed Sabrinas.)* **Right** *The first Hawker-built Dutch Hunter T Mark 7 streams its drag chute on landing. This aircraft was later purchased by Hawker for refurbishing and resale as an Abu Dhabian Hunter T Mark 77.*

OVERLEAF
Top *Second of the two Danish Hunter T Mark 53s, 272; these aircraft were unique in being the only two-seat Hunters not fitted with wing leading-edge extensions (as the Danish single-seaters were also without them). After being phased out of service in Denmark they were repurchased by Hawker having flown more than 3,000 hours apiece.* **Centre** *The effect of napalm. During the vital trials in Switzerland undertaken by the Hunter all manner of weapons were discharged to investigate the capabilities of the aircraft when operating in the mountainous surroundings.* **Bottom** *A Hunter 58 of the Swiss aerobatic team, The Acro-Hunters, on its visit to Greenham Common in 1979 during the Hunter's anniversary celebrations.*

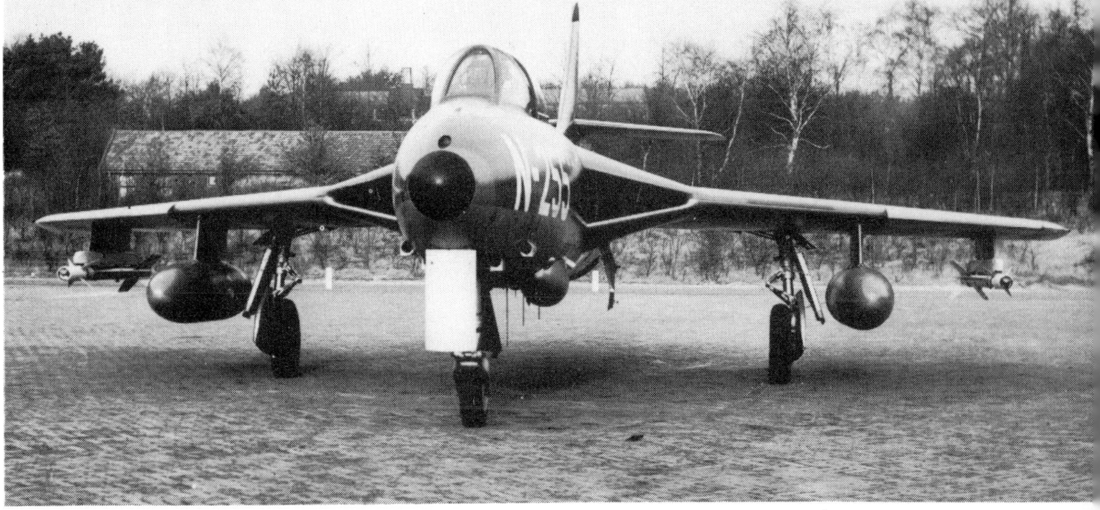

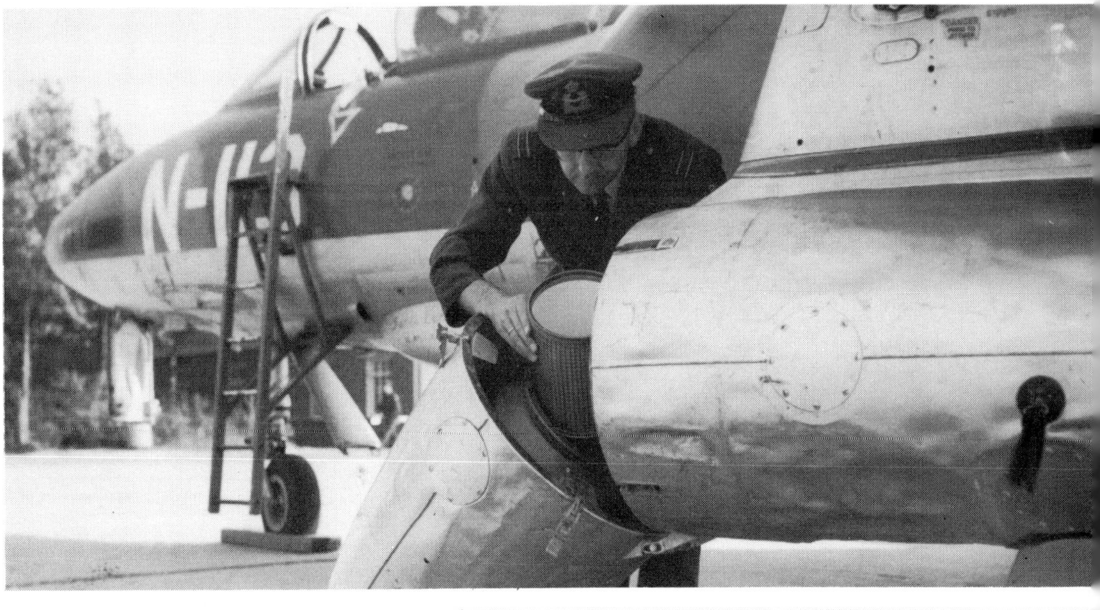

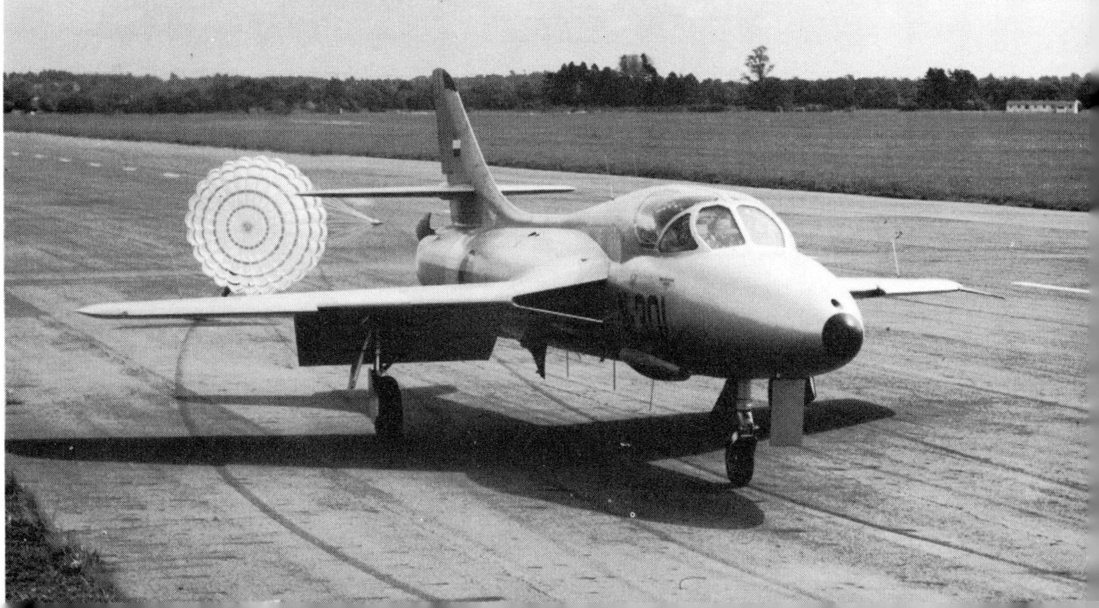

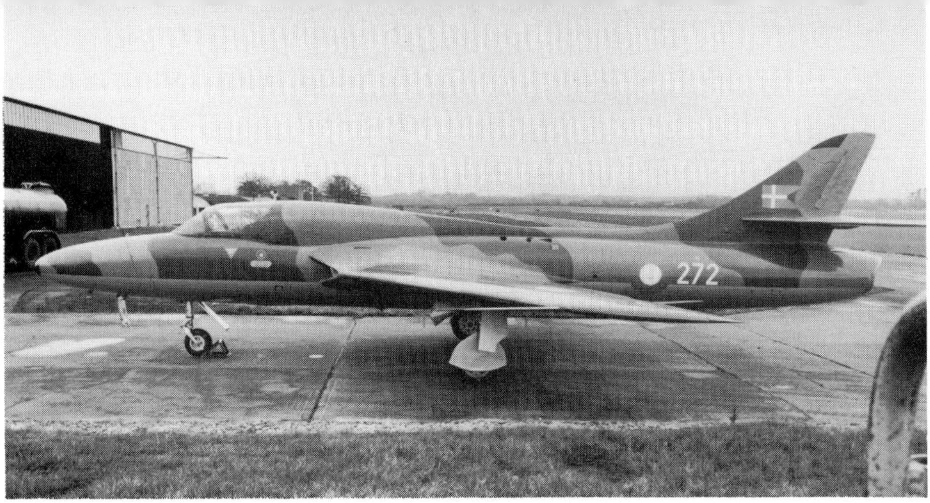
272

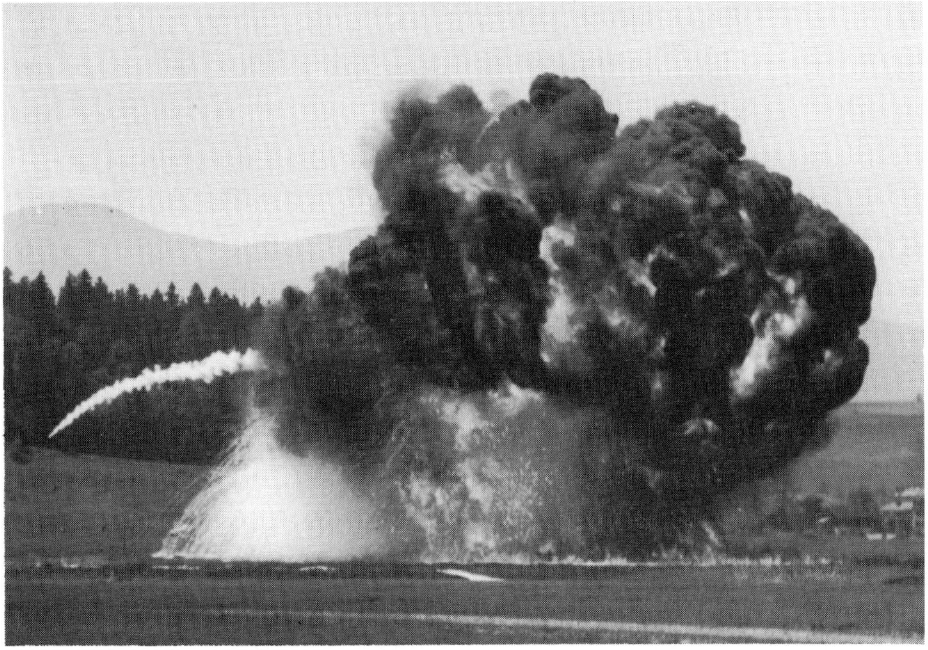

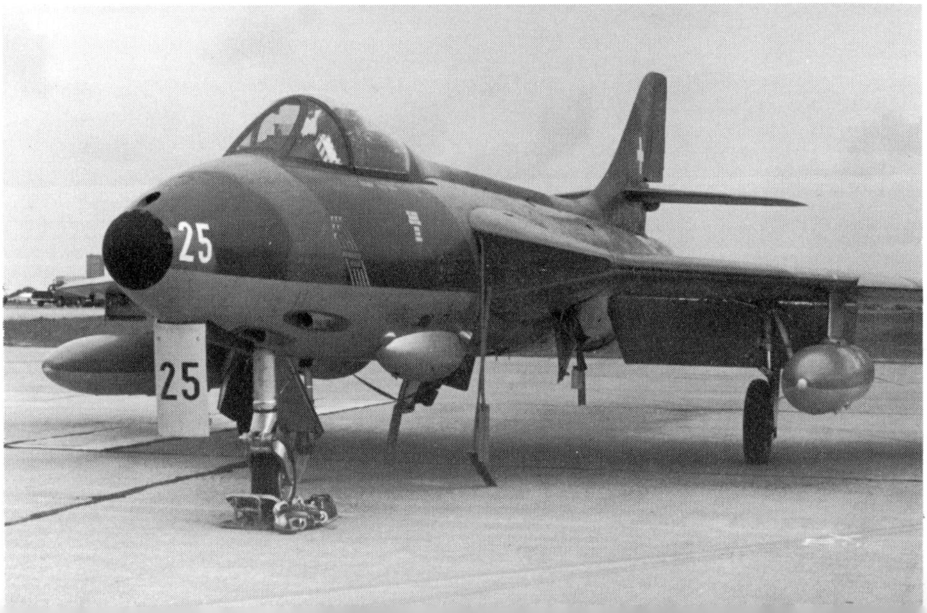
25
25

Chapter 10

Hunters overseas—the second phase

Taking stock of the survival of Hunters available for possible sale overseas, the Mark 1s and 2s had almost all been scrapped as having no further useful value—although for several years the remains of half a dozen airframes had been giving up minor components as spare parts. The Mark 4s had been subject of fairly continuous programmes of conversion to two-seat Mark 7s and 8s, as well as to Mark 11s for the Fleet Air Arm. Some scrapping of Mark 4s had taken place but this was halted in 1963. Almost all the Hunter 5s had been scrapped or fatigue tested to destruction, while the RAF was intent on converting all remaining Mark 6s to FGA Mark 9s and FR Mark 10s.

It thus seemed to Hawker that only one expedient remained to support its export of Hunters, to try to negotiate the purchase of Dutch- and Belgian-built aircraft, of which more than 200 Mark 6s had been produced. In the Belgian Air Force the Hunter was being withdrawn from service in 1962, and the following year the Mark 6 was declared redundant in the Royal Netherlands Air Force.

The difficulty appeared to lie in the fact that production of the Hunter on the Continent had been funded by the United States of America, and it was expected that any attempt by Hawker to acquire these aircraft for offer on the world market would meet with strong opposition from American manufacturers—always active in fighter sales to foreign governments. On the other hand Hawker sales contracts had always included the stipulation that the aircraft, when due for disposal at the end of their useful life with the customer, must invariably be first offered for re-purchase by the parent company. This was a safety clause aimed at preventing British aircraft from 'falling into the wrong hands', but it was seldom anticipated that Hawker would support the expense of collecting time-expired airframes from distant countries.

However, such was the potential market for Hunters still considered to exist that strenuous efforts were made in 1962 to negotiate the purchase of the Belgian and Dutch Mark 6s. Little opposition was, in fact, encountered from American manufacturers when it became apparent that the Hunter's markets lay within countries or areas already committed to the purchase of British aircraft, or whose air forces employed RAF personnel for training and maintenance purposes.

Having overcome these likely obstacles, Hawker started collecting the large number of redundant Hunter 6s from Belgium towards the end of 1962, and the following year aircraft started flying in to Dunsfold from Holland. It was soon apparent that the Belgian Hunters in particular still possessed a considerable life expectancy, their airframe hours seldom exceeding 600, and more often than not averaging around half that figure.

Fatigue tests carried out on single-seaters at Kingston had confirmed that for a weight penalty of less than 10 lb, the front transport joint could be strengthened so as to greatly extend the normal fatigue life, and that such local strengthening need not necessitate re-jigging of the fuselage.

Notwithstanding the generally good condition of the redundant Hunters, Hawker set about an elaborate and painstaking refurbishing programme to make available aircraft whose value to potential customers could be expected to extend for many years to come.

Iraq

The first overseas customer to receive Hunters converted from the Belgian aircraft was Iraq whose government ordered 24 ground-attack fighters at full FGA Mark 9 standard early in 1963; these were delivered (as Mark 59s) in the following year, and were followed by 22 further aircraft (termed Mark 59s and 59Bs) in 1965 and 1966.

Five two-seaters (also converted from Belgian single-seaters) were sold to Iraq in 1965-66, although there is some evidence that these ostensibly training aircraft were also employed in the combat rôle. One or two of the single-seaters were also converted for use as reconnaissance fighters.

At the beginning of the 'Six-Day War' against Israel in 1967 the Iraqi Air Force had on strength a total of 64 single-seat Hunters and four two-seaters, including nine Mark 6s previously transferred from RAF stocks. Some of these aircraft fought in the vicious air battles of the short campaign, but it is believed that not more than six were lost, almost all to ground fire.

In the Yom Kippur War of October 1973 Iraq still flew a total of 48 Hunters, of which three were two-seaters. The IrAF Hunters joined Syrian MiG-21s flying top cover over the Northern Front while Syrian Sukhoi Su-7s carried out their ground attack strikes. Wisely, the Iraqi pilots tended to avoid combat with the Israeli Phantoms, but frequently engaged enemy A-4 Skyhawks and Super Mystères. Seven Iraqi Hunters were lost during this war (at least two by ground fire), but they are known to have destroyed at least a dozen Israeli aircraft between October 12 and 24. In 1979 Iraq was still flying at least 30 Hunters.

India

As told in the previous chapter, India's initial order for 160 single-seat Hunter 56s and 22 Mark 66 two-seaters had completed delivery early in the 1960s, but these totals were eroded fairly quickly by flying accidents during the first four years of service, so that on the eve of the Indo-Pakistani conflict of September 1965 the first-line strength of combat-ready Mark 56s had fallen to no more than 118. Moreover, on the second day of the war,

Below *An Iraqi Hunter FGA Mark 59.* **Above right** *Last of the Swiss Hunter T Mark 68s to be delivered, J-4208, pictured here in Switzerland. Note the windscreen wipers, fitted to the Swiss two-seaters.*

on September 7, no fewer than five Indian Hunters from one formation were shot down in as many minutes by a Pakistani F-86F-40 Sabre flown by Squadron Leader Mohammed Alam of No 11 Squadron, Pakistani Air Force. From all accounts the Hunter pilots were caught by surprise, and after the first aircraft was shot down by a Sidewinder missile the Pakistani pilot simply picked off the stragglers using his guns.

The high attrition of Indian Hunters continued after the conclusion of the war and prompted the negotiation of further orders from Hawker, amounting to 53 Mark 56A aircraft delivered between June 1966 and March 1970. At the beginning of the second Indo-Pakistani conflict of December 3-17 1971, single-seat Hunter strength of the Indian Air Force stood at 127, plus 28 two-seaters (comprising 17 of the original T Mark 66s and eleven of twelve T Mark 66Ds delivered to India during 1966-67). Twenty-two further Hunters were lost in this latest war.

Notwithstanding these high losses, the Indian Air Force remained a staunch advocate of the Hunter in the ground-attack rôle, and a new order for five T Mark 66Es (converted in this instance from ex-RAF Hunter F Mark 6s) was completed in 1973.

By 1979 80 Mark 56s remained in front-line service with Nos 14, 20, 27 and 37 Strike Squadrons of the Indian Air Force, while almost a score of others (mostly old Mark 56s) were employed on target towing duties with Nos 3 and 31 Squadrons of the Armament Training Wing at Jamnagar. The 23 surviving T Mark 66s, 66Ds and 66Es were serving at the Operational Conversion Unit at Kalaikunda.

Switzerland

It has been suggested that of all world air forces to fly Hunters the Swiss *Flugwaffe* will eventually employ them longer than any other. It has been stated recently that it is the present intention to retain them until the end of the century, although presumably not in an operational rôle!

After the completion of the initial order for 100 Mark 58s no further production contracts were placed with Hawker until 1969 when 30 further single-seaters were called for delivery between 1971 and 1973. Among these Mark 58As were the first Mark 4 Hunters to be re-framed to accommodate Avon 200-series engines. 22 further Mark 58As followed between January 1974 and April 1975, and these were accompanied by eight two-seat T Mark 68s (the first two-seaters to be delivered to Switzerland). These Hunters were equipped in Switzerland with provision to carry Sidewinder missiles, and some aircraft carried the SAAB BT9K bombing computer. In 1979 the Mark 58A was flying with *Fliegerstaffeln 4, 5, 7, 8, 18, 19* and *21*; they are maintained by full back-up facilities based at Emmen.

Rhodesia

It is convenient here to mention an order for a dozen Hunter FGA Mark 9s for Rhodesia signed early in 1963. These ex-RAF Mark 6s equipped No 1 Squadron of the Rhodesian Air Force at about the time of the Colony's Unilateral Declaration of Independence but, following the embargo placed upon trade with the country, no follow-up servicing of its Hunters nor delivery of spare parts were permissible.

All the more remarkable therefore was the fact that nine of the original twelve Hunters were still flying with the Zimbabwe-Rhodesian Air Force at the end of the 1970s with only local facilities available for maintenance and repair; the aircraft had moreover been continuously engaged throughout their life in rigorous ground attack flying. No 1 Squadron even created a four-man formation aerobatic team which gave displays in the late 1960s and early '70s.

Kuwait

As part of a defence agreement between the British Government and Kuwait, four ex-Belgian Hunter 6s were sold to that nation under the designation FGA Mark 57 during 1965-66, together with five T Mark 67s (all with Avon 200-series engines) converted from Belgian, Dutch and RAF Mark 6s. The single-seaters were withdrawn from service late in 1976 to be replaced by American A-4KU Skyhawks, but the two-seaters continued to serve on in the training rôle.

Jordan

The Air Force of the Hashemite Kingdom of Jordan flew Hunters almost as long as any other in the Middle East. As already mentioned, the first Hunters to be delivered had been a number of ex-RAF Mark 6s supplied from RAF stocks in 1958. These had been joined by a number of other Mark 6s during the early 1960s, but the entire strength of the JAF's No 1 Squadron, including a number of Hunter FGA Mark 9s (transferred from No 43 (Fighter) Squadron in 1964) was destroyed by the Israeli Air Force's heavy strike attack on Mafraq during the Six-Day War of 1967; only two Hunters survived the attack and these were badly damaged.

These losses were made good by the presentation of three single-seaters by Saudi Arabia and the placing of further orders with Hawker. Under the designations FGA Marks 73, 73A and 73B, eighteen further single-seaters were delivered to Jordan between June 1968 and November 1971.

In June 1972 the Hunters on strength with the JAF amounted to 35 single-seaters and three two-seaters, and these aircraft were scheduled for replacement when the Yom Kippur War broke out. Replacement was, however, still awaited early in 1975 when Sultan Qaboos of Abu Dhabi presented to King Hussein his entire strength of twelve Hunters to join the nineteen surviving Jordanian aircraft. Later in 1975 King Hussein in turn presented all his 31 Hunters now accumulated from various sources to the Sultan of Oman.

Lebanon

The third recipient of American-funded Hunters back in 1958-59 was the Lebanon, this country receiving six Hunter 6s from RAF stocks as part of a military aid package deal. To these were added three T Mark 66Cs and four FGA Mark 70s, all converted from Belgian Mark 6s for delivery during 1965-66. Of these, five were lost in training accidents and six more Mark 70s were ordered in 1975 from RAF stocks. Three of the final batch were delivered in the spring of 1976 but the remainder were detained in Britain to await

Above *First of the Rhodesian Hunter FGA Mark 9s. Despite 15 years of constant use under most difficult conditions, almost entirely without external support and spares back-up, the Rhodesian Hunters maintained an extraordinarily high serviceability rate.* **Below** *Fine picture of a Kuwaiti Hunter T Mark 67 two-seater.* **Bottom** *An early Jordanian Hunter 6, presented to the Jordanian Government from RAF stocks; note the absence of tail parachute, later deemed essential for operation in the tropics.*

HAWKER HUNTER F. MARK 6
Rolls-Royce Avon 203

HAWKER HUNTER T. MARK 7
Rolls-Royce Avon 121

FRANCIS K. MASON © 1980

HUNTER T. MARK 7. The fuselage datum is inclined approximately 0° 30' nose-up when stationary on the ground with full internal fuel, full ammunition and two pilots aboard. Carriage of external stores does not affect on-ground attitude.

100-gallon drop tank on inboard pylon; landing gear details identical to Mark 6 below.

STENCIL UNDER STARBOARD WING LEADING EDGE

S4-A8763
DTD900/4263

BLOCK SECTION B
(HUNTER T. MK. 7)

Mark 7 wing with 1,000-lb bomb inboard and four 3-inch R.P.s (60-lb warheads) outboard

100-GALLON DROP TANKS

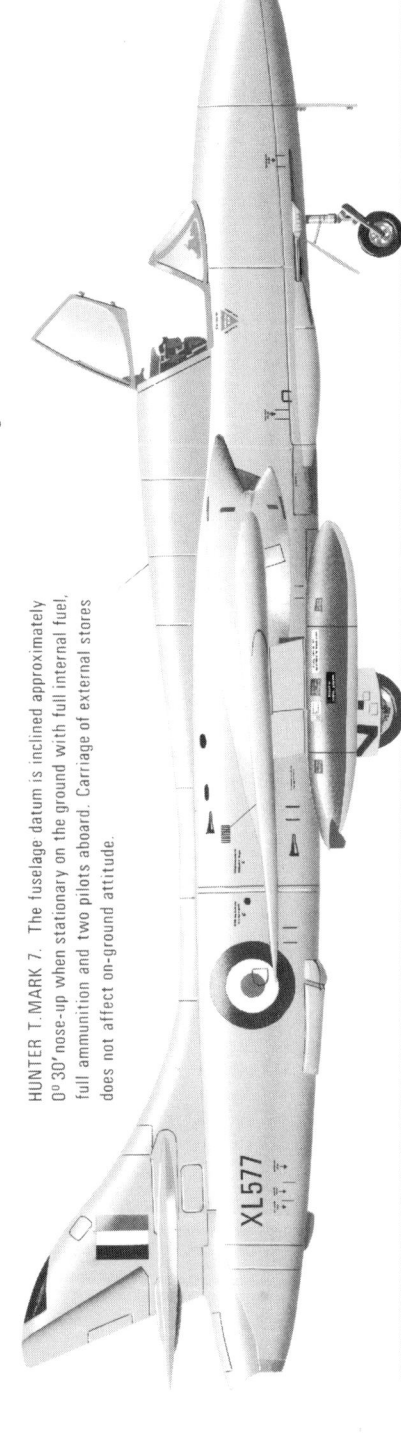

TANK STENCIL DETAILS

SOME HUNTERS CARRIED THEIR UNDERWING SERIAL NUMBERS RAKED

Mark 6 wing with 230-gallon drop tank inboard and 100-gallon drop tank outboard

WING SECTION CC THROUGH OUTBOARD PYLON AND 100-GALLON DROP TANK

SECTION A

SECTION C

TRESTLE HERE

STENCIL ADJACENT TO T-MARKS ON WINGS AND FUSELAGE

OIL SYNTHETIC CX-58
SPEC.D.ENG.R.D. 2447

STENCIL ON LOWER STARBOARD SIDE OF FUSELAGE 32 INS. FORWARD OF REAR TRANSPORT JOINT

WING SECTION AA SHOWING LANDING GEAR OLEO CAVITY AND LANDING FLAP PROFILE

BLOCK SECTION ON REAR TRANSPORT JOINT

BLOCK SECTION ON REAR CONE JOINT

0 1 2 3 4 5 6 7 8 9 10 11 12 13 14 15   FEET

See also page 76/77

HUNTER F. MARK 6. The fuselage datum is inclined approximately 0° 45' nose-up when stationary on the ground with full internal fuel, (no external stores), full ammunition and with pilot aboard.

The last three Lebanese Hunter FGA Mark 70s to be delivered, shown here at Bitteswell. Note the large blade aerials just aft of the cockpit canopies.

the outcome of Lebanon's bloody civil war; they eventually left for the Lebanon in December 1977. It has been stated that *Al Quwwat Aljawwiya Allubnamiya* plans to retain one squadron of Hunters operational on fighter/strike duties until well into the 1980s.

Saudi Arabia

As part of the so-called 'Magic Carpet' arms deal with Saudi Arabia, Hawker was contracted to supply the Royal Saudi Air Force with four Hunter Mark 6s and two Mark 7s early in 1966. This contract, arranged through HM Government, referred to 'Hunter F Mark 60s and T Mark 70s', and these designations persisted in some quarters, although they were not used by the manufacturers who were already supplying Hunters to the Lebanon under the designation FGA Mark 70.

While pilots of the RSAF were given Hunter flying training in Britain, their aircraft reached Riyadh in May 1966, and were deployed at Khamis Mushayt to form No 6 Squadron, RSAF. Soon afterwards MiG-21s and Il-28s of the Egyptian Air Force carried out a number of attacks in the northern areas of Saudi Arabia, but owing to an almost total lack of ground control the Hunters were unable to intercept any of the raiders, and their pilots were therefore sent on retaliatory ground strikes.

One of the single-seaters was lost early in 1967, and later that year the three survivors were presented to King Hussein of Jordan whose air force had suffered so severely in the Six-Day War with Israel. As mentioned in Chapter 6, the two two-seaters were returned to Britain in 1974.

Chile

Chile was one of Britain's unfortunate customers to fall victim of doctrinaire embargos applied after the conclusion of legitimate commercial negotiations. After fairly lengthy discussions—in the face of considerable competition from elsewhere—an order for fifteen single-seat Hunters (culled from RAF, Dutch and Belgian sources) was finalised with Hawker in 1966, and these deliveries were completed in June 1968. These FGA Mark 71s were followed by thirteen more by September 1973, together with six single-seat fighter-reconnaissance Mark 71As. At the same time six two-seaters (including conversions of the old second prototype P.1101, XJ627, and Hawker's famous G-APUX), T Mark 72s, were also delivered.

In 1974, however, prompted by opinions being expressed in some quarters in Britain, an embargo on the supply of spares to Chile was imposed—thereby creating a market vacuum which was quickly filled by the United States, Brazil and Argentina. Chile's effective strength of Hunters thereafter quickly declined as a result of this restriction, so that by 1978 only twenty aircraft remained serviceable, and these were serving with *Grupos 8* and *9* of *Ala 1* (Support Wing) at Cerro Moreno air force base, Antofagasta.

Hunters overseas—the second phase

Singapore

In July 1968 the Republic of Singapore contracted to purchase sixteen refurbished ex-RAF Hunter 6s, twelve of them at FGA Mark 9 and four at FR Mark 10 standard. Delivered during 1970 and 1971 these aircraft entered service with No 140 (Osprey) Squadron, RSAF, commanded by Major Chris Strong, a former RAF Hunter pilot of considerable experience; these FGA Mark 74s and FR Mark 74As were based at Tengah, their pilots responsible for air defence duties, army support and tactical reconnaissance, and customarily flew with SNEB-Matra rocket batteries on the outboard wing pylons and 230-gallon drop tanks inboard.

Further orders followed for 22 Mark 74B single-seaters and nine T 75As and 75Bs (some of these being converted from ex-RAF Mark 4s) during the next two years, and these were delivered by October 1973, although one aircraft ditched in the Bristol Channel in November 1972 and was lost. A second Squadron, No 141 (Merlin) Squadron, was then formed to fly these late deliveries.

Abu Dhabi

The withdrawal of Britain's stabilising influence from the Persian Gulf area during the late 1960s was accompanied by efforts to secure some measure of security by the small oil

Below *A Saudi Arabian Hunter Mark 60.* **Bottom** *Final chapter in the saga of the famous demonstration Hunter G-APUX, shown here as a Chilean T Mark 72, as it was sold in 1967.*

states and Emirates in arranging defence measures under British guidance. The resulting creation of small air forces, trained and often supervised by RAF personnel, was typified by Abu Dhabi's formation of an air force equipped with Hunters ordered from Hawker in 1969. Seven Hunter FGA Mark 76s, three FR Mark 76As (converted from RAF aircraft) and two T Mark 77s (converted from Dutch T Mark 7s) were delivered during 1970 and 1971 to equip a single squadron based at Sharjah. These served until 1975 when Sultan Qaboos presented them to King Hussein of Jordan to help in making good his losses sustained in the Yom Kippur War of 1973.

Qatar

Two Hunter FGA Mark 78s and one T Mark 79 were delivered for service in the Qatar Public Safety Forces in December 1971 and were followed later by a further four refurbished aircraft.

Kenya

Latest customer for refurbished Hunters is Kenya whose air force was supplied with four single-seat FGA Mark 80s (converted from RAF Hunter 4s and a Mark 6) and two T Mark 81s (previously Fleet Air Arm Hunter T Mark 8s). These aircraft left Dunsfold during 1974 and 1975.

Oman

The Sultan of Oman's Air Force received from Jordan all the surviving Hunters collected from various sources by that country in 1975. About 31 such aircraft were transferred and in 1979 twelve of these were serving with the Sultan's No 6 Squadron at Thumrait, his Air Force's principal strike base. The remaining aircraft were being retained in storage as replacements and to provide spares for the operational aircraft.

* * *

It is difficult to see where further surplus Hunters will become available to Hawker (or British Aerospace, as the new nationalised aircraft conglomerate is now termed), unless the currently-serving RAF aircraft are deemed to possess a worthwhile remaining lease of life. Little has, however, been stated regarding the final disposal of the majority of the old Swedish Hunter Mark 50s which were phased out of service with the *Flygvapnet* in the mid-1960s; four such aircraft were returned to Hawker (to become Swiss Hunter T Mark 68s in 1975), and there have been unconfirmed reports that others are now in America. □

Top Right *Hunter 6s supplied to the Lebanese Air Force by the British Government awaiting delivery in Britain.* **Centre right** *Swiss Hunter Mark 58As at the Federal Aircraft Factory, Emmen. Most of the Mark 58As were delivered as major components by land to Switzerland where they were assembled and flight tested.* **Right** *This Hunter started life as an RAF Mark 4 in 1956 and after apparently ending its useful flying life was presented to an Air Training Corps Squadron. It was, however, purchased by Hawker in the early 1970s, completely refurbished and sold to Switzerland as a Mark 58A.*

OVERLEAF
Top *An Iraqi Hunter 59 suffered a mid-air collision in February 1967 with a similar aircraft; both pilots landed safely despite considerable damage to their aircraft. The pilot of this Hunter evidently attempted to stream his landing chute but it failed to deploy owing to damage to the fairing doors. Note the two Iraqi Tupolev Tu-16 'Badger-A' bombers in the background.* **Centre** *A Jordanian Hunter FR Mark 10, 712. Fighter reconnaissance Hunters have been widely used by the Middle East air forces during the past 20 years.* **Bottom** *A Jordanian Hunter T Mark 66B.*

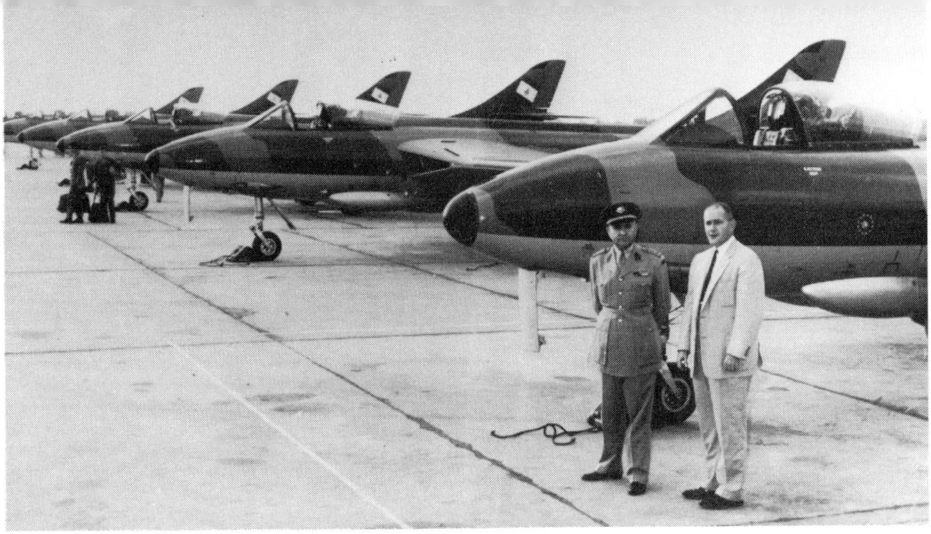

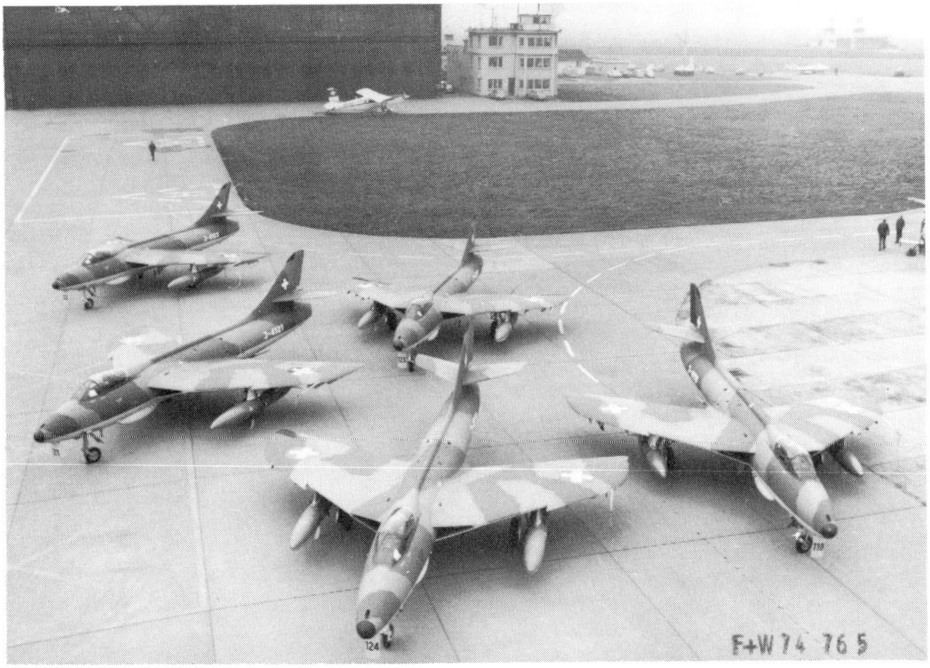
F+W 74 76 5

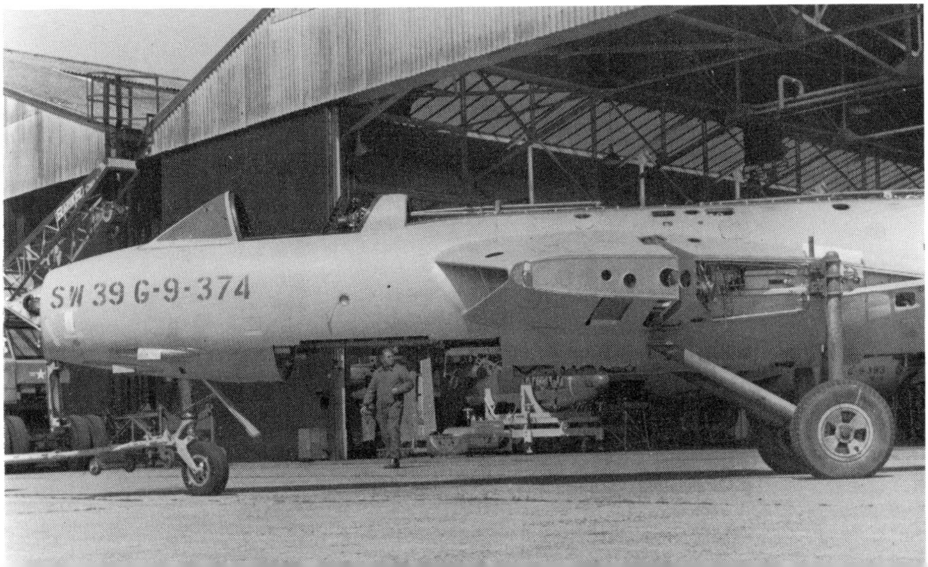
SW 39 G-9-374

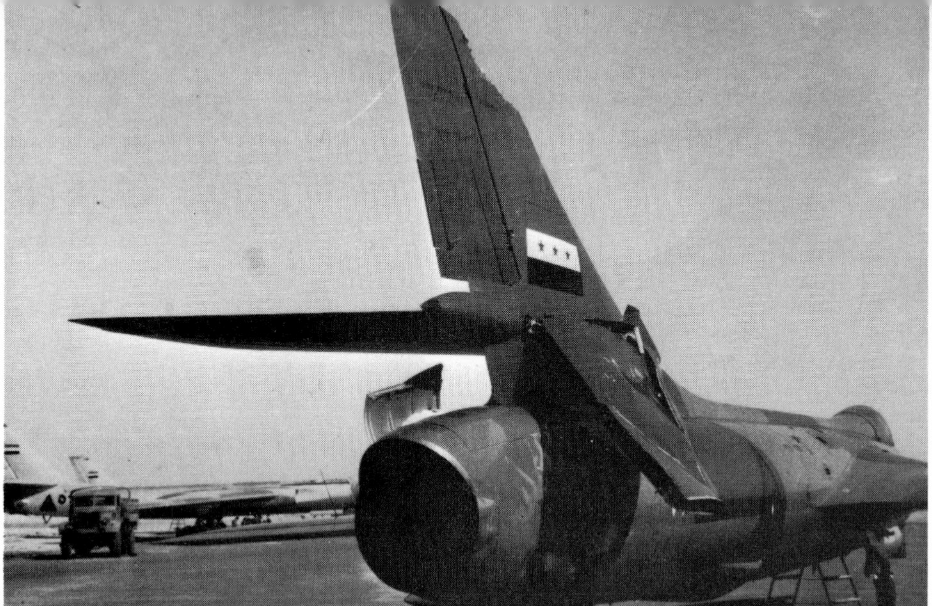

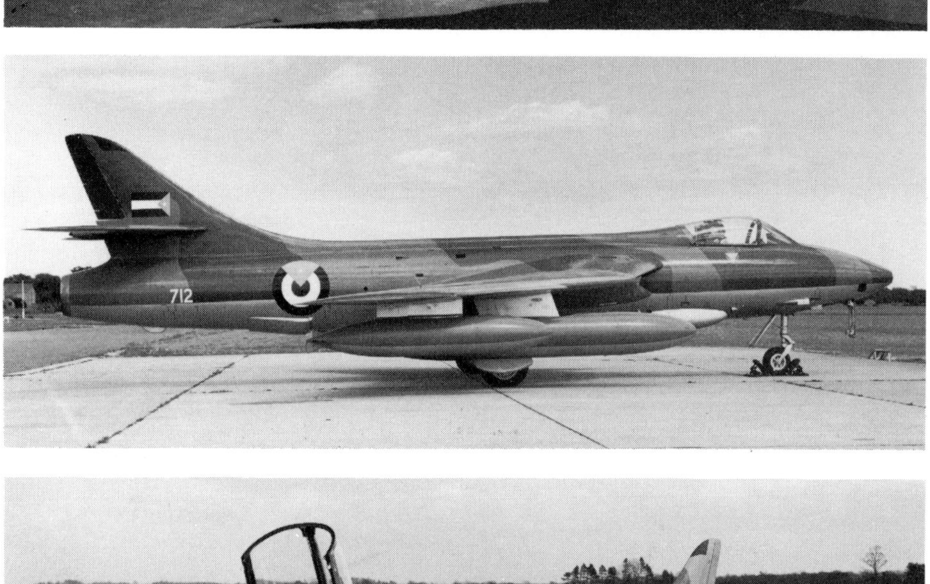
712

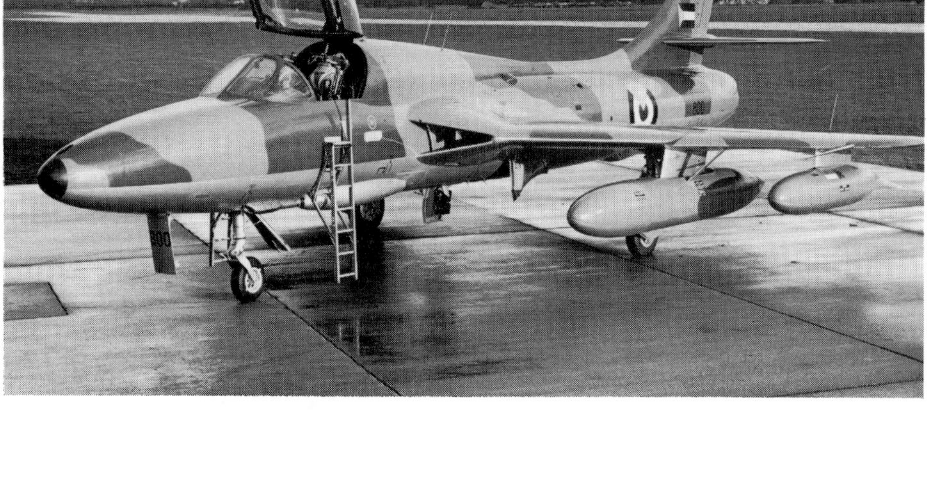
800

Chapter 11

The Hunter described

The following description of the Hawker Hunter is applicable to the Fighter Ground Attack Mark 9 and its overseas equivalents. Within the space available it is not possible to describe all the minor variations in the specification applicable to the various Marks, although many of these are referred to in other chapters.

General

The Hunter is a single-seat mid-wing fighter with swept-back wings and tail surfaces, variable incidence tailplane, power-operated aileron and elevator controls and pressurised cockpit. It is powered by a Rolls-Royce Avon 200-Series turbojet with a fifteen-stage axial-flow compressor. The engine is located centrally within the fuselage with its air intakes in the leading edges of the stub wings and its straight-through jet pipe exhausting through the rear fuselage.

The armament consists of four electrically fired and controlled 30 mm Aden automatic guns carried together with their ammunition in a removable, pre-armed pack located in the underside of the front fuselage. The guns are sighted by means of a gyro gunsight which is provided with manual or radar ranging control, and is positioned above the centre instrument panel in the cockpit. A cine camera, which ordinarily operates in conjunction with the guns, but can be operated separately if necessary, is located in the extreme nose of the aircraft. Pylons, on which to attach overload fuel tanks, weapons and other ordnance according to the aircraft's operational duty, may be fitted to four strongpoints under the wings, two on each side.

The pressurised cockpit, which accommodates a fully-automatic Martin-Baker pilot-ejection seat complete with survival equipment, is protected forward of the pilot by heavy plating; it is provided with an electrically-operated canopy which slides fore and aft, and may be jettisoned in an emergency. The flying controls are of normal stick and rudder-bar type and operate the control surfaces by push-pull tubes. The rudder and left aileron are provided with small electrically-operated trim tabs; the rudder actuator tab operates in conjunction with an autostabiliser. Hydraulic boosters are also provided to assist operation of ailerons and elevators.

Front fuselage

The fuselage is an all-metal monocoque structure composed of three main sections to facilitate manufacture, transport and storage. The front fuselage is provided with a detachable nosepiece and accommodates the cockpit, armament package and radio equipment, while the centre fuselage, which is built with the stub wings as an integral part, houses the engine and the forward fuel tanks. The rear fuselage, which is built with the lower part of the fin integrally and terminates with a detachable tail cone surmounted

Front fuselage nose piece

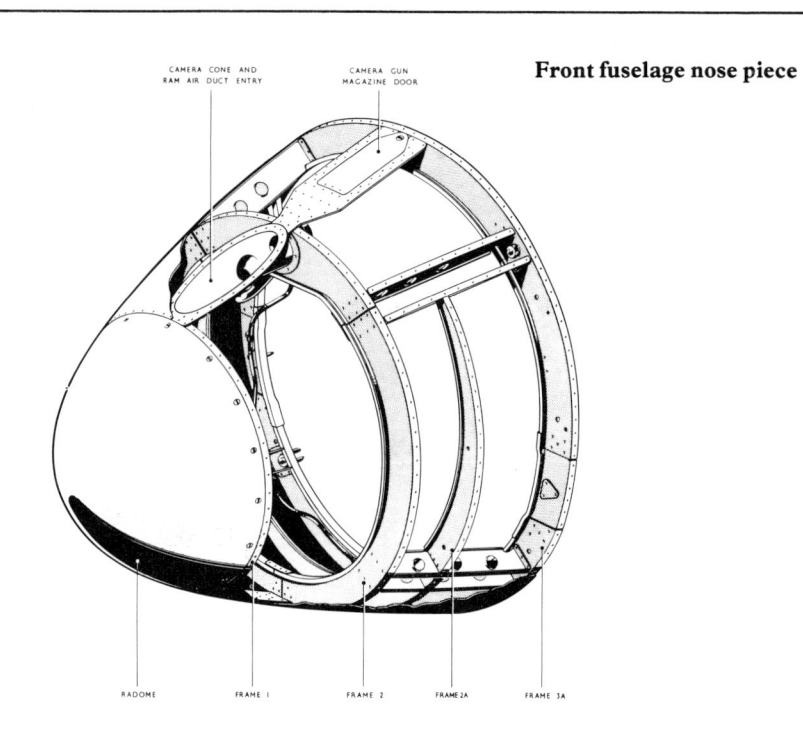

Front fuselage

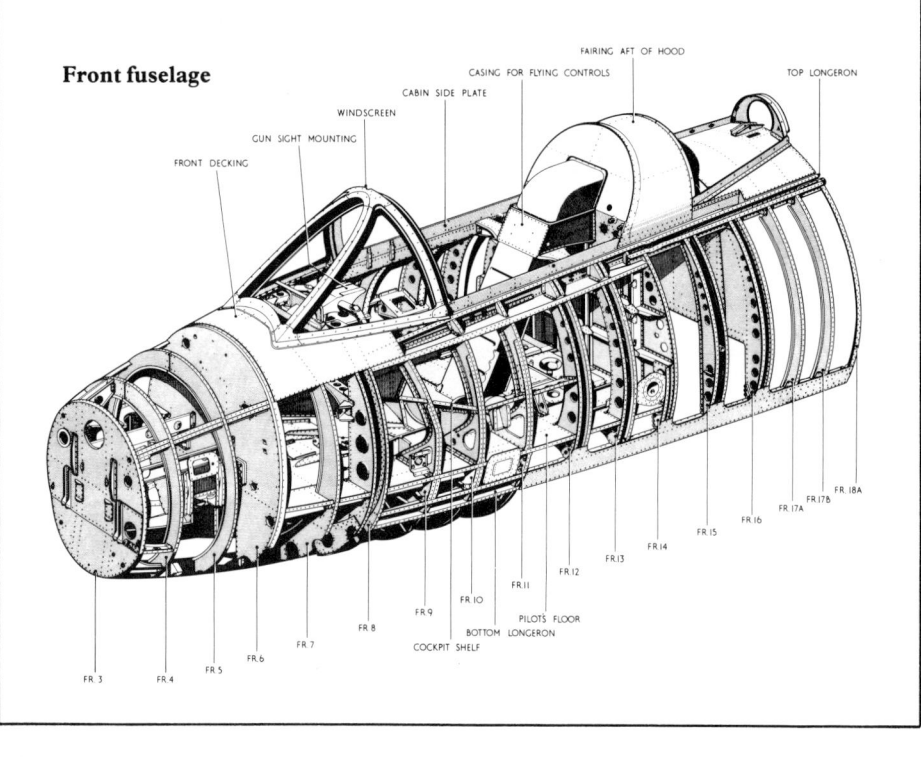

by the drag chute fairing, houses the engine tail pipe, the rear fuel tanks and carries the hydraulically operated air brake in the ventral position.

The detachable nosepiece, which extends from the radome to frame 3, consists of a light alloy skin supported by frames and contains the radar scanner and camera gun. In the Hunter FR Mark 10 the scanner equipment is omitted and a forward-looking reconnaissance camera is fitted instead, operating through automatic eyelids to protect the camera lens from dirt, flies, etc, when not in operation.

The front fuselage continues aft from frame 3 to frame 18 which constitutes the front frame of the front transport joint. The structure consists of a number of frames and four longerons reinforced by a box-sectioned keel member extending between frames 6 and 11, the whole assembly being covered by a light alloy skin. The nosewheel member is hinged to the keel member at frame 8 and when retracted is enclosed in the front fuselage by fairing doors. The pilot's cockpit is located between frames 6 and 14, and the gun pack is located between frames 15 and 17A with the gun barrels projecting forward under the cabin floor. The radio bay is situated immediately forward of the transport joint.

The cockpit, being pressurised, is sealed from the remainder of the airframe by a floor extending from frame 6, which is a solid bulkhead, to a diaphragm at frame 14. Ejector-seat leg restraint anchorages in the form of a pair of fork fittings are fitted to the cockpit floor. Above the floor the fuselage structure is enclosed to form side walls, and above these walls are shelves for instruments and controls. The centre instrument panel, together with the left and right panels, are situated at the forward end of the cockpit above the shelves on a structure which extends across the top of frame 8, and is strengthened by two tubular struts reaching forward to frame 7. The gunsight is carried on a mounting above the centre instrument panel.

The windscreen consists of a flat bullet-proof centre panel and two curved quarterlights, all three being held in a cast light alloy frame attached to the fuselage decking. The centre panel comprises two plates of glass between which is a layer of dry air to prevent misting, the air being kept dry by silica gel located in a container on the forward face of frame 8, and connected through a valve by rubber tubing to the base of the windscreen. An adjustable convex rear-view mirror is attached to the top of the windscreen frame.

The hood is moulded from a single sheet of transparent plastic mounted in a frame consisting of a steel arch member at the forward end and two edge members. A rack and roller assembly is bolted to each edge member and the complete hood slides in rails attached to the main structure by locks. The hood is opened and closed by an electric actuator which drives a cross-shaft carrying pinions which engage with the racks on each side of the hood. In an emergency the hood may be jettisoned by use of an operating handle which projects upwards from the left-hand cockpit shelf; pulling this handle fires the hood jettison gun which opens the locks securing the hood side channel members, and gases from the gun are used to force the hood away.

The armament pack consists of a removable container, which carries the four Aden guns together with their ammunition. This container features guide spigots at the forward end which engage with brackets attached to the bottom longerons and is supported by six spherical-ended mounting spigots, three on each side projecting downwards to engage with sockets integral with the pack. The forward sections of the gun barrels, which are detachable from the pack, are staggered and extend foward under the cockpit floor to blast tubes in the underside of the front fuselage structure. The guns are electrically fired and controlled by a trigger on the control column handgrip.

The radio bay contains an upper and lower mounting structure, each supporting anti-

Front fuselage sections awaiting final assembly in 1953. Note Sea Furies being refurbished in the background.

vibration mountings not only for the transmitter-receivers and their associated equipment but also various components of the aircraft's electrical system.

The front and centre fuselage structures are assembled together at a butt joint formed by the flanges of frames 18A and 18B, which are bolted together, and by special attachments on the four longerons, these attachments consisting of large threaded fittings, bolted to the front fuselage longerons, which extend aft through frame 18A to engage in captive nuts; these nuts are locked to the spigots with nickel-alloy wire when assembled to the front fuselage fittings.

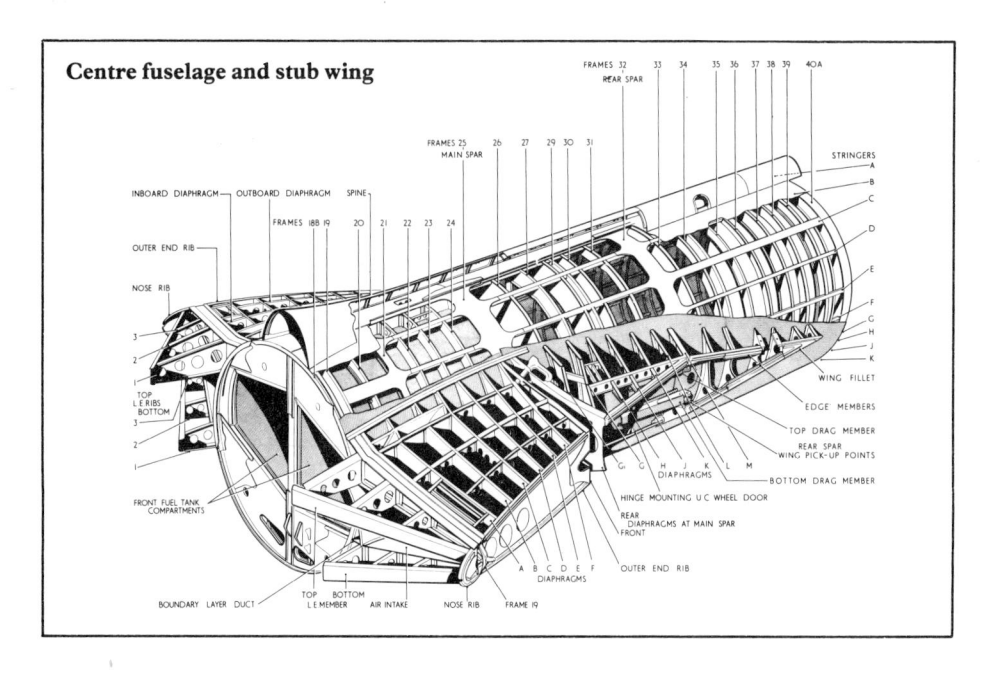

Centre fuselage

The centre fuselage extends back from frame 18B to frame 40A, both of these frames forming transport joints. It is a monocoque structure consisting of a number of frames and stringers and covered with a light alloy skin, at the top of which is a spine member enclosing the flying control rods. Frames 19, 25 and 32 are of heavier construction than the remaining frames and continue outwards to form the front, main and rear spars of the stub wings which are an integral part of the centre fuselage structure. The stub wing consists of these three spars, together with a number of ribs and diaphragms which are covered externally with light alloy skin, and internally by the engine air-intake and boundary layer ducting. The spars feature high-tensile steel fittings to which the outer wings are attached.

The structure between frames 19 and 25 is double-skinned to provide a compartment in which the forward flexible bag-type fuel tanks are supported.

The engine is located aft of the main spar frame, being mounted at frames 34 and 40A, with the engine-driven accessories gearbox between frames 29 and 30. A diaphragm at frame 38 engages with the engine to provide a firewall and to divide the engine compartment into two zones for cooling purposes. Another firewall at frames 29 and 30 isolates the engine bay from the engine starter bay.

The centre and rear fuselage structures are assembled together at frames 40A and 40B by special attachments at fifteen points between these frames. These attachments consist of large threaded fittings bolted to the stringers of the centre fuselage and extending aft through frame 40A to engage with captive nuts bolted to the stringers of the rear fuselage. When assembled these nuts are locked together with nickel-alloy wire, and the gap between the two frames is covered by a fairing strap.

Rear fuselage

The rear fuselage extends from frame 40B to frame 57 and consists of a number of frames and stringers covered with light alloy skin to form a monocoque structure at the top of which is a spine member enclosing the flying controls. Frames 52 and 55 are of more substantial construction and extend upwards to form the primary structure of the lower fin assembly; this lower fin structure consists of these major frames together with a dorsal fin extending forward to the spine member and aft to an anti-buffet fairing below the rudder. The upper portion of the fin, which carries the rudder, is attached to the lower part by fittings at the top of frames 52 and 55, while the tailplane is pivoted on a fitting on frame 55 and anchored at the leading edge to the tailplane actuator accommodated in the lower fin structure.

A small bumper block is attached to the bottom of frame 55 to take the load in the event of the tail striking the ground during take-off or landing. The bottom skin between frames 47 and 50 is discontinued and the gap so formed is boxed-in by side members and a top skin to form a recess for the hydraulic air-brake jack.

The tail cone, which is detachable, incorporates the drag chute housing and is secured to the rear fuselage by four toggle fasteners together with locating spigots. It extends from frame 58 to frame 63 and consists of the drag chute housing, which is a fairing with two upward-opening spring-loaded doors extending rearwards over the top of the tailpiece, surmounting a structure of six frames and a tailpiece covered with light alloy skin stiffened by butt straps. The tailpiece also incorporates a stainless steel duct which engages with the jet pipe.

Internal structure between frames 41 and 45, consisting of tank support beams and skinning, forms an annular compartment around the rear of the engine in which the rear

Rear fuselage and tail cone

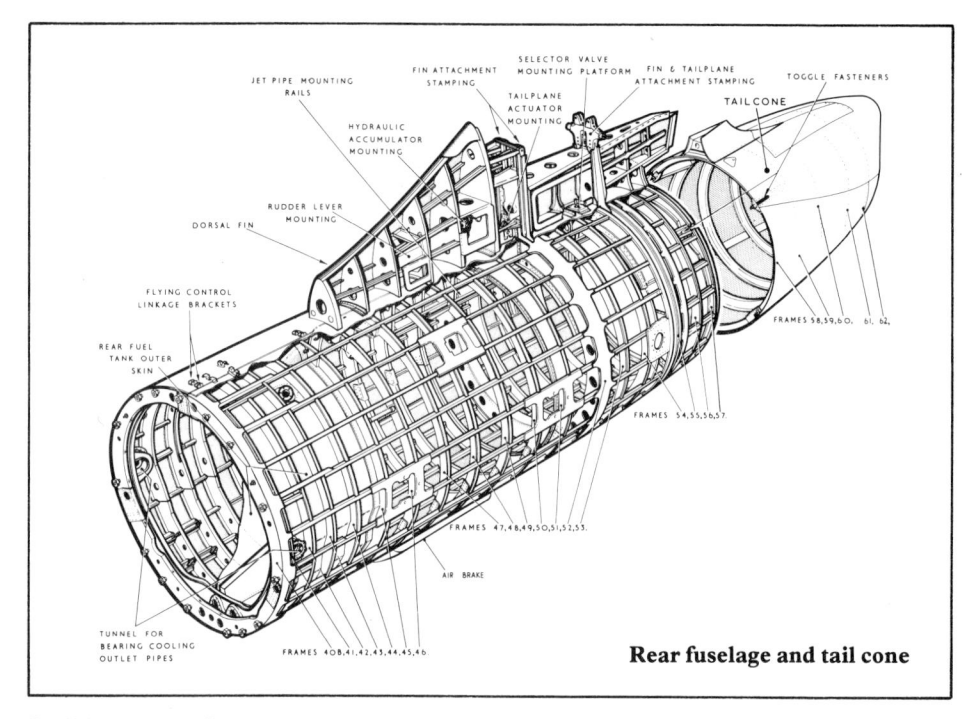

flexible bag-type fuel tanks are housed.

The structure of the airbrake, which in the closed position embraces the rear under-fuselage, consists of a series of curved formers attached to a channel-section central rib. This centre rib incorporates the anchorage fitting to which the operating jack is attached and the entire structure is hinged on the forward edge.

The engine jet pipe is rigidly secured at its forward end to the engine and extends aft to terminate at the end of the tail cone. The pipe is supported at frame 55 by blocks attached to each side of the pipe, which engage in adjustable slides secured to the fuselage structure thereby allowing for expansion of the pipe.

Wings

The wings are built in three sections: the centre-section stub wings (described above), and left and right outer wings. The outer wings are swept back with slight anhedral and accommodate the wing fuel tanks, store pylons, ailerons, flaps and main undercarriage. The ailerons are provided with hydroboosters to assist their operation at high speeds.

Each outer wing is an all-metal stressed-skin cantilever structure consisting of leading-edge, front and rear spars, undercarriage girder, nose ribs, inter-spar ribs and rail ribs, all covered by a heavy-gauge light alloy skin which is additionally strengthened by stringers and stiffeners. A detachable wing tip, which extends from the leading edge to aft of the rear spar, completes the basic structure.

The wing fuel tanks are carried forward of the main spar in compartments formed between nose ribs A and G; the leading edge of this portion is removable for access to the tanks. Inboard store pylons, when fitted, are bolted to the underside of the wing outboard of the fuel compartments, and outboard pylons just inboard of the wing tip.

Both wing spars are fabricated in three sections, but are continuous when assembled.

The undercarriage girder is attached to the inboard end of the rear spar and extends outward and forward to the inter-spar rib G, thus forming a box-like compartment between the spars into which the mainwheel assembly retracts. The undercarriage pivot block is accommodated at the outer end of this structure, being attached to the front spar, inter-spar rib G and the undercarriage girder.

The trailing edge structure aft of the rear spar comprises a number of tail ribs extending from the wing root to the aileron shroud; these ribs are recessed to form the flap housing. The flaps are of conventional design, each consisting of a single spar with a number of ribs covered on the underside only with light alloy skin. Each flap is hinged at four points on bearing brackets. Each aileron consists of a main spar, ribs and stiffeners covered by light alloy skin; each is hinged at three points, the centre point including a double hinge. The ailerons are provided with hydroboosters.

The leading edge extension is a fixed structural section consisting of heavy gauge skins attached to the outboard portion of the leading edge of the wing structure between ribs H-J and R. The chord-line of this extension is angled downwards in relation to the wing chord-line, thereby minimising in-flight 'pitch-up'.

Tail unit

The tail unit comprises conventional fin, rudder, tailplane and elevator assembly mounted on the lower fin structure which is an integral part of the rear fuselage. The tailplane incidence may be varied in flight by means of an electrically operated actuator, and hydraulic boost is provided for elevator movement. An interconnection between the full-power elevators and the tailplane actuator makes provision for operation of the units as an electrically operated flying tail which may be cut out by use of a switch in the cockpit. The rudder incorporates an electrically operated trimming tab which operates in conjunction with a Mark 2 autostabiliser.

The fin is a two-part structure, the lower part being integral with the rear fuselage and

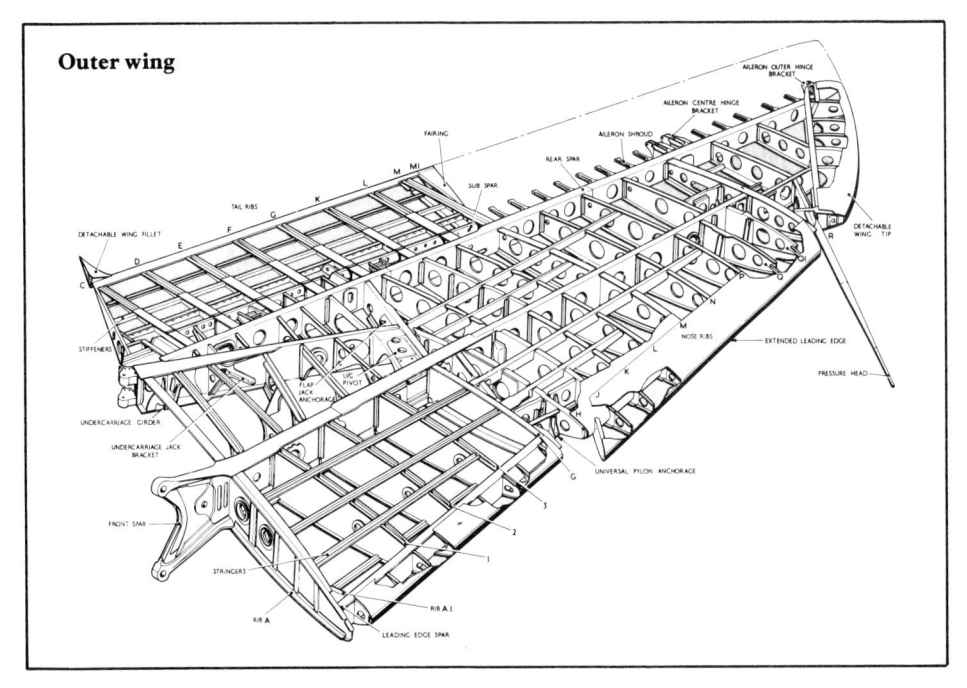

Outer wing

Tail unit

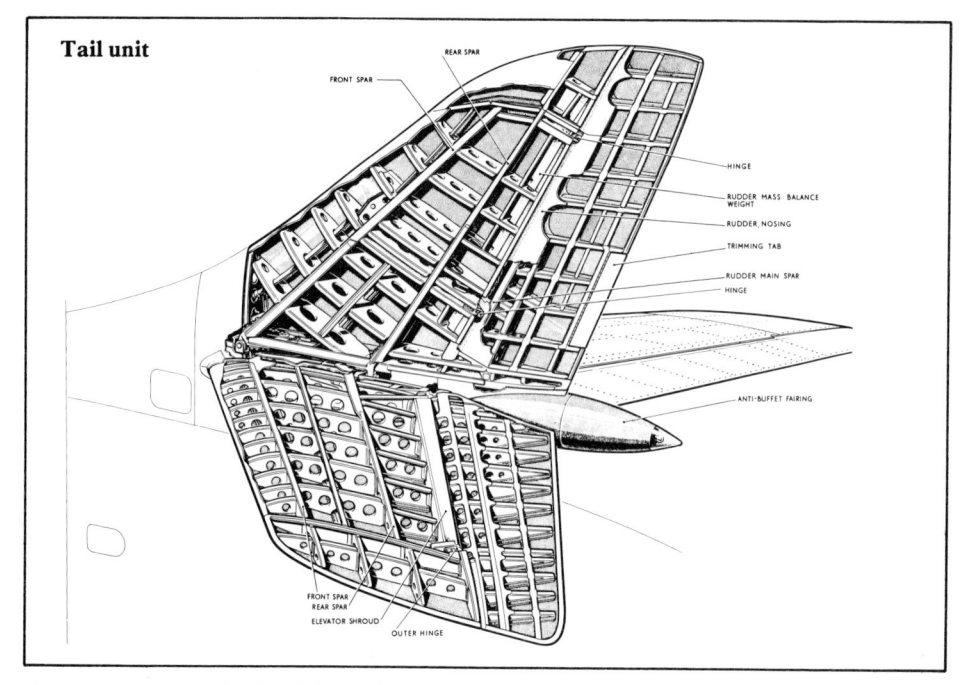

the upper part attached to it by fittings bolted to it on the front spar, inter-spar bottom rib and rear spar. The upper fin is a structure of front spar, inter-spar ribs and rear spar, nose ribs and rudder shroud, the latter carrying the rudder on two hinges. The whole structure is light alloy skin-covered.

The tailplane is an all-metal cantilever structure of swept-back planform, and is constructed in one piece. The structure consists of front and rear spars with nose ribs, inter-spar ribs and tail ribs together with an elevator shroud, the whole assembly being light alloy skin-covered. The unit is anchored at the front spar to an electrically operated actuator and is hinged at the rear spar on trunnions on top of frame 55. Operation of the actuator therefore raises or lowers the leading edge to provide variable incidence. The elevator shroud structure carries the inner and outer hinges for each elevator.

Undercarriage

The alighting gear is composed of twin inwards-retracting mainwheel units and a forwards-retracting nosewheel, retraction being effected hydraulically and activated electrically by a pushbutton control in the cockpit. All three components are of the liquid-spring cantilever type, the nosewheel being fully castoring and self-centering during retraction.

When fully extended, the wing-mounted mainwheel units are secured in the 'down' position by mechanical locks incorporated in the hydraulic jacks that operate them. The nosewheel is also locked down mechanically.

To enclose the wheels and legs when retracted into their bays, fairing doors are provided, these being operated by hydraulic jacks which are harmonised with those of the alighting gear by means of sequence valves. Undercarriage position indicator lamps are located in a common indicator in the cockpit.

The mainwheels are provided with hydraulically-operated brakes, controlled by a lever-operated control fitted to the pilot's control column handgrip. Differential control is obtained by means of a relay valve connected to the rudder bar. In addition, Maxaret units are fitted, one in each mainwheel leg, which allow the maximum braking efforts to be applied without the risk of wheel locking.

Airbrake

The ventral airbrake is operated by a hydraulic jack anchored at frame 50 and controlled by a thumb-switch on the throttle twist grip in the cockpit. Full extension or retraction of the airbrake is by selection, using the throttle-mounted switch, and no intermediate position is normally obtainable. A magnetic indicator in the cockpit gives a white indication when the airbrake is extended and black when retracted.

On selecting the undercarriage down, the airbrake control switch is automatically rendered inoperative, owing to limited ground clearance; if in the 'out' position when the undercarriage is selected down, the airbrake is automatically retracted.

Hydraulic system

The hydraulic system operates the undercarriage retraction gear, wheelbrakes, airbrake, landing flaps and power operation of ailerons and elevators. High pressure air bottles are provided for emergency operation of the undercarriage and flaps, while emergency operation of the wheelbrakes, ailerons and elevators is achieved by means of energy stored in hydraulic accumulators.

The hydraulic supply circuit is composed of a reservoir, engine-driven pump and filter. For the operation of the system on the ground, when the engine is not running, a hand-pump is incorporated in the circuit. External supply couplings are also provided.

Both the engine-driven pump and hand-pump deliver hydraulic fluid under pressure through their own non-return valves to the main delivery line and thence to the various circuits. The main delivery line branches to a pressure switch which operates to illuminate a warning light in the cockpit if the pressure falls below 600 psi, thereby warning the pilot to reduce airspeed sufficiently to permit manual operation of the flying controls. There is also an aural warning note generated in the pilot's headphones.

Cockpit air conditioning and pressurisation

The Hunter is provided with an air conditioning system and pressurised cockpit, pressure air being tapped from the engine compressor. A switch in the cockpit is provided to select pressurisation, the 'off' position enabling ram-air, received from an air intake in the nose of the aircraft, to be used instead of engine air if desired.

Temperature control is obtained by use of a control switch, which is gated for hotter or colder selections in manual, an intermediate position maintaining the selected condition. A fourth position provides for automatic control.

The cockpit canopy is fitted with a rubber seal which is automatically inflated from the engine supply when the hood is closed, and automatically deflated when the hood is opened, partial deflation occurring before the hood actuation gear operates.

Oxygen system

The Hunter's oxygen system consists of a pressure-demand installation and an emergency supply. The demand supply is obtained from two high-pressure cylinders and is fed to the pilot's oxygen mask through a pressure-reducing valve and a demand regulator. The cylinders are charged *in situ*, and a gauge indicates their content. The emergency supply is obtained from an oxygen set carried in the pilot's dinghy pack.

Hunters in final assembly. Most are in their factory primer finish, before receiving their final paint scheme. Their intial flights were carried out in the primer finish.

Pilot's ejector seat

The aircraft emergency equipment installed in the Hunter consists of a cartridge-operated Martin-Baker ejector seat and a hood jettison mechanism which incorporates a cartridge-operated hood gun, the gases from which are piped to a pair of gas guns mounted below each canopy rail, port and starboard. The seat is of the fully-automatic type and an interconnection with the hood release mechanism ensures automatic jettisoning of the canopy when ejection action is taken, a time-delay ensuring that the seat is not discharged until the hood is clear of the aircraft. The hood may be jettisoned independently of seat ejection if desired.

Anti-G system

The anti-G system consists of two high-pressure air bottles mounted side-by-side above the two hydraulic emergency air bottles behind the ejector seat; these are brought into operation by a selector valve and automatically supply air to inflate the pilot's anti-G suit when G-loads are applied, thereby raising the pilot's blackout threshhold, considerably reducing fatigue by repeated application of G-loads and enabling him to perform normal physical actions under high-G conditions. The air from the bottles is fed, via a filter, selector valve, pressure-reducing valve and an anti-G valve, to a quick-release connector on a flexible hose attached to the pilot's seat.

Armament

The gun installation of a single-seat Hunter consists of four electrically fired and controlled 30 mm Aden automatic guns carried with their ammunition in a removable, pre-armed pack located in the underside of the front fuselage. The inboard guns are housed slightly forward of the outboard guns.

The empty cartridge cases are ejected into the airstream through chutes extending aft from the rear of the gun pack, two on each side, while the belt-links pass down chutes extending from the guns to collector tanks fitted beneath the fuselage. Whenever the guns are fired the pack is automatically ventilated by the opening of a small electrically operated air-scoop in the starboard gun-bay access panel.

The Hunter described

The guns are cocked pneumatically before flight from a ground-supply and are fired by a trigger on the forward face of the pilot's control column hand-grip. Ammunition for approximately 7.4 seconds' firing time by all four guns is normally carried.

Except under certain mixed-store circumstances (wherein rocket projectiles are carried in addition to outboard wing pylons), the rocket projectiles are normally carried either singly or in tiers of up to three on each of four sets of launcher rails under each outer wing. The rocket projectiles are fired by depressing the Bomb/RP push-switch on the control column hand-grip, after the Bomb/RP selector switch has been placed in the RP position, the method of fire being selected by setting the Normal/Ripple switch and the salvo size selected. Alternatively, 2-in rocket projectiles may be carried in expendable containers (each carrying up to 36 missiles) on inboard and/or outboard pylons.

Powerplant

The power unit of the Hunter is a single Rolls-Royce Avon (or in the Marks 2 and 5, an Armstrong-Siddeley Sapphire) axial-flow turbojet mounted centrally in the fuselage with its air intakes in the leading edge of the stub wings, and a straight-through jet pipe which exhausts at the tail end of the fuselage.

A Plessey isopropyl-nitrate liquid-fuel starter unit is attached to the front of the engine, and its ancillaries are mounted adjacent to it. Fuel flow to the engine burners is controlled by a manually operated throttle valve, the initial opening of which opens the high-pressure fuel cock.

The accessories gearbox is housed in the engine bay and driven by the engine through two shafts and universal joints and a turret drive arm mounted between them. A firewall at frames 29 and 30 seals the engine bay from the engine starter bay, and a similar firewall at frame 38 isolates the engine from the rear fuel tanks. Air extractors and cooling ducts are provided to maintain the temperature of the engine bay within predetermined limits.

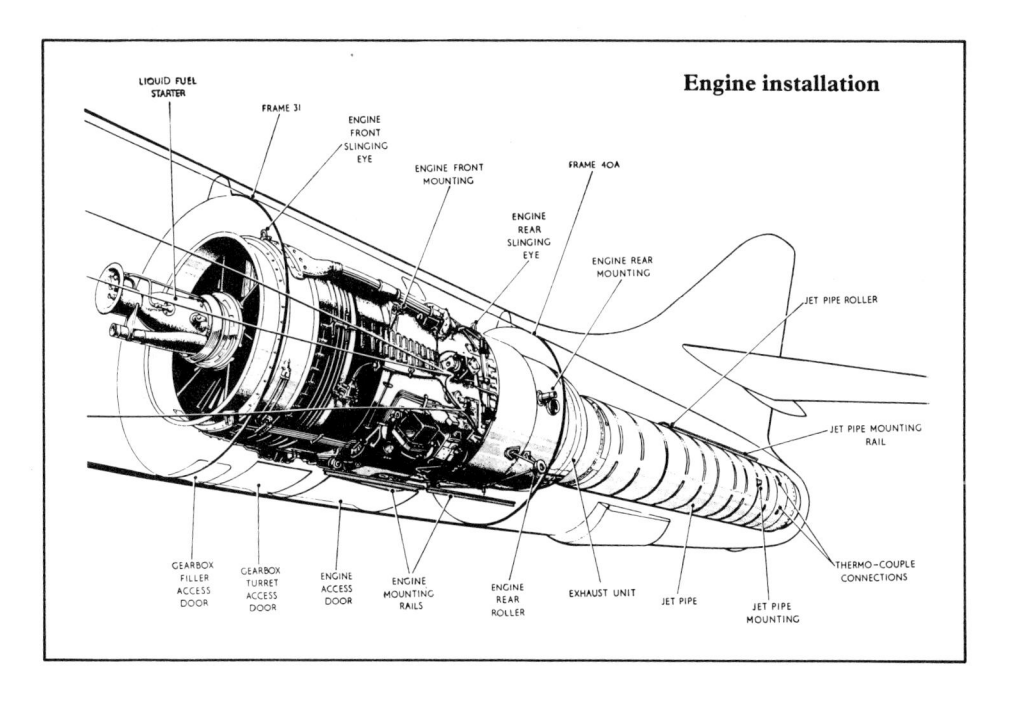

Engine installation

The Hunter two-seater

The two-seat versions of the Hunter differ principally in the structure of the front fuselage section, but are otherwise essentially similar elsewhere in the aircraft structure, powerplant, systems, undercarriage, wing stores and controls. The gun armament is reduced to one or two Aden guns according to customer requirements (generally speaking, those versions powered by Avon 200-series engines are armed with two guns, the remainder with a single gun). An enlarged canopy fairing is attached dorsally to the centre fuselage to accommodate the bulkier cockpit contours, and the front fuselage nose piece forward of frame 1C is also of slightly altered shape to accommodate the wider fuselage contours of the two-seater.

The front fuselage continues from frame 1C aft to frame 18A which forms the front frame of the forward transport joint. The cockpit, which is protected by heavy plating and provided with two ejector seats, is enclosed by a windscreen and hydraulically-operated hood. The canopy opens upwards, hinging on its rear edge for entry and exit, and may be jettisoned in emergency. To allow the cockpit to be pressurised, it is sealed from the remainder of the airframe by a floor extending from frame 6, which is a solid bulkhead, to a diaphragm at frame 14. The twin instrument panels, together with the port and starboard side panels, are located at the forward end of the cockpit on a structure extending across the top of frame 8 which also carries the two gunsights.

The windscreen consists of two flat bullet-proof centre panels and two curved side panels, all four of which are secured to the fuselage decking. The hood is moulded from two sheets of transparent plastic mounted in a frame consisting of front and back arch members, a longitudinal roof member and two edge members at the sides. The complete hood lifts upwards, hinging on its rear arch member on a pivot point between frames 14 and 14A. It opens and closes by electro-hydraulic jacks located in the hood fairing, and is secured in the fully open position by an internal mechanical lock in the jack. The hood is

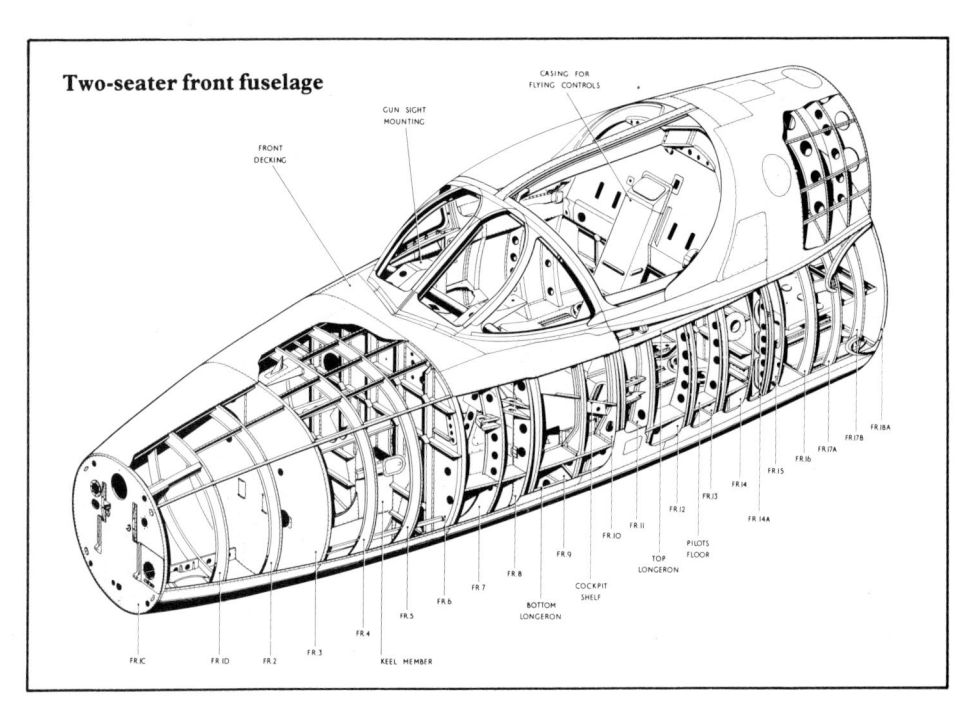

Two-seater front fuselage

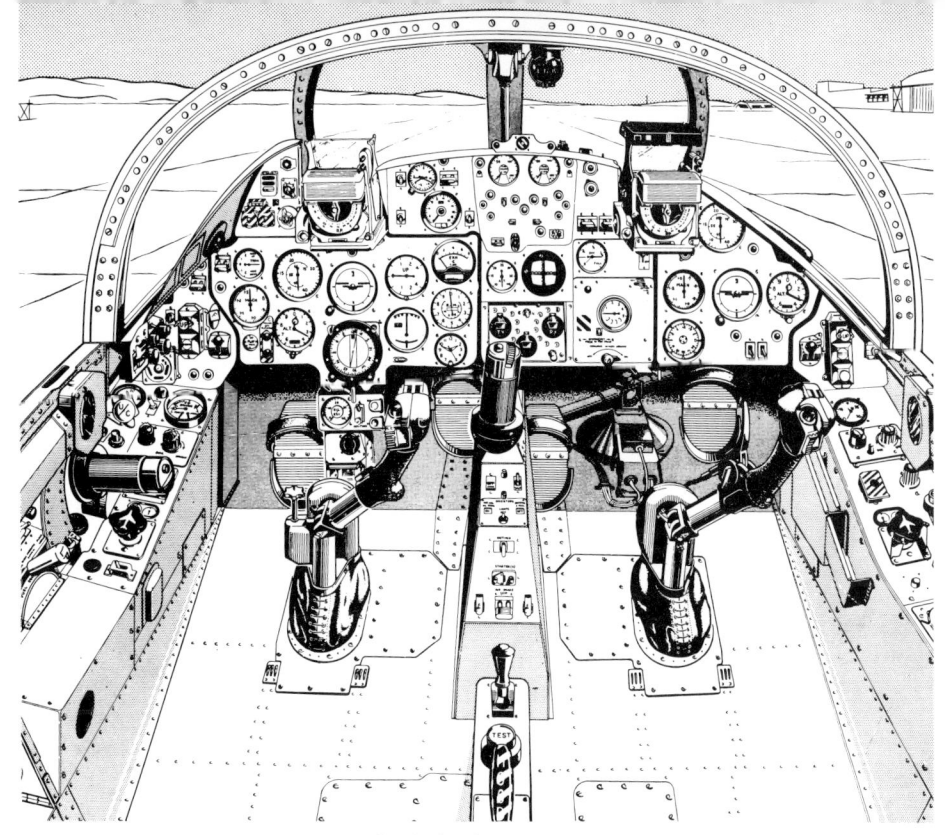

Cockpit of T Mark 66

provided with a rubber seal which is automatically inflated when the canopy is closed and deflated when it is open, partial deflation occurring before the hood actuation gear operates. A modification was introduced to allow the hood to be partially opened during taxiing.

The gun installation consists of two 30 mm Aden automatic guns, semi-buried in the undersurface of the front fuselage, together with an ammunition box and empty-link collector tanks. Each gun is covered by a fairing made up in three sections between frames 10 and 17B; the barrel of each gun lies along a blast trough extending forward in the front fuselage skin. The guns are electrically fired and controlled by a trigger on each of the control column handgrips.

Geometric and performance specification of the F6/FGA 9/FR 10

Geometric data

Wing Span: 33 ft 8 in (10.25 m); Overall length: 45 ft 10½ in (13.98 m); Overall height: 13 ft 2 in (4.0 m). Gross area: 349 sq ft (32.42 m^2); Quarter-chord sweepback: 40.0°; Thickness/chord ratio: 0.085 constant; Aspect ratio: 3.33; Aileron movement (normal to hinge): ±13°; Aileron area, aft of hinge (both): 26.52 sq ft (2.46 m^2); Landing flap movement (normal to hinge): 0 to 80°; Landing flap area, aft of hinge (both): 31.2 sq ft (2.89 m^2).

Tailplane and elevator Total gross area: 53.92 sq ft (4.90 m^2); Elevator area, aft of hinge: 16.34 sq ft (1.51 m^2); Tailplane span: 11 ft 10 in (3.61 m); Quarter-chord sweepback: 41.5°; Tailplane movement, normal to hinge: ± 2½°; Elevator movement, normal to hinge: 23° up, 9° down.

Fin and rudder Nett area, excluding body: 35.0 sq ft (3.24 m^2); Rudder area, aft of

hinge line: 6.07 sq ft (0.56 m^2); Quarter-chord sweepback: 48.0°; Rudder movement, normal to hinge: ± 23½°.
Undercarriage Track: 14 ft 9 in (4.48 m).
Airbrake Area: 10.2 sq ft (0.94 m^2); Movement, normal to hinge: 0 to 67°.
Tail parachute Diameter: 10 ft 6 in (3.2 m) (when fitted).

All-up weights—various configurations

Assuming Internal fuel capacity of aircraft: 392 gall (1,780 litres); Specific gravity of fuel: 0.77; Weight of inboard pylons (pair): 115 lb (52 kg); Weight of outboard pylons (pair): 70 lb (32 kg); Weight of empty 100-gall (454 litre) drop tanks (pair): 300 lb (136 kg); Weight of empty 230-gall (1,044 litre) drop tanks (pair): 480 lb (218 kg).
Interceptor rôle Clean aircraft: 17,750 lb (8,060 kg); With two 100-gall (454 litre) drop tanks: 19,700 lb (8,940 kg); With two 230-gall (1,044 litre) drop tanks: 21,900 lb (9,940 kg).
Ground attack rôle With two 500 lb (227 kg) bombs: 18,950 lb (8,500 kg); With two 1,000 lb (454 kg) bombs: 20,050 lb (9,100 kg); With 24 3-in (7.62 cm) rocket projectiles: 19,300 lb (8,760 kg); With two 500 lb (227 kg) bombs and 24 3-in (7.62 cm) rocket projectiles: 20,550 lb (9,330 kg); With two 1,000 lb (454 kg) bombs and 24 3-in (7.62 cm) rocket projectiles: 21,650 lb (9,830 kg); With two 100-gall drop tanks and two 500 lb bombs: 20,850 lb (9,470 kg); With two 100-gall drop tanks and two 1,000 lb bombs: 22,000 lb (9,990 kg); With two 100-gall drop tanks and 24 3-in rocket projectiles: 21,300 lb (9,670 kg); With two 230-gall (1,044 litre) drop tanks and 24 3-in rocket projectiles: 23,450 lb (10,650 kg).
Long-range ferry or fighter-reconnaissance rôle With two 230-gall (1,044 litre) drop tanks and two 100-gall (454 litre) drop tanks: 23,800 lb (10,810 kg).

Engine performance and aircraft sorties

Rolls-Royce Avon Mark 207 engine.
Maximum take-off and operational necessity Engine speed: 8,000 rpm; Thrust: 10,150 lb (4,610 kg); Specific fuel consumption: 0.880; Time limit: 10 min combined duration.
Intermediate condition Engine speed: 7,800 rpm; Thrust: 9,550 lb (4,340 kg); Specific fuel consumption: 0.865; Time limit: 30 min.
Maximum continuous Engine speed: 7,600 rpm; Thrust: 8,850 lb (4,020 kg); Specific fuel consumption: 0.850; Time limit: Unrestricted.
Ground idling Engine speed: 2,500 rpm; Thrust: 220 lb (100 kg); Specific fuel consumption: 4.00; Time limit: Unrestricted.

Performance

Maximum speeds Clean aircraft: Mach 0.95 at 36,000 ft, Mach 0.938 at sea level; Aircraft with two 100-gall (454 litre) drop tanks: Mach 0.94 at 35,000 ft, Mach 0.925 at sea level; Aircraft with two 230-gall (1,044 litre) drop tanks: Mach 0.936 at 35,000 ft, Mach 0.913 at sea level; Aircraft with two 230- and two 100-gall drop tanks: Mach 0.905 at 30,000 ft, Mach 0.87 at sea level.
Time to 40,000 feet Clean aircraft: 5 min 30 sec; Aircraft with two 100-gall drop tanks: 7 min 20 sec; Aircraft with two 230- and two 100-gall drop tanks: 12 min 30 sec.
Take-off ground run Example: Take-off weight 20,500 lb (9,299 kg); 10-knot wind component: 3,000-ft runway altitude; 20°C outside air temperature; unstick at 10 knots above minumum IAS; *Ground run* 1,090 yds.
Landing ground run Example: Landing weight 15,500 lb (7,031 kg); 15-knot wind

component; 3,000-ft runway altitude; 10°C outside air temperature; minimum touchdown speed; *Ground run* 720 yds.

Representative operational sorties
High altitude intercept mission: clean aircraft

Phase	Time (min)	Distance Nautical miles	km	Fuel lb	kg
Take-off and acceleration	1.25	—	—	190	86
Climb to 46,000 ft (14,000 m)	6.75	58	108	570	259
Cruise at 46,000 ft (14,000 m)	26.30	218	403	665	301
Combat	10.00	—	—	435	197
Cruise at 46,000 ft (14,000 m)	33.20	276	511	780	353
Reserve	—	—	—	480	218
Totals	**1 hr 18 min**	**2 × 276**	**2 × 511**	**3,120**	**1,414**

Ground attack (Hi-Lo-Hi): aircraft with two 230-gall tanks and 24 × 3-in rockets

Phase	Time (min)	Distance Nautical miles	km	Fuel lb	kg
Take-off and acceleration	2.00	—	—	310	141
Climb to 39,000 ft (12,000 m)	12.40	101	187	1,160	525
Cruise out at 39,000 ft	42.80	336	622	1,765	800
Descent to sea level	5.00	35	65	115	52
Attack	5.00	—	—	915	415
Climb to 39,000 ft (12,000 m)	5.10	43	80	510	231
Cruise back at 39,000 ft	52.50	429	794	1,545	701
Reserve	—	—	—	480	218
Totals	**2 hr 5 min**	**2 × 472**	**2 × 874**	**6,800**	**3,083**

One of the Blue Fox-equipped Hunter T Mark 8Ms, XL602, produced in 1980 to train Fleet Air Arm pilots for the Sea Harrier. Note rose radome and pitot boom.

Chapter 12

In the cockpit

There can be few pilots who, on climbing into an aeroplane for their first flight on type, are not appreciably influenced by a knowledge of its manufacturer's authority and experience in the particular field of design, or of its reputation. In other words there is bound to be an attitude of mind which embraces a knowledge with confidence that each new aircraft that stems from a long-established design office will embody the experience of countless pilots of previous generations.

Of course, there have been outstanding exceptions to this in both opposing senses; the brilliant Martin-Baker MB 5 fighter of the mid-1940s emerged from an agency that had never succeeded in producing a fighter that had been accepted for operational service; whereas the Supermarine Swift, with a long line of distinguished antecedents, proved a failure.

Thus, despite the tedious problems which were largely eliminated in the pre-service period, the Hunter was eagerly awaited by RAF Fighter Command and quickly showed itself to be a 'pilot's aeroplane'. One sensed from the first moments in the cockpit that the pilot had been uppermost in the designers' minds when the aeroplane was being evolved. A superb field of vision from the cockpit on the ground and in the air was inherent in the design, together with simple-action controls and a well-ordered instrument presentation.

Unlike the previous generation of RAF fighters, the Hunter's cockpit tended to follow the American practice of arranging the instruments and secondary controls in tidy consoles which, absent from aircraft such as the Meteor and Vampire, no longer gave the impression that many items had been 'screwed on' as afterthoughts.

Flying controls consisted of a split-action control column whose lateral movement was confined to its upper ten inches without interfering with the pilot's leg movement on the rudder pedals. The wheelbrake lever was mounted on the control column and operated in conjunction with differential use of the pedals. The tailplane incidence control was a button located on the rear face of the control column grip as a logical extension of the normal use of elevator control, while fine trimming of the controls was achieved by means of switches positioned immediately below the throttle adjacent to their relevant indicators. Otherwise all other flight instruments and indicators were located well forward of the pilot's seat and demanded no extensive 'eye-balling' inside the cockpit—a vital consideration for a fighter pilot whose maximum attention must lie outside the cockpit.

Engine controls were confined to the throttle lever mounted high on the left of the cockpit, movement of this also opening and closing the high pressure fuel cock. Secondary engine controls, not needed for normal flight operation, were relegated to more remote locations, although the re-light switch was positioned adjacent to the throttle. Again, engine speed and temperature instruments, and fuel indicators, were placed well forward of the pilot's eyes. The airbrake control, used in conjunction with the throttle to adjust

In the cockpit

the aircraft's speed, was a switch mounted for thumb operation on the stub-end of the throttle lever.

All other instruments, navigation and armament controls were located in groups arranged in easily accessible positions around the upper levels of the cockpit.

In the air

Taxiing the Hunter was entirely straightforward with a superlative view from the cockpit and powerful, positive action of the wheelbrakes which were normally only fitted to the mainwheels.

Opening up on the runway prior to take-off, despite plenty of power from either 'large' or 'small' Avon, produced no forward creep against the brakes, but on releasing these the surge of acceleration—particularly with the Avon 200-Series—was exhilarating to say the least, and is today only otherwise associated with fighters equipped with re-heat.

Speed built up rapidly after unstick and the aircraft crould be trimmed into the climb almost immediately. Once more, the exceptional rate of climb of the Avon 200-powered Hunter was more than a trifle exciting for pilots previously accustomed to the Meteor or Vampire.

At altitude one's first impression was that of lightness of control response, the aileron boosters imparting a positive crispness which, with plenty of engine power available, rendered the Hunter a magnificent aerobatic mount. Maximum level speed at altitude was 0.94 Mach, but supersonic speed required that the aircraft be dived gently from around 30,000 feet or above, speed building up quickly in a 30-degree dive. There was no sensation in exceeding Mach 1, with no tendency towards control reversal or buffet, while recovery was effected simply by throttling back and easing out of the dive. Actuation of the airbrake brought rapid deceleration with little change of trim.

As a weapon platform the Hunter proved eventually to be outstanding after the early

Cockpit of the Hunter F Mark 6.

pitch-up problems during high-altitude gun-firing had been cured, and after the surge-free Avons had been introduced. Engine surge during those early days was rather alarmingly manifest by the loud rumbling in the engine intake ducts, sometimes followed by a loud bang and then silence as the 'flame went out'. Engine re-light was, however, entirely straightforward.

Spinning in the Hunter was also without problems, the aircraft tending to stall without wing-drop, so that the spin had to be positively initiated with assistance from rudder and ailerons. Erect spin recovery was normal with forward movement of control column and centralised rudder.

On re-joining the airfield circuit to land it was customary to employ the airbrake to reduce speed to about 160 knots, arriving on the approach at 140 knots, wheels down and part flap. After touchdown the drag chute would be employed by operating the control on the left of the cockpit, and this in conjunction with the Maxaret wheelbrakes quickly reduced the ground run.

Normal flight endurance of Hunters carrying a couple of 100-gallon drop tanks (in which configuration the aircraft was fully stressed for all normal manoeuvres and aerobatics, though entry speeds needed to be rather higher than on a 'clean' aircraft owing to quicker deceleration) was about 90 minutes at altitude, although descent to a target for ground attack reduced this considerably.

Flying the Hunter came to be regarded as being almost entirely viceless, so that it was of little wonder that, in its old age, it was a natural choice to become the operational trainer for such modern aircraft as the Jaguar and Harrier. □

Mr. Letcher's civil-registered Hunter 4 in America, N72602.

Chapter 13

The future

The last two RAF squadrons to fly Hunters, Nos 45 and 58 based at Wittering, were finally disbanded in August 1976 and their aircraft handed over to the Tactical Weapons Unit at Brawdy. This unit and No 337 OCU at Honington are, at the time of writing, the only RAF units still flying the Hunter—the last examples of which were produced for the RAF over twenty years ago.

Hunters will continue to serve in the operational rôle in half a dozen air forces well into the 1980s, while those of Switzerland will continue flying in the '90s. It also seems likely that Hunters will continue to be painstakingly preserved in flying condition by private individuals who are fortunate to have access to fairly elaborate maintenance facilities. At least one owner in the USA, Mr Letcher, has acquired a Hunter and restored it superbly for flying under limited civil permit conditions.

It is always sad to see fine aeroplanes pass into history and disappear from the skies—overtaken and perhaps eclipsed by more modern shapes with the advance of technology. Yet who will say that Sydney Camm's most graceful Hunter will ever be surpassed? Most surely it will live on as apt memorial to the man who led British fighter design for forty long and eventful years.

Notwithstanding the aestheticism of the Hunter as a surviving tribute to its designers, its builders and those who flew it, a far more beneficial attribute would unquestionably accrue if one could be convinced that its path through history had bestowed tangible evidence of experience among the agencies responsible for the provision of military aircraft in this country. As has been told, the early troubles of the Hunter were directly attributable to Treasury parsimony, and it became incumbent upon a handful of dedicated people, often working within the strict limits of commercial finance—by implication infinitely more cost-effective for the nation than public funds—to employ their professional skills to produce the necesssary remedies.

Now that the British aircraft industry has passed into State ownership as the result of doctrinaire pressures—not least that of accountability to the nation—one is bound to wonder whether an aeroplane such as the Hunter could ever again be created within such a conglomerate as British Aerospace, and whether the same motivation will or can exist among individuals to minister to the strengths and weaknesses of modern aircraft.

In the event that the aircraft industry *does* return to the realms of private enterprise, one must ensure that the lessons of continuity of research and wholehearted Government support for overseas sales have been learned and are acted upon. If political capital must be made from an arms industry, let that capital lie in the benefit of world leadership, of stable manpower employment and labour relations, and pride of achievement. Therein lies the Hawker Hunter's stature.

Appendices

Notes to the appendices

The following is a summary of the individual Hunter aircraft histories, including manufacturer, contracts, dates of first flight and the test pilots involved, dates of delivery to customer, record of Service life, conversion to subsequent Marks, record of trials on which the aircraft were engaged and, where known, the eventual fate of the aircraft. First flight details of Coventry- and Blackpool-built Hunters have not apparently survived.

The 'G-9-..' registration is allocated to aircraft by the manufacturer to cover restricted flying, delivery flights, etc. The GIA numerals apply to those aircraft confined solely to maintenance training use. Normally once an aircraft has been employed in this category it seldom flies again, but in the instance of the Hunter there were numerous aeroplanes which were refurbished and resumed full flying duties.

The following abbreviations have been used:

A&AEE	Aircraft & Armament Experimental Establishment, Boscombe Down
AFDS	Air Fighting Development Squadron, West Raynham
APS	Armament Practice Squadron (Acklington, and later Sylt)
AQAA	*Al Quwwat Aljawwiya Aliraqiya* (Iraqi Air Force)
ASM	Armstrong Siddeley Motors Limited
AWA	Sir W.G. Armstrong Whitworth Aircraft Limited, Coventry
(B)	Bomber
BRD	Base Repair Depot, Indian Air Force
CA	Comptroller (Air), Ministry of Supply
CAACU	Combined Anti-Aircraft Co-operation Unit
CFE	Central Fighter Establishment, West Raynham
CFS	Central Flying School
Deld	Delivered (followed by delivery date)
DFCS	Day Fighters' Conversion Squadron, West Raynham
DFLS	Day Fighter Leaders' School, West Raynham
ESK	*Eskadrille*/Squadron, Danish Air Force
ETPS	Empire Test Pilots' School, Farnborough
F, (F)	Fighter
FAA	Fleet Air Arm
FAB/BL	*Force Aérienne Belge/Belgische Luchtmacht*
FAC	*Fuerza Aerea Chilena*
FAP	*Fuerza Aerea Peruana*
ff	First flight (with date and pilot, where known)
FGA	Fighter, Ground Attack
FH	Flying hours (total flown by aircraft)

Appendix 1

FRADU	Fleet Requirements and Direction Unit
FR, (FR)	Fighter Reconnaissance
FTS	Flying Training School
FWS	Fighter Weapons School
GA	Ground Attack
GIA	Ground Instruction Airframe (or Aircraft)
HAL	Hawker Aircraft Limited, Kingston-upon-Thames and Dunsfold (used prior to March 1958)
HSA	Hawker Siddeley Aviation Limited (used from March 1958)
IAF	Indian Air Force
IRS	Instrument Rating Squadron, West Raynham
KAF	Kenyan Air Force
KDF	*Kongelige Dansk Flyvevabnet* (Danish Air Force)
KL	*Koninklijke Luchtmacht* (Royal Netherlands Air Force)
MU	Maintenance Unit
OCU	Operational Conversion Unit (No 229 OCU, Chivenor)
RAE	Royal Aircraft Establishment, Farnborough and Bedford
RJAF	Royal Jordanian Air Force
RNAMU	Royal Naval Air Maintenance Unit
RNAS	Royal Naval Air Station
RR	Rolls-Royce Limited
RSAF	Republic of Singapore Air Force
SOC	Struck Off Charge
Sqn	Squadron
Stn Flt	Station Flight
STT	School of Technical Training
T	Trainer
TAF	Tactical Air Force
TI	Trial Installation
TWU	Tactical Weapons Unit
WTS	Weapon(s) Training Squadron

1 Hunter prototypes

Hawker P.1067 1st prototype. Designed to Air Ministry Specification F.3/48. Contract placed June 25 1948. WB188. Unarmed aircraft. First flown at Boscombe Down by Sqn Ldr Neville Duke on July 20 1951; duration of flight 47 min. Employed on prototype performance and handling trials until mid-1953 when fitted with Rolls-Royce Avon RA7R with reheat for attack on World Air Speed Records, September 1953. Also engaged in trials to decide optimum airbrake. Became GIA, No 1 School of Technical Training, Halton, and afterward passed to RAF Melksham. (During record flight aircraft was designated the Hunter Mark 3.)

Hawker P.1067 2nd prototype. WB195. Armed with full four-Aden gun armament and radar ranging. First flight, May 5 1952. Employed in airbrake development programme and initial spinning trials. Passed to No 1 School of Technical Training as GIA, 7284M, March 1959.

Hawker P.1067 3rd prototype. WB202. Armstrong-Siddeley Sapphire engine. Was in effect prototype for Hunter F Mark 2. First flight, November 30 1952. Fully armed with four Aden guns. Employed in airbrake trials and drop tank trials at Dunsfold. Later fitted with four dummy Firestreaks.

Hawker P.1083. WN470. Single experimental prototype ordered under Contract No 6296 and covered by Works Orders 013021 to 013034. Aircraft was Hunter development with Avon RA14R and 50° swept wing. Reached advanced manufacture but cancelled by HM Government, July 9 1953.

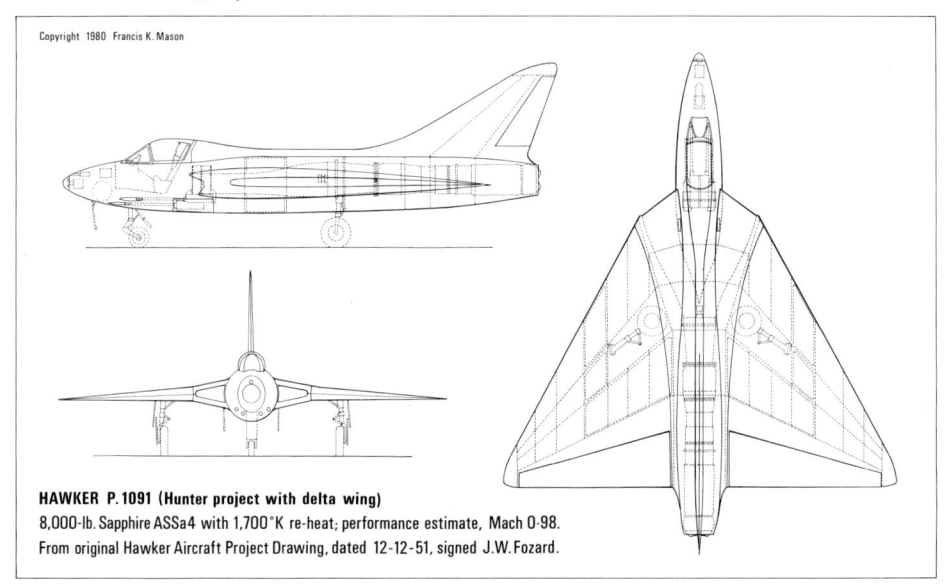

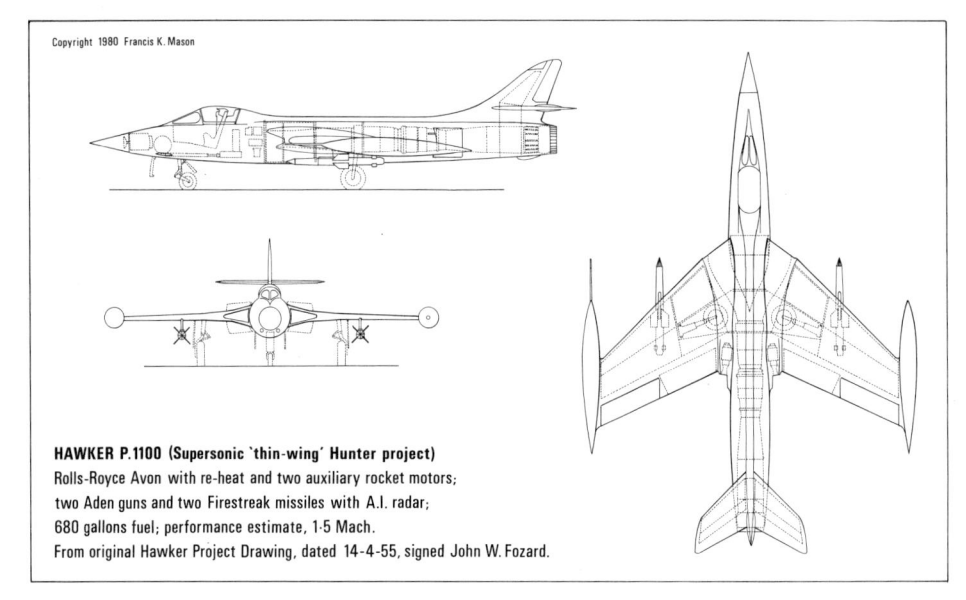

HAWKER P.1091 (Hunter project with delta wing)
8,000-lb. Sapphire ASSa4 with 1,700°K re-heat; performance estimate, Mach 0·98.
From original Hawker Aircraft Project Drawing, dated 12-12-51, signed J.W. Fozard.

HAWKER P.1100 (Supersonic 'thin-wing' Hunter project)
Rolls-Royce Avon with re-heat and two auxiliary rocket motors; two Aden guns and two Firestreak missiles with A.I. radar; 680 gallons fuel; performance estimate, 1·5 Mach.
From original Hawker Project Drawing, dated 14-4-55, signed John W. Fozard.

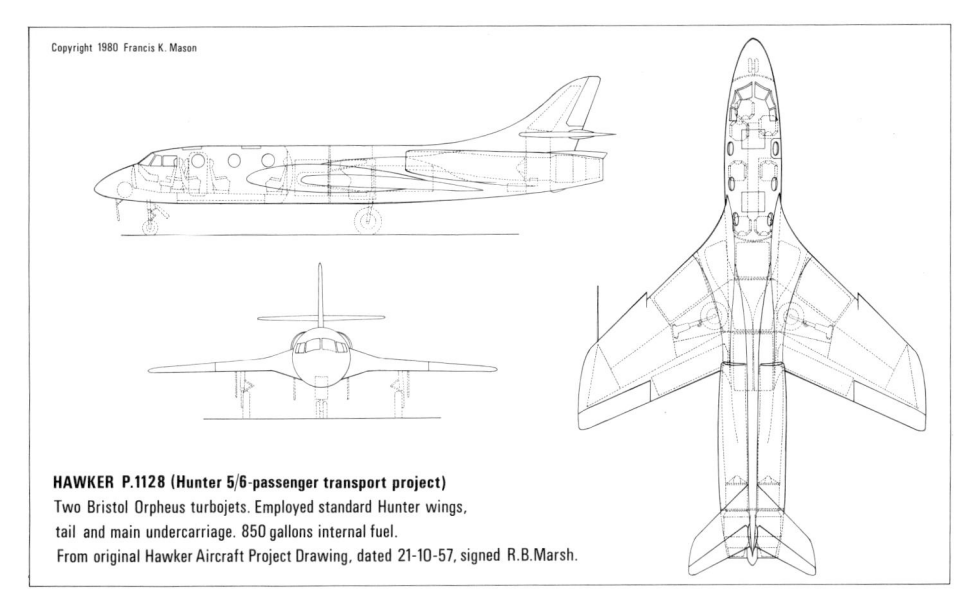

HAWKER P.1128 (Hunter 5/6-passenger transport project)
Two Bristol Orpheus turbojets. Employed standard Hunter wings, tail and main undercarriage. 850 gallons internal fuel.
From original Hawker Aircraft Project Drawing, dated 21-10-57, signed R.B.Marsh.

Hawker P.1099. Prototype Hunter F Mark 6, XF833. Aircraft used front and centre fuselage components of cancelled P.1083. Ordered under Contract No 10032. First flight, January 22 1954. Extensive flying trials at Dunsfold and Boscombe Down. Delivered to Miles Aircraft Ltd, Shoreham, June 5 1956 to be fitted with Rolls-Royce thrust-reversal equipment.

Hawker P.1101. First prototype. XJ615. Ordered under Contract No 11595. Rolls-Royce Avon RA21 engine. Initially armed with two, but later one Aden gun. First flight, July 8 1955. Employed on numerous trials including hood development, spinning, gun firing, etc. Delivered to RAE May 1 1959.

Hawker P.1101. Second prototype. XJ627. Rolls-Royce Avon RA28 engine. First flight, November 17 1956. To Boscombe Down December 6 1957; returned to HAL July 4 1958. Delivered to Martin-Baker Limited, Chalgrove, November 19 1958 for prolonged ejector seat trials. Re-purchased by HSA September 27 1968, with 224.45 FH. Refurbished and flown in Class 2 markings, G-9-296. Converted to full Chilean Hunter T Mark 72, 721, and delivered via Chester to Chile on May 19 1971.

2 Hunter production

Hawker Hunter F Mark 1

First production batch of 113 aircraft built by Hawker Aircraft Ltd, Kingston-upon-Thames. Instruction to Proceed received on October 20 1950. Contract dated March 14 1951, No SP/6/5910/CB.7a.

WT555 ff 16-5-53 Frank Murphy. Handling and performance trials, HAL and A&AEE, 1953-54.

WT556 ff 16-6-53. CA aircraft. Demonstrations in Europe, 1953; to RR for engine trials; used for familiarisation flying at Boscombe Down, 7-53.
WT557 ff 17-7-53 Frank Murphy. CA aircraft. Demonstrations in Denmark. To RRE for radio trials.
WT558 ff 24-8-53 Frank Murphy. Gun firing trials. Fitted with wing fences. A&AEE, 11-53. No 54 (F) Sqn ('T').
WT559 ff 2-9-53 Frank Murphy. CA aircraft. Flown by Belgian evaluation team. To A&AEE for hood jettison trials.
WT560 ff 28-9-53 Frank Bullen. CA aircraft, Dunsfold. Minor trial installations. To RR for Avon 119.
WT561 ff 23-10-53 Frank Bullen. CA aircraft, Dunsfold. Minor trial installations.
WT562 ff 29-10-53 Frank Murphy. CA aircraft, Dunsfold. Trial installation of one-third-span flaps.
WT563 ff 2-11-53 Frank Murphy. CA aircraft, Dunsfold. Trial installation of interim flying tail.
WT564 ff 28-11-53 Frank Murphy. CA aircraft, Dunsfold. Used by A&AEE for practice interception trials, 1954.
WT565 ff 7-12-53 Frank Murphy. To RR for Avon 119.
WT566 ff 12-12-53 Frank Bullen. CA aircraft, Dunsfold. Used for airbrake development.
WT567 ff 18-12-53 Frank Bullen. Gun firing trials, A&AEE.
WT568 ff 16-12-53 Frank Murphy. CA aircraft, Dunsfold. TI of wing leading edge extensions. To A&AEE, 1-54.
WT569 ff 18-12-53 Frank Bullen. To A&AEE, 15-7-54. TI of full-power ailerons. Tropical trials, Khartoum, 9-54.
WT570 ff 22-12-53 Neville Duke. CA aircraft, Dunsfold. TI of full-power ailerons. To A&AEE and RAE, 27-7-54.
WT571 ff 8-1-54 Frank Murphy. Experimental 'area rule' application. To RAE, Farnborough, 1-7-55.
WT572 ff 5-1-54 Frank Bullen. Miscellaneous company trials.
WT573 ff 5-1-54 Frank Bullen. CA aircraft, Dunsfold & A&AEE. To RR for Avon 119.
WT574 ff 22-1-54 Frank Bullen. To RR, 12-5-54.
WT575 ff 8-1-54 Neville Duke. To Boscombe Down, 5-7-54. No 229 OCU.
WT576 ff 18-1-54 Frank Murphy. To Boscombe Down, 3-6-54. AFDS.
WT577 ff 19-1-54 Neville Duke. To CFE, 5-7-54. AFDS.
WT578 ff 20-1-54 Don Lucey. To CFE, 5-7-54. AFDS.
WT579 ff 23-1-54 Frank Bullen. To CFE, 8-6-54. No 229 OCU.
WT580 ff 25-1-54 Frank Murphy. To No 5 MU, 7-7-54. No 43 (F) Sqn.
WT581 ff 3-2-54 Frank Bullen. To No 5 MU, 5-8-54. No 43 (F) Sqn ('S').
WT582 ff 8-2-54 Frank Bullen. To No 5 MU, 5-7-54. No 43 (F) Sqn.
WT583 ff 10-2-54 Don Lucey. First aircraft with modified Avon 113. To No 5 MU, 9-7-54. No 43 (F) Sqn.
WT584 ff 20-2-54 Bill Bedford. To No 5 MU, 7-7-54. No 43 (F) Sqn. No 229 OCU.
WT585 ff 20-2-54 Neville Duke. To No 5 MU, 7-7-54. No 43 (F) Sqn.
WT586 ff 22-2-54 Frank Murphy. To No 5 MU, 9-7-54. No 229 OCU.
WT587 ff 24-2-54 Frank Murphy. To No 5 MU, 21-7-54. No 43 (F) Sqn.
WT588 ff 24-2-54 Bill Bedford. To CFE, AFDS.
WT589 ff 15-6-54 Frank Murphy. To No 5 MU, 9-7-54. No 43 (F) Sqn.
WT590 ff 21-6-54 Frank Bullen. To No 5 MU, 22-7-54.
WT591 ff 21-6-54 Don Lucey. To CFE, 16-7-54. DFLS.
WT592 ff 22-6-54 Don Lucey. No 54 (F) Sqn. No 233 OCU.

Appendix 2

WT593 ff 1-7-54 Frank Murphy. To No 5 MU, 17-9-54. DFLS.
WT594 ff 2-7-54 Frank Bullen. To No 5 MU, 17-9-54. No 43 (F) Sqn ('N').
WT595 ff 2-7-54 Hugh Merewether. To No 5 MU, 27-7-54. No 43 (F) Sqn.

WT611 ff 8-7-54 Hugh Merewether. Trials with Avon 115 with HAL and RR.
WT612 ff 13-7-54 Frank Bullen. Second aircraft with Avon 115. To No 5 MU, 7-9-54.
WT613 ff 16-7-54 Hugh Merewether. To No 5 MU, 5-8-54. No 43 (F) Sqn ('R'). DFLS.
WT614 ff 12-7-54 Hugh Merewether. To No 5 MU, 17-9-54. FWS.
WT615 ff 20-7-54 Hugh Merewether. To No 5 MU, 21-10-54. No 233 OCU.
WT616 ff 20-7-54 Frank Bullen. CA aircraft. Trials with Avon 115.
WT617 ff 29-7-54 Hugh Merewether. To No 5 MU, 4-10-54. DFLS.
WT618 ff 28-7-54 Hugh Merewether. To No 5 MU, 7-9-54. No 43 (F) Sqn.
WT619 ff 28-7-54 Frank Bullen. To No 5 MU, 13-9-54. No 43 (F) Sqn. No 222 (F) Sqn ('B'). No 233 OCU.
WT620 ff 29-7-54 Frank Murphy. To No 5 MU, 22-9-54. No 233 OCU.
WT621 ff 10-8-54 Hugh Merewether. To ETPS, 21-9-54.
WT622 ff 8-7-54 Hugh Merewether. To No 5 MU, 27-7-54. No 43 (F) Sqn ('G').
WT623 ff 15-7-54 Hugh Merewether. To No 5 MU, 5-8-54. No 43 (F) Sqn.
WT624 ff 13-7-54 Frank Murphy. To No 5 MU, 12-8-54. No 229 OCU.
WT625 ff 7-8-54 Hugh Merewether. To No 5 MU, 20-9-54. No 229 OCU. No 233 OCU.
WT626 ff 28-7-54 Don Lucey. To No 5 MU, 7-9-54. No 229 OCU.
WT627 ff 7-8-54 Don Lucey. To No 5 MU, 4-10-54. DFLS.
WT628 ff 5-8-54 Don Lucey. To No 5 MU, 27-9-54. ETPS.
WT629 ff 6-8-54 Frank Bullen. To No 5 MU, 22-9-54. DFLS.
WT630 ff 1-9-54 Hugh Merewether. To No 5 MU, 12-10-54. No 43 (F) Sqn. No 222 (F) Sqn. No 233 OCU.
WT631 ff 29-7-54 Hugh Merewether. To No 5 MU, 22-9-54. No 229 OCU.
WT632 ff 4-9-54 Frank Murphy. To No 5 MU, 27-9-54. Crashed and SOC, Kemble, 8-12-55.
WT633 ff 12-8-54 Hugh Merewether. To RAE, 29-9-54, for miscellaneous trials.
WT634 ff 10-8-54 Don Lucey. To No 5 MU, 28-9-54. No 222 (F) Sqn. No 233 OCU.
WT635 ff 1-9-54 Hugh Merewether. Deld 4-10-54, No 233 OCU.
WT636 ff 9-9-54 Frank Murphy. Deld 4-11-54, No 233 OCU.
WT637 ff 15-9-54 Hugh Merewether. Deld 11-10-54, No 43 (F) Sqn. No 222 (F) Sqn ('F'). No 229 OCU.
WT638 ff 7-9-54 Hugh Merewether. No 233 OCU.
WT639 ff 3-9-54 Hugh Merewether. Deld 27-10-54, DFLS.
WT640 ff 9-9-54 Frank Bullen. Deld 19-10-54, No 54 (F) Sqn. No 229 OCU.
WT641 ff 2-9-54 Frank Bullen. Deld 11-10-54, No 43 (F) Sqn ('T'). DFLS.
WT642 ff 10-9-54 Don Lucey. Deld 7-10-54, No 43 (F) Sqn. No 229 OCU.
WT643 ff 9-9-54 Hugh Merewether. Deld 15-10-54, No 43 (F) Sqn. No 233 OCU.
WT644 ff 4-9-54 Hugh Merewether. Deld 7-10-54, No 43 (F) Sqn.
WT645 ff 16-9-54 Frank Bullen. Deld 7-10-54, DFLS.
WT646 ff 16-9-54 Frank Bullen. Deld 19-10-54, No 222 (F) Sqn.
WT647 ff 11-9-54 Don Lucey. Deld 17-11-54, No 222 (F) Sqn.
WT648 ff 4-10-54 Frank Bullen. Deld 4-11-54, No 222 (F) Sqn.
WT649 ff 21-9-54 Hugh Merewether. Deld 12-11-54, No 43 (F) Sqn ('N'). No 222 (F) Sqn.
WT650 ff 17-9-54 Frank Murphy. Deld 15-10-54, No 222 (F) Sqn.

WT651 ff 23-9-54 Hugh Merewether. Deld 21-10-54, No 222 (F) Sqn ('C').
WT652 ff 18-9-54 Frank Murphy. Deld 12-10-54, DFLS.
WT653 ff 27-9-54 Frank Bullen. Deld 9-11-54, No 229 OCU.
WT654 ff 24-9-54 Hugh Merewether. Deld 3-11-54, No 229 OCU.
WT655 ff 4-10-54 Frank Bullen. Deld 24-11-54, No 233 OCU.
WT656 ff 14-10-54 Hugh Merewether. Experimental TI of flap blowing, HAL and RAE.
WT657 ff 2-10-54 Frank Bullen. Deld 10-12-54, No 229 OCU. No 233 OCU.
WT658 ff 6-10-54 Hugh Merewether. Deld 24-11-54, DFLS.
WT659 ff 29-9-54 Frank Bullen. Deld 3-11-54, No 54 (F) Sqn ('U').
WT660 ff 11-10-54 Frank Murphy. Deld 17-11-54, DFLS.

WT679 ff 28-9-54 Hugh Merewether. Deld 12-11-54, No 229 OCU.
WT680 ff 6-10-54 Hugh Merewether. Deld 10-11-54, West Raynham Stn Flt.
WT681 ff 11-10-54 Frank Bullen. Deld 24-11-54.
WT682 ff 6-10-54 Frank Murphy. Deld 17-11-54, No 229 OCU.
WT683 ff 8-10-54 Hugh Merewether. Deld 24-11-54, DFLS.
WT684 ff 14-10-54 Hugh Merewether. Deld 24-11-54, DFLS.
WT685 ff 9-10-54 Frank Murphy. Deld 10-12-54, No 229 OCU.
WT686 ff 14-10-54 Frank Bullen. Deld 12-11-54.
WT687 ff 20-10-54 Hugh Merewether. Deld 15-12-54, No 54 (F) Sqn.
WT688 ff 19-10-54 Frank Bullen. Deld 10-12-54, No 229 OCU.
WT689 ff 20-10-54 Frank Bullen. Deld 10-12-54, No 229 OCU. Crashed and SOC, 2-9-55.
WT690 ff 13-10-54 Frank Bullen. Deld 24-11-54, DFLS.
WT691 ff 21-10-54 Frank Bullen. Deld 10-12-54, No 229 OCU. No 233 OCU.
WT692 ff 23-10-54 Frank Bullen. Deld 10-12-54, No 54 (F) Sqn ('S'). DFLS.
WT693 ff 21-10-54 Hugh Merewether. Deld 10-12-54, No 54 (F) Sqn.
WT694 ff 29-10-54 Hugh Merewether. Deld 2-2-55, No 54 (F) Sqn. DFLS.
WT695 ff 8-11-54 Hugh Merewether. Deld 15-12-54, No 229 OCU. No 233 OCU.
WT696 ff 4-11-54 Hugh Merewether. Deld 4-2-55, No 54 (F) Sqn. No 229 OCU.
WT697 ff 1-11-54 Hugh Merewether. Deld 17-12-54. Returned to HAL for demonstration use.
WT698 ff 4-11-54 Frank Bullen. Deld 10-12-54, No 54 (F) Sqn. DFLS.
WT699 ff 3-11-54 Hugh Merewether. Deld 10-12-54, No 229 OCU.
WT700 ff 10-11-54 Duncan Simpson. Deld 1-2-55, No 229 OCU.

Second production batch of 26 aircraft built by Hawker Aircraft (Blackpool) Ltd. Contract dated August 15 1953, No SP/6/8435/CB.7a.
WW599 No 43 (F) Sqn ('B').
WW600 ff 7-7-54. No 43 (F) Sqn. DFLS.
WW601 DFLS.
WW602 No 229 OCU.
WW603 DFLS.
WW604 No 233 OCU.
WW605 No 233 OCU.
WW606 No 222 (F) Sqn. No 229 OCU.
WW607 No 229 OCU.
WW608 DFLS.
WW609 No 233 OCU.

Appendix 2

WW610 No 54 (F) Sqn ('A'). FWS.

WW632 No 229 OCU.
WW633 DFLS.
WW634 No 229 OCU.
WW635 DFLS. Crashed and SOC, 8-2-55.
WW636 No 54 (F) Sqn. No 229 OCU.
WW637 No 229 OCU. No 233 OCU.
WW638 No 247 (F) Sqn ('J'). DFLS.
WW639 DFLS.
WW640 No 54 (F) Sqn ('C').
WW641 No 54 (F) Sqn ('B'). DFLS.
WW642 AFDS.
WW643 No 229 OCU.
WW644 No 229 OCU.
WW645 DFLS.

Hawker Hunter F Mark 2

One production batch of 45 aircraft built by Sir W.G. Armstrong Whitworth Aircraft Ltd, Coventry. Contract No SP/6/6315/CB.7a.

WN888 ff 14-10-53. Retained by AWA as CA aircraft for performance and handling trials. To Dunsfold, 3-11-53.
WN889 CA aircraft. To Baginton, 18-1-54. Trials with Sapphire ASSa.12 engine.
WN890 CA aircraft, AWA. Boscombe Down for de-tuner trials, 11-62.
WN891 CA aircraft, Baginton. A&AEE. CEPE, Canada, for winterisation trials.
WN892 CA aircraft. A&AEE, Boscombe Down, 1-10-54.
WN893 CA aircraft. RAE, Farnborough & Bedford, 31-8-54.
WN894 CA aircraft. A&AEE, Boscombe Down, 26-8-54.
WN895 First Service aircraft. CFE and AFDS. No 263 (F) Sqn, 2-2-55.
WN896 Crashed and SOC, 1954.
WN897 No 263 (F) Sqn. No 257 (F) Sqn, 24-7-54.
WN898 No 257 (F) Sqn ('A'). No 263 (F) Sqn. No 1 (F) Sqn ('A').
WN899 No 263 (F) Sqn. GIA, Henlow, 7542M.
WN900 No 263 (F) Sqn ('U').
WN901 No 257 (F) Sqn ('B'). No 12 STT, Melksham.
WN902 No 257 (F) Sqn ('D').
WN903 No 257 (F) Sqn. No 263 (F) Sqn ('B').
WN904 No 257 (F) Sqn ('Q').
WN905 Crashed and SOC, 1955.
WN906 Deld 23-9-54, No 5 MU. CFE. No 12 STT, Melksham.
WN907 No 257 (F) Sqn ('H'). RAF Colerne, 8-68.
WN908 Deld 8-9-57, No 5 MU. No 263 (F) Sqn.
WN909 Deld 27-9-54, No 45 MU. No 257 (F) Sqn ('S').
WN910 Trials, AWA. Deld No 41 MU. RAF Halton, 1964.
WN911 Deld 13-9-54, No 5 MU. CFE. AFDS.
WN912 Deld 23-9-54, No 5 MU. No 263 (F) Sqn. CFE.
WN913 Deld 9-10-54, No 5 MU. No 263 (F) Sqn. No 257 (F) Sqn ('U').
WN914 Deld 28-9-54, No 5 MU. No 257 (F) Sqn ('V').
WN915 Deld 21-9-54, No 5 MU. No 257 (F) Sqn ('T'). No 263 (F) Sqn ('L'), 18-3-55. Fire Fighting School, Sutton-on-Hull.

WN916 Deld 14-10-54, No 45 MU. CFE. AFDS.
WN917 Deld 7-10-54, No 45 MU. No 257 (F) Sqn ('E'), 17-11-54.
WN918 Deld 23-9-54, No 5 MU. No 257 (F) Sqn ('W'). No 1 (F) Sqn.
WN919 Deld 27-9-54, No 45 MU. No 257 (F) Sqn ('Q'). No 263 (F) Sqn ('F'). No 1 (F) Sqn.
WN920 Deld 28-9-54, CFE. AFDS.
WN921 Deld 1-10-54, No 5 MU. No 263 (F) Sqn ('S'). CFE.

WN943 Deld 22-10-54, No 5 MU. No 257 (F) Sqn.
WN944 Deld 7-10-54, No 45 MU. No 263 (F) Sqn ('H'), 21-4-55.
WN945 Deld 21-10-54, No 45 MU. CFE, 1-12-54. No 257 (F) Sqn ('M').
WN946 Deld 28-10-54, No 5 MU. No 263 (F) Sqn ('N'), 4-2-55. CFE.
WN947 Deld 9-11-54, No 5 MU. No 263 (F) Sqn ('R'), 31-5-55. No 257 (F) Sqn ('W').
WN948 Deld 27-9-54, No 45 MU. No 257 (F) Sqn ('R'), 12-11-54. No 263 (F) Sqn.
WN949 Deld 15-10-54, No 5 MU. No 257 (F) Sqn ('M'), 30-12-54.
WN950 Deld 1-10-54, No 5 MU. No 257 (F) Sqn ('F'), 30-12-54.
WN951 Deld 22-10-54, No 5 MU. No 257 (F) Sqn. No 263 (F) Sqn.
WN952 Deld 14-10-54, No 5 MU. No 257 (F) Sqn ('G'), 13-1-55.
WN953 Deld 4-11-54, No 45 MU. No 257 (F) Sqn ('C'), 25-1-55.

Hawker Hunter F Mark 4

First production batch of 85 aircraft built by Hawker Aircraft Ltd, Kingston-upon-Thames. Second part of Contract No SP/6/5910/CB.7a.

WT701 ff 20-10-54 Frank Murphy. CA aircraft. Trials with drop tanks and other stores. *Converted to Hunter T Mark 8.* No 764 Sqn, FAA. Collided with XL599, 23-8-61, and SOC.
WT702 ff 9-12-54 Hugh Merewether. CA aircraft. HAL and A&AEE radio trials. *Converted to Hunter T Mark 8.* RNAS, Lossiemouth. No 703 Sqn, FAA.
WT703 ff 11-54 Bill Bedford. CA aircraft. External store trials, HAL and A&AEE. Broken up, Dunsfold, 1964. 244.25 FH.
WT704 ff 26-11-54 Duncan Simpson. CA aircraft. Broken up, 1959.
WT705 ff 12-11-54 Hugh Merewether. CA aircraft. Handling and gunnery trials, A&AEE. Collided with banner target and damaged, 16-10-57. Broken up, 11-64.
WT706 ff 13-12-54 Hugh Merewether. CA aircraft. Handling trials at A&AEE. *Converted to Peruvian Hunter T Mark 62 (681).* ff 15-9-59 Don Lucey. Deld 10-59, Peru.
WT707 ff 13-1-55 Don Lucey. Crashed at Ford (Frank Murphy unhurt), 25-1-55, and SOC.
WT708 ff 15-12-54 Frank Bullen. Deld 9-2-55, No 33 MU. No 54 (F) Sqn ('F'). FWS.
WT709 ff 15-12-54 Frank Bullen. Deld 15-2-55, No 33 MU. No 54 (F) Sqn. Crashed at Slinfold, Sussex, 3-11-55, owing to fuel shortage in bad weather; pilot ejected safely. (Was one of four aircraft similarly lost on this day.)
WT710 ff 17-12-54 Frank Bullen. Deld 15-2-55, No 33 MU. No 54 (F) Sqn. No 111 (F) Sqn ('N'). Broken up, HAL, 1964. 484.30 FH.
WT711 ff 10-2-55 Hugh Merewether. Deld 19-3-55, No 33 MU. No 54 (F) Sqn. No 14 (F) Sqn ('A'). *Converted to Hunter GA Mark 11, 11-62.*
WT712 ff 19-1-55 Hugh Merewether. Deld 1-3-55, No 33 MU. No 54 (F) Sqn. *Converted to Hunter GA Mark 11, 5-63.* Collided with WT810, 1965, and SOC; pilot safe.
WT713 ff 25-1-55 Frank Bullen. Deld 2-3-55, No 33 MU. No 111 (F) Sqn. *Converted to Hunter GA Mark 11, 2-63.* Returned to HAL, 1970, as G-9-336. 819.55 FH.

Hunter 4, XF975, of No 229 OCU, Chivenor.

WT714 ff 25-1-55 Duncan Simpson. Deld 29-4-55, Lyneham. No 111 (F) Sqn. No 14 (F) Sqn. Collided with WT807, 18-8-55, and crashed near Bremen; Fg Off Deluce killed.
WT715 ff 25-1-55 Duncan Simpson. Deld 14-3-55, No 33 MU. No 111 (F) Sqn. No 229 OCU ('L'). Broken up, HAL, 1964. 271.00 FH.
WT716 ff 27-1-55 Duncan Simpson. Deld 29-3-55, No 5 MU. No 111 (F) Sqn. Became G-9-385, 4-72. GIA, 7790M. 550.45 FH.
WT717 ff 25-1-55 Hugh Merewether. Deld 16-6-55, North Weald Stn Flt. *Converted to Peruvian Hunter Mark 52 (630).* ff 1-12-55 Frank Bullen. Deld 2-56, Peru.
WT718 ff 29-1-55 Hugh Merewether. Deld 14-3-55, No 33 MU. No 111 (F) Sqn. No 245 (F) Sqn. No 229 OCU (RS-I). *Converted to Hunter GA Mark 11, 9-62.* RNAS, Lossiemouth.
WT719 ff 27-1-55 Hugh Merewether. Deld 17-3-55, No 5 MU. No 43 (F) Sqn. No 92 (F) Sqn. No 118 (F) Sqn. GIA, 1958, 7596M.
WT720 ff 27-1-55 Frank Bullen. Deld 1-3-55, No 33 MU. No 74 (F) Sqn ('B'). No 111 (F) Sqn. Broken up, HAL, 11-64. 613.10 FH.
WT721 ff 2-2-55 Hugh Merewether. Deld 15-2-55, No 33 MU. No 54 (F) Sqn. *Converted to Hunter GA Mark 11.* Deld 21-12-62, A&AEE, for trials. *Converted to Hunter PR Mark 11.* Lossiemouth, 1-66.
WT722 ff 4-2-55 Hugh Merewether. Deld 24-5-55, No 54 (F) Sqn. No 26 (F) Sqn ('S'). *Converted to Hunter T Mark 8.* Deld 10-4-59, FAA. No 703 Sqn, FAA. No 764 Sqn, FAA.
WT723 ff 16-2-55 Duncan Simpson. Deld 25-3-55, No 5 MU. No 54 (F) Sqn. No 14 (F) Sqn ('T'). No 229 OCU. *Converted to Hunter GA Mark 11.* Deld 17-8-62, Lossiemouth.

WT734 ff 5-2-55 Hugh Merewether. Deld 9-5-55. Returned to HAL. *Converted to Peruvian Hunter Mark 52 (638).* ff 18-1-56 Duncan Simpson. Deld 3-56, Peru. Damaged in collision but repaired in Peru.
WT735 ff 12-2-55 Duncan Simpson. Retained by HAL for radio trials. Fitted with American electronic equipment. SOC, 8-4-60.
WT736 ff 4-2-55 Hugh Merewether. To RR for engine trials with Avon 121. To Ferranti, 4-12-56. Broken up, 11-64. 385.30 FH.
WT737 ff 1-3-55 Hugh Merewether. Deld 29-3-55, No 5 MU. No 118 (F) Sqn. No 4 (F) Sqn. No 222 (F) Sqn. No 229 OCU ('B'). Scrapped, Coleys, 11-62. 543.50 FH.
WT738 ff 17-2-55 Hugh Merewether. Deld 25-3-55, No 5 MU. No 118 (F) Sqn. Collided with WT757, 23-10-55, near Hamburg; pilot killed.
WT739 ff 10-2-55 Duncan Simpson. Deld 2-3-55, No 33 MU. No 111 (F) Sqn. FWS ('E'). Broken up, 11-62. 528.15 FH.

WT740 ff 17-2-55 Duncan Simpson. Deld 29-3-55, No 5 MU. No 54 (F) Sqn. No 247 (F) Sqn ('F'). No 229 OCU. Broken up, HAL, 11-64. 439.50 FH.
WT741 ff 1-3-55 Sqn Ldr Sowrey. Deld 28-3-55, No 5 MU. No 118 (F) Sqn ('Q'). *Converted to Hunter GA Mark 11.* Deld 11-62, FAA. 457.55 FH. *Converted to Singaporean Hunter T Mark 75A (541).* Deld, 10-73.
WT742 ff 28-2-55 Sqn Ldr J.A. Sowrey. Deld 29-3-55, No 5 MU. No 98 (F) Sqn ('A'). Broken up and SOC, 10-57.
WT743 ff 28-2-55 Duncan Simpson. Deld 29-3-55, No 5 MU. No 118 (F) Sqn ('R'). Damaged due to acid from burst battery, 10-57, and broken up.
WT744 ff 28-2-55 Duncan Simpson. Deld 25-3-55, No 5 MU. AFDS. No 247 (F) Sqn. *Converted to Hunter GA Mark 11.* Deld 13-2-63, No 738 Sqn, FAA.
WT745 ff 2-3-55 Neville Duke. Deld 14-4-55, No 5 MU. No 14 (F) Sqn. Deld 1959, AWA. *Converted to Hunter T Mark 8.* Yeovilton Instrument Flight, 12-4-60. No 764 Sqn, FAA.
WT746 ff 1-3-55 Duncan Simpson. Deld 17-3-55, No 5 MU. AFDS. GIA, 7770M.
WT747 ff 4-3-55 Hugh Merewether. Deld 25-3-55, No 5 MU. No 98 (F) Sqn ('B'). Broken up, HAL, 11-64. 445.55 FH.
WT748 ff 3-3-55 Frank Bullen. No 118 (F) Sqn ('S'). Broken up, HAL, 1962. 709.25 FH.
WT749 ff 15-3-55 Hugh Merewether. Deld 1-4-55, No 247 (F) Sqn ('P'). No 229 OCU. Broken up, HAL, 11-64. 378.05 FH.
WT750 ff 4-3-55 Duncan Simpson. Deld 20-4-55, No 247 (F) Sqn. No 245 (F) Sqn ('A'). Broken up, HAL, 11-64. 545.00 FH.
WT751 ff 9-3-55 Duncan Simpson. Deld 28-3-55, No 5 MU. No 247 (F) Sqn. No 118 (F) Sqn. A&AEE, 1962, for jettison trials with 230-gallon drop tanks (empty).
WT752 ff 3-3-55 Duncan Simpson. Deld 1-4-55, No 247 (F) Sqn. No 118 (F) Sqn ('D'). Broken up, HAL, 11-64. 592.10 FH.
WT753 ff 10-3-55 Duncan Simpson. Deld 1-4-55, No 118 (F) Sqn ('E'). No 247 (F) Sqn. Broken up, HAL, 1962. 415.30 FH.
WT754 ff 10-3-55 Duncan Simpson. Deld 29-3-55, No 5 MU. No 118 (F) Sqn.
WT755 ff 18-3-55 M. Anderson, Avions Fairey. Deld 14-4-55, No 14 (F) Sqn. Returned to HAL, 1959. *Converted to Hunter T Mark 8.* RNAS Lossiemouth. RNAS Brawdy, 8-64. Returned to HAL, 3-73, as G-9-417. 2,240 FH at this date. *Converted to Kenyan Hunter T Mark 81 (801).* Deld 24-6-74, Kenya.
WT756 ff 11-3-55 M. Anderson, Avions Fairey. Deld 20-4-55. *Converted to Peruvian Hunter Mark 52 (639).* ff 17-1-56 Duncan Simpson. Deld 4-56, Peru.
WT757 ff 15-3-55 Sqn Ldr J.A. Sowrey. Deld 1-4-55, No 118 (F) Sqn. Collided with WT738, 23-10-55, near Hamburg; pilot killed and aircraft SOC.
WT758 ff 17-3-55 Frank Bullen. Deld 14-4-55, No 5 MU. *Converted to Peruvian Hunter Mark 52 (633).* ff 15-12-55 Duncan Simpson. Deld 3-56, Peru.
WT759 ff 16-3-55 M. Anderson, Avions Fairey. Deld 20-5-55. *Converted to Peruvian Hunter Mark 52 (642).* ff 26-1-56 Frank Bullen. Deld 3-56, Peru.
WT760 ff 17-3-55 Frank Bullen. Deld 14-4-55, No 5 MU. No 118 (F) Sqn. Broken up, HAL, 11-64. 697.45 FH.
WT761 ff 28-3-55 M. Anderson, Avions Fairey. Deld 15-4-55, No 5 MU. No 14 (F) Sqn. No 98 (F) Sqn. Broken up, HAL, 11-64.
WT762 ff 29-3-55 Hugh Merewether. Deld 15-4-55, No 247 (F) Sqn. Returned to 'manual' on take-off and dived into wood near Farnborough, 7-7-55, and SOC.
WT763 ff 25-3-55 Duncan Simpson. Deld 20-4-55, No 26 (F) Sqn ('F'). Broken up, HAL, 11-64. 459.25 FH.
WT764 ff 16-3-55 Frank Bullen. Deld 14-4-55, No 5 MU. No 111 (F) Sqn. No 54 (F) Sqn

Appendix 2

('G'). No 74 (F) Sqn ('J'). No 247 (F) Sqn. Broken up, HAL, 11-64. 600.10 FH.
WT765 ff 5-4-55 Duncan Simpson. Deld 29-4-55. *Converted to Peruvian Hunter Mark 52 (645)*. ff 7-2-56 Frank Bullen. Deld 4-56, Peru.
WT766 ff 24-3-55 Sqn Ldr J.A. Sowrey. Deld 2-5-55. *Converted to Peruvian Hunter Mark 52 (635)*. ff 30-12-55 Duncan Simpson. Deld 3-56, Peru.
WT767 ff 12-4-55 Flt Lt N.J. Carver. Deld 26-4-55, No 14 (F) Sqn. No 229 OCU, 1957. Broken up, 1962.
WT768 ff 23-5-55 Sqn Ldr J.A. Sowrey. Deld 25-4-55, No 118 (F) Sqn ('C'). No 247 (F) Sqn ('G'). *Converted to Peruvian Hunter Mark 52 (641)*. ff 20-1-56 Neville Duke. Deld 4-56, Peru.
WT769 ff 30-3-55 Duncan Simpson. Deld 20-5-55, No 26 (F) Sqn ('B'). Broken up, HAL, 1962. 361.35 FH.
WT770 Not flown in the UK; sold to Sweden for evaluation. *Became Swedish Hunter Mark 50 (34001)*.
WT771 ff 14-4-55 Flt Lt N.J. Carver. Deld 20-5-55, No 111 (F) Sqn. No 222 (F) Sqn ('C'). Broken up, HAL, 11-64.
WT772 ff 30-3-55 M. Anderson, Avions Fairey. TI of extended-span tailplane. CA aircraft, HAL. *Converted to Hunter T Mark 8 by AWA, 1959*. No 764 Sqn, FAA.
WT773 ff 19-4-55 Hugh Merewether. Deld 29-4-55. *Converted to Peruvian Hunter Mark 52 (644)*. ff 13-2-56 Hugh Merewether. Deld 5-56. Damaged in collision, 21-7-56, but repaired in Peru.
WT774 ff 6-4-55 Frank Bullen. Deld 2-5-55. *Converted to Peruvian Hunter Mark 52 (637)*. ff 9-1-56 Hugh Merewether. Deld 5-56, Peru.
WT775 ff 4-4-55 Frank Bullen. Deld 25-4-55, No 247 (F) Sqn ('Q'). Badly damaged in take-off accident, 26-3-56. Broken up, HAL, 1964.
WT776 ff 1-4-55 M. Anderson, Avions Fairey. Deld 24-5-55. *Converted to Peruvian Hunter Mark 52 (631)*. ff 5-12-55 Hugh Merewether. Deld 5-56.
WT777 ff 21-4-55 Flt Lt N.J. Carver. Deld 2-6-55, No 4 (F) Sqn ('U'). No 98 (F) Sqn ('F'). Broken up 1962.
WT778 ff 5-4-55 Duncan Simpson. Deld 25-5-55, No 26 (F) Sqn ('W'). GIA, 7791M, 1960. Flown back to HAL, 3-73, as G-9-419. Scrapped, HAL, 1979.
WT779 ff 19-4-55 Hugh Merewether. Deld 25-5-55. *Converted to Peruvian Hunter Mark 52 (643)*. ff 27-1-56 Hugh Merewether. Deld 4-56, Peru.
WT780 ff 6-4-55 Duncan Simpson. Retained by HAL; TIs included 5-camera nose (used by Warwick Films to make the film *High Flight*); tail hook, drag chute development, ram-air turbine, etc. Broken up. HAL, 11-64.

WT795 ff 21-4-55 Duncan Simpson. Deld 4-5-55, No 247 (F) Sqn ('A'). No 229 OCU. Broken up, HAL, 9-64.
WT796 ff 22-4-55 Flt Lt N.J. Carver. Deld 4-5-55. *Converted to Peruvian Hunter Mark 52 (640)*. ff 18-1-56 Hugh Merewether. Deld 5-56, Peru.
WT797 ff 21-4-55 Frank Bullen. Deld 20-5-55, No 14 (F) Sqn. No 111 (F) Sqn. GIA, 7792M. Flown back to HAL, 5-72, as G-9-388. *Converted to Swiss Hunter Mark 58A (J4148)*. Deld 30-4-74.
WT798 ff 13-4-55 Flt Lt N.J. Carver. Deld 22-3-56, A&AEE for performance trials. Broken up, HAL, 11-64.
WT799 ff 26-4-55 Duncan Simpson. Deld 1-6-55, No 111 (F) Sqn. No 4 (F) Sqn. Damaged in wheels-up landing, 6-3-56. *Converted to Hunter T Mark 8 by HAL, 1959*. RNAS Lossiemouth. RAE, Bedford. No 759 Sqn, Brawdy, 8-64.
WT800 ff 4-4-55 Duncan Simpson. Deld 26-4-55, No 54 (F) Sqn. *Converted to Peruvian*

Hunter Mark 52 (636). ff 13-12-55 Duncan Simpson. Deld 4-56, Peru.
WT801 ff 23-3-55 Duncan Simpson. Deld 1-6-55, No 4 (F) Sqn. Was one of only three Mark 4s with wing leading-edge extensions. No 229 OCU. GIA, 1960, 7789M. Flown back to HAL, 10-71, as G-9-379. *Converted to Chilean Hunter FGA Mark 71 (J-731).* Deld 3-9-73, Chile.
WT802 ff 24-3-55 M. Anderson, Avions Fairey. Deld 20-4-55, No 98 (F) Sqn. No 247 (F) Sqn. Broken up, 1962.
WT803 ff 23-3-55 M. Anderson, Avions Fairey. Deld 29-4-55. *Converted to Peruvian Hunter Mark 52 (634).* ff Duncan Simpson. Deld 5-56, Peru.
WT804 ff 23-3-55 Sqn Ldr J.A. Sowrey. Deld 14-4-55, No 247 (F) Sqn ('R'). *Converted to Hunter GA Mark 11.* Deld 9-63, Lossiemouth.
WT805 ff 18-4-55 Duncan Simpson. Deld 2-5-55, No 130 (F) Sqn ('X'). No 234 (F) Sqn ('F'). *Converted to Hunter GA Mark 11.* Deld 3-63, No 738 Sqn, FAA. Crashed at St Bride's Bay, Brawdy, 22-3-67.
WT806 ff 31-3-55 Duncan Simpson. Deld 25-4-55, No 14 (F) Sqn. Aircraft over-trimmed in tight turn; accelerometer jammed at 10 g. Aircraft returned to HAL, stripped and re-built. *Converted to Hunter GA Mark 11, c 1962.*
WT807 ff 4-4-55 Frank Bullen. Deld 2-5-55, No 14 (F) Sqn. Collided with WT714, 18-8-55, near Bremen; pilot, Sergeant Stone, ejected safely. Aircraft SOC.
WT808 ff 5-5-55 Hugh Merewether. Deld 24-5-55, No 111 (F) Sqn ('G'). No 222 (F) Sqn ('G'). *Converted to Hunter GA Mark 11.* A&AEE, 1966. Returned to HAL, 24-4-70. 1,096.15 FH.
WT809 ff 13-4-55 Hugh Merewether. Deld 28-6-55, No 66 (F) Sqn ('G'). Linton-on-Ouse Stn Flt. FWS ('G'), 10-57. *Converted to Hunter GA Mark 11.* No 738 Sqn, 1964. No 764 Sqn, FAA.
WT810 ff 19-4-55 Duncan Simpson. Deld 18-5-55, No 54 (F) Sqn. No 247 (F) Sqn ('W'). *Converted to Hunter GA Mark 11.* Collided with WT712, 1965; pilot ejected safely; aircraft SOC.
WT811 23-4-55 Flt Lt N.J. Carver. Deld 24-5-55, No 111 (F) Sqn ('H'). No 222 (F) Sqn ('D'). Broken up, 1962. 498.05 FH.

Second production batch of 85 aircraft built by Hawker Aircraft Ltd, Kingston-upon-Thames. Contract, dated May 9 1951, No SP/6/6867/CB.7a.
WV253 ff 29-4-55 Flt Lt N.J. Carver. Deld 26-5-55, No 4 (F) Sqn. Returned to HAL. *Converted to Hunter T Mark 7 (Special).* Deld 12-6-62, for spinning trials, ETPS, Farnborough.
WV254 ff 27-4-55 Duncan Simpson. Deld 20-5-55, No 247 (F) Sqn. No 229 OCU. Scrapped, 6-61.
WV255 ff 30-4-55 Duncan Simpson. Deld 24-5-55, No 26 (F) Sqn ('X').
WV256 ff 5-5-55 Duncan Simpson. Deld 20-5-55, No 26 (F) Sqn. No 229 OCU. *Converted to Hunter GA Mark 11.* Deld 2-4-63, Lossiemouth. No 738 Sqn, RNAS Brawdy, 8-64.
WV257 ff 5-5-55 Hugh Merewether. Deld 24-5-55, No 26 (F) Sqn ('E'). Stalled on landing approach, 22-7-55; destroyed two fire tenders and control van, killed two and injured three; pilot safe. Aircraft repaired. *Converted to Hunter GA Mark 11.* No 738 Sqn, FAA. Re-purchased by HAL, as G-9-341, 4-70. *Converted to Swiss Hunter Mark 58A (J-4125).* Deld 29-1-73.
WV258 ff 10-5-55 Hugh Merewether. Deld 1-6-55, No 54 (F) Sqn. No 111 (F) Sqn ('T'). GIA 7779M. Flown back to HAL, 27-9-71, as G-9-368. *Converted to Singaporean Hunter Mark 74B (539).* Deld 13-6-73.

Appendix 2 147

WV259 ff 26-4-55 Hugh Merewether. Deld 23-5-55, No 14 (F) Sqn. Scrapped by Coleys, c 1963.
WV260 ff 29-4-55 Flt Lt N.J. Carver. Deld 24-5-55, Oldenburg Stn Flt. No 26 (F) Sqn. Scrapped, 6-61.
WV261 ff 23-4-55 Duncan Simpson. Deld 1-6-55, No 26 (F) Sqn. Crash-landed, 13-1-56. GIA, 7780M, Halton. Flown back to HAL, 3-73, as G-9-400. *Converted to Swiss Hunter Mark 58A (J-4147).* Deld 6-12-74.
WV262 ff 7-5-55 Bill Bedford. Deld 20-5-55, No 247 (F) Sqn ('D'). No 74 (F) Sqn ('K'). Scrapped, Kemble, 6-61.
WV263 ff 29-4-55 Flt Lt N.J. Carver. Deld 1-6-55, No 4 (F) Sqn. No 118 (F) Sqn. Scrapped, Kemble, 6-61.
WV264 ff 30-4-55 Frank Bullen. Deld 16-5-55, No 111 (F) Sqn ('A'). FWS. Scrapped, Kemble, 6-61.
WV265 ff 6-5-55 Duncan Simpson. Deld 24-5-55, No 26 (F) Sqn ('V'). GIA, 7684M, Melksham.
WV266 ff 2-5-55 Flt Lt N.J. Carver. Deld 23-5-55, No 4 (F) Sqn ('T'). No 67 (F) Sqn ('B'). No 234 (F) Sqn ('B'). GIA, 7781M, Halton. Flown back to HAL, 7-72, as G-9-399. *Converted to Swiss Hunter Mark 58A (J-4146).* Deld 24-10-74.
WV267 ff 5-5-55 Duncan Simpson. No 93 (F) Sqn ('R'). No 247 (F) Sqn. No 98 (F) Sqn. *Converted to Hunter GA Mark 11.* No 738 Sqn, FAA, 11-64.
WV268 ff 16-5-55 Hugh Merewether. Deld 14-6-55, No 93 (F) Sqn. No 26 (F) Sqn ('T'). GIA, 7701M, Manston.
WV269 ff 12-5-55 Duncan Simpson. Deld 2-6-55, No 54 (F) Sqn. No 74 (F) Sqn ('H'). Scrapped, Kemble, c 1961.
WV270 ff 12-5-55 Flt Lt N.J. Carver. Deld 14-6-55, No 54 (F) Sqn. No 26 (F) Sqn ('Z'). Scrapped, Kemble, 6-61.
WV271 ff 12-5-55 Duncan Simpson. Deld 21-6-55, No 4 (F) Sqn. Crashed during beat-up of Oldenburg airfield, 23-10-55; pilot, Sergeant Williams, killed. Aircraft SOC.
WV272 ff 11-5-55 Flt Lt N.J. Carver. Deld 6-6-55, No 54 (F) Sqn. No 74 (F) Sqn ('L'). GIA, 7782M, Halton. Flown back to HAL, 23-9-71, as G-9-369. *Converted to Singaporean Hunter T Mark 75A (540).* Deld, 18-7-73.
WV273 ff 26-5-55 Flt Lt N.J. Carver. Deld 23-6-55, No 67 (F) Sqn ('D'). Scrapped, Kemble, 6-61.
WV274 ff 12-5-55 Frank Bullen. Deld 20-6-55, No 4 (F) Sqn. No 118 (F) Sqn. Badly damaged after fire during landing in heavy rainstorm, 16-7-57; repairs never completed, and aircraft SOC, 11-57.
WV275 ff 13-5-55 Flt Lt N.J. Carver. Deld 15-6-55, No 4 (F) Sqn. No 111 (F) Sqn. No 229 OCU. Scrapped, 6-61.
WV276 ff 20-5-55 Frank Bullen. Deld 15-6-55. Trials at A&AEE with Avon 121 engine. No 74 (F) Sqn ('P'). Fate unknown.
WV277 ff 13-5-55 Frank Bullen. Deld 6-6-55, No 14 (F) Sqn ('K'). No 93 (F) Sqn. No 111 (F) Sqn. No 229 OCU. Scrapped, Kemble, 6-61.
WV278 ff 18-5-55 Frank Bullen. Paris Air Show, 6-55. Deld 30-6-55, No 66 (F) Sqn ('H'). Scrapped, Kemble, 6-61
WV279 ff 20-5-55 Hugh Merewether. Deld 17-6-55, No 4 (F) Sqn. No 229 OCU. Scrapped, Kemble, 6-61.
WV280 ff 24-5-55 Hugh Merewether. Deld 16-6-55, RAF College, Manby. Scrapped, Kemble, 6-61.
WV281 ff 24-5-55 Frank Murphy. Deld 14-6-55, No 54 (F) Sqn ('M'). No 74 (F) Sqn ('Q'). Scrapped, Kemble, 6-61.

WV314 ff 19-5-55 Flt Lt N.J. Carver. Deld 20-6-55, No 66 (F) Sqn. No 43 (F) Sqn. No 92 (F) Sqn ('B'). No 74 (F) Sqn ('JH'). No 222 (F) Sqn ('J').
WV315 ff 24-5-55 Hugh Merewether. Deld 20-6-55, No 66 (F) Sqn. No 43 (F) Sqn ('J'). Scrapped, Kemble, 6-61.
WV316 ff 25-5-55 Frank Bullen. Deld 17-6-55, No 4 (F) Sqn. No 98 (F) Sqn. GIA, 7676M. Derelict, 6-64.
WV317 ff 27-5-55 Flt Lt N.J. Carver. Deld 23-6-55, No 54 (F) Sqn. No 247 (F) Sqn ('S'). No 74 (F) Sqn ('D').
WV318 ff 23-5-55 Flt Lt N.J. Carver. Deld 16-6-55, No 14 (F) Sqn. No 26 (F) Sqn. No 93 (F) Sqn. One of only three Hunter Mark 4s with wing leading-edge extensions. Returned to HAL, 1960. *Converted to Hunter T Mark 7, and later to Hunter T Mark 7A.* No 15 (B) Sqn.
WV319 ff 3-6-55 Bill Bedford. Deld 28-6-55. Crashed at Kemble, 13-1-56, by CFS pilot. Repaired, No 32 MU; returned to HAL. *Converted to Hunter T Mark 8.* No 764 Sqn, FAA.
WV320 ff 26-5-55 Frank Bullen. Deld 28-6-55, No 222 (F) Sqn ('S'). GIA, 7685M, Melksham.
WV321 ff 6-6-55 Hugh Merewether. Deld 11-7-55, No 4 (F) Sqn ('B'). No 111 (F) Sqn ('E'). No 222 (F) Sqn. Scrapped, 6-61.
WV322 ff 8-6-55 Duncan Simpson. Deld 28-6-55, No 43 (F) Sqn ('G'). No 92 (F) Sqn. Returned to HAL, 1959. *Converted to Hunter T Mark 8.* No 764 Sqn, FAA.
WV323 ff 8-6-55 Duncan Simpson. Deld 28-6-55, No 43 (F) Sqn ('H'). GIA, 7668M, Devizes (No 2397 Sqn, ATC).
WV324 ff 31-5-55 Hugh Merewether. Deld 27-6-55, No 43 (F) Sqn ('U'). No 74 (F) Sqn ('C'). GIA, 7668M, Halton.
WV325 ff 13-6-55 Hugh Merewether. Deld 15-7-55, CFS. Stored by No 5 MU. Returned to HAL, 19-10-67, as G-9-250. *Converted to Jordanian Hunter FGA Mark 73A (846).* Deld 7-10-71.
WV326 ff 7-6-55 Frank Bullen; Deld 5-7-55, No 54 (F) Sqn. No 74 (F) Sqn ('R'). GIA, 7669M, Halton. Flown back to HAL, 1-72, as G-9-396. *Converted to Chilean Hunter FR Mark 71A (J-735).* Deld 11-1-74, Chile.
WV327 ff 13-6-55 Duncan Simpson. Deld 11-7-55, No 111 (F) Sqn ('U'). No 222 (F) Sqn ('U'). GIA, 7670M, Halton.
WV328 ff 8-6-55 Duncan Simpson. Deld 30-6-55, No 247 (F) Sqn. Destroyed by fire, 25-1-56, following starter explosion.
WV329 ff 2-6-55 Hugh Merewether. Deld 1-7-55, No 54 (F) Sqn ('D'). No 245 (F) Sqn. No 229 OCU. GIA, 7671M, Halton. Flown back to HAL, 7-72, as G-9-407. *Converted to Swiss Hunter Mark 58A (J-4144).* Deld 10-9-74.
WV330 ff 4-6-55 Frank Bullen. Deld 17-7-55, No 54 (F) Sqn. No 247 (F) Sqn ('G'). No 245 (F) Sqn ('D'). No 229 OCU. GIA, 7672M, Larkhill.
WV331 ff 10-6-55 Hugh Merewether. Deld 12-7-55. Stored by No 5 MU. GIA, 7783M, Halton. Flown back to HAL, 8-71, as G-9-372. *Converted to Singaporean Hunter Mark 74B (543).* Deld 16-8-73.
WV332 ff 7-6-55 Hugh Merewether. Deld 27-6-55, No 67 (F) Sqn ('X'). No 234 (F) Sqn ('P'). GIA, 7673M, Halton. Flown back to HAL, 7-72, as G-9-406. *Converted to Swiss Hunter T Mark 68 (J-4201).* Deld 2-8-74.
WV333 ff 10-6-55 Frank Bullen. Deld 1-7-55, No 43 (F) Sqn ('A'). Stored by No 47 MU, 14-3-58.
WV334 ff 14-6-55 David Lockspeiser. Deld 5-7-55, No 54 (F) Sqn ('C'). No 74 (F) Sqn ('E'). Scrapped, Kemble, c 1961.

Appendix 2 149

WV363 ff 22-6-55 David Lockspeiser. Deld 8-7-55, No 234 (F) Sqn ('K'). *Converted to Hunter T Mark 8.* No 764 Sqn, FAA. A&AEE, 9-63.

WV364 ff 17-6-55 David Lockspeiser. Deld 30-6-55, No 26 (F) Sqn. No 93 (F) Sqn ('S'). No 98 (F) Sqn. No 118 (F) Sqn. GIA, 7674M, Halton. Flown back to HAL, 3-71, as G-9-347. *Converted to Singaporean Hunter Mark 74B (530).* Deld 17-1-73.

WV365 ff 27-6-55 David Lockspeiser. Deld 23-8-55, No 54 (F) Sqn. No 247 (F) Sqn. Stored by No 5 MU, 7-7-58.

WV366 ff 16-6-55 Hugh Merewether. Deld 5-7-55, No 43 (F) Sqn ('T'). GIA, Halton. Flown back to HAL, 2-71, as G-9-350. *Converted to Singaporean Hunter Mark 74B (537).* Deld 9-4-73.

WV367 ff 27-6-55 David Lockspeiser. Deld 8-8-55, No 67 (F) Sqn ('X'). No 234 (F) Sqn ('J'). GIA, 7677M, Larkhill.

WV368 ff 24-6-55 Frank Bullen. Deld 12-7-55, No 93 (F) Sqn. No 98 (F) Sqn. No 118 (F) Sqn. Scrapped, 6-61.

WV369 ff 27-6-55 Frank Bullen. Deld 14-7-55, No 26 (F) Sqn. GIA, 7675M, Halton.

WV370 ff 23-6-55 David Lockspeiser. Deld 5-8-55, No 54 (F) Sqn. No 74 (F) Sqn ('M'). Stored, Kemble, 6-58.

WV371 ff 30-6-55 David Lockspeiser. Deld 11-8-55, No 54 (F) Sqn ('O'). No 74 (F) Sqn ('N'). GIA, 7678M, Larkhill.

WV372 ff 15-7-55 Hugh Merewether. Deld 2-9-55, No 222 (F) Sqn ('H'). Damaged by fire in the air when jet pipe became detached from engine, 9-11-56. *Converted to Hunter T Mark 7.* Deld 7-5-59, No 5 MU. Jever Stn Flt, 8-1-60. Gutersloh Stn Flt, 1963.

WV373 ff 29-6-55 Hugh Merewether. Deld 14-7-55, No 98 (F) Sqn. No 118 (F) Sqn. Written off, 8-12-55.

WV374 ff 4-7-55 Hugh Merewether. To RAE, 5-8-55. No 67 (F) Sqn ('T'). *Converted to Hunter GA Mark 11.* Deld 20-8-62, No 738 Sqn, FAA. Returned to HAL, 24-4-70. 1,827.20 FH.

WV375 ff 30-6-55 Hugh Merewether. Deld 27-9-55, No 54 (F) Sqn ('A'). GIA, 7679M, Weeton.

WV376 ff 4-7-55 David Lockspeiser. Deld 23-8-55, No 222 (F) Sqn ('W'). FWS ('J'). GIA, 7680M, Weeton.

WV377 ff 4-7-55 Duncan Simpson. Deld 9-8-55, No 14 (F) Sqn. No 26 (F) Sqn. No 93 (F) Sqn ('V'). GIA, 7681M, Larkhill.

WV378 ff 5-7-55 David Lockspeiser. Deld 17-8-55, No 222 (F) Sqn. No 43 (F) Sqn ('H'). GIA, 7682M, Weeton.

WV379 ff 15-7-55 David Lockspeiser. Deld 23-8-55, No 111 (F) Sqn ('V'). GIA, 7683M, Larkhill.

WV380 ff 7-7-55 Hugh Merewether. Deld 11-8-55, RAF College, Manby. Returned to HAL, 1960. *Converted to Hunter GA Mark 11.* Deld 29-5-62, Lossiemouth, No 738 Sqn, FAA. 1,152 FH. Returned to HAL, 24-4-70, as G-9-335. *Converted to Swiss Hunter Mark 58A (J-4119).* Deld 3-11-72.

WV381 ff 3-8-55 Duncan Simpson. Deld 17-8-55, No 222 (F) Sqn ('Q'). FWS ('F'). *Converted to Hunter GA Mark 11.* Deld 7-62, Lossiemouth.

WV382 ff 11-7-55 Duncan Simpson. Deld 15-3-55, No 67 (F) Sqn ('C'). *Converted to Hunter GA Mark 11.* Deld 14-8-62, Lossiemouth. Brawdy, 1-66.

WV383 ff 12-7-55 Hugh Merewether. Deld 23-8-55. RAF College, Manby, 19-12-55. Severely damaged in belly landing, 27-1-56. Returned to HAL, 1958. *Converted to Hunter T Mark 7.* Deld 3-7-59. Gutersloh Stn Flt, 8-1-60. Jever Stn Flt, 14-4-61. To Kai Tak, No 28 (F) Sqn, c 1964. RAE, Farnborough, 7-77.

WV384 ff 10-8-55 Duncan Simpson. Deld 2-9-55, No 71 (F) Sqn. Engine failed on

landing approach, 5-4-57; pilot ejected but was killed when the drogue gun failed.
WV385 ff 5-8-55 Frank Bullen. Trials with Avon 115. Deld 17-10-55, No 66 (F) Sqn ('L'). AFDS. No 229 OCU. No 3 CAACU, Exeter, 5-60. GIA, 7775M.
WV386 ff 12-8-55 Duncan Simpson. Deld 5-9-55, No 222 (F) Sqn ('G'). No 229 OCU. Returned to HAL, 2-71, as G-9-348. 723.00 FH. *Converted to Singaporean Hunter T Mark 75A (532).* Deld 15-12-72.
WV387 ff 11-8-55 Duncan Simpson. Deld 5-9-55, No 43 (F) Sqn ('Q'). No 67 (F) Sqn. No 71 (F) Sqn. Broken up, Kemble, 9-58.
WV388 ff 16-8-55 Duncan Simpson. Deld 16-9-55, No 222 (F) Sqn ('R'). Crashed into sea at night during GCA landing, 25-3-57; pilot killed.
WV389 ff 16-8-55 David Lockspeiser. Deld 7-9-55, No 222 (F) Sqn. No 66 (F) Sqn. No 98 (F) Sqn. No 247 (F) Sqn. No 229 OCU. Returned to HAL, 1968, as G-9-245. *Converted to Abu Dhabian Hunter FGA Mark 76 (703).* Deld 6-11-70.
WV390 ff 16-8-55 David Lockspeiser. Deld 7-9-55, No 20 (F) Sqn. No 26 (F) Sqn, 12-6-57. RAF College, Manby. Written off, 29-3-58.
WV391 ff 23-8-55 Hugh Merewether. Deld 13-9-55, No 20 (F) Sqn. No 229 OCU. Crashed on landing approach, 5-6-58; pilot killed.
WV392 ff 19-8-55 Duncan Simpson. Deld 9-9-55, Linton-on-Ouse Stn Flt. No 66 (F) Sqn. Aircraft crashed during air firing sortie, 17-7-56; pilot ejected safely.
WV393 ff 19-8-55 David Lockspeiser. Deld 9-9-55, Linton-on-Ouse Stn Flt. Returned to HAL, 1-73, as G-9-410. *Converted to Swiss Hunter Mark 58A (J-4151).* Deld 19-2-75.
WV394 ff 23-8-55 Hugh Merewether. Deld 21-9-55, No 20 (F) Sqn ('E'). No 229 OCU. Broken up, HAL, 9-64.
WV395 ff 2-9-55 Duncan Simpson. Deld 12-9-55, No 20 (F) Sqn ('W'). Pilot experienced fire in the air following rear engine bearing failure, but landed at base successfully, 11-3-57. Aircraft re-purchased by HAL, 1-8-75, as G-9-428. Awaiting final disposal, 2-80.
WV396 ff 24-8-55 David Lockspeiser. Deld 23-9-55, No 20 (F) Sqn. No 229 OCU. Returned to HAL, 1963. 951.55 FH. *Converted to Hunter T Mark 8C.* RNAS, Brawdy, 1-66.
WV397 ff 25-8-55 Duncan Simpson. Deld 27-9-55, No 20 (F) Sqn. No 229 OCU. Returned to HAL, 1963. *Converted to Hunter T Mark 8C.* No 759 Sqn, FAA. Crashed into sea near Brawdy, 23-11-65. Fire warning light came on, instructor ejected safely, but student pilot killed. 1,768.10 FH.
WV398 ff 29-8-55 Duncan Simpson. Deld 19-9-55, No 20 (F) Sqn. No 26 (F) Sqn. No 229 OCU. Returned to HAL, 1-73, as G-9-411. *Converted to Swiss Hunter T Mark 68 (J-4203).* Deld 4-3-75.
WV399 ff 26-8-55 David Lockspeiser. Deld 23-9-55, No 222 (F) Sqn ('B'). No 229 OCU. Derelict at Lasham, 1963.
WV400 ff 30-8-55 David Lockspeiser. Deld 20-9-55, No 66 (F) Sqn. AFDS. No 229 OCU. Iraqi pilot omitted to lower wheels for landing at Chivenor, 6-3-59. Aircraft returned to HAL, 13-6-68, as G-9-259. *Converted to Abu Dhabian Hunter FR Mark 76A (710).* Deld 19-1-71.
WV401 ff 1-9-55 Frank Bullen. No 20 (F) Sqn ('T'). No 26 (F) Sqn. No 229 OCU. Returned to HAL, 2-11-67, as G-9-246. *Converted to Jordanian Hunter FGA Mark 73B (851).* Deld 13-11-71.
WV402 ff 6-9-55 Hugh Merewether. Deld 7-10-55. No 222 (F) Sqn ('T'). No 229 OCU. Returned to HAL, 28-8-68, as G-9-247. *Converted to Abu Dhabian Hunter FGA Mark 76 (704).* Deld 5-12-70.
WV403 ff 2-9-55 Duncan Simpson. Deld 27-9-55, No 67 (F) Sqn ('J'). Broken up, Kemble, 9-58.

Appendix 2 151

WV404 ff 15-9-55 Neville Duke. Deld 27-9-55, No 54 (F) Sqn. No 247 (F) Sqn ('T'). No 229 OCU. GIA, 7768M. Returned to HAL, 2-5-72, as G-9-384. *Converted to Swiss Hunter Mark 58A (J-4137).* Deld 5-6-74. 612.25 FH.

WV405 ff 9-9-55 Duncan Simpson. Deld 23-9-55, No 222 (F) Sqn ('A'). No 229 OCU. Transferred to FAA; HMS *Condor*, Arbroath, 1-66. Returned to HAL, 1970, as G-9-316. *Converted to Swiss Hunter Mark 58A (J-4106).* Deld 23-3-72.

WV406 ff 9-9-55 David Lockspeiser. No 222 (F) Sqn ('F'). No 229 OCU. No 3 CAACU, Exeter.

WV407 ff 14-9-55 Hugh Merewether. Deld 4-10-55, No 20 (F) Sqn. RAF College, Manby. Returned to HAL, 14-8-68, as G-9-248. *Converted to Jordanian Hunter FGA Mark 73A (849).* Deld 21-12-71.

WV408 ff 19-9-55 David Lockspeiser. No 20 (F) Sqn. No 229 OCU. Returned to HAL, 16-11-67, as G-9-249. 614.25 FH. *Converted to Jordanian Hunter FGA Mark 73A (845).* Deld 26-8-71.

WV409 ff 20-9-55 Frank Bullen. Deld 7-10-55, No 66 (F) Sqn ('N'). No 234 (F) Sqn ('K'). No 229 OCU (ES-A). Aircraft jumped chocks on engine run, 3-61, and collided with Hunter Mark 6, XG210, and destroyed.

WV410 ff 21-9-55 Hugh Merewether. Deld 18-10-55, No 20 (F) Sqn ('X'). No 229 OCU. Iraqi pilot (the same as involved in accident to WV400, qv) experienced difficulty in landing at Chivenor, 20-3-59, and touched down on the bed of the River Taw; aircraft eventually disintegrated, and pilot slightly hurt.

WV411 ff 26-9-55 David Lockspeiser. Deld 10-10-55, No 20 (F) Sqn ('D'). No 229 OCU. Transferred to FAA; HMS *Condor*, Arbroath, 1-66. Returned to HAL, 1970, as G-9-314. 1,185.55 FH. *Converted to Swiss Hunter Mark 58A (J-4108).* Deld 27-4-72.

WV412 ff 23-9-55 Duncan Simpson. Deld 10-10-55, No 112 (F) Sqn ('A'). Aircraft suffered flame-out in landing circuit and crashed, 13-9-56; pilot ejected safely from 900 feet.

Third production batch of three aircraft built by Hawker Aircraft Ltd, Kingston-upon-Thames. Instruction to Proceed, July 12 1951. Contract dated July 19 1951, No SP/6/7144/CB.7a. (Remainder of this contract transferred to Blackpool, see Contract No 8435.)

WW589 ff 6-10-55 David Lockspeiser. Deld 9-11-55, No 20 (F) Sqn. No 229 OCU. GIA, 7943M, Halton. Repurchased by HAL, 2-71, as G-9-343. *Converted to Swiss Hunter Mark 58A (J-4130).* Deld 13-4-73.

WW590 ff 6-10-55 David Lockspeiser. Deld 9-11-55, No 20 (F) Sqn. No 229 OCU. Returned to HAL, 4-72, as G-9-386. 689.50 FH. *Converted to Swiss Hunter Mark 58A (J-4138).* Deld 19-6-74.

WW591 ff 4-10-55 Duncan Simpson. Deld 2-11-55, Denmark, as the first *Danish Hunter Mark 51.*

First production batch of 20 aircraft built by Hawker Aircraft (Blackpool) Ltd, Blackpool. Contract, dated August 15 1952, No SP/6/8435/CB.7a.

WW646 ff 20-1-55. Deld 11-3-55, A&AEE, for check on manufacturer's standard of production. No 111 (F) Sqn ('P'). No 222 (F) Sqn ('P').

WW647 Deld 29-3-55, No 5 MU. No 98 (F) Sqn ('C'). No 247 (F) Sqn ('A'). 552.35 FH.

WW648 Deld 15-3-55, No 33 MU. No 98 (F) Sqn ('D'). No 247 (F) Sqn ('C'). No 229 OCU.

WW649 Deld 15-3-55, No 33 MU. No 98 (F) Sqn ('E'). Scrapped, Dunsfold, 8-64.

WW650 Deld 16-3-55, No 33 MU. No 98 (F) Sqn ('F'). No 222 (F) Sqn ('R'). Scrapped, Dunsfold, 8-64.
WW651 Deld 28-3-55, No 5 MU. No 98 (F) Sqn. No 111 (F) Sqn ('F'). No 222 (F) Sqn. Written off, 5-1-57.
WW652 Deld 29-3-55, No 5 MU. No 98 (F) Sqn ('G'). No 247 (F) Sqn. No 222 (F) Sqn ('H'). Stored, Kemble, 12-57.
WW653 Deld 30-3-55, No 33 MU. No 98 (F) Sqn. GIA, 7784M, Halton. Repurchased by HAL, 1-72, as G-9-398. *Converted to Chilean Hunter FGA Mark 71 (J-737).* Deld 11-1-74, Chile.
WW654 Deld 28-3-55, No 5 MU. No 98 (F) Sqn ('L'). No 229 OCU, 14-11-57. *Converted to Hunter GA Mark 11.* Deld 4-9-62, Lossiemouth.
WW655 Deld 30-3-55, No 5 MU. No 98 (F) Sqn ('M'). Stored, Kemble, 7-57.
WW656 Deld 30-3-55, No 5 MU. No 98 (F) Sqn ('N'). Scrapped, Dunsfold, 8-64.
WW657 Deld 30-3-55, No 5 MU. No 118 (F) Sqn ('G'). Stored by No 47 MU, Hawarden, 1-58.
WW658 Deld 6-4-55, No 33 MU. No 98 (F) Sqn ('O'). No 229 OCU (RS-5). Scrapped, Dunsfold, 6-64. 609.40 FH.
WW659 Deld 1-4-55, No 33 MU. No 247 (F) Sqn ('V'). Returned to HAL, 1960. *Converted to Hunter GA Mark 11.* No 738 Sqn, FAA. 1,808.05 FH. Returned to HAL, 24-4-70, as G-9-342. *Converted to Swiss Hunter Mark 58A (J-4126).* Deld 7-2-73.
WW660 Deld 6-4-55, No 33 MU. No 118 (F) Sqn ('B'). No 229 OCU, 28-6-57. Reduced to spares, 5-61.
WW661 No 33 MU. No 98 (F) Sqn. Returned to HAL, 24-2-58. *Converted to Hunter T Mark 8.* Deld 12-3-59, RNAS, Lossiemouth. No 764 Sqn, FAA.
WW662 No 54 (F) Sqn. Returned to HAL, 12-55. *Converted to Peruvian Hunter Mark 52 (632).* ff 9-12-55 Duncan Simpson. Deld 4-56.
WW663 Deld 27-4-55, No 5 MU. No 14 (F) Sqn ('H'). Broken up at Chilbolton, 1962.
WW664 No 26 (F) Sqn ('C'). Damaged in forced landing at Ahlhorn, 28-5-56; returned for repair by HAL. *Converted to Hunter T Mark 8B Prototype.* CA aircraft. No 764 Sqn, FAA; returned to HAL. *Converted to Singaporean Hunter T Mark 75 (514),* 1969.
WW665 Deld 3-5-55, No 5 MU. No 247 (F) Sqn ('E'). No 245 (F) Sqn. Broken up at No 47 MU, Hawarden, 1-61.

Second production batch of 100 aircraft built by Hawker Aircraft (Blackpool) Ltd, Blackpool. Contract, dated August 24 1953, No SP/6/9817/CB.7a.
XE657 Deld 3-5-55, No 5 MU. No 14 (F) Sqn ('Y'). Broken up at Dunsfold, 11-64.
XE658 Deld 3-5-55, No 5 MU. No 54 (F) Sqn ('R'). No 74 (F) Sqn. Reduced to spares, 5-61.
XE659 Deld 4-5-55, No 33 MU. No 54 (F) Sqn. No 66 (F) Sqn. No 92 (F) Sqn ('J'). No 229 OCU (RS-23). GIA, 7785M, Halton. Returned to HAL, 3-72, as G-9-401. *Converted to Swiss Hunter Mark 58A (J-4149).* Deld 10-1-75.
XE660 Deld 18-5-55, No 5 MU. No 247 (F) Sqn ('H'). Aircraft broke from formation at 4,000 feet and dived into the ground between Alton and Lasham, 5-12-56; pilot killed.
XE661 Deld 6-6-55, No 33 MU. No 54 (F) Sqn ('B'). No 74 (F) Sqn ('F').
XE662 Deld 18-5-55, No 5 MU. No 247 (F) Sqn ('Z'). No 74 (F) Sqn ('S'). Landing accident, 25-5-57, Horsham St Faith, due to undercarriage failure; pilot unhurt but aircraft SOC.
XE663 Deld 1-6-55, No 5 MU. No 4 (F) Sqn ('V'). No 43 (F) Sqn ('V'). Scrapped, Dunsfold, 8-64.

Appendix 2 153

XE664 Deld 23-5-55, No 5 MU. No 26 (F) Sqn ('F'). Returned to HAL, 1958. *Converted to Hunter T Mark 8*. Deld 12-3-59, No 764 Sqn, FAA. *Converted to Singaporean Hunter T Mark 75 (516)*. Deld 9-70.

XE665 Deld 24-5-55, No 5 MU. No 118 (F) Sqn ('A'). Jever Stn Flt. Returned to HAL, 1957. *Converted to Hunter T Mark 8*. Deld 20-4-59, No 764 Sqn, FAA; RNAS Yeovilton, 1-66.

XE666 Deld 6-6-55, No 5 MU. No 4 (F) Sqn ('X'). No 111 (F) Sqn. No 245 (F) Sqn ('R'). No 229 OCU (ES-D).

XE667 Deld 6-6-55, No 5 MU. No 4 (F) Sqn ('Z'). Broken up, Dunsfold, 11-64.

XE668 Deld 6-6-55, No 5 MU. No 4 (F) Sqn ('X'). No 26 (F) Sqn ('G'). *Converted to Hunter GA Mark 11*. No 738 Sqn, FAA, 11-64.

XE669 Deld 16-6-55, RAE. No 98 (F) Sqn. On 4-12-56 aircraft suffered explosion after take-off causing jet pipe to move aft six feet out of rear fuselage; pilot ejected but was killed when barostat failed; aircraft SOC.

XE670 Deld 21-6-55, No 5 MU. No 26 (F) Sqn. No 93 (F) Sqn ('D'). GIA, 7762M. No 71 MU, Bicester, 11-7-63.

XE671 Deld 6-6-55, No 33 MU. No 54 (F) Sqn ('K'). Aircraft crashed after flame-out, 1-5-56; pilot ejected safely.

XE672 Deld 6-6-55, No 33 MU. No 112 (F) Sqn ('B'). Reduced to spares, 19-5-61.

XE673 Deld 27-6-55, No 33 MU. No 112 (F) Sqn ('C'). No 234 (F) Sqn. *Converted to Hunter GA Mark 11*. Deld 14-6-62, Lossiemouth.

XE674 Deld 21-6-55, No 33 MU. No 112 (F) Sqn ('D'). *Converted to Hunter GA Mark 11*. Deld 5-6-62, No 738 Sqn, FAA. Purchased by HAL, 27-4-70, as G-9-340. *Converted to Swiss Hunter Mark 58A (J-4124)*. Deld 19-1-73.

XE675 Deld 27-6-55, No 33 MU. No 26 (F) Sqn ('H'). No 93 (F) Sqn ('E'). Was one of only three Hunter Mark 4s with wing leading-edge extensions. No 111 (F) Sqn. No 229 OCU.

XE676 Deld 1-7-55, No 5 MU. No 222 (F) Sqn ('U'). FWS. Scrapped, 11-62.

XE677 Deld 11-7-55, No 5 MU. No 4 (F) Sqn ('M'). No 93 (F) Sqn ('Q'). Was one of only three Hunter Mark 4s with wing leading edge extensions. No 111 (F) Sqn. No 229 OCU. Refurbished at Dunsfold, 11-61, and presented to Loughborough College. 752.40 FH.

XE678 Deld 4-7-55, No 5 MU. No 222 (F) Sqn ('X'). GIA, Halton. Returned to HAL, 6-72, as G-9-404. *Converted to Swiss Hunter Mark 58A (J-4145)*. Deld 7-10-74.

XE679 Deld 4-7-55, No 5 MU. No 111 (F) Sqn ('B'). Detached to Malta, 10-56. No 222 (F) Sqn ('Y'). GIA, 7887M, Halton, Returned to HAL, 9-71, as G-9-370. *Converted to Singaporean Hunter Mark 74B (541)*. Deld 13-6-73.

XE680 Deld 11-7-55, No 5 MU. No 130 (F) Sqn ('Y'). No 234 (F) Sqn ('L'). *Converted to Hunter GA Mark 11*. Deld 29-4-63.

XE681 Deld 1-7-55, No 33 MU. No 66 (F) Sqn ('J'). Reduced to spares, 19-5-61.

XE682 Deld 5-7-55, No 33 MU. No 118 (F) Sqn. *Converted to Hunter GA Mark 11*. Deld 1-7-63, No 738 Sqn, FAA.

XE683 Deld 20-7-55, No 5 MU. No 54 (F) Sqn ('S'). No 74 (F) Sqn ('G'). Scrapped, Coleys, c 1963.

XE684 Deld 20-7-55, No 33 MU. No 4 (F) Sqn. No 93 (F) Sqn. No 98 (F) Sqn. No 111 (F) Sqn. No 229 OCU. Reduced to spares, 5-61.

XE685 Deld 18-7-55, No 33 MU. No 93 (F) Sqn. No 98 (F) Sqn. *Converted to Hunter GA Mark 11*. Deld 6-5-63, No 738 Sqn, FAA.

XE686 Deld 22-7-55, No 5 MU. CFE, AFDS; trials with drop tanks, 1955-56. No 247 (F) Sqn ('H'). No 245 (F) Sqn ('O'). No 229 OCU (ES-C). Scrapped, 11-62.

XE687 Deld 22-7-55, No 5 MU. No 118 (F) Sqn ('F'). NO 93 (F) Sqn ('C'). No 98 (F) Sqn. Scrapped, 11-62.
XE688 Deld 24-8-55, No 45 MU. No 222 (F) Sqn. No 74 (F) Sqn ('A'). Reduced to spares, 19-5-61.
XE689 Deld 22-7-55, No 5 MU. No 67 (F) Sqn ('W'). No 234 (F) Sqn. *Converted to Hunter GA Mark 11.* Deld 4-7-63.

XE702 Deld 22-7-55, No 5 MU. To A&AEE for trials with various external stores. No 92 (F) Sqn ('E'). No 43 (F) Sqn ('B'). GIA, 7794M, Sealand, 11-7-63. To HAL, 9-71, as G-9-375. *Converted to Swiss Hunter T Mark 68 (J-7204).* Deld 15-4-75.
XE703 Deld 10-8-55, No 5 MU. No 4 (F) Sqn ('J'). No 93 (F) Sqn ('P'). No 118 (F) Sqn ('B'). Scrapped, 11-62.
XE704 Deld 7-10-55, No 45 MU. No 112 (F) Sqn ('S'). GIA, 7788M, Halton. To HAL, 1-72, as G-9-397. *Converted to Chilean Hunter T Mark 72 (J-736).* Deld 15-2-74.
XE705 Deld 24-8-55, No 45 MU. No 111 (F) Sqn. No 92 (F) Sqn ('F'). No 43 (F) Sqn ('P'). On 3-10-56 pilot abandoned take-off and bellied into River Eden; was rescued by helicopter, but aircraft written off.
XE706 Deld 11-10-55, No 45 MU. No 43 (F) Sqn ('P'). No 92 (F) Sqn ('L'). Scrapped, 11-62.
XE707 Deld 1-9-55, No 5 MU. No 93 (F) Sqn. No 118 (F) Sqn. *Converted to Hunter GA Mark 11.* No 738 Sqn, 8-64. No 764 Sqn, 11-64.
XE708 Deld 29-8-55, No 5 MU. No 14 (F) Sqn. No 229 OCU. GIA, Halton.
XE709 Deld 5-9-55, No 45 MU. No 222 (F) Sqn ('D'). No 43 (F) Sqn ('Q'). Scrapped, 11-62.
XE710 Deld 2-9-55, No 5 MU. No 14 (F) Sqn ('R'). No 229 OCU. Scrapped, 11-62.
XE711 Deld 11-10-55, No 45 MU. RAF College, Manby. JHSS 'A' Flt, Benson. Scrapped, 11-62.
XE712 Deld 2-9-55, No 5 MU. No 222 (F) Sqn ('E'). No 43 (F) Sqn ('U'). *Converted to Hunter GA Mark 11.* Deld 6-4-62, No 738 Sqn, FAA.
XE713 Deld 18-10-55, No 45 MU. No 66 (F) Sqn ('E'). No 67 (F) Sqn. Scrapped, Dunsfold, 9-64.
XE714 Deld 19-10-55, No 5 MU. Bruggen Stn Flt. No 234 (F) Sqn. No 112 (F) Sqn. Scrapped, 11-62.
XE715 Deld 1-11-55, No 45 MU. No 3 (F) Sqn ('L'). No 71 (F) Sqn. No 130 (F) Sqn. GIA, 7807M.
XE716 Deld 28-10-55, No 5 MU. No 67 (F) Sqn ('A'). No 112 (F) Sqn ('A'). *Converted to Hunter GA Mark 11.* Deld 6-7-62.
XE717 Deld 28-10-55, No 5 MU. No 67 (F) Sqn ('G'). No 234 (F) Sqn ('G'). *Converted to Hunter GA Mark 11.* Deld 5-6-63, No 738 Sqn. Yeovilton Stn Flt. Returned to HAL, 24-4-70, as G-9-338. *Converted to Swiss Hunter Mark 58A (J-4122).* Deld 14-2-72.
XE718 Deld 2-11-55, No 5 MU. No 93 (F) Sqn ('A'). No 98 (F) Sqn ('A'). Scrapped, 11-62.

XF289 Deld 2-11-55, No 5 MU. No 67 (F) Sqn. Returned to HAL, 1958. *Converted to Hunter T Mark 7 and later to Hunter T Mark 8.* No 764 Sqn, FAA.
XF290 Deld 29-11-55, No 5 MU. No 67 (F) Sqn. Crashed and SOC, 14-8-56; engine failure on take-off; pilot ejected safely from 670 feet.
XF291 Deld 29-11-55, No 5 MU. No 67 (F) Sqn. *Converted to Hunter GA Mark 11.* Deld 5-6-63. No 738 Sqn, FAA, 8-64.
XF292 Deld 12-12-55, No 5 MU. No 130 (F) Sqn ('A'). Scrapped, 9-64.

Appendix 2 155

XF293 Deld 8-12-55, No 5 MU. No 112 (F) Sqn ('N'). No 234 (F) Sqn ('N'). Scrapped, 11-62. 267.19 FH.
XF294 Deld 8-12-55, No 5 MU. No 130 (F) Sqn ('B').
XF295 Deld 29-11-55, No 5 MU. No 130 (F) Sqn ('C'). FTU, Benson. Scrapped, 11-62. 202.50 FH.
XF296 Deld 9-1-56, No 5 MU. No 67 (F) Sqn ('Z'). No 234 (F) Sqn ('H'). Scrapped, 11-62. 330.10 FH.
XF297 Deld 8-12-55, No 5 MU. No 130 (F) Sqn. No 234 (F) Sqn ('D'). *Converted to Hunter GA Mark 11*. Deld 14-8-62. No 738 Sqn, FAA, 8-64.
XF298 Deld 29-12-55, No 5 MU. No 130 (F) Sqn ('G'). No 112 (F) Sqn. Scrapped, 11-62.
XF299 Deld 29-12-55, No 5 MU. No 43 (F) Sqn ('O'). Scrapped, Dunsfold, 9-64.
XF300 Deld 9-1-56, No 5 MU. No 234 (F) Sqn ('P'). No 130 (F) Sqn ('W'). *Converted to Hunter GA Mark 11*. Deld 12-2-63. No 738 Sqn, FAA, 8-64.
XF301 Deld 30-12-55, No 5 MU. No 43 (F) Sqn ('L'). *Converted to Hunter GA Mark 11*. Deld 19-10-62. No 738 Sqn, FAA, 11-64.
XF302 Deld 30-12-55, No 5 MU. No 43 (F) Sqn ('S'). GIA, 7774M, Halton. Returned to AWA, 16-12-71, as G-9-382. *Converted to Chilean Hunter FGA Mark 71 (J-733)*. Deld 15-2-74.
XF303 Deld 9-1-56, No 5 MU. No 66 (F) Sqn ('A'). Transferred to FAA. GIA, A2565; HMS *Condor*, Arbroath. Returned to HAL, 4-2-70, as G-9-315. *Converted to Swiss Hunter Mark 58A (J-4105)*. Deld 10-3-72.
XF304 Deld 16-1-56, No 5 MU. No 66 (F) Sqn ('B'). No 43 (F) Sqn. Turnhouse Stn Flt (MR).
XF305 Deld 9-1-56, No 5 MU. No 67 (F) Sqn. Aircraft destroyed by fire at Sylt, 28-11-56, due to simultaneous firing of two starter cartridges.
XF306 Deld 9-1-56, No 5 MU. No 112 (F) Sqn ('E'). GIA, 7776M. Returned to HAL, 6-72, as G-9-402. *Converted to Swiss Hunter Mark 58A (J-4133)*. Deld 22-2-74.
XF307 Deld 16-1-56, No 5 MU. No 112 (F) Sqn ('F'). No 26 (F) Sqn. Stored, Kemble, 5-66.
XF308 Deld 25-1-56, No 5 MU. No 130 (F) Sqn ('F'). GIA, 7777M. Returned to HAL, 8-72, as G-9-381. *Converted to Swiss Hunter Mark 58A (J-4135)*. Deld 27-3-74.
XF309 Deld 10-1-56, No 5 MU. No 112 (F) Sqn ('C'). GIA, 7771M, Finningley. Returned to HAL, 5-73, as G-9-420. *Converted to Kenyan Hunter Mark 80 (805)*. Deld 8-12-74.
XF310 Deld 20-7-56, Fairey Aviation Limited. Experimental Fairey Fireflash missile installation. *Converted to Hunter T Mark 7*. ff 24-4-59 Frank Bullen. Deld 29-5-59, No 20 (F) Sqn ('T').
XF311 Deld 10-1-56, No 5 MU. No 130 (F) Sqn ('V'). GIA, A2566, HMS *Condor*, Arbroath. Transferred as GIA to Singapore, 31-1-70.
XF312 Deld 18-1-56, No 5 MU. No 71 (F) Sqn. No 112 (F) Sqn ('T'). No 26 (F) Sqn. Purchased by HSA, 6-72, as G-9-405. *Converted to Swiss Hunter Mark 58A (J-4150)*. Deld 30-1-75.
XF313 Deld 18-1-56, No 5 MU. No 71 (F) Sqn ('G'). No 112 (F) Sqn.
XF314 Deld 27-1-56, No 5 MU. No 43 (F) Sqn ('N'). No 229 OCU (RS-24), 9-57. Derelict, Lasham, 9-63.
XF315 Deld 27-1-56, No 5 MU. No 93 (F) Sqn. Jever Stn Flt. No 4 (FR) Sqn. No 43 (F) Sqn.
XF316 Deld 24-1-56, No 33 MU. HQ Flt, 2nd TAF. No 71 (F) Sqn. No 112 (F) Sqn ('R'). GIA, 7778M, Halton. Purchased by HSA, 6-72, as G-9-403. *Converted to Swiss*

Hunter Mark 58A (J-7134). Deld 12-3-74.

XF317 Deld 30-1-56, No 33 MU. No 67 (F) Sqn ('U'). GIA, 7773M, Halton. Purchased by HSA, 12-71, as G-9-383. *Converted to Chilean Hunter FR Mark 71A (J-734).* Deld 11-1-74.

XF318 Deld 27-2-56, No 33 MU. No 118 (F) Sqn ('Z'). No 130 (F) Sqn ('Z'). GIA, A2567, HMS *Condor*, Arbroath. Purchased by HSA, 1-4-70, as G-9-328. *Converted to Swiss Hunter Mark 58A (J-7110).* Deld 6-6-72.

XF319 Deld 25-1-56, No 5 MU. No 66 (F) Sqn ('F'). No 112 (F) Sqn.

XF320 Deld 9-2-56, No 33 MU. No 247 (F) Sqn ('R'). No 229 OCU (RS-4).

XF321 Deld 27-2-56, No 33 MU. No 130 (F) Sqn ('G'). Returned to HSA, 1958. *Converted to Hunter T Mark 7.* No 56 (F) Sqn.

XF322 Deld 15-2-56, No 45 MU. No 112 (F) Sqn. Returned to HSA, 1957. *Converted to Hunter T Mark 8 for FAA.*

XF323 Deld 17-2-56, No 45 MU. RAF College, Manby. Purchased by HSA, 30-10-71, as G-9-380. *Converted to Chilean FGA Mark 71 (J-732).* Deld 7-9-73.

XF324 Deld 5-3-56, No 33 MU. No 92 (F) Sqn ('D'). No 222 (F) Sqn ('K'). Derelict, Lasham, 9-63.

XF357 Deld 1-3-56, No 33 MU. No 130 (F) Sqn. Returned to HSA, 1959. *Converted to Hunter T Mark 8.* RNAS Lossiemouth.

XF358 Deld 6-3-56, No 33 MU. No 112 (F) Sqn ('P'). Returned to HSA, 1959. *Converted to Hunter T Mark 8.* RNAS Lossiemouth.

XF359 Deld 27-2-56, No 33 MU. No 130 (F) Sqn. No 3 (F) Sqn. Derelict, Lasham, 9-63.

XF360 Deld 5-3-56, No 33 MU. No 130 (F) Sqn. No 234 (F) Sqn. No 3 (F) Sqn. No 229 OCU (ES-K). Purchased by HSA, 19-8-71, as G-9-371. *Converted to Singaporean FR Mark 74B (542).* Deld 13-6-73.

XF361 Deld 1-3-56, No 33 MU. No 130 (F) Sqn. No 229 OCU (RS-22). Purchased by HSA, 20-6-68, as G-9-260. *Converted to Swiss Hunter Mark 58A (J-4117).* Deld 30-10-71.

XF362 Deld 27-2-56, No 33 MU. No 112 (F) Sqn ('Q'). Purchased by HSA, 19-9-68, as G-9-251. *Converted to Abu Dhabian Hunter FGA Mark 76 (705).* Deld 5-12-70.

XF363 Deld 1-3-56, No 33 MU. No 234 (F) Sqn. No 3 (F) Sqn. No 229 OCU. Transferred to FAA.

XF364 Deld 6-3-56, No 33 MU. No 130 (F) Sqn. No 234 (F) Sqn. No 229 OCU. Purchased by HSA, 6-6-68, as G-9-262. *Converted to Jordanian Hunter FGA Mark 73A (843).* Deld 15-7-71.

XF365 Deld 19-3-56, No 33 MU. No 71 (F) Sqn. No 229 OCU. Purchased by HSA, 8-69, as G-9-297. *Converted to Swiss Hunter Mark 58A (J-4109).* Deld 11-5-72.

XF366 Deld 7-3-56, No 33 MU. No 112 (F) Sqn ('R'). No 71 (F) Sqn. No 229 OCU. Stored, Kemble, 1966.

XF367 Deld 19-3-56, No 33 MU. No 4 (FR) Sqn. RAF College, Manby. No 71 (F) Sqn. Purchased by HSA, 21-8-68, as G-9-252. *Converted to Abu Dhabian Hunter FGA Mark 76 (706).* Deld 5-12-70.

XF368 Deld 7-3-56, No 33 MU. No 3 (F) Sqn ('C'). No 71 (F) Sqn. No 4 (FR) Sqn ('N'). No 118 (F) Sqn ('N'). No 229 OCU.

XF369 Deld 8-3-56, No 33 MU. No 234 (F) Sqn ('M'). RAF College, Manby. GIA, 7941M, Halton. Purchased by HSA, 2-71, as G-9-351. *Converted to Singaporean Hunter FR Mark 74B (538).* Deld 9-4-73.

XF370 Deld 15-3-56, No 33 MU. No 4 (FR) Sqn. No 118 (F) Sqn. Sylt Stn Flt. RAF Staff College, Strubby. GIA, 7772M. Purchased by HSA, 4-70, as G-9-387. *Converted to*

Appendix 2 157

Swiss Hunter Mark 58A (J-4136). Deld 30-4-74.

Third production batch of 56 aircraft built by Hawker Aircraft (Blackpool) Ltd, Blackpool. Contract No SP/6/10344/CB.7a.

XF932 Deld 23-3-56, No 45 MU. No 234 (F) Sqn ('A'). Engine failure during take-off from Kleim-Brogel, 22-9-56; aircraft SOC.

XF933 Deld 23-3-56, No 33 MU. Purchased by HSA, 3-72, as G-9-392. *Converted to Swiss Hunter Mark 58A (J-4132).* Deld 28-1-74.

XF934 Deld 3-4-56, No 5 MU. No 234 (F) Sqn ('C'). CFS Type Sqn. Scrapped at Kemble, 3-7-63.

XF935 Dcld 23-3-56, No 45 MU. No 234 (F) Sqn ('D'). Purchased by HSA, 6-9-68, as G-9-253. *Converted to Abu Dhabian Hunter FGA Mark 76 (707).* Deld 9-1-71.

XF936 Deld 11-4-56, No 33 MU. No 234 (F) Sqn ('E'). No 14 (F) Sqn. Purchased by HSA, 15-11-67, as G-9-255. *Converted to Jordanian Hunter FGA Mark 73A (844).* Deld 26-8-71.

XF937 Deld 23-3-56, No 5 MU. No 112 (F) Sqn ('K'). No 71 (F) Sqn. No 234 (F) Sqn. RAF College, Manby. Purchased by HSA, 16-10-68, as G-9-256. *Converted to Swiss Hunter Mark 58A (J-4116).* Deld 19-9-72.

XF938 Deld 27-3-56, No 5 MU. No 71 (F) Sqn ('D'). No 229 OCU. Returned to HSA, 1960. *Converted to Hunter T Mark 8B.* RNAS, Brawdy (6-62).

XF939 Deld 4-4-56, No 5 MU. No 71 (F) Sqn. No 229 OCU. Returned to HSA, 1960. *Converted to Hunter T Mark 8B.* No 759 Sqn, FAA.

XF940 Deld 6-4-56, No 5 MU. No 71 (F) Sqn. No 74 (F) Sqn ('F'). ETPS, Farnborough. Crashed after running short of fuel, 13-10-61, near Farnborough; pilot safe.

XF941 Deld 19-4-56, No 45 MU. No 71 (F) Sqn. No 229 OCU. GIA, 8006M. No 2030 ATC Sqn, Birmingham, 18-3-68. Purchased by HSA, 3-72, as G-9-374. *Converted to Swiss Hunter Mark 58A (J-4139).* Deld 7-74.

XF942 Deld 27-3-56, No 5 MU. No 71 (F) Sqn. No 229 OCU. Returned to HSA, 1964. *Converted to Hunter T Mark 8C.* No 759 Sqn, FAA. Crashed into sea on take-off, 6-11-68. 2,137.50 FH.

XF943 Deld 6-4-56, No 5 MU. No 234 (F) Sqn ('F'). CFS. Written off, 29-6-62.

XF944 Deld 9-4-56, No 45 MU. No 234 (F) Sqn ('G'). CFS. Purchased by HSA, 3-72, as G-9-393. *Converted to Swiss Hunter Mark 58A (J-4142).* Deld 21-8-74.

XF945 Deld 11-4-56, No 5 MU. No 234 (F) Sqn ('H'). Engine flamed-out at 20,000 feet at night, 20-11-56; pilot ejected safely.

XF946 Deld 6-4-56, No 5 MU. No 234 (F) Sqn ('L'). No 3 (F) Sqn. GIA, 7804M, at No 71 MU.

XF947 Deld 20-4-56, No 5 MU. No 3 (F) Sqn ('S'). No 229 OCU. Transferred to FAA. GIA, A2568, HMS *Condor*, Arbroath. Purchased by HSA, 1970, as G-9-317. *Converted to Swiss Hunter Mark 58A (J-4104).* Deld 2-2-72.

XF948 Deld 9-4-56, No 5 MU. No 3 (F) Sqn ('J'). No 229 OCU. Aircraft crashed into sea, 7-11-57, near Lundy Isle, after take-off; pilot ejected but was killed.

XF949 Deld 24-4-56, No 33 MU. No 3 (F) Sqn ('C'). Two cartridges fired on starting, 13-1-57; aircraft destroyed by fire.

XF950 Deld 17-4-56, No 33 MU. Geilenkirchen Stn Flt. No 3 (F) Sqn ('M'). Purchased by HSA, 20-3-71, as G-9-349. *Converted to Singaporean Hunter T Mark 75A (536).* Deld 13-4-73.

XF951 Deld 1-5-56, No 33 MU. No 3 (F) Sqn ('P'). No 111 (F) Sqn. No 229 OCU. Purchased by HSA, 5-72, as G-9-389. *Converted to Swiss Hunter T Mark 68 (J-4202).* Deld 12-74.

XF952 Deld 23-4-56, No 33 MU. No 234 (F) Sqn. No 229 OCU. Purchased by HSA, 18-7-68, as G-9-263. *Converted to Jordanian Hunter FGA Mark 73A (848).* Deld 7-10-71.
XF953 Deld 26-4-56, No 5 MU. RAF College, Manby.

XF967 Deld 1-5-56, No 5 MU. No 3 (F) Sqn ('Z'). Returned to HSA, 1963. *Converted to Hunter T Mark 8C.* RNAMU, Changi, 1-66.
XF968 Deld 2-5-56, No 5 MU. No 3 (F) Sqn ('R'). No 229 OCU. Purchased by HSA, 25-7-68, as G-9-264. *Converted to Jordanian Hunter FGA Mark 73A (847).* Deld 21-12-71.
XF969 Deld 1-5-56, No 5 MU. No 3 (F) Sqn ('D'). ETPS (26). Purchased by HSA, 2-71, as G-9-346. *Converted to Singaporean Hunter FR Mark 74B (529).* Deld 15-12-72.
XF970 Deld 2-5-56, No 33 MU. A&AEE, tropical trials, Idris, 18-6-56. No 130 (F) Sqn. No 234 (F) Sqn. No 26 (F) Sqn. No 229 OCU. Purchased by HSA, 2-71, as G-9-345. *Converted to Singaporean Hunter T Mark 75A (528).* Deld 10-11-72.
XF971 Deld 2-5-56, No 33 MU. No 3 (F) Sqn ('K'). Purchased by HSA, 2-10-68, as G-9-257. *Converted to Abu Dhabian Hunter FR Mark 76A (709).* Deld 19-1-71.
XF972 Deld 15-5-56, No 33 MU. No 3 (F) Sqn ('V'). No 71 (F) Sqn. No 14 (F) Sqn. No 26 (F) Sqn. No 229 OCU. GIA, 7948M. Purchased by HSA, 2-73, as G-9-418. *Converted to Kenyan Hunter FGA Mark 80 (804).* Deld 8-12-74.
XF973 Deld 28-5-56, No 5 MU. No 66 (F) Sqn. No 71 (F) Sqn. CFS ('E'). Purchased by HSA, 3-72, as G-9-394. 1,189.45 FH. *Converted to Swiss Hunter Mark 58A (J-4143).* Deld 18-9-74.
XF974 Deld 15-5-56, No 33 MU. No 3 (F) Sqn ('G'). No 229 OCU.
XF975 Deld 17-5-56, No 5 MU. No 3 (F) Sqn ('W'). No 229 OCU (RS-27). GIA, 7945M, St Athan. Purchased by HSA, 5-73, as G-9-421. *Converted to Kenyan Hunter FGA Mark 80 (806).* Deld 13-1-75.
XF976 Deld 14-5-56, No 5 MU. No 3 (F) Sqn. No 111 (F) Sqn. No 229 OCU (RS-15). *Converted to Swiss Hunter Mark 58A (J-4112).* Deld 29-6-72.
XF977 Deld 17-5-56, No 33 MU. No 118 (F) Sqn ('A'). Sylt Stn Flt. Returned to HSA, 1962. *Converted to Hunter GA Mark 11.* RNAS Lossiemouth, 2-10-62.
XF978 Deld 17-5-56, No 33 MU. No 20 (F) Sqn. No 26 (F) Sqn. Returned to HSA, 1963. *Converted to Hunter T Mark 8B.* RNAS Lossiemouth (110), 10-64.
XF979 Deld 28-5-56, No 5 MU. RAF College, Manby ('A'). Staff College, Strubby ('A'). Purchased by HSA, 22-10-68 as G-9-258. *Converted to Jordanian Hunter FGA Mark 73B (850).* Deld 13-11-71.
XF980 Deld 28-5-56, No 33 MU. RAF College, Manby. Suffered mid-air collision with Gloster Javelin, 24-8-56.
XF981 Deld 5-6-56, No 5 MU. RAF College, Manby. Purchased by HSA, 18-11-67, as G-9-254. *Converted to Swiss Hunter Mark 58A (J-7114).* Deld 10-8-72.
XF982 Deld 1-6-56, No 5 MU. No 43 (F) Sqn ('D'). No 229 OCU. Purchased by HSA, 2-72, as G-9-391. *Converted to Chilean Hunter FR Mark 71A (738).* Deld 15-2-74.
XF983 Deld 1-6-56, No 33 MU. Oldenburg Stn Flt. No 20 (F) Sqn. No 26 (F) Sqn. No 229 OCU. Returned to HSA, 1963. *Converted to Hunter T Mark 8C.* No 759 Sqn, FAA. Crashed at Brawdy, 29-9-66, and SOC.
XF984 Deld 5-6-56, No 5 MU. No 4 (FR) Sqn. No 71 (F) Sqn. No 229 OCU (ES-55). Transferred to FAA. GIA, A2570, HMS *Condor*, Arbroath. Purchased by HSA, 1970, as G-9-330. *Converted to Swiss Hunter Mark 58A (J-4113).* Deld 12-7-72.
XF985 Deld 6-6-56, No 33 MU. No 71 (F) Sqn. Returned to HSA, 1963. *Converted to Hunter T Mark 8B.* No 759 Sqn, FAA.
XF986 Deld 12-6-56, No 33 MU. No 112 (F) Sqn ('A'). No 234 (F) Sqn. No 229 OCU. Aircraft crashed, 7-8-59, at Milton Demeral; pilot ejected safely.

Appendix 2

XF987 Deld 6-6-56, No 33 MU. No 93 (F) Sqn. No 118 (F) Sqn. No 229 OCU. No 3 CAACU. *Converted to Jordanian Hunter FGA Mark 73A (842).* Deld 15-7-71.
XF988 Deld 14-6-56, No 5 MU. RAF College, Manby. Scrapped, 7-63.
XF989 Deld 20-6-56, No 33 MU. No 26 (F) Sqn ('A'). No 229 OCU. Scrapped, Kemble, 7-63.
XF990 Deld 22-6-56, No 33 MU. No 3 (F) Sqn ('K'). No 111 (F) Sqn. No 229 OCU (RS-16). Purchased by HSA, 8-72, as G-9-408. *Converted to Swiss Hunter Mark 58A (J-4139).* Deld 29-7-74.
XF991 Deld 31-8-56, No 5 MU. No 234 (F) Sqn ('A'). No 229 OCU. Returned to HSA, 1963. *Converted to Hunter T Mark 8B.* RNAS Brawdy, 1 66.
XF992 Deld 23-7-56, No 45 MU. No 43 (F) Sqn ('C'). Returned to HSA, 1963, *Converted to Hunter T Mark 8B.* Repurchased by HSA, 1-68, and cannibalised for spares.
XF993 Deld 17-7-56, No 45 MU. No 43 (F) Sqn. No 229 OCU. No 74 (F) Sqn. Engine seized during ground run, 1960; aircraft SOC.
XF994 Deld 23-7-56, No 33 MU. No 66 (F) Sqn. AFDS. No 229 OCU. Returned to HSA, 1963. *Converted to Hunter T Mark 8B.* No 759 Sqn, FAA.
XF995 Deld 20-7-56, No 33 MU. No 247 (F) Sqn. No 229 OCU. Returned to HSA, 1963. *Converted to Hunter T Mark 8C.* Deld 11-6-64.
XF996 Deld 6-11-56, No 5 MU. No 98 (F) Sqn. No 247 (F) Sqn. No 229 OCU, 1959. Aircraft suffered jammed ailerons in landing circuit and crashed at Saunton Sands, 6-5-59; pilot ejected safely.
XF997 Deld 20-7-56, No 5 MU. No 43 (F) Sqn ('F'). Pilot overshot on landing to avoid flock of birds, 28-6-56; aircraft crashed and SOC; pilot rescued unhurt from mudflats.
XF998 Deld 20-7-56, No 33 MU. No 54 (F) Sqn ('A'). No 245 (F) Sqn. No 229 OCU. GIA, 7950M. Purchased by HSA, 2-72, as G-9-390. *Converted to Swiss Hunter Mark 58A (J-4140).* Deld 17-7-74.
XF999 Deld 20-7-56, No 45 MU. CFS. Aircraft suffered control failure in landing circuit, 24-10-56; pilot ejected but was killed.

XG341 Deld 20-7-56, No 5 MU. No 43 (F) Sqn ('H'). RAF College, Manby. Purchased by HSA, 20-6-68, as G-9-260. *Converted to Abu Dhabian Hunter FGA Mark 76 (702).* Deld 6-11-70.
XG342 Deld 20-7-56, No 5 MU. No 66 (F) Sqn. No 111 (F) Sqn ('A'). No 222 (F) Sqn ('W'). No 247 (F) Sqn. No 229 OCU. Scrapped, Kemble, 7-63.

Hawker Hunter F Mark 5

One production batch of 105 aircraft built by Sir W.G. Armstrong Whitworth Aircraft Ltd, Coventry. Contract No SP/6/6315/CB.7a, Second Part.
WN954 ff 19-10-54. A&AEE, Boscombe Down; later used for target towing.
WN955 ASM; flight trials with Sapphire ASSa.7 engines.
WN956 A&AEE for fuel system trials. No 1 (F) Sqn ('P'). No 41 (F) Sqn ('G').
WN957 RAE, Farnborough; miscellaneous flight trials.
WN958 A&AEE; trials with various external stores.
WN959 Deld 26-4-55, No 5 MU. No 1 (F) Sqn ('A').
WN960 Deld 26-4-55, No 5 MU. Damaged and stored, No 45 MU.
WN961 Deld 5-5-55, No 5 MU. RAE, Farnborough, miscellaneous trials. No 257 (F) Sqn. No 41 (F) Sqn ('G').
WN962 Deld 28-4-55, No 5 MU. No 1 (F) Sqn ('N'). No 41 (F) Sqn.
WN963 Deld 20-5-55, No 5 MU. No 257 (F) Sqn ('T'). No 41 (F) Sqn ('F'). No 34 (F) Sqn.

WN964 Deld 11-5-55, No 5 MU. No 41 (F) Sqn ('C').
WN965 Deld 16-5-55, No 5 MU. No 41 (F) Sqn ('P').
WN966 Deld 28-4-55, No 5 MU. No 41 (F) Sqn ('M').
WN967 Deld 20-5-55, No 5 MU. No 34 (F) Sqn. No 41 (F) Sqn ('A'). Fatigue tested, HSA, 3-62.
WN968 Deld 25-3-55, No 5 MU. No 56 (F) Sqn ('P'). No 41 (F) Sqn.
WN969 Deld 11-5-55, No 5 MU. No 41 (F) Sqn ('N').
WN970 Deld 16-5-55, No 45 MU. No 34 (F) Sqn ('L'). No 54 (F) Sqn ('M'). Purchased by HSA and scrapped, 1963.
WN971 Deld 30-3-55, No 45 MU. No 56 (F) Sqn ('T').
WN972 Deld 28-3-55, No 45 MU. No 263 (F) Sqn. No 41 (F) Sqn ('U').
WN973 Deld 18-4-55, No 45 MU. No 1 (F) Sqn ('B').
WN974 Deld 26-5-55, No 5 MU. No 1 (F) Sqn ('H'). Scrapped, 1-59.
WN975 Deld 18-5-55, No 5 MU. No 263 (F) Sqn. No 1 (F) Sqn ('C'). Scrapped, 1-59.
WN976 Deld 28-3-55, No 45 MU. No 263 (F) Sqn ('P'). No 56 (F) Sqn ('P'). Wattisham Stn Flt. Scrapped, 1-59.
WN977 Deld 26-5-55, No 5 MU. No 1 (F) Sqn ('P'). Collided with WP137, 5-5-58, and SOC.
WN978 Deld 29-5-55, No 5 MU. No 34 (F) Sqn ('B'). No 1 (F) Sqn ('F').
WN979 Deld 29-3-55, No 5 MU. No 56 (F) Sqn ('E'). Purchased by HSA and scrapped, 1963.
WN980 Deld 31-3-55, No 45 MU. No 263 (F) Sqn. No 1 (F) Sqn ('F').
WN981 Deld 16-3-55, No 45 MU. No 263 (F) Sqn ('V').
WN982 Deld 31-3-55, No 5 MU. No 56 (F) Sqn ('H'). No 1 (F) Sqn.
WN983 Deld 16-3-55, No 45 MU. No 263 (F) Sqn. No 41 (F) Sqn ('T').
WN984 Deld 31-5-55, No 5 MU. No 56 (F) Sqn ('O'). No 41 (F) Sqn ('C').
WN985 Deld 16-3-55, No 45 MU. AFDS, Tactical evaluation trials. No 41 (F) Sqn ('P').
WN986 Deld 22-4-55, No 45 MU. No 1 (F) Sqn ('P'). No 56 (F) Sqn ('H'). No 41 (F) Sqn ('M').
WN987 Deld 25-4-55, No 45 MU. No 56 (F) Sqn ('C'). Purchased by HSA and scrapped, 1962.
WN988 Deld 13-4-55, No 45 MU. No 1 (F) Sqn ('A'). No 41 (F) Sqn ('H').

Hunter F Mark 5, WN979, of No 56 (F) Squadron.

Appendix 2

WN989 Deld 6-4-55, No 45 MU. No 263 (F) Sqn. Crashed and SOC.
WN990 Deld 6-4-55, No 45 MU. No 263 (F) Sqn ('F'). No 56 (F) Sqn ('U'). Wattisham Stn Flt. Purchased by HSA and scrapped, 1962.
WN991 Deld 23-3-55, No 45 MU. AFDS, tactical evaluation trials, 4-55.
WN992 Deld 25-4-55, No 45 MU. No 56 (F) Sqn ('D').

WP101 Deld 14-4-55, No 45 MU. No 56 (F) Sqn ('N').
WP102 Deld 28-4-55, No 45 MU. No 56 (F) Sqn ('Q'). No 257 (F) Sqn. No 263 (F) Sqn. Purchased by HSA and scrapped, 1962.
WP103 Deld 25-4-55, No 45 MU. No 1 (F) Sqn ('C'). No 41 (F) Sqn. No 263 (F) Sqn. No 56 (F) Sqn ('J'). Scrapped, HSA, 1962.
WP104 Deld 28-4-55, No 5 MU. No 56 (F) Sqn ('A'). Purchased by HSA and scrapped, 1963.
WP105 Deld 6-4-55, No 45 MU. No 263 (F) Sqn. No 1 (F) Sqn ('R').
WP106 Deld 26-4-55, No 45 MU. No 56 (F) Sqn ('F').
WP107 Deld 1-4-55, No 5 MU. No 263 (F) Sqn ('A'). Crashed near Wymeswold, 25-11-56, and SOC.
WP108 Deld 2-4-55, No 5 MU. No 263 (F) Sqn ('T'). No 41 (F) Sqn ('S').
WP109 Deld 6-4-55, No 5 MU. No 56 (F) Sqn ('B').
WP110 Deld 21-4-55, No 5 MU. No 56 (F) Sqn ('M').
WP111 Deld 14-4-55, No 45 MU. No 34 (F) Sqn ('M').
WP112 Deld 28-4-55, No 45 MU. No 1 (F) Sqn ('D'). No 34 (F) Sqn ('E'). No 41 (F) Sqn. Scrapped, 1961.
WP113 Deld 19-4-55, ASM. No 34 (F) Sqn ('V'). No 1 (F) Sqn ('Q').
WP114 Deld 19-4-55, ASM. Test bed for various Sapphire engines.
WP115 Deld 22-4-55, No 45 MU. No 56 (F) Sqn ('G').
WP116 Deld 28-4-55, No 45 MU. No 1 (F) Sqn ('D'). No 56 (F) Sqn ('W').
WP117 Deld 22-4-55, No 45 MU. No 1 (F) Sqn ('R'). No 41 (F) Sqn ('N').
WP118 Deld 18-5-55, No 5 MU. No 1 (F) Sqn ('S'). No 257 (F) Sqn ('W').
WP119 Deld 25-4-55, No 45 MU. No 1 (F) Sqn ('T'). No 41 (F) Sqn ('L'). Aircraft fatigue tested, HSA, 3-62.
WP120 Deld 2-5-55, No 5 MU. No 56 (F) Sqn ('S'). No 1 (F) Sqn ('R'). Aircraft fatigue tested, HSA, 3-62.
WP121 Deld 10-6-55, No 45 MU. No 1 (F) Sqn ('W').
WP122 Deld 10-6-55, No 45 MU. No 41 (F) Sqn ('A').
WP123 Deld 10-5-55, No 5 MU. No 41 (F) Sqn ('O'). No 56 (F) Sqn ('B'). Purchased by HSA and scrapped, 1963.
WP124 Deld 26-5-55, No 45 MU. No 34 (F) Sqn.
WP125 Deld 12-5-55, No 5 MU. No 56 (F) Sqn ('R'). Scrapped, 1962.
WP126 Deld 16-5-55, No 5 MU. No 1 (F) Sqn. No 34 (F) Sqn ('R').
WP127 Deld 10-5-55, No 5 MU. No 1 (F) Sqn ('G'). No 34 (F) Sqn ('O').
WP128 Deld 13-6-55, No 45 MU. No 41 (F) Sqn ('C'). Crashed and SOC.
WP129 Deld 10-6-55, No 45 MU. No 41 (F) Sqn ('J').
WP130 Deld 6-6-55, No 5 MU. No 34 (F) Sqn ('S'). No 56 (F) Sqn ('S').
WP131 Deld 12-5-55, No 5 MU. No 1 (F) Sqn ('V').
WP132 Deld 19-5-55, No 5 MU. No 34 (F) Sqn ('T').
WP133 Deld 2-5-55, No 45 MU. No 41 (F) Sqn ('D'). No 34 (F) Sqn ('L').
WP134 Deld 23-5-55, No 5 MU. No 41 (F) Sqn. No 263 (F) Sqn.
WP135 Deld 2-6-55, No 45 MU. No 41 (F) Sqn ('E'). Crashed, Anglesey, 5-5-56.
WP136 Deld 30-6-55, No 45 MU. No 34 (F) Sqn ('N'). No 56 (F) Sqn ('D'). Purchased

by HSA and scrapped, 1962.
WP137 Deld 25-5-55, No 5 MU. No 1 (F) Sqn ('S'). Crashed after collision with WN977, 5-5-58.
WP138 Deld 24-5-55, No 5 MU. No 1 (F) Sqn.
WP139 Deld 26-5-55, No 45 MU. No 34 (F) Sqn ('J'). No 56 (F) Sqn ('O'). Purchased by HSA and scrapped, 1962.
WP140 Deld 22-6-55, No 45 MU. No 34 (F) Sqn ('R').
WP141 Deld 19-5-55, No 45 MU. No 41 (F) Sqn ('B'). No 1 (F) Sqn ('GRC').
WP142 Deld 18-5-55, No 5 MU. No 34 (F) Sqn ('L', later 'W').
WP143 Deld 23-6-55, RAE. A&AEE. No 1 (F) Sqn. No 257 (F) Sqn ('M'). Crashed and SOC, 1956.
WP144 Deld 24-5-55, No 5 MU. No 1 (F) Sqn ('PJS'). No 34 (F) Sqn ('JRG').
WP145 Deld 10-6-55, No 45 MU. No 34 (F) Sqn ('X').
WP146 Deld 11-5-55, No 45 MU. No 1 (F) Sqn ('H').
WP147 Deld 13-6-55, No 45 MU. No 41 (F) Sqn ('L'). No 1 (F) Sqn ('G').
WP148 Deld 13-6-55, No 45 MU. No 41 (F) Sqn ('K'). No 56 (F) Sqn ('G').
WP149 Deld 22-6-55, No 45 MU. No 34 (F) Sqn ('H'). No 56 (F) Sqn ('H').
WP150 AWA and A&AEE, miscellaneous trials.

WP179 Deld 15-6-55, No 45 MU. No 263 (F) Sqn ('W').
WP180 Deld 16-6-55, No 45 MU. No 41 (F) Sqn ('H'). No 1 (F) Sqn ('F').
WP181 Deld 30-6-55, No 5 MU. No 263 (F) Sqn. No 41 (F) Sqn ('P').
WP182 Deld 23-6-55, No 45 MU. No 34 (F) Sqn ('C'). No 1 (F) Sqn ('V').
WP183 Deld 30-6-55, No 5 MU. No 56 (F) Sqn ('V').
WP184 Deld 28-6-55, No 45 MU. No 34 (F) Sqn ('A').
WP185 Deld 4-7-55, No 45 MU. No 34 (F) Sqn ('E'). GIA, 7583M.
WP186 Deld 19-7-55, No 5 MU. No 56 (F) Sqn ('AW').
WP187 Deld 8-7-55, No 5 MU. No 41 (F) Sqn ('R').
WP188 Deld 12-7-55, No 5 MU. No 1 (F) Sqn ('X').
WP189 Deld 19-7-55, No 45 MU. Metropolitan Sector Cdr's aircraft.
WP190 Deld 22-7-55, No 5 MU. No 1 (F) Sqn ('K'). No 41 (F) Sqn.
WP191 Deld 3-8-55, No 5 MU. No 1 (F) Sqn ('Z'). No 34 (F) Sqn.
WP192 Deld 3-8-55, No 45 MU. No 34 (F) Sqn ('D'). Crashed, 9-57.
WP193 Deld 18-8-55, No 45 MU. No 34 (F) Sqn.
WP194 Deld 29-7-55, No 5 MU. No 41 (F) Sqn. No 56 (F) Sqn ('H').

Hawker Hunter F Mark 6
First production batch of seven aircraft (employing Pre-Mod. 228 Mark 4 wings), built by Hawker Aircraft Ltd, Kingston-upon-Thames. Instruction to proceed, originally dated July 12 1951. Contract No 7144, second part.
WW592 ff 23-5-55 Bill Bedford. HAL & A&AEE, performance trials, 1955-56. Repurchased by HSA, 1968. *Converted to Abu Dhabian Hunter FR Mark 76A (708)*. Crashed and SOC, 1971.
WW593 ff 19-8-55 Frank Bullen. HAL and A&AEE for miscellaneous TIs. Returned to HSA, 1960. *Converted to Hunter FR Mark 10*. Deld 26-4-61, No 19 MU.
WW594 ff 23-9-55 Frank Bullen. HAL; P.1109A: aerodynamic test aircraft for DH Firestreak installation; missiles not fitted. Returned to HSA, 25-1-60. *Converted to Hunter FR Mark 10*. Deld 5-5-61, No 19 MU. Purchased by HSA, 7-74, as G-9-423. *Converted to Lebanese FGA Mark 70A (L.282)*. Deld 8-12-75. 1,028.25 FH.
WW595 ff 29-9-55 Hugh Merewether. HAL, Blackpool, TIs. HSA, Dunsfold, 13-10-59.

Appendix 2

Converted to Hunter FR Mark 10. Deld 22-12-60, No 19 MU. Written off, Gutersloh, 24-1-67.
WW596 ff 10-10-55 Frank Bullen. CA aircraft; TIs at Blackpool. DFCS. Returned to HSA, 14-10-59. *Converted to Hunter FR Mark 10.* Deld 2-3-61, No 19 MU. Purchased by HSA, 2-3-71, as G-9-352. 2,375.20 FH. *Converted to Indian Hunter T Mark 66E (S.1390).* Deld 13-6-73.
WW597 ff 10-10-55 Duncan Simpson. No 19 MU, St Athan. Stored 1955-58. *Became Jordanian Hunter F Mark 6 (712).* Deld 12-11-58.
WW598 ff 31-12-55 Frank Bullen. HAL, TIs, Dunsfold. To RAE, Farnborough and Bedford, High Speed Flt. Converted to P.1109A standard (see WW594) and employed for tropical low-altitude gust investigation. Repurchased by HSA, 14-5-74, as G-9-424. 1,291.00 FH. *Converted to Lebanese Hunter FGA Mark 70A (L.280).* Deld 8-12-75.

Second production batch of 100 aircraft built by Hawker Aircraft Ltd, Kingston-upon-Thames. (Aircraft not initially fitted with wing leading-edge extensions, but later modified.)
XE526 ff 11-10-55 Hugh Merewether. Deld 11-1-56, No 5 MU. Returned to HAL, 1957. *Converted to Swiss Hunter Mark 58 (J-4008).* ff 8-9-58 Duncan Simpson. Deld 3-10-58.
XE527 ff 29-12-55 Duncan Simpson. Deld 11-1-56, No 19 MU. Returned to HAL, 1957. *Converted to Swiss Hunter Mark 58 (J-4006).* ff 26-8-58 Duncan Simpson. Deld 2-10-58.
XE528 ff 28-12-55 Frank Bullen. Deld 17-1-56, No 5 MU. Returned to HAL, 1957. *Converted to Swiss Hunter Mark 58 (J-4009).* ff 9-9-58 David Lockspeiser. Deld 8-11-58.
XE529 ff 25-12-55 Hugh Merewether. Deld 17-1-56, No 5 MU. Returned to HAL, 1957. *Converted to Swiss Hunter Mark 58 (J-4005).* ff 25-7-58 Duncan Simpson. Deld 25-9-58.
XE530 ff 28-12-55 Hugh Merewether. CA aircraft, RR. Deld 3-2-56; trials with various Avon engines; tropical trials, 1956. No 26 (F) Sqn ('A'). Returned to HSA, 1-2-61. *Converted to Hunter FGA Mark 9.* Purchased by HSA, 11-67, as G-9-267. 2,170.45 FH. *Converted to Kuwaiti Hunter T Mark 67 (220).* Deld 22-5-69.
XE531 ff 9-1-56 Hugh Merewether. CA aircraft, RR. Tropical trials, 1956. Returned to HSA, 1959. *Converted to Hunter FGA Mark 9; later converted to Hunter Mark 12 two-seater.* Trials with head-up display and vertical nose camera, RAE, 1965.
XE532 ff 10-1-56 David Lockspeiser. CA aircraft, RR. Deld 3-2-56; trials with various Avon engines; tropical trials, 1956. No 92 (F) Sqn ('L'). Returned to HSA, 5-11-64. *Converted to Hunter FGA Mark 9.* No 8 (F) Sqn. Crashed, 2nd TAF, 6-5-68; pilot safe.
XE533 ff 12-1-56 Frank Bullen. Deld 4-2-56, No 5 MU. Returned to HAL, 1957. *Converted to Swiss Hunter Mark 58 (J-4002).* ff 14-6-58 Frank Bullen. Deld 25-7-58.
XE534 ff 12-1-56 Duncan Simpson. Deld 4-2-56, No 5 MU. *Converted to Lebanese Hunter F Mark 6 (L.172),* 22-5-62.
XE535 ff 17-1-56 David Lockspeiser. Deld 4-2-56, No 5 MU. No 20 (F) Sqn. No 26 (F) Sqn ('F'). Returned to HSA, 2-2-61. *Converted to Hunter FGA Mark 9.* No 28 (F) Sqn ('C'). Crashed, 28-12-62.
XE536 ff 27-1-56 David Lockspeiser. Deld 23-2-56, No 5 MU. Returned to HAL, 1957. *Converted to Swiss Hunter Mark 58 (J-4001).* ff 29-3-58 Frank Bullen. Deld 3-4-58.
XE537 ff 18-1-56 Hugh Merewether. Deld 23-2-56, No 5 MU. Returned to HAL, 1957. *Converted to Indian Hunter Mark 56 (BA233).* ff 21-1-58 Flt Lt Chopra. Deld 6-2-58.
XE538 ff 20-1-56 Hugh Merewether. Deld 14-2-56, No 5 MU. Returned to HAL, 1957. *Converted to Indian Hunter Mark 56 (BA234).* ff 17-1-58 Fg Off Dey. Deld 6-2-58.
XE539 ff 20-1-56 Duncan Simpson. Deld 14-2-56. No 5 MU. Returned to HAL, 1957.

Converted to Indian Hunter Mark 56 (BA235). ff 27-1-58 Flt Lt Chopra. Deld 6-2-58.

XE540 ff 8-2-56 Frank Bullen. Deld 23-2-56, No 5 MU. Returned to HAL, 1957. *Converted to Indian Hunter Mark 56 (BA236).* ff 29-1-58 Fg Off Dey. Deld 5-3-58.

XE541 ff 9-2-56 David Lockspeiser. Deld 23-2-56, No 5 MU. Returned to HAL, 1957. *Converted to Swiss Hunter Mark 58 (J-4003).* ff 9-7-58 David Lockspeiser. Deld 10-58.

XE542 ff 2-2-56 David Lockspeiser. Deld 14-2-56, No 5 MU. Returned to HAL, 1957. *Converted to Swiss Hunter Mark 58 (J-4004).* ff 17-10-58 David Lockspeiser. Deld 10-58. Crashed at Interlaken, 22-10-58.

XE543 ff 13-2-56 Frank Bullen. No 19 MU. A&AEE, Boscombe Down, for armament trials. *Became Jordanian Hunter F Mark 6 (707),* 12-11-58.

XE544 ff 27-1-56 David Lockspeiser. Deld 26-3-56, No 5 MU. No 66 (F) Sqn ('V'). Returned to HSA, 1960. *Converted to Hunter FGA Mark 9.*

XE545 ff 14-2-56 Hugh Merewether. Deld No 5 MU. Returned to HAL, 1957. *Converted to Swiss Hunter Mark 58 (J-4007).* ff 27-8-58 Duncan Simpson. Deld 3-10-58.

XE546 ff 16-2-56 David Lockspeiser. Deld 8-3-56, No 5 MU. No 93 (F) Sqn ('Z'). No 26 (F) Sqn ('M'). Returned to HSA, 1-2-61. 881.55 FH. *Converted to Hunter FGA Mark 9.* No 43 (F) Sqn ('B'). Transferred to FAA, RNAS Brawdy, 10-76.

XE547 ff 9-2-56 Hugh Merewether. Deld 8-3-56, No 5 MU. Returned to HAL, 1957. *Converted to Indian Hunter Mark 56 (BA237).* ff 3-1-58 Frank Bullen. Deld 3-58.

XE548 ff 6-2-56 Duncan Simpson. Deld 23-2-56, No 5 MU. No 4 (FR) Sqn ('H'). *Converted to Rhodesian Hunter FGA Mark 9 (120).*

XE549 ff 1-2-56 Hugh Merewether. Deld No 5 MU. Returned to HAL, 1957. *Converted to Indian Hunter Mark 56 (BA238).* ff 9-1-58 Fg Off Dey. Deld 3-58.

XE550 ff 23-2-56 Frank Bullen. Deld 14-2-56, No 5 MU. No 93 (F) Sqn ('R'). *Converted to Hunter FGA Mark 9.* 931.05 FH. Deld 5-10-61, No 43 (F) Sqn ('X'). Transferred to Kuwaiti Air Force, 12-67.

XE551 ff 14-2-56 Frank Bullen. Deld No 5 MU. A&AEE for miscellaneous trials, 1956-57. *Became Jordanian Hunter F Mark 6 (700),* 7-11-58.

XE552 ff 23-2-56 David Lockspeiser. Deld 26-3-56, No 5 MU. No 65 (F) Sqn. No 263 (F) Sqn. Returned to HSA, 1960. *Converted to Hunter FGA Mark 9.* No 54 (F) Sqn ('M').

XE553 ff 28-2-56 Frank Bullen. Deld 26-3-56, No 5 MU. Returned to HAL, 1957. *Converted to Swiss Hunter Mark 58 (J-4012).* ff 4-10-58 Duncan Simpson. Deld 12-12-58.

XE554 ff 29-2-56 David Lockspeiser. Deld 8-3-56, No 19 MU. Returned to HAL, 1957. *Converted to Swiss Hunter Mark 58 (J-4010).* ff 18-9-58 David Lockspeiser. Deld 10-11-58.

XE555 ff 15-2-56 David Lockspeiser. Deld 14-3-56, No 5 MU. Returned to HAL, 1957. *Converted to Swiss Hunter Mark 58 (J-4011).* ff 22-9-58 David Lockspeiser. Deld 4-12-58.

XE556 ff 24-2-56 Frank Bullen. Deld 14-3-56, No 19 MU. No 208 (F) Sqn ('B'). Returned to HSA, 1961. *Converted to Hunter FR Mark 10.* Purchased by HSA, 2-3-71, as G-9-353. *Converted to Indian Hunter T Mark 66E (S.1391).* Deld 13-6-73.

XE557 ff 1-3-56 David Lockspeiser. Deld 26-3-56, No 5 MU. No 263 (F) Sqn ('I'). No 19 (F) Sqn ('O'). Purchased by HSA, 16-3-70, as G-9-319. *Converted to Chilean Hunter Mark 71 (727).* Deld 3-6-71.

XE558 ff 14-3-56 Frank Bullen. Deld No 5 MU. A&AEE for air firing trials, 1956-57. *Became Jordanian Hunter F Mark 6 (701),* 1-11-58. Destroyed and SOC, 1-7-60.

XE559 ff 2-3-56 Frank Bullen. Deld 4-4-56, No 33 MU. *Converted to Rhodesian Hunter FGA Mark 9 (116).*

XE560 ff 1-3-56 Hugh Merewether. CA aircraft, HAL; various TIs. No 43 (F) Sqn ('E'). No 65 (F) Sqn. 620.00 FH. *Converted to Rhodesian Hunter FGA Mark 9 (126).*

XE561 ff 9-3-56 Hunter Merewether. Deld 4-4-56, No 33 MU. No 19 (F) Sqn ('Z'). No

Appendix 2 165

43 (F) Sqn ('D'). No 54 (F) Sqn. No 111 (F) Sqn. No 1 (F) Sqn. No 229 OCU. Purchased by HSA, 16-3-70, as G-9-318. *Converted to Chilean Hunter FGA Mark 71 (726)*. Deld 4-5-71.

XE579 ff 15-3-56 David Lockspeiser. Deld 4-4-56, No 19 MU. No 208 (F) Sqn ('A'). Returned to HSA, 15-2-60. *Converted to Hunter FR Mark 10*. Deld 15-3-61, No 19 MU. No 8 (F) Sqn. Crashed near Zinjibah, Eastern Aden Protectorate, 8-8-61; Fg Off E.J. Volkers killed.

XE580 ff 15-3-56 Frank Bullen. Deld 4-4-56, No 19 MU. Returned to HSA, 28 9-59. *Converted to Hunter FR Mark 10*. Deld 1-12-60, No 19 MU. No 4 (FR) Sqn ('D'). Purchased by HSA, 3-6-70, as G-9-332. 2,758.10 FH. *Converted to Chilean Hunter FGA Mark 71 (730)*. Deld 2-9-71.

XE581 No 33 MU, 1956. No 247 (F) Sqn ('T'). Returned to HSA, 25-2-59. *Converted to Hunter FGA Mark 9*. Deld 30-10-59, No 19 MU. No 8 (F) Sqn. Crashed following full tail trim runaway, 22-11-61; pilot killed.

XE582 No 33 MU, 1956. No 66 (F) Sqn ('J'). No 247 (F) Sqn. Returned to HSA, 16-11-60. *Converted to Hunter FGA Mark 9*. No 20 (F) Sqn ('J').

XE583 No 33 MU, 1956. No 19 (F) Sqn ('D'). Crashed off Danish coast, 12-9-61.

XE584 ff 20-3-56 Hugh Merewether. Deld 10-4-56, No 19 MU. CFE. DFLS ('G'). No 263 (F) Sqn ('W'). No 1 (F) Sqn ('W'). *Converted by RAF to Hunter Interim Mark 9*. No 8 (F) Sqn. Repurchased by HSA, 2-76, as G-9-450. 3,262.00 FH. Awaiting final disposal, 1979.

XE585 ff 6-4-56 Hugh Merewether. Deld 1-5-56, No 5 MU. CFE. DFLS ('Q'). Returned to HAL, 16-9-59. *Converted to Hunter FR Mark 10*. Deld 28-11-60, No 19 MU. Purchased by HSA, 2-3-71, as G-9-354. 2,810.00 FH. *Converted to Indian Hunter T Mark 66E (S.1392)*. Deld 13-12-73.

XE586 ff 19-3-56 Frank Bullen. Deld 17-4-56, No 5 MU. No 263 (F) Sqn. Crashed in spin, 2-8-57; pilot ejected safely.

XE587 ff 23-3-56 David Lockspeiser. Deld 1-5-56, No 19 MU. Demonstrations in Switzerland; tail parachute development.

XE588 ff 6-4-56 Hugh Merewether. Deld 15-5-56, No 19 MU. Demonstrations in Switzerland, 1957. Spinning trials, HAL and A&AEE. Crashed and SOC, 9-11-57.

XE589 ff 3-4-56 Frank Bullen. Deld 17-4-56, No 33 MU. No 74 (F) Sqn. Returned to HSA, 1962. *Converted to Hunter FR Mark 10*. Deld 24-2-61, No 8 (F) Sqn. No 1417 Flt. Purchased by HSA, 2-68, as G-9-270. *Converted to Abu Dhabian Hunter FGA Mark 76 (701)*. Deld 9-3-70.

XE590 ff 6-4-56 Hugh Merewether. Deld 7-5-56, No 33 MU. No 19 (F) Sqn ('R'). No 263 (F) Sqn. No 93 (F) Sqn. No 4 (FR) Sqn. Crashed, 10-11-60, following bird strikes; pilot safe.

XE591 ff 28-3-56 Hugh Merewether. Deld No 33 MU. No 74 (F) Sqn ('G'). No 65 (F) Sqn. No 229 OCU. Repurchased by HSA, 4-4-66, as G-9-212. *Converted to Saudi Arabian Hunter F Mark 60 (60/602)*. Deld 2-5-66.

XE592 ff 5-4-56 Hugh Merewether. Deld 7-5-56, No 33 MU. No 43 (F) Sqn. No 111 (F) Sqn ('P'). Returned to HSA, 14-7-59. *Converted to Hunter FGA Mark 9*. No 54 (F) Sqn ('Y'). No 8 (F) Sqn. Crashed into sea, 16-10-64; pilot killed.

XE593 ff 6-4-56 Frank Bullen. Deld 7-5-56, No 19 MU. No 65 (F) Sqn ('P'). Aircraft destroyed in starter explosion at Duxford, 23-1-61.

XE594 ff 9-4-56 David Lockspeiser. Deld 7-5-56, No 5 MU. No 65 (F) Sqn ('J'). No 56 (F) Sqn ('N'). No 229 OCU. Collided with XF433 during formation aerobatics, 7-3-63; pilot ejected safely.

XE595 ff 9-4-56 David Lockspeiser. Deld No 33 MU. No 66 (F) Sqn. No 65 (F) Sqn. Crashed and written off after pilot abandoned take-off, 26-7-57; pilot unhurt.
XE596 ff 9-4-56 David Lockspeiser. Deld No 33 MU. No 63 (F) Sqn. No 66 (F) Sqn. Returned to HSA, 14-10-59. *Converted to Hunter FR Mark 10.* Deld 31-5-61, No 19 MU.
XE597 ff 16-4-56 David Lockspeiser. Deld No 19 MU. No 63 (F) Sqn ('A'). Returned to HSA, 6-5-59. *Converted to Hunter FGA Mark 9.* No 208 (F) Sqn ('G'). No 1 (F) Sqn ('A'). Transferred to FAA, RNAS Brawdy ('F'), 10-56.
XE598 ff 16-4-56 David Lockspeiser. Deld 11-5-56, A&AEE. Trials with gun-blast deflectors. *Became Lebanese Hunter F Mark 6 (L.170),* 31-10-58.
XE599 ff 19-4-56 Frank Bullen. Deld 1-5-56, A&AEE, intensive gun firing trials. No 208 (F) Sqn ('C'). Trials with wing leading edge extensions, HAL and A&AEE. Returned to HSA, 9-12-59. *Converted to Hunter FR Mark 10.* Deld 15-3-61, No 19 MU. Purchased by HSA, 10-71, as G-9-376. *Converted to Singaporean Hunter Mark 74B (535).* Deld 14-3-73.
XE600 ff 20-4-56 David Lockspeiser. Deld 15-5-56, A&AEE. Damaged in accident and returned to HAL, 1957. *Converted to Indian Hunter Mark 56 (BA239).* ff 14-2-58 Flt Lt Chopra. Deld 3-58. Refused by IAF and returned to HSA, 15-4-59, and reverted to XE600. Trials with nosewheel brake, HSA. *Converted to Hunter FGA Mark 9.* Crashed, 25-6-62; pilot killed.
XE601 ff 2-5-56 Frank Bullen. CA aircraft, HAL, 1956; progressively modified up to Hunter FGA Mark 9 standard, though it was never officially designated as such.
XE602 ff 4-5-56 Frank Bullen. Deld 14-8-56, No 5 MU. No 63 (F) Sqn. No 92 (F) Sqn. No 56 (F) Sqn ('G'). No 229 OCU ('41'). Crashed on landing at Chivenor, 8-3-61; throttle jammed open by groundcrew's screwdriver; pilot safe.
XE603 ff 15-5-56 Frank Bullen. Deld 21-6-56, No 5 MU. CFE, AFDS and DFLS. No 19 (F) Sqn ('R'). Purchased by HSA, 3-66, as G-9-209. 1,577.25 FH. *Converted to Jordanian Hunter FGA Mark 73 (832).* Deld 13-6-68.
XE604 ff 5-6-56 Frank Bullen. Deld 28-6-56, No 33 MU. No 263 (F) Sqn ('D'). No 1 (F) Sqn ('Z'). North Weald Stn Flt. *Converted by RAF to Hunter Interim Mark 9.* No 1 (F) Sqn ('Z'). Crashed into sea, 2-3-61, during rocket firing.
XE605 ff 14-5-56 Frank Bullen. TIs, HAL and A&AEE. Returned to HSA, 4-12-59.

This Indian Hunter Mark 56, BA239, seen here carrying four rocket batteries, was interesting in that during its RAF service it had suffered a serious accident; it was fully repaired and was one of the aircraft selected for conversion and sale to India. When the Indians heard of the aircraft's previous history, however, they refused acceptance and BA239 reverted to its RAF identity, XE600. A newly-built BA239 was added to the end of the first Indian contract.

Appendix 2 167

Converted to Hunter FR Mark 10. Returned to HSA, 5-71, as G-9-360. *Converted to Singaporean Hunter FR Mark 74B (523).* Deld 15-8-72.

XE606 ff 17-5-56 David Lockspeiser. Deld 21-6-56, No 33 MU. AFDS. No 54 (F) Sqn. No 229 OCU. Transferred to FAA, RNAS Brawdy, 10-76.

XE607 ff 25-5-56 David Lockspeiser. Deld 21-6-56, No 5 MU. No 263 (F) Sqn. Returned to HSA, 1963. *Converted to Hunter FGA Mark 9.* No 208 (F) Sqn ('F'). Crashed, 30-3-62.

XE608 ff 8-6-56 David Lockspeiser. Deld 3-7-56, No 33 MU. DFLS and AFDS. DFCS, 1962. No 229 OCU. Transferred to FAA, RNAS Brawdy, 10-76.

XE609 ff 10-6-56, No 33 MU. No 54 (F) Sqn ('R'). Returned to HSA, 1959. *Converted to Hunter FGA Mark 9.* No 8 (F) Sqn ('A'). No 208 (F) Sqn ('E'). Written off, 7-4-66.

XE610 CA aircraft, Bitteswell. No 5 MU. No 74 (F) Sqn ('J'). Returned to HSA, 7-11-60. *Converted to Hunter FGA Mark 9.* Deld 17-7-61, No 20 (F) Sqn ('C').

XE611 CA aircraft, Bitteswell. No 5 MU. No 208 (F) Sqn. DFCS. No 43 (F) Sqn ('Q'). Returned to HSA, 1960. *Converted to Hunter FGA Mark 9.* No 43 (F) Sqn. Purchased by HSA, 25-3-69, as G-9-295. *Converted to Swiss Hunter Mark 58A (J-4103).* Deld 17-1-72.

XE612 CA aircraft, Bitteswell. No 5 MU. No 74 (F) Sqn ('M'). Crashed on landing at Horsham St Faith, 17-5-60, following brake fire; pilot safe.

XE613 CA aircraft, Bitteswell. No 5 MU. No 74 (F) Sqn ('C'). *Converted to Rhodesian Hunter FGA Mark 9 (118).*

XE614 No 5 MU. No 263 (F) Sqn ('R'). Returned to HSA, 1-7-60. *Converted to Hunter FR Mark 10.* Deld 27-2-61. Purchased by HSA, 6-71, as G-9-366. *Converted to Singaporean Hunter FR Mark 74B (533).* Deld 21-2-73.

XE615 ff 22-5-56 Hugh Merewether. Deld 21-6-56, No 263 (F) Sqn ('A'). Returned to HSA, 1959. *Converted to Hunter FGA Mark 9.* No 1 (F) Sqn ('A'). Repurchased by HSA, 30-10-69, as G-9-305. 2,662.15 FH. *Converted to Singaporean Hunter FGA Mark 74 (508).* Deld 14-1-71.

XE616 ff 5-5-56 David Lockspeiser. Deld 25-6-56, No 5 MU. No 263 (F) Sqn ('E'). *Converted to Hunter Interim Mark 9.* No 1 (F) Sqn ('E').

XE617 ff 11-6-56 David Lockspeiser. Deld 3-7-56, No 65 (F) Sqn. No 92 (F) Sqn ('D'). *Converted to Hunter FGA Mark 9.* Written off, Aden, 5-66.

XE618 ff 12-6-56 Hugh Merewether. Deld 4-7-56, No 66 (F) Sqn. Church Fenton Stn Flt. Returned to HSA, 1959. *Converted to Hunter FGA Mark 9.* Deld 4-2-60, No 208 (F) Sqn ('L'). Transferred to Kuwaiti Air Force, 12-67.

XE619 ff 7-6-56 David Lockspeiser. Deld 28-6-56, No 263 (F) Sqn ('S'). Written off at Honington, 2-3-59.

XE620 ff 12-6-56 Frank Bullen. Deld 4-7-56, No 111 (F) Sqn. No 263 (F) Sqn. Returned to HSA, 1959. *Converted to Hunter FGA Mark 9.* Purchased by HSA, 4-68 as G-9-273. 2,391.20 FH. *Converted to Indian Hunter Mark 56A (A967).* Deld 31-7-69.

XE621 ff 17-6-56 David Lockspeiser. Deld 4-7-56, No 56 (F) Sqn. No 92 (F) Sqn. No 111 (F) Sqn. Returned to HSA, 6-8-59. 135.30 FH. *Converted to Hunter FR Mark 10.* Deld 22-12-60. Crashed at Gutersloh, 30-1-62.

XE622 ff 7-6-56 David Lockspeiser. Deld 2-7-56, No 263 (F) Sqn. No 1 (F) Sqn ('E'). *Converted to Hunter FGA Mark 9.* No 28 (F) Sqn ('A'). Destroyed 12-7-66, after starter explosion.

XE623 ff 12-6-56 David Lockspeiser. Deld 3-7-56, No 263 (F) Sqn ('G'). Returned to HSA, 7-4-59. *Converted to Hunter FGA Mark 9.* No 208 (F) Sqn ('C'). Crashed, 11-8-64.

XE624 ff 17-6-56 David Lockspeiser. Deld 3-7-56, No 263 (F) Sqn. *Converted to Hunter FGA Mark 9,* 2-60. No 1 (F) Sqn ('B'). Transferred to FAA, RNAS Brawdy ('G'), 10-76.

XE625 ff 17-6-56 Frank Bullen. Deld 11-7-56, No 263 (F) Sqn. *Converted to Hunter FR*

Mark 10. No 4 (FR) Sqn ('E'). Purchased by HSA, 3-6-70, as G-9-331. 2,717.25 FH. *Converted to Chilean Hunter FGA Mark 71 (729).* Deld 22-7-71.

XE626 ff 17-6-56 Frank Bullen. Deld 20-7-56, No 263 (F) Sqn ('P'). Returned to HSA, 28-9-59. *Converted to Hunter FR Mark 10.* Deld 2-12-60, No 4 (FR) Sqn ('E'). Purchased by HSA, 22-8-72, as G-9-409. 1,815.10 FH. *Converted to Kenyan Hunter FGA Mark 80 (803).* Deld 24-6-74.

XE627 ff 13-6-56 Don Lucey. Deld 20-7-56, No 65 (F) Sqn ('T'). No 92 (F) Sqn. No 54 (F) Sqn ('D'). No 229 OCU. No 1 (F) Sqn.

XE628 ff 20-6-56 Frank Bullen. Deld 11-7-56, No 111 (F) Sqn. No 263 (F) Sqn. *Converted to Hunter FGA Mark 9.* No 1 (F) Sqn ('G'). Crashed at El Adem, 24-4-63.

XE643 ff 26-6-56 David Lockspeiser. Deld 17-7-56, No 45 MU. No 63 (F) Sqn. No 66 (F) Sqn. *Converted to Hunter FGA Mark 9.* No 208 (F) Sqn ('K'). Scrapped, HSA, 5-62.

XE644 ff 21-6-56 David Lockspeiser. Deld 20-7-56, No 5 MU. No 65 (F) Sqn ('B'). No 92 (F) Sqn. No 229 OCU. Purchased by HSA, 23-5-70, as G-9-322. 2,869.20 FH. *Converted to Chilean Hunter FGA Mark 71 (728).* Deld 7-7-71.

XE645 ff 28-6-56 Hugh Merewether. Deld 20-8-56, No 33 MU. No 92 (F) Sqn. No 56 (F) Sqn ('B'). Returned to HSA, 12-3-59. *Converted to Hunter FGA Mark 9.* No 208 (F) Sqn ('M'). *Became Jordanian Hunter FGA Mark 71 (827)*, 12-67.

XE646 ff 21-6-56 David Lockspeiser. Deld 20-7-56, No 33 MU. No 263 (F) Sqn. Returned to HSA, 1960. *Converted to Hunter FGA Mark 9.* No 1 (F) Sqn ('V'). Crashed in Leconfield village, 30-12-66; pilot ejected safely.

XE647 ff 28-6-56 Frank Bullen. Deld 20-8-56, No 5 MU. No 92 (F) Sqn. No 56 (F) Sqn ('E'). Returned to HSA, 14-5-59. *Converted to Hunter FGA Mark 9.* Deld 4-4-60, No 208 (F) Sqn. Crashed, 30-6-64.

XE648 ff 29-6-56 Mr. Stone. Deld 22-8-56, No 33 MU. No 63 (F) Sqn. No 66 (F) Sqn. No 56 (F) Sqn ('H'). Written off, 16-10-59.

XE649 ff 30-6-56 David Lockspeiser. Deld 14-8-56, No 5 MU. Returned to HSA, 23-2-59. *Converted to Hunter FGA Mark 9.* Transferred to FAA, RNAS Brawdy, 10-76.

XE650 ff 2-7-56 Mr. Stone. Deld 20-7-56, No 33 MU. No 263 (F) Sqn. No 1 (F) Sqn ('U'). *Converted to Hunter FGA Mark 9.* No 208 (F) Sqn. No 8 (F) Sqn ('A'). Returned to HSA, 2-76, as G-9-449. 3,643.00 FH. Awaiting disposal, 2-80.

XE651 ff 5-7-56 David Lockspeiser. Deld 14-8-56, No 33 MU. No 63 (F) Sqn ('R'). No 66 (F) Sqn. No 56 (F) Sqn. Returned to HSA, 10-3-59. *Converted to Hunter FGA Mark 9.* No 1 (F) Sqn ('L'). Transferred to FAA, RNAS Brawdy, 10-76.

XE652 ff 16-8-56 David Lockspeiser. Deld 4-9-56, No 5 MU. No 66 (F) Sqn. DFLS. Returned to HSA, 1960. *Converted to Hunter FGA Mark 9.* No 20 (F) Sqn ('A'). Purchased by HSA, 6-4-70, as G-9-323. 2,661.05 FH. *Converted to Singaporean Hunter FGA Mark 74 (519).* Deld 20-5-71.

XE653 ff 6-7-56 David Lockspeiser. Deld 24-8-56, No 5 MU. No 43 (F) Sqn. No 111 (F) Sqn ('S'). No 229 OCU, 6-64.

XE654 ff 8-8-56 Hugh Merewether. Deld 31-8-56, No 5 MU. No 65 (F) Sqn ('G'). No 92 (F) Sqn. Returned to HSA, 12-3-59. *Converted to Hunter FGA Mark 9.* Crashed, 20-11-67; pilot killed.

XE655 ff 8-8-56 Fg Off W.D.E. Eggleton. Deld 24-8-56, No 5 MU. No 63 (F) Sqn. No 92 (F) Sqn. No 56 (F) Sqn. Returned to HSA, 1-4-59. *Converted to Hunter FGA Mark 9.* No 43 (F) Sqn, 1964. *Became Jordanian Hunter FGA Mark 73 (817),* 1968.

XE656 ff 9-8-56 Duncan Simpson. Deld 24-8-56, No 19 MU. No 65 (F) Sqn ('R'). No 92 (F) Sqn ('B'). DFLS. No 229 OCU.

Appendix 2 169

Third production batch of 110 aircraft built by Hawker Aircraft Ltd, Kingston-upon-Thames (except those marked with a star (*) which were transferred to Sir W.G. Armstrong Whitworth Aircraft Ltd, Coventry). Aircraft later modified with gun-blast deflectors and wing leading-edge extensions.

XG127 ff 18-7-56 Fg Off W.D.E. Eggleton. Deld 24-8-56, No 19 MU. No 63 (F) Sqn. No 66 (F) Sqn. Returned to HSA, 1962. *Converted to Hunter FR Mark 10.* Deld 30-1-61, No 19 MU. Purchased by HSA, 10-6-68, as G-9-294. 1,987.00 FH. *Converted to Swiss Hunter Mark 58A (J-4101).* Deld 7-12-71.

XG128 ff 14-8-56 Fg Off W.D.E. Eggleton. Deld 4-10-56, No 33 MU. No 20 (F) Sqn ('Y'). No 65 (F) Sqn ('S'). DFLS. Returned to HSA, 1963. *Converted to Hunter FGA Mark 9.* No 8 (F) Sqn. Crashed, date unknown.

XG129 ff 14-8-56 Fg Off W.D.E. Eggleton. Deld 3-10-56, No 19 MU. No 43 (F) Sqn. No 111 (F) Sqn ('F'). Returned to HSA, 6-9-67, as G-9-240. 2,071 FH. *Converted to Indian Hunter Mark 56A (A936).* Deld 15-11-68.

XG130 ff 14-8-56 Duncan Simpson. Deld 3-9-56, No 19 MU. No 63 (F) Sqn ('J'). No 66 (F) Sqn. Returned to HSA, 2-4-59. *Converted to Hunter FGA Mark 9.* No 1 (F) Sqn ('E').

XG131 ff 16-8-56 David Lockspeiser. TI of wing-tip tanks, HAL. Deld 10-10-56, No 5 MU. No 14 (F) Sqn ('N'). No 229 OCU.

XG132 ff 14-8-56 Hugh Merewether. Deld 12-9-56, No 5 MU. AFDS. Transferred to Jordanian Air Force, 6-62 to 10-62.

XG133 ff 20-8-56 Frank Bullen. Deld 24-9-56, No 5 MU. No 19 (F) Sqn. No 263 (F) Sqn. Crashed on take-off at Duxford, 7-9-58, and SOC; pilot killed.

XG134 ff 21-8-56 Duncan Simpson. Deld 14-9-56, No 19 MU. No 63 (F) Sqn. Returned to HSA, 1960. *Converted to Hunter FGA Mark 9.* No 208 (F) Sqn ('A'). Crashed in Kuwait, 16-7-61, during rocket attack in local crisis; pilot killed.

XG135 ff 24-8-56 Fg Off W.D.E. Eggleton. Deld 24-9-56, No 5 MU. No 19 (F) Sqn. No 263 (F) Sqn. Returned to HSA, 1960. *Converted to Hunter FGA Mark 9.*

XG136 ff 28-8-56 Duncan Simpson. Deld 17-9-56, No 5 MU. AFDS. Returned to HSA, 1960. *Converted to Hunter FGA Mark 9.* No 20 (F) Sqn. Aircraft failed to recover from spin and crashed, 19-10-64; pilot ejected safely.

XG137 ff 27-8-56 David Lockspeiser. Deld 18-9-56, No 19 MU. DFLS ('D'). No 92 (F) Sqn ('E'). No 229 OCU. *Became Jordanian Hunter FGA Mark 73 (813),* 2-68.

XG150* Deld No 5 MU. Despatched to HAL, 6-11-57. *Converted to Indian Hunter Mark 56 (BA247).* ff 28-3-58 Flt Lt Chopra. Deld 19-5-58.

XG151* No 19 MU. No 54 (F) Sqn ('H'). *Converted to Hunter FGA Mark 9.* No 54 (F) Sqn.

XG152* No 19 MU. DFLS. No 19 (F) Sqn ('X'). No 229 OCU.

XG153* No 5 MU. No 66 (F) Sqn ('L'). No 92 (F) Sqn. APS. Returned to HSA, 14-11-60. *Converted to Hunter FGA Mark 9.* No 20 (F) Sqn ('L'). Purchased by HSA, 5-71, as G-9-357. *Converted to Singaporean Hunter FR Mark 74B (520).* Deld 8-6-72.

XG154* No 19 MU. No 66 (F) Sqn ('T'). Returned to HSA, 1960. *Converted to Hunter FGA Mark 9.* No 8 (F) Sqn ('H'). No 43 (F) Sqn ('B'). Transferred to FAA, RNAS Brawdy, 10-76.

XG155* No 19 MU. No 54 (F) Sqn ('T'). *Converted to Hunter FGA Mark 9.*

XG156* No 5 MU. No 54 (F) Sqn. *Converted to Hunter Interim Mark 9.* No 54 (F) Sqn ('F').

XG157* No 33 MU. No 54 (F) Sqn ('H'). No 1 (F) Sqn ('Y'). No 229 OCU. Crashed into hill in bad weather, 16-6-66.

XG158* No 19 MU. No 65 (F) Sqn ('O').

XG159★ No 5 MU. No 19 (F) Sqn. No 263 (F) Sqn. No 56 (F) Sqn ('P'). No 229 OCU. *Became Jordanian Hunter FGA Mark 73*, 1-68.
XG160★ No 5 MU. No 43 (F) Sqn. No 111 (F) Sqn ('U'). No 229 OCU. Transferred to FAA, RNAS Brawdy, 10-76.
XG161★ No 33 MU. AFDS. DFLS ('P'). Stored by No 5 MU.
XG162★ No 5 MU. No 111 (F) Sqn. DFLS ('W'). Crashed at West Raynham, and SOC, 7-11-57; pilot killed.
XG163★ No 5 MU. Returned to HAL, 1957. *Converted to Indian Hunter Mark 56 (BA248).* ff Flt Lt Chopra. Deld 9-6-58.
XG164★ No 33 MU. No 111 (F) Sqn. No 74 (F) Sqn ('H'). West Raynham Stn Flt. Transferred to FAA, RNAS Brawdy, 10-76.
XG165★ No 33 MU. No 208 (F) Sqn ('GW'; Sqn Cdr's aircraft). Middleton St George Stn Flt. Crashed after flame-out, 18-4-58, and SOC; pilot ejected safely.
XG166★ Deld 3-12-56, No 5 MU. No 14 (F) Sqn. No 229 OCU. Crashed into sea, 17-2-64; pilot killed.
XG167★ Deld 18-2-57, No 5 MU. No 19 (F) Sqn ('F'). Supplied to Lebanon as L.174, 13-10-58.
XG168★ Deld 2-4-57, No 5 MU. No 208 (F) Sqn. Returned to HSA, 6-8-59. *Converted to Hunter FR Mark 10.* Deld 30-1-61, No 2 (FR) Sqn ('N').

XG169 ff 21-8-56 Fg Off W.D.E. Eggleton. Deld 14-9-56, No 19 MU. No 19 (F) Sqn ('Q'). Returned to HSA, 1960. *Converted to Hunter FGA Mark 9.* No 8 (F) Sqn ('B').
XG170 ff 30-8-56 David Lockspeiser. Deld 3-10-56, No 19 MU. No 43 (F) Sqn. No 111 (F) Sqn ('G'). No 229 OCU. Purchased by HSA, 6-9-67, as G-9-241. 2,344.40 FH. *Converted to Indian Hunter Mark 56A (A940).* Deld 27-1-69.
XG171 ff 23-8-56 Duncan Simpson. Deld 24-9-56, No 5 MU. No 43 (F) Sqn. No 111 (F) Sqn. To Jordanian Air Force, 6-62 to 10-62.
XG172 ff 27-8-56 Duncan Simpson. Deld 19-9-56, No 5 MU. No 19 (F) Sqn ('B'). No 263 (F) Sqn. Transferred to FAA, RNAS Brawdy, 10-76.

XG185 ff 4-9-56 David Lockspeiser. Deld 3-10-56, No 19 MU. No 19 (F) Sqn ('T'). No 4 FTS. RNAS Brawdy, 1976. Aircraft crashed, 21-4-76, after fire in the air; pilot ejected safely.
XG186 ff 2-9-56 Duncan Simpson. Deld 17-9-56, No 5 MU. No 19 (F) Sqn. No 66 (F) Sqn. No 92 (F) Sqn.('J'). DFLS. Purchased by HSA, 6-10-67, as G-9-237. 1,452.30 FH. *Converted to Indian Hunter Mark 56A (A941).* Deld 22-3-69.
XG187 ff 27-8-56 David Lockspeiser. Deld 17-9-56, No 5 MU. No 63 (F) Sqn. No 66 (F) Sqn. No 56 (F) Sqn ('V'). *Became Jordanian Hunter F Mark 6 (811)*, 6-62.
XG188 ff 12-9-56 Frank Bullen. Deld 3-10-56, No 19 MU. No 19 (F) Sqn ('C'). Air collision, 15-5-61; pilot ejected safely.
XG189 ff 4-9-56 David Lockspeiser. Deld 3-10-56, No 19 MU. No 111 (F) Sqn ('D'). No 92 (F) Sqn. Purchased by HSA, 4-10-67, as G-9-238. 1,370.00 FH. *Converted to Indian Hunter Mark 56A (A942).* Deld 18-4-69.
XG190 ff 31-8-56 Duncan Simpson. Deld 10-10-56, No 19 MU. No 43 (F) Sqn. No 111 (F) Sqn ('C'). Purchased by HSA, 13-9-67, as G-9-244. 1,494.20 FH. *Converted to Indian Hunter Mark 56A (A939).* Deld 27-1-69.
XG191 ff 2-9-56 David Lockspeiser. Deld 3-10-56, No 19 MU. No 19 (F) Sqn ('E'). No 263 (F) Sqn. No 229 OCU, 5-64.
XG192 ff 21-9-56 Frank Bullen. Deld 17-10-56, No 19 MU. DFLS ('F'). FTU, Benson. DFCS. Damaged in forced landing, 7-3-57; written off, 16-1-62.

Appendix 2 171

XG193 ff 6-9-56 Don Lucey. Deld 10-10-56, No 19 MU. No 43 (F) Sqn. No 111 (F) Sqn ('A'). Collided with XG200, 10-6-60, during aerobatic practice; pilot did not eject and was killed.

XG194 ff 6-9-56 David Lockspeiser. Deld 3-10-56, No 19 MU. No 43 (F) Sqn. No 111 (F) Sqn. No 92 (F) Sqn. *Converted to Hunter FGA Mark 9 by RAF,* 3-65. No 1 (F) Sqn ('Q'). RNAS Brawdy, 10-76.

XG195 ff 4-9-56 David Lockspeiser. Deld 3-10-56, No 19 MU. No 19 (F) Sqn ('V'). No 1 (F) Sqn ('C'). *Converted to Hunter FGA Mark 9.* No 208 (F) Sqn ('K'). Purchased by HSA, 2-76, as G-9-453. 3,234.00 FH. Awaiting final disposal, 2-80.

XG196 ff 10-9-56 Don Lucey. Deld 3-10-56, No 19 MU. No 19 (F) Sqn ('U'). No 229 OCU, 9-64.

XG197 ff 11-9-56 Frank Bullen. Deld 23-10-56, No 5 MU. DFLS ('A'). DFCS ('A'). RNAS Brawdy, 10-76.

XG198 ff 24-9-56 Frank Bullen. Deld 30-10-56, No 19 MU. No 74 (F) Sqn ('Q'). No 111 (F) Sqn. No 263 (F) Sqn. Eastern Sector Commander's aircraft, 19-1-58. No 92 (F) Sqn. No 229 OCU, 24-3-61. Crashed during rocket firing training, Pembrey, 4-9-67; pilot killed. 2,083.50 FH.

XG199 ff 11-9-56 David Lockspeiser. Deld 2-10-56, No 33 MU. No 19 (F) Sqn ('J'). No 229 OCU, 3-64. Purchased by HSA, 2-12-69, as G-9-312. 2,620.21 FH. *Converted to Chilean Hunter FGA Mark 71 (724).* Deld 18-2-71.

XG200 ff 13-9-56 David Lockspeiser. Deld 2-10-56, No 33 MU. No 43 (F) Sqn. No 111 (F) Sqn ('Q'). FTU, Benson. No 229 OCU, 7-64. Collided with XG235, 5-67, while flying from Chivenor.

XG201 ff 22-9-56 David Lockspeiser. Deld 23-10-56, No 5 MU. No 43 (F) Sqn. No 111 (F) Sqn ('B'). No 92 (F) Sqn ('B'). Purchased by HSA, 6-9-67, as G-9-242. 2,026.25 FH. *Converted to Indian Hunter Mark 56A (A937).* Deld 15-11-68.

XG202 ff 18-9-56 David Lockspeiser. Deld 11-10-56, No 19 MU. No 66 (F) Sqn. Crashed near Morpeth after flame-out on landing approach, 13-2-57; pilot ejected safely.

XG203 ff 18-9-56 David Lockspeiser. Deld 17-10-56, No 5 MU. No 43 (F) Sqn. No 111 (F) Sqn ('H'). On 30-4-57 aircraft failed to overshoot, crashed and exploded; explosion activated the ejector seat which blew the pilot clear with only slight injuries.

XG204 ff 25-9-56 David Lockspeiser. Deld 25-10-56, No 19 MU. DFLS ('B'). RAF Valley, 1968. Aircraft hit ground while flying at 600 knots, 15-8-69; Lebanese pilot, Lieut Shamsaddine, killed.

XG205 ff 17-9-56 David Lockspeiser. Deld 3-10-56, No 19 MU. No 247 (F) Sqn ('Y'). No 43 (F) Sqn ('E'). No 229 OCU. *Converted to Hunter FGA Mark 9.* No 54 (F) Sqn ('E'). Purchased by HSA, 5-4-70, as G-9-325. 2,892.25 FH. *Converted to Singaporean Hunter Mark 74A (506).* Deld 24-6-71.

XG206 ff 28-9-56 David Lockspeiser. Deld 22-10-56, No 19 MU. DFLS. DFCS ('E'). Crashed into sea, 2-6-65; pilot killed.

XG207 ff 4-10-56 David Lockspeiser. Deld 29-10-56, No 19 MU. No 93 (F) Sqn. No 1 (F) Sqn ('F'). *Converted to Hunter FGA Mark 9.* Deld 1-60. No 54 (F) Sqn ('C'), 10-65.

XG208 ff 2-10-56 David Lockspeiser. Deld 22-10-56, No 19 MU. No 93 (F) Sqn. No 26 (F) Sqn. Aircraft crashed after flame-out during aerobatic display, 24-3-59; pilot ejected safely.

XG209 ff 27-9-56 David Lockspeiser. Deld 25-10-56, No 33 MU. No 14 (F) Sqn. No 111 (F) Sqn. DFLS. DFCS ('C').

XG210 ff 5-10-56 David Lockspeiser. Deld 1-11-56, No 33 MU. No 14 (F) Sqn. No 66 (F) Sqn.

XG211 ff 24-9-56 David Lockspeiser. Deld 31-10-56, No 5 MU. No 92 (F) Sqn ('A'). No

111 (F) Sqn. Purchased by HSA, 12-10-67, as G-9-239. 1,773.55 FH. *Converted to Indian Hunter Mark 56A (A943)*. Deld 18-4-69.

XG225 ff 20-10-56 David Lockspeiser. Deld 1-11-56, No 5 MU. No 20 (F) Sqn ('P'). No 74 (F) Sqn. No 92 (F) Sqn ('M'). No 229 OCU, 9-64. Transferred to FAA, RNAS Brawdy, 10-76.
XG226 ff 28-9-56 Frank Bullen. Deld 29-10-56, No 5 MU. No 66 (F) Sqn ('B'). Transferred to FAA, RNAS Brawdy, 10-76.
XG227 ff 28-9-56 Frank Bullen. Deld 15-10-56, No 5 MU. No 111 (F) Sqn. No 92 (F) Sqn ('B'). Written off, 31-12-58.
XG228 ff 2-10-56 Neville Duke. Deld 25-10-56, No 5 MU. No 92 (F) Sqn ('C'). *Converted to Hunter FGA Mark 9*, 1965. Transferred to FAA, RNAS Brawdy, 10-76.
XG229 ff 3-10-56 Neville Duke. Deld 22-10-56, No 5 MU. No 74 (F) Sqn. No 92 (F) Sqn ('F'). No 56 (F) Sqn ('M'). No 229 OCU. Crashed, 3-9-71; pilot ejected safely.
XG230 ff 4-10-56 Frank Bullen. Deld 22-10-56, No 5 MU. No 92 (F) Sqn. Written off in accident probably due to control icing at altitude, 15-11-56; pilot ejected safely.
XG231 ff 17-10-56 David Lockspeiser. Deld 30-10-56, No 5 MU. No 74 (F) Sqn. No 111 (F) Sqn. No 92 (F) Sqn ('A'). Purchased by HSA, 19-4-66, as G-9-207. *Converted to Jordanian Hunter F Mark 6 (715)*. Deld 13-6-67.
XG232 ff 13-10-56 David Lockspeiser. Deld 30-10-56, No 5 MU. No 92 (F) Sqn ('G'). A&AEE, 1964. Purchased by HSA, 21-6-66, as G-9-216. *Converted to Chilean Hunter FGA Mark 71 (J-714)*. Deld 19-6-68.
XG233 ff 5-10-56 David Lockspeiser. Deld 30-10-56, No 5 MU. No 66 (F) Sqn. Crashed into Famagusta Bay, Cyprus, 20-8-58; pilot killed.
XG234 ff 11-10-56 Duncan Simpson. Deld 25-10-56, No 5 MU. No 74 (F) Sqn. No 92 (F) Sqn ('E'). Purchased by HSA, 9-5-68, as G-9-272. *Converted to Jordanian Hunter FGA Mark 73A (830)*. Deld 22-7-69.
XG235 ff 20-10-56 Duncan Simpson. Deld 5-11-56, No 5 MU. No 74 (F) Sqn. No 92 (F) Sqn ('R'). No 56 (F) Sqn ('O'). No 229 OCU, 5-64. Collided with XG200, 5-67.
XG236 ff 19-10-56 Duncan Simpson. Deld 9-11-56, No 5 MU. No 66 (F) Sqn ('N'). Crashed near Scottish border, 14-2-58, and SOC; pilot killed.
XG237 ff 5-11-56 Duncan Simpson. Deld 16-11-56, No 5 MU. No 66 (F) Sqn ('C'). *Converted to Hunter FGA Mark 9*. No 43 (F) Sqn ('C'). Purchased by HSA, 15-1-68 as G-9-268. *Converted to Jordanian Hunter FGA Mark 73A (828)*. Deld 22-7-69.
XG238 ff 16-10-56 Frank Bullen. Deld 9-11-56, No 5 MU. No 74 (F) Sqn. No 92 (F) Sqn ('F'). Crashed into sea off Cyprus, 5-5-61; pilot killed.
XG239 ff 20-10-56 David Lockspeiser. Deld 26-11-56, No 5 MU. No 92 (F) Sqn. Crashed on take-off, Nicosia, 11-1-58, and SOC; pilot safe.

XG251 ff 20-10-56 David Lockspeiser. Deld 26-11-56, No 5 MU. No 66 (F) Sqn. Returned to HSA, c 1960. *Converted to Hunter FGA Mark 9*. Purchased by HSA, 30-10-69, as G-9-304. 2,072.45 FH. *Converted to Singaporean Hunter FGA Mark 74 (507)*. Deld 10-12-70.
XG252 ff 25-10-56 Frank Bullen. Deld 6-11-56, No 5 MU. No 66 (F) Sqn ('D'). *Converted to Hunter FGA Mark 9*. Transferred to FAA, RNAS Brawdy, 10-76.
XG253 ff 1-11-56 David Lockspeiser. Deld 27-11-56, No 5 MU. No 66 (F) Sqn ('A'). *Converted to Hunter FGA Mark 9*. No 54 (F) Sqn ('W'). Transferred to FAA, RNAS Brawdy, 10-76.
XG254 ff 1-11-56 Duncan Simpson. Deld 26-11-56, No 5 MU. No 54 (F) Sqn ('A'). *Converted to Hunter FGA Mark 9*. No 54 (F) Sqn ('A').

Appendix 2 173

XG255 ff 23-10-56 David Lockspeiser. Deld 14-11-56, No 5 MU. No 66 (F) Sqn. *Converted to Hunter FGA Mark 9. Became Jordanian Hunter FGA Mark 73 (825),* 12-67.

XG256 ff 27-10-56 Duncan Simpson. Deld 26-11-56, No 5 MU. No 66 (F) Sqn ('K'). *Converted to Hunter FGA Mark 9.* No 43 (F) Sqn ('G').

XG257 ff 25-10-56 David Lockspeiser. Deld 27-11-56, No 5 MU. No 66 (F) Sqn ('H'). No 93 (F) Sqn. Transferred to Jordanian Air Force *(812),* 6-62 to 10-62.

XG258 ff 31-10-56 Duncan Simpson. Deld 3-1-57, No 5 MU. No 93 (F) Sqn. Jever Aerobatic Team; crashed during aerobatics at Spangdahlen, 17-5-57, and SOC; pilot killed.

XG259 ff 6-11-56 David Lockspeiser. Deld 30-11-56, No 5 MU. No 54 (F) Sqn ('G'). Extensively damaged during night taxiing collision, 14-7-58; partly repaired and shipped to Jordan for ground instruction purposes.

XG260 ff 26-10-56 Duncan Simpson. No 54 (F) Sqn. *Converted to Hunter FGA Mark 9,* 1-60. No 54 (F) Sqn ('B'). Purchased by HSA, 13-9-69, as G-9-300. 2,357.45 FH. *Converted to Singaporean Hunter FGA Mark 74 (501).* Deld 12-11-70.

XG261 ff 19-11-56 David Lockspeiser. Deld 3-12-56, No 5 MU. No 54 (F) Sqn ('C'). No 43 (F) Sqn ('G'). *Converted to Hunter FGA Mark 9,* 11-60. No 43 (F) Sqn ('G').

XG262 ff 8-11-56 Duncan Simpson. Deld 3-1-57, No 5 MU. No 4 (FR) Sqn. Returned to HSA, 1960. *Converted to Jordanian Hunter FR Mark 10 (712).* Deld 11-60.

XG263 ff 1-11-56 Duncan Simpson. Deld 3-12-56, No 5 MU. No 4 (FR) Sqn. Transferred to Jordanian Air Force, 6-62 to 10-62.

XG264 ff 9-11-56 Duncan Simpson. Deld 30-11-56, No 5 MU. No 111 (F) Sqn. Returned to HSA, 1960. *Converted to Hunter FGA Mark 9.* No 54 (F) Sqn ('D'). Transferred to FAA, RNAS Brawdy, 10-76.

XG265 ff 31-10-56 David Lockspeiser. Deld 27-11-56, No 5 MU. No 66 (F) Sqn ('P'). Returned to HSA, 14-11-60. *Converted to Hunter FGA Mark 9.* Deld 17-7-61, No 20 (F) Sqn ('K'). Crashed, 1-3-64, in Labuan, Borneo, after fire in the air; pilot ejected but was killed.

XG266 ff 7-11-56 Duncan Simpson. Deld 26-11-56, No 5 MU. No 66 (F) Sqn ('R'). Returned to HSA, 16-11-60. *Converted to Hunter FGA Mark 9.* Deld 17-8-61, No 20 (F) Sqn ('N'). Purchased by HSA, 6-5-71, as G-9-358. 3,211.25 FH. *Converted to Singaporean Hunter FR Mark 74B (521).* Deld 8-6-72.

XG267 ff 14-11-56 Duncan Simpson. Deld 3-12-56, No 5 MU. No 4 (FR) Sqn. Transferred to Jordanian Air Force *(801),* 6-62 to 10-62.

XG268 ff 9-11-56 David Lockspeiser. Deld 3-12-56, No 5 MU. No 4 (FR) Sqn. Transferred to Jordanian Air Force *(806),* 6-62 to 10-62.

XG269 ff 14-11-56 David Lockspeiser. Deld 4-12-56, No 5 MU. No 4 (FR) Sqn. Transferred to Jordanian Air Force *(807),* 6-62 to 10-62.

XG270 ff 10-11-56 David Lockspeiser. Deld 4-12-56, No 5 MU. Forced landed on Isle of Baltrum after flame out, 28-6-57; pilot unhurt, but aircraft swamped by rising sea before salvage, and SOC.

XG271 ff 19-11-56 Frank Bullen. Deld 3-12-56, No 5 MU. No 54 (F) Sqn ('F'). *Converted to Hunter FGA Mark 9.* Take-off accident at Sylt, 25-7-61; burnt out and SOC.

XG272 ff 4-12-56 David Lockspeiser. Deld 9-1-57, No 5 MU. No 20 (F) Sqn. No 93 (F) Sqn. Returned to HSA, 3-1-61. *Converted to Hunter FGA Mark 9.* Deld 11-1-61. Purchased by HSA, 19-3-70 as G-9-310. 2,759.40 FH. *Converted to Swiss Hunter Mark 58A (J-4111).* Deld 22-6-72.

XG273 ff 15-11-56 David Lockspeiser. Deld 30-11-56, No 5 MU. No 54 (F) Sqn ('L'). No 66 (F) Sqn ('E'). *Converted to Hunter Interim Mark 9.* No 54 (F) Sqn ('U'). Collided with XF446 near El Adem and crashed into sea; pilot killed.

XG274 ff 15-11-56 David Lockspeiser. Deld 3-1-57, No 5 MU. No 14 (F) Sqn ('P'). No 66 (F) Sqn. No 229 OCU. No 4 FTS ('71').

XG289 ff 26-11-56 Frank Bullen. Deld 6-2-57, No 33 MU. No 93 (F) Sqn. Crashed on take-off at Sylt, 29-10-57; pilot safe.

XG290 ff 20-11-56 David Lockspeiser. Deld 18-12-56, No 19 MU. A&AEE, miscellaneous trials.

XG291 ff 21-11-56 Duncan Simpson. Deld 3-1-57, No 19 MU. No 14 (F) Sqn. *Converted to Hunter FGA Mark 9*. Transferred to FAA, RNAS Brawdy, 10-76.

XG292 ff 27-11-56 David Lockspeiser. Deld 2-1-57, No 19 MU. No 14 (F) Sqn ('R'). No 26 (F) Sqn ('D'). Returned to HSA, 30-1-61. *Converted to Hunter FGA Mark 9*. Purchased by HSA, 5-4-70, as G-9-326. 2,894.55 FH. *Converted to Singaporean Hunter FR Mark 74A (512)*. Deld 4-8-71.

XG293 ff 3-12-56 David Lockspeiser. Deld 9-1-57, No 33 MU. No 4 (FR) Sqn ('V'). No 20 (F) Sqn ('D'). *Converted to Hunter FGA Mark 9*. Deld 23-1-62. Crashed and SOC, 21-4-64.

XG294 ff 29-11-56 David Lockspeiser. Deld 24-1-57, No 5 MU. No 93 (F) Sqn ('A'). No 2 (FR) Sqn ('W'). *Converted to Rhodesian Hunter FGA Mark 9 (122)*.

XG295 ff 27-11-56 Duncan Simpson. Deld 18-12-56, No 19 MU. No 14 (F) Sqn ('S'). Collided with XJ643, 11-5-57 (pilot unhurt); crashed but aircraft repaired. *Converted to Rhodesian Hunter FGA Mark 9 (121)*.

XG296 ff 30-11-56 David Lockspeiser. Deld 29-1-57, No 33 MU. No 93 (F) Sqn ('X'). Returned to HSA, 1960. *Converted to Hunter FGA Mark 9*. Deld 20-10-61, No 43 (F) Sqn ('A'). Purchased by HSA, 22-10-69, as G-9-303. 2,517.00 FH. *Converted to Singaporean Hunter FGA Mark 74 (510)*. Deld 4-3-71.

XG297 ff 3-12-56 Duncan Simpson. Deld 3-1-57, No 33 MU. No 4 (FR) Sqn ('Y'). *Converted to Hunter FGA Mark 9*. Deld 19-9-61, No 20 (F) Sqn ('Y'). No 28 (F) Sqn ('B'). Purchased by HSA, 8-3-76, as G-9-452. 3,099.00 FH. Awaiting final disposal, 7-79.

XG298 ff 29-11-56 Duncan Simpson. Deld 3-1-57, No 5 MU. No 4 (FR) Sqn ('X'). *Converted to Hunter FGA Mark 9*. Deld 25-10-61, No 43 (F) Sqn. ('J'). Transferred to Jordanian Air Force as Hunter FGA Mark 9 *(826)*, 12-67.

Fourth production batch of 45 aircraft built by Hawker Aircraft Ltd, Kingston-upon-Thames. First aircraft to be fitted with wing leading-edge extension from outset; gun-blast deflectors fitted retrospectively.

XJ632 ff 3-1-57 David Lockspeiser. Deld 24-1-57, No 5 MU. No 93 (F) Sqn ('H'). No 26 (F) Sqn ('H'). Returned to HSA, 30-1-61. *Converted to Hunter FGA Mark 9*. Deld 29-11-61, No 208 (F) Sqn ('K'). Purchased by HSA, 31-10-69, as G-9-302. 3,304.05 FH. *Converted to Singaporean Hunter FGA Mark 74 (505)*. Deld 10-12-70.

XJ633 ff 4-12-56 David Lockspeiser. Deld 15-2-57, No 5 MU. No 93 (F) Sqn. No 65 (F) Sqn ('Z'). Returned to HSA, 30-9-59. *Converted to Hunter FR Mark 10*. No 2 (FR) Sqn. Purchased by HSA, 2-3-71, as G-9-356. 2,495.10 FH. *Converted to Singaporean Hunter FR Mark 74B (534)*. Deld 21-2-73.

XJ634 ff 3-1-57 David Lockspeiser. Deld 24-1-57, No 33 MU. No 93 (F) Sqn ('V'). Transferred to FAA, RNAS, Brawdy, 10-76.

XJ635 ff 3-1-57 Duncan Simpson. Deld 1-3-57, No 5 MU. No 93 (F) Sqn ('F'). *Converted to Hunter FGA Mark 9*. Deld 27-7-65. Rebuilt by HSA, 1976. RNAS Brawdy ('B'), 1976. Crashed and SOC, 4-5-76; pilot killed.

XJ636 ff 18-12-56 Duncan Simpson. Deld 22-1-57, No 33 MU. No 4 (FR) Sqn. No 26 (F) Sqn ('K'). No 1 (F) Sqn ('D'), 1965. RNAS Brawdy. Aircraft crashed, 26-10-76, after fire

Appendix 2 175

in the air; pilot ejected safely.
XJ637 ff 3-1-57 Hugh Merewether. Deld 28-1-57, No 5 MU. No 4 (FR) Sqn. No 2 (FR) Sqn. No 229 OCU, 1964. Transferred to FAA, RNAS Brawdy, 10-76.
XJ638 ff 10-1-57 Duncan Simpson. Deld 27-5-57, No 5 MU. No 4 (FR) Sqn ('D'). *Converted to Rhodesian Hunter FGA Mark 9 (123).*
XJ639 ff 18-12-56 David Lockspeiser. Deld 11-3-57, No 33 MU. No 4 (FR) Sqn. No 229 OCU, 12-64.
XJ640 ff 3-1-57 Duncan Simpson. Deld 21-1-57, No 33 MU. No 4 (FR) Sqn. Returned to HSA, 1963. *Converted to Hunter FGA Mark 9.* Deld 2-7-65, No 1 (F) Sqn ('F'). Purchased by HSA, 15-1-75, as G-9-425. *Converted to Lebanese Hunter FGA Mark 70A (L.285).* Deld 1-6-77.
XJ641 ff 3-1-57 Duncan Simpson. Deld 5-2-57, No 33 MU. No 93 (F) Sqn. Lost at sea off Dutch coast, 11-11-59; pilot presumed drowned.
XJ642 ff 15-1-57 David Lockspeiser. Deld 29-1-57, No 5 MU. No 14 (F) Sqn ('A'). No 54 (F) Sqn ('L'). *Converted to Hunter FGA Mark 9.* Purchased by HSA, 9-2-70, as G-9-311. 2,700.50 FH. *Converted to Singaporean Hunter FGA Mark 74 (518).* Deld 20-5-71.
XJ643 ff 15-1-57 Duncan Simpson. Deld 4-3-57, No 5 MU. No 14 (F) Sqn. Damaged in collision with XG295, 11-5-57. Returned to HSA, 11-5-59. *Converted to Hunter FGA Mark 9.* No 208 (F) Sqn ('M'). No 28 (F) Sqn. Purchased by HSA, 6-2-70, as G-9-309. *Converted to Singaporean Hunter FGA Mark 74 (515).* Deld 24-3-71.
XJ644 ff 9-1-57 Duncan Simpson. Deld 11-2-57, No 33 MU. No 14 (F) Sqn. *Converted to Hunter FGA Mark 9.* No 54 (F) Sqn ('K'). Purchased by HSA, 20-1-75, as G-9-427. 2,635.45 FH. *Converted to Lebanese Hunter FGA Mark 70A (L.284).* Deld 17-5-77.
XJ645 ff 10-1-57 David Lockspeiser. Deld 5-2-57, No 33 MU. No 93 (F) Sqn. *Converted to Hunter FGA Mark 9.* Purchased by HSA, 11-4-68, as G-9-274. *Converted to Jordanian Hunter FGA Mark 73A (831).* Deld 19-5-69.
XJ646 ff 9-1-57 Duncan Simpson. Deld 5-2-57, No 19 MU. No 14 (F) Sqn ('D'). No 66 (F) Sqn. *Converted to Hunter FGA Mark 9.* Purchased by HSA, 25-4-68, as G-9-275. *Converted to Indian Hunter Mark 56A (A968).* Deld 31-7-69.

XJ673 ff 7-1-57 David Lockspeiser. Deld 11-2-57, No 33 MU. No 14 (F) Sqn ('E'). No 66 (F) Sqn. Returned to HSA, 8-60. *Converted to Hunter FGA Mark 9.* No 20 (F) Sqn ('XX').
XJ674 ff 16-1-57 David Lockspeiser. Deld 11-2-57, No 5 MU. No 4 (FR) Sqn. No 26 (F) Sqn ('L'). *Converted to Hunter FGA Mark 9.* Deld 11-6-65.
XJ675 ff 15-1-57 Hugh Merewether. Deld 15-2-57, No 5 MU. No 93 (F) Sqn. Aircraft crashed on take-off after flame-out, 8-1-60; pilot ejected safely.
XJ676 ff 6-2-57 Don Lucey. Deld 1-3-57, No 5 MU. No 93 (F) Sqn. No 2 (FR) Sqn, 2-61. No 229 OCU.
XJ677 ff 25-1-57 Duncan Simpson. Deld 4-3-57, No 5 MU. *Presented to Iraq by HM Government, 15-4-57 (394).*
XJ678 ff 10-1-57 Duncan Simpson. Deld 5-2-57, No 33 MU. *Presented to Iraq by HM Government, 15-4-57 (395).*
XJ679 ff 17-1-57 David Lockspeiser. Deld 20-3-57, No 5 MU. *Presented to Iraq by HM Government, 15-4-57 (396).*
XJ680 ff 18-2-57 Hugh Merewether. Deld 26-3-57, No 5 MU. No 20 (F) Sqn ('A'). Returned to HSA, 2-6-61. *Converted to Hunter FGA Mark 9.* Deld 11-10-61. Purchased by HSA, 16-12-69, as G-9-307. 3,127.00 FH. *Converted to Singaporean Hunter FGA Mark 74 (511).* Deld 4-3-71.
XJ681 ff 24-1-57 David Lockspeiser. Deld 21-2-57, No 5 MU. *Presented to Iraq by HM*

Government, 15-4-57 (397).

XJ682 ff 16-1-57 David Lockspeiser. Deld 26-3-57, No 5 MU. *Presented to Iraq by HM Government, 15-4-57 (398).*

XJ683 ff 7-2-57 Don Lucey. Deld 29-5-57, No 5 MU. No 93 (F) Sqn ('D'). *Converted to Hunter FGA Mark 9.* No 43 (F) Sqn ('L').

XJ684 ff 11-2-57 David Lockspeiser. Deld 26-3-57, No 5 MU. No 20 (F) Sqn ('B'). Returned to HSA, 2-1-61. *Converted to Hunter FGA Mark 9.* Deld 26-10-61, No 43 (F) Sqn ('D'). Purchased by HSA, 16-12-69, as G-9-308. *Converted to Singaporean Hunter FGA Mark 74 (513).* Deld 12-11-70.

XJ685 ff 8-2-57 Don Lucey. Deld 1-4-57, No 5 MU. No 20 (F) Sqn ('C'). Returned to HSA, 30-1-61. *Converted to Hunter FGA Mark 9.* Deld 9-1-62. Purchased by HSA, 4-11-69, as G-9-306. 2,801.15 FH. *Converted to Singaporean Hunter FGA Mark 74 (502).* Deld 12-11-70.

XJ686 ff 22-1-57 Duncan Simpson. Deld 26-3-57, No 5 MU. No 20 (F) Sqn ('D'). *Converted to Hunter FGA Mark 9.* Deld 11-12-61. Transferred to FAA, RNAS Brawdy, 10-76.

XJ687 ff 26-2-57 Frank Bullen. Deld 12-8-57, No 5 MU. No 66 (F) Sqn ('H'). Returned to HSA, 17-4-59. *Converted to Hunter FGA Mark 9.* Deld 19-1-60, No 208 (F) Sqn ('B'). Transferred to FAA, RNAS Brawdy, 10-76.

XJ688 ff 8-2-57 David Lockspeiser. Deld 26-3-57, No 5 MU. No 20 (F) Sqn ('E'). *Converted to Hunter FGA Mark 9.* Deld 9-1-62.

XJ689 ff 6-2-57 Duncan Simpson. Deld 20-3-57, No 5 MU. No 14 (F) Sqn. No 66 (F) Sqn. Returned to HSA, 30-1-61. *Converted to Hunter FGA Mark 9.* Deld 14-12-64. Purchased by HSA, 5-4-70, as G-9-327. 3,072.00 FH. *Converted to Singaporean Hunter FR Mark 74A (517).* Deld 4-8-71.

XJ690 ff 12-2-57 Duncan Simpson. Deld 26-3-57, No 5 MU. No 14 (F) Sqn ('H'). *Converted to Hunter FGA Mark 9.* Deld 27-10-64, No 20 (F) Sqn ('G'). Purchased by HSA, 2-76, as G-9-451. 2,637.00 FH. Awaiting final disposal, 1979.

XJ691 ff 8-2-57 Duncan Simpson. Deld 26-3-57, No 5 MU. No 14 (F) Sqn. No 66 (F) Sqn. *Converted to Hunter FGA Mark 9.* Deld 15-12-67, No 208 (F) Sqn. Missing in the Middle East, 4-67; believed crashed into sea.

XJ692 ff 18-2-57 Hugh Merewether. Deld 8-5-57, No 5 MU. No 20 (F) Sqn. Returned to HSA, 30-1-61. *Converted to Hunter FGA Mark 9.* Deld 7-12-61. Purchased by HSA, 6-4-68, as G-9-276. *Converted to Indian Hunter Mark 56A (A969).* Deld 23-9-69.

XJ693 ff 11-2-57 Duncan Simpson. Deld 8-5-57, No 5 MU. No 20 (F) Sqn ('X'). Written off in landing accident at Gutersloh, 3-10-60; pilot safe.

XJ694 ff 20-2-57 Hugh Merewether. CA aircraft, Dunsfold, 1957. No 208 (F) Sqn ('D'). Returned to HSA, 27-11-59. *Converted to Hunter FR Mark 10.* Deld 14-4-61, No 2 (FR) Sqn. Purchased by HSA, 17-2-71, as G-9-344. *Converted to Indian Hunter T Mark 66E (S.1389).* Deld 13-6-73.

XJ695 ff 11-2-57 Duncan Simpson. Deld 17-4-57, No 5 MU. No 20 (F) Sqn ('U'). No 14 (F) Sqn. *Converted to Hunter FGA Mark 9.* Deld 15-1-65. Transferred to FAA, RNAS Brawdy, 10-76.

XJ712 ff 22-2-57 Duncan Simpson. Deld 5-57, No 5 MU. No 20 (F) Sqn ('F'). No 14 (F) Sqn. No 1 (F) Sqn. Purchased by HSA, 1-4-66, as G-9-210. *Converted to Saudi Arabian Hunter F Mark 60 (60/601).* Deld 1966.

XJ713 ff 22-2-57 Duncan Simpson. Deld 5-57, No 5 MU. No 20 (F) Sqn. No 14 (F) Sqn. No 1 (F) Sqn. Purchased by HSA, 10-9-69, as G-9-298. *Converted to Chilean Hunter FGA Mark 71 (722).* Deld 21-12-70.

Appendix 2 177

XJ714 ff 13-2-57 Duncan Simpson. Deld 26-3-57, No 5 MU. Tropical trials, Idris, 6-57. No 208 (F) Sqn ('B'). Returned to HSA, 21-8-59. *Converted to Hunter FR Mark 10.* Deld 28-11-60. Purchased by HSA, 29-6-71, as G-9-365. 2,907.05 FH. *Converted to Singaporean Hunter FR Mark 74B (531).* Deld 17-1-73.

XJ715 ff 22-2-57 Frank Bullen. Deld 30-5-57, No 5 MU. No 111 (F) Sqn ('H'). No 229 OCU. Returned to HSA, 6-4-66, as G-9-213. *Converted to Saudi Arabian Hunter F Mark 60 (60/604),* 1966.

XJ716 ff 20-2-57 Duncan Simpson. Deld 5-57, No 5 MU. No 20 (F) Sqn ('T'). *Converted to Rhodesian Hunter FGA Mark 9 (124).*

XJ717 ff 25-2-57 Duncan Simpson. Deld 27-5-57, No 5 MU. No 20 (F) Sqn. No 26 (F) Sqn. No 1 (F) Sqn. No 54 (F) Sqn. Purchased by HSA, 5-7-67, as G-9-234. *Converted to Chilean Hunter FR Mark 71A (J-717).* Deld 24-9-68.

XJ718 ff 20-3-57 David Lockspeiser. Deld 8-5-57, No 5 MU. No 93 (F) Sqn ('B'). No 118 (F) Sqn. *Converted to Rhodesian Hunter FGA Mark 9 (117).*

Fifth production batch of 53 aircraft built by Hawker Aircraft Ltd, Kingston-upon-Thames. The original contract was for 153 aircraft, but the final 100 (XK225-XK241, XK257-XK306 and XK323-XK355) were cancelled by HM Government. Only the first 21 aircraft were originally delivered to the RAF.

XK136 ff 21-3-57 David Lockspeiser. Deld 19-8-57, No 5 MU. No 74 (F) Sqn. Returned to HSA, 1960. *Converted to Hunter FGA Mark 9.* No 20 (F) Sqn ('O'). Crashed in spin, 19-10-64; pilot ejected safely.

XK137 ff 11-3-57 Duncan Simpson. Deld 8-5-57, No 5 MU. No 20 (F) Sqn. Returned to HSA, 2-1-61. *Converted to Hunter FGA Mark 9.* No 43 (F) Sqn ('P'). No 54 (F) Sqn ('E'), 1965.

XK138 ff 21-3-57 Duncan Simpson. Deld 27-5-57, No 5 MU. No 14 (F) Sqn ('Y'). No 20 (F) Sqn.

XK139 ff 11-4-57 Duncan Simpson. Deld 12-8-57, No 5 MU. No 66 (F) Sqn ('G'). Returned to HSA, 2-1-61. *Converted to Hunter FGA Mark 9.* Deld 19-9-61, No 1 (F) Sqn ('X').

XK140 ff 29-3-57 Duncan Simpson. Deld 8-57, No 5 MU. No 74 (F) Sqn. Returned to HSA, 15-4-59. *Converted to Hunter FGA Mark 9.* Deld 4-2-60.

XK141 ff 15-4-57 David Lockspeiser. Deld 12-8-57, No 5 MU. No 74 (F) Sqn. No 229 OCU. Transferred to FAA, RNAS Brawdy, 10-76.

XK142 ff 8-4-57 Duncan Simpson. Deld 11-9-57, No 5 MU. No 74 (F) Sqn ('L'). Returned to HSA, 28-11-60. *Converted to Hunter FGA Mark 9.* Deld 7-9-61, No 20 (F) Sqn ('P'). Purchased by HSA, 5-5-71, as G-9-359. *Converted to Singaporean Hunter FR Mark 74B (522).* Deld 18-8-72.

XK143 fr 16-5-57 Duncan Simpson. Deld 8-57, No 5 MU. *Presented to Iraq by HM Government, 19-12-57 (400).*

XK144 ff 25-4-57 Duncan Simpson. Deld 8-57, No 5 MU. *Presented to Iraq by HM Government, 19-12-57 (401).*

XK145 ff 15-4-57 Duncan Simpson. Deld 21-8-57, No 5 MU. *Presented to Iraq by HM Government, 19-12-57 (402).*

XK146 ff 26-4-57 Duncan Simpson. Deld 8-57, No 19 MU. *Presented to Iraq by HM Government, 19-12-57 (403).*

XK147 ff 24-4-57 Duncan Simpson. Deld 8-57, No 19 MU. *Presented to Iraq by HM Government, 19-12-57 (404).*

XK148 ff 9-5-57 Duncan Simpson. Deld A&AEE. Purchased by HSA, 13-7-67, as G-9-235. *Converted to Chilean Hunter FR Mark 71A (J-715).* Deld 15-7-68.

XK149 ff 20-5-57 Duncan Simpson. Deld 26-9-57, No 5 MU. AFDS; tactical evaluation, 1958. No 1 (F) Sqn, 3-63. No 54 (F) Sqn, 7-63. No 229 OCU. Transferred to FAA, RNAS Brawdy, 10-76.

XK150 ff 30-5-57 Duncan Simpson, Deld 9-57, No 5 MU. AFDS; operational trials, Aden, 1958. *Converted to Hunter FGA Mark 9.* No 208 (F) Sqn. No 8 (F) Sqn, 1965. Transferred to Jordanian Air Force, 1968.

XK151 ff 16-6-57 Duncan Simpson. Deld 9-57, No 5 MU. AFDS; operational trials, Aden, 1958. *Converted to Hunter FGA Mark 9.* Transferred to FAA, RNAS Brawdy, 10-76.

XK152 ff 3-6-57 Duncan Simpson. Deld 17-9-57, No 19 MU. *Presented to Iraq by HM Government, 19-12-57 (405).*

XK153 ff 7-6-57 Duncan Simpson. Deld 17-9-57, No 19 MU. *Presented to Iraq by HM Government, 19-12-57 (406).*

XK154 ff 20-6-57 David Lockspeiser. Deld 23-8-57, No 19 MU. *Presented to Iraq by HM Government, 19-12-57 (407).*

XK155 ff 5-7-57 David Lockspeiser. Deld 23-9-57, No 19 MU. *Presented to Iraq by HM Government, 19-12-57 (408).*

XK156 ff 9-7-57 Duncan Simpson. Deld 1-10-57, No 19 MU. *Presented to Iraq by HM Government, 19-12-57 (409).*

XK157 *Completed as Indian Hunter Mark 56 (BA201).* ff 11-10-57 Flt Lt Carson. Deld 17-12-57, No 7 Sqn, IAF, Ambala.

XK158 *Completed as Indian Hunter Mark 56 (BA202).* ff 11-10-57 Flt Lt Carson. Deld 17-12-57, No 7 Sqn, IAF, Ambala.

XK159 *Completed as Indian Hunter Mark 56 (BA203).* ff 15-10-57 Duncan Simpson. Deld 17-12-57, No 17 Sqn, IAF, Poona.

XK160 *Completed as Indian Hunter Mark 56 (BA204).* ff 15-10-57 Duncan Simpson. Deld 17-12-57, No 7 Sqn, IAF, Ambala.

XK161 *Completed as Indian Hunter Mark 56 (BA205).* ff 19-10-57 Fg Off Karnik. Deld 25-10-57, No 7 Sqn, IAF, Ambala.

XK162 *Completed as Indian Hunter Mark 56 (BA206).* ff 21-10-57 Hugh Merewether. Deld 25-10-57, No 7 Sqn, IAF, Ambala.

XK163 *Completed as Indian Hunter Mark 56 (BA207).* ff 26-11-57 IAF pilot. Deld 26-11-57, No 7 Sqn, IAF, Ambala. No 17 Sqn, IAF, Poona.

XK164 *Completed as Indian Hunter Mark 56 (BA208).* ff 26-11-57 IAF pilot. Deld 26-11-57, No 17 Sqn, IAF, Poona.

XK165 *Completed as Indian Hunter Mark 56 (BA209).* ff 6-12-57 IAF pilot. Deld 6-12-57, No 17 Sqn, IAF, Poona.

XK166 *Completed as Indian Hunter Mark 56 (BA210).* ff 26-11-57 IAF pilot. Deld 26-11-57, No 17 Sqn, IAF, Poona.

XK167 *Completed as Indian Hunter Mark 56 (BA211).* ff 28-11-57 IAF pilot. Deld 28-11-57, No 17 Sqn, IAF, Poona.

XK168 *Completed as Indian Hunter Mark 56 (BA212).* ff 26-11-57 IAF pilot. Deld 26-11-57; crashed and SOC, 1958 (see *BA216*).

XK169 *Completed as Indian Hunter Mark 56 (BA213).* ff 28-11-57 IAF pilot. Deld 28-11-57, No 17 Sqn, IAF, Poona.

XK170 *Completed as Indian Hunter Mark 56 (BA214).* ff 28-11-57 IAF pilot. Deld 28-11-57, No 7 Sqn, IAF, Ambala.

XK171 *Completed as Indian Hunter Mark 56 (BA215).* ff 28-11-57 IAF pilot. Deld 28-11-57, No 17 Sqn, IAF; pilot abandoned take-off after loss of power, 14-5-58; aircraft badly damaged, but pilot safe. No 1 BRD.

XK172 *Completed as Indian Hunter Mark 56 (BA216).* ff 6-12-57 IAF pilot. Deld 6-12-57; collided with BA212 during formation aerobatics, 1958; both pilots ejected safely.
XK173 *Completed as Indian Hunter Mark 56 (BA217).* ff 6-12-57 IAF pilot. Deld 6-12-57, No 17 Sqn, IAF, Poona.
XK174 *Completed as Indian Hunter Mark 56 (BA218).* ff 6-12-57 IAF pilot. Deld 6-12-57, No 17 Sqn, IAF, Poona.
XK175 *Completed as Indian Hunter Mark 56 (BA219).* ff 9-12-57 David Lockspeiser. Deld 31-12-57, No 7 Sqn, IAF, Ambala.
XK176 *Completed as Indian Hunter Mark 56 (BA220).* ff 24-10-57 David Lockspeiser. Deld 6-12-57, No 17 Sqn, IAF, Poona.

XK213 *Completed as Indian Hunter Mark 56 (BA221).* ff 9-12-57 Frank Bullen. Deld 20-12-57, No 17 Sqn, IAF, Poona.
XK214 *Completed as Indian Hunter Mark 56 (BA222).* ff 6-12-57 Frank Bullen. Deld 6-12-57, No 7 Sqn, IAF, Ambala.
XK215 *Completed as Indian Hunter Mark 56 (BA223).* ff 6-12-57 IAF pilot. Deld 6-12-57, No 7 Sqn, IAF; aircraft seriously damaged, 3-6-58, after pilot abandoned take-off; pilot safe.
XK216 *Completed as Indian Hunter Mark 56 (BA224).* ff 6-12-57 IAF pilot. Deld 6-12-57, No 7 Sqn, IAF, Ambala.
XK217 *Completed as Indian Hunter Mark 56 (BA225).* ff 10-12-57 IAF pilot. Deld 10-12-57, No 7 Sqn, IAF, Ambala.
XK218 *Completed as Indian Hunter Mark 56 (BA226).* ff 10-12-57 IAF pilot. Deld 10-12-57, No 17 Sqn, IAF, Poona.
XK219 *Completed as Indian Hunter Mark 56 (BA227).* ff 6-12-57 Duncan Simpson. Deld 23-12-57, No 7 Sqn, IAF, Ambala.
XK220 *Completed as Indian Hunter Mark 56 (BA228).* ff 6-12-57 Duncan Simpson. Deld 23-12-57, No 7 Sqn, IAF, Ambala.
XK221 *Completed as Indian Hunter Mark 56 (BA229).* ff 20-12-57 IAF pilot. Deld 20-12-57, No 17 Sqn, IAF; aircraft destroyed in crash after flame-out, 4-6-58.
XK222 *Completed as Indian Hunter Mark 56 (BA230).* ff 11-12-57 David Lockspeiser. Deld 23-12-57, No 7 Sqn, IAF, Ambala.
XK223 *Completed as Indian Hunter Mark 56 (BA231).* ff 9-12-57 Duncan Simpson. Deld 31-12-57, No 7 Sqn, IAF, Ambala.
XK224 *Completed as Indian Hunter Mark 56 (BA232).* ff 19-12-57 Frank Bullen. Deld 31-12-57, No 7 Sqn, IAF, Ambala.

Single production batch of 100 aircraft built by Sir W.G. Armstrong Whitworth Aircraft Ltd, Coventry. Aircraft retrospectively fitted with wing leading-edge extensions and gun-blast deflectors. Contract No SP/6/9818/CB.7a. Production and delivery completed December 31 1956.
XF373 RR engine trials, Wymeswold, 1956. *Supplied to Jordan, 1958 (703) under US Offshore Payment.*
XF374 CA aircraft, Dunsfold, 1956-59; fuel system trials with early 230-gallon drop tanks. *Converted to Rhodesian Hunter FGA Mark 9 (127).*
XF375 CA aircraft, AWA, Wymeswold and Bittesfell, 1956-57. To English Electric Co, Warton, 1-59. ETPS, 23-4-63.
XF376 No 5 MU. A&AEE trials, 1956-57. Returned to HSA, 8-5-59. *Converted to Hunter FGA Mark 9.* Deld 26-2-60, No 208 (F) Sqn ('J'). Transferred to FAA, RNAS

Brawdy ('D'), 10-76.
XF377 CA aircraft, AWA, Bitteswell, 1956-57. *Supplied to Lebanon, 1958 (L.173) under US Offshore Payment.* Crashed, 26-3-62, on Bekka Plain while flying from Rayak, Lebanon; pilot ejected but killed.
XF378 CA aircraft, HAL, Dunsfold. P.1109B aircraft with complete DH Firestreak missile system. Trials at Hatfield and Valley, 1957. Cannibalised, 1959, after fuselage fire.
XF379 CA aircraft, HAL, Dunsfold, 1956-57; TI of lateral fuselage airbrakes. *Supplied to Jordan, 1958 (709), under US Offshore Payment.*
XF380 No 19 MU. CA aircraft, Dunsfold, 1957. *Supplied to Jordan, 1958 (710), under US Offshore Payment.*
XF381 A&AEE, Boscombe Down, for miscellaneous trials, 1957. *Supplied to Jordan, 1958 (711), under US Offshore Payment.*
XF382 No 65 (F) Sqn ('Q'). No 92 (F) Sqn. DFCS ('R'). Transferred to FAA, RNAS Brawdy, 10-76.
XF383 No 1 (F) Sqn. No 65 (F) Sqn ('V'). No 263 (F) Sqn ('F'). No 229 OCU ('14').
XF384 No 92 (F) Sqn. No 111 (F) Sqn. DFLS. DFCS ('U'). No 229 OCU. No 4 FTS. Collided with XF387 at Valley, 10-8-72; pilot killed.
XF385 No 92 (F) Sqn. No 65 (F) Sqn ('M').
XF386 No 65 (F) Sqn ('C'). No 92 (F) Sqn ('C'). No 229 OCU, 4-61.
XF387 No 5 MU. No 63 (F) Sqn ('D'). No 229 OCU. No 4 FTS. Collided with XF384 at Valley, 10-8-72; pilot and one person on the ground killed.
XF388 RR engine trials. CA aircraft, Bitteswell, 1957. No 65 (F) Sqn. Returned to HSA, 13-5-59. *Converted to Hunter FGA Mark 9.* Deld 5-4-60, No 19 MU.
XF389 No 92 (F) Sqn. DFLS. No 56 (F) Sqn. No 229 OCU. Purchased by HSA, 23-5-68, as G-9-271. *Converted to Jordanian Hunter FGA Mark 73A (829).* Deld 19-5-69.

XF414 No 19 MU. No 56 (F) Sqn ('P'). No 63 (F) Sqn ('P'). Returned to HSA, 1961. *Converted to Hunter FGA Mark 9.* No 20 (F) Sqn ('E'). Crashed after engine failure near Tengah, 20-2-67; pilot safe.
XF415 No 19 MU, St Athan. Stored 1957-58. No 26 (F) Sqn, 1959. Transferred to Jordanian Air Force, 6-62 to 10-62.
XF416 No 33 MU. No 43 (F) Sqn. No 111 (F) Sqn ('T'). *Converted to Hunter FGA Mark 9.* Transferred to FAA, RNAS Brawdy, 10-76.
XF417 No 19 MU, St Athan. Stored, 1957-58. No 26 (F) Sqn, 1958. Transferred to Jordanian Air Force, 6-62 to 10-62.
XF418 No 33 MU. AFDS. DFLS ('T'). DFCS. Transferred to FAA, RNAS Brawdy, 10-76.
XF419 No 19 MU. No 74 (F) Sqn ('C'). *Converted to Hunter FGA Mark 9.* No 1 (F) Sqn ('Q', later 'X').
XF420 No 5 MU. DFLS ('R'). No 54 (F) Sqn, 11-62.
XF421 No 5 MU. No 54 (F) Sqn ('P'). Returned to HSA, 27-4-59. *Converted to Hunter FGA Mark 9.* No 208 (F) Sqn ('H').
XF422 No 5 MU. Stored, 1957-58. No 208 (F) Sqn ('X'). Returned to HSA, 4-12-59. *Converted to Hunter FR Mark 10.* Deld 11-4-61. Purchased by HSA, 2-3-71, as G-9-361. 2,491.45 FH. *Converted to Singaporean Hunter FR Mark 74B (524).* Deld 22-8-72.
XF423 No 5 MU. Stored by No 33 MU, 1957-58. No 93 (F) Sqn. Transferred to Jordanian Air Force, 6-62 to 10-62.
XF424 No 5 MU. No 43 (F) Sqn. No 111 (F) Sqn. No 247 (F) Sqn ('V'). Returned to HSA, 1959. *Converted to Hunter FGA Mark 9.* ff 25-9-59 Duncan Simpson. Deld 3-11-59, No 8 (F) Sqn; believed to have crashed.

Striking picture of Hunter 6, XF389, with drop tanks and 24 three-in rockets. This late production aircraft is fitted with wing leading-edge extensions, and gun-blast deflectors.

XF425 No 5 MU. Stored by No 33 MU, 1958. No 74 (F) Sqn. Collided with XF502 at night near Norwich, 26-8-59, and SOC.
XF426 No 5 MU. Returned to HSA, 1960. No 208 (F) Sqn ('Y'). *Converted to Hunter FR Mark 10.* Deld 24-1-61. *Presented to Jordan (853); later passed to Oman, 1976.*
XF427 No 5 MU. No 54 (F) Sqn. Crashed on Isle of Wight, 13-3-57; pilot, who was killed, had been passed wrong weather information.
XF428 No 5 MU. No 208 (F) Sqn ('S'). Returned to HSA, 1960. *Converted to Hunter FR Mark 10.* ff 2-11-60 David Lockspeiser. Deld 21-4-61. Purchased by HSA, 7-7-71, as G-9-362. 2,717.25 FH. *Converted to Singaporean Hunter FR Mark 74B (525).* Deld 11-10-72.
XF429 No 33 MU. Returned to HAL, 1957. *Converted to Prototype Hunter FR Mark 10.* ff 7-11-58. Passed to RAF, 7-3-66. Purchased by HSA, 4-71, as G-9-373. *Converted to Swiss Hunter Mark 58A (J-4131).* Deld 10-1-74.
XF430 No 5 MU. No 43 (F) Sqn. No 111 (F) Sqn. Returned to HSA, 1964. *Converted to Hunter FGA Mark 9.* Deld 9-7-65. Purchased by HSA, 16-1-75, as G-9-426. *Converted to Lebanese Hunter FGA Mark 70A (L.283).* Deld 17-5-77.
XF431 No 5 MU. No 54 (F) Sqn ('D'). No 43 (F) Sqn. *Converted to Hunter FGA Mark 9.* No 43 (F) Sqn.
XF432 No 5 MU. Returned to HSA, 14-10-59. *Converted to Hunter FR Mark 10.* ff 11-60 Don Lucey. Deld 21-12-60. Purchased by HSA, 14-5-71, as G-9-363. 2,674.05 FH. *Converted to Singaporean Hunter FR Mark 74B (526).* Deld 10-11-72.
XF433 No 19 MU. No 65 (F) Sqn ('G'). No 263 (F) Sqn. No 229 OCU. Collided with XE594 during formation aerobatics, 7-3-63; pilot ejected safely.
XF434 No 5 MU. No 247 (F) Sqn. No 43 (F) Sqn. Aircraft dived into the sea off Akrotiri, Cyprus, 11-4-60; pilot killed.
XF435 No 5 MU. No 247 (F) Sqn. No 43 (F) Sqn ('P'). *Converted to Hunter FGA Mark 9.* No 8 (F) Sqn ('E'). Transferred to FAA, RNAS Brawdy, 10-76.

XF436 No 5 MU. Returned to HSA, 14-11-59. *Converted to Hunter FR Mark 10.* Deld 24-2-61. Purchased by HSA, 27-3-70, as G-9-321. 2,200.00 FH. *Converted to Swiss Hunter Mark 58A (J-4115).* Deld 1-9-72.

XF437 No 5 MU. No 247 (F) Sqn ('A'). No 43 (F) Sqn. *Converted to Hunter FGA Mark 9.* Purchased by HSA, 6-4-70 as G-9-324. *Converted to Singaporean Hunter FR Mark 74A (503).* Deld 24-6-71.

XF438 No 5 MU. No 208 (F) Sqn ('H'). Returned to HSA, 14-10-59. *Converted to Hunter FR Mark 10.* ff 11-60 Duncan Simpson. Deld 11-1-61. Purchased by HSA, 3-6-70, as G-9-333. 2,709.30 FH. *Converted to Swiss Hunter Mark 58A (J-4102).* Deld 24-12-71.

XF439 No 5 MU. No 247 (F) Sqn. No 43 (F) Sqn. No 19 (F) Sqn. No 54 (F) Sqn. No 1 (F) Sqn.

XF440 No 5 MU. No 247 (F) Sqn ('D'). No 43 (F) Sqn ('U'). *Converted to Hunter FGA Mark 9.* Written off in Middle East; pilot safe.

XF441 No 5 MU. No 19 MU. No 208 (F) Sqn ('P'). Returned to HSA, 2-11-59. *Converted to Hunter FR Mark 10.* Deld 7-2-61. Purchased by HSA, 1-10-71, as G-9-377. *Converted to Singaporean Hunter FR Mark 74B (545).* Deld 16-8-73.

XF442 No 19 MU. No 247 (F) Sqn ('Z'). No 43 (F) Sqn. Returned to HSA, 1-6-59. *Converted to Hunter FGA Mark 9.* ff 10-3-60 Flt Lt Tilak. Used for air firing trials with rocket projectiles, 1962.

XF443 No 5 MU. No 65 (F) Sqn ('E'). No 92 (F) Sqn. No 229 OCU. Crashed on night landing approach at Chivenor, 3-8-67; pilot ejected safely.

XF444 No 5 MU. *Supplied to Jordan, 14-11-58 (705) under US Offshore Payment.*

XF445 No 5 MU. No 263 (F) Sqn. No 1 (F) Sqn ('Z'). *Converted to Hunter FGA Mark 9.* No 43 (F) Sqn ('R'). No 1 (F) Sqn.

XF446 No 19 MU. No 111 (F) Sqn ('R'). Returned to HSA, 12-64. *Converted to Hunter FGA Mark 9.* Damaged in collision and returned to HSA, 6-68 as G-9-277. *Converted to Indian Hunter Mark 56A (A1010).* Deld 23-9-69.

XF447 No 33 MU. No 65 (F) Sqn ('H'). No 92 (F) Sqn. Purchased by HSA, 17-9-69, as G-9-299. *Converted to Chilean Hunter FGA Mark 71 (J-723).* Deld 31-12-70.

XF448 No 5 MU. Stored by No 19 MU, 1958. No 74 (F) Sqn. Crashed into sea during tailchase, 21-8-58; pilot killed.

XF449 No 5 MU. No 263 (F) Sqn. No 19 (F) Sqn. Written off, 18-10-63.

XF450 No 5 MU. DFCS. No 74 (F) Sqn. No 229 OCU. Returned to HSA, 1-4-66 as G-9-211. *Converted to Saudi Arabian Hunter F Mark 60 (60/603), 1966.*

XF451 No 5 MU. No 247 (F) Sqn. No 229 OCU. SOC after landing accident, 20-7-62, Chivenor; pilot unhurt.

XF452 No 19 MU. CA aircraft, AWA, Bitteswell, 1957. A&AEE, miscellaneous trials, 1958. *Supplied to Jordan, 12-11-58 (708) under US Offshore Payment.*

XF453 No 5 MU. No 54 (F) Sqn. No 247 (F) Sqn. DFCS. Purchased by HSA, 14-7-67, as G-9-233. *Converted to Chilean Hunter FR Mark 71A (J-716).* Deld 1-8-68.

XF454 No 19 MU. No 247 (F) Sqn. No 43 (F) Sqn. Returned to HSA, 17-3-59. *Converted to Hunter FGA Mark 9.* ff 24-11-59 David Lockspeiser. Deld 18-12-59, No 208 (F) Sqn. No 43 (F) Sqn, 1965. Transferred to Jordanian Air Force *(816)*, 1968.

XF455 No 5 MU. No 247 (F) Sqn ('B'). No 43 (F) Sqn. *Converted to Hunter FGA Mark 9.* ff 7-11-59 Bill Bedford. Deld 3-12-59, No 20 (F) Sqn. Crashed into sea off Singapore, 19-9-64; pilot killed.

XF456 No 5 MU. No 247 (F) Sqn. No 43 (F) Sqn ('A'). *Converted to Hunter FGA Mark 9.* No 43 (F) Sqn. Purchased by HSA, 9-10-69, as G-9-301. 2,967.05 FH. *Converted to Singaporean Hunter FGA Mark 74 (509).* Deld 14-1-71.

XF457 No 19 MU. Stored by No 5 MU, 1958. No 208 (F) Sqn ('V'). *Converted to Hunter*

Appendix 2 183

FR Mark 10. Deld 30-1-61, No 2 (FR) Sqn ('A'). Purchased by HSA, 23-7-74, as G-9-422. 2,682.10 FH. *Converted to Lebanese Hunter FGA Mark 70A (L.281).* Deld 8-12-75.
XF458 No 5 MU. Stored, 1958. No 208 (F) Sqn ('Z'). *Converted to Hunter FR Mark 10.* No 2 (FR) Sqn ('W'). Purchased by HSA, 5-71, as G-9-364. *Converted to Singaporean Hunter FR Mark 74B (527).* Deld 11-10-72.
XF459 No 5 MU. Returned to HSA, 1960. *Converted to Hunter FR Mark 10.* ff 19-9-60 David Lockspeiser. Deld 1-12-60. Purchased by HSA, 2-3-71, as G-9-355. 2,694.25 FH. *Converted to Indian Hunter T Mark 66E (S.1393).* Deld 13-12-73.
XF460 Deld 6-2-57, No 5 MU. No 208 (F) Sqn ('T'). *Converted to Hunter FR Mark 10.* Deld 28-3-61. Repurchased by HSA, 10-71, as G-9-378. *Converted to Singaporean Hunter FR Mark 74B (546).* Deld 11-10-73.
XF461 No 5 MU. *Supplied to Lebanon, 1958 (L.171) under US Offshore Payment.*
XF462 No 5 MU. No 66 (F) Sqn. Returned to HSA, 17-4-59. *Converted to Hunter FGA Mark 9.* ff 30-12-59 Don Lucey. Deld 4-2-60. Purchased by HSA, 24-3-70, as G-9-320. *Converted to Swiss Hunter Mark 58A (J-4107).* Deld 12-4-72.
XF463 No 5 MU. Returned to HAL, 1957. *Converted to Indian Hunter Mark 56 (BA241).* ff 21-2-58 Fg Off Dey. Deld 13-5-58, No 27 Sqn, IAF, Ambala.

XF495 No 5 MU. *Supplied to Lebanon, 13-10-58 (L.175) under US Offshore Payment.*
XF496 No 5 MU. *Supplied to Jordan, 12-11-58 (706) under US Offshore Payment.*
XF497 No 5 MU. Returned to HAL, 1957. *Converted to Indian Hunter Mark 56 (BA242).* ff 27-2-58 Fg Off Dey. Deld 12-5-58, No 27 Sqn, IAF, Ambala.
XF498 No 5 MU. *Supplied to Jordan, 12-11-58 (704) under US Offshore Payment.*
XF499 No 5 MU. Returned to HAL, 1957. *Converted to Indian Hunter Mark 56 (BA243).* ff 10-3-58 Duncan Simpson. Deld 15-5-58. Crashed and SOC, 1959.
XF500 No 5 MU. Returned to HAL, 1957. *Converted to Indian Hunter Mark 56 (BA240).* ff 14-2-58 Flt Lt Chopra. Deld 12-5-58, No 27 Sqn, IAF, Ambala.
XF501 No 5 MU. Returned to HAL, 1957. *Converted to Indian Hunter Mark 56 (BA244).* ff 6-3-58 Flt Lt Chopra. Deld 15-5-58, No 27 Sqn, IAF, Ambala.
XF502 No 5 MU. Stored, 1958. No 74 (F) Sqn ('K'). Collided with XF425 at night in the Norwich area, and SOC, 26-8-59.
XF503 No 5 MU. Returned to HAL, 1957. *Converted to Indian Hunter Mark 56 (BA245).* ff 27-3-58 Frank Bullen. Deld 9-6-58, No 27 Sqn, IAF, Ambala.
XF504 No 5 MU. Stored, 1958. No 74 (F) Sqn ('B'). *Converted to Rhodesian Hunter FGA Mark 9 (125).*
XF505 No 5 MU. Returned to HAL, 1957. *Converted to Indian Hunter Mark 56 (BA246).* ff 21-3-58 Flt Lt Chopra. Deld 19-5-58, No 27 Sqn, IAF, Ambala.
XF506 No 5 MU. No 111 (F) Sqn ('X'). No 263 (F) Sqn. *Converted to Rhodesian Hunter FGA Mark 9 (119).*
XF507 No 5 MU. No 65 (F) Sqn ('A')' Written off, 30-5-60.
XF508 No 19 MU. No 54 (F) Sqn. No 111 (F) Sqn. AFDS. Returned to HSA, 15-11-60. *Converted to Hunter FGA Mark 9.* Deld 19-7-61, No 5 MU. No 20 (F) Sqn ('D').
XF509 No 5 MU. No 54 (F) Sqn ('M'). To Bristol, 17-4-63, for use as chase plane for Fairey FD-2 conversion. No 4 FTS, c 1965.
XF510 No 19 MU. North Weald Stn Flt. Crashed on landing at North Weald, 30-7-57; pilot killed and aircraft SOC.
XF511 No 19 MU. No 74 (F) Sqn ('P'). No 111 (F) Sqn. *Converted to Hunter FGA Mark 9.* No 8 (F) Sqn. Transferred to FAA, RNAS Brawdy, 10-76.
XF512 No 33 MU. DFLS. Damaged in accident, 19-3-57, and repaired. Purchased by HSA, 2-12-69 as G-9-313. *Converted to Chilean Hunter FGA Mark 71 (725).* Deld 24-3-71.

XF513 No 5 MU. No 54 (F) Sqn. Aircraft crashed on landing and SOC, 1-9-58; pilot escaped.
XF514 No 5 MU. No 247 (F) Sqn ('P'). No 43 (F) Sqn. DFCS ('F'). Transferred to Jordanian Air Force, 1-68.
XF515 Deld 4-12-56, No 5 MU. No 247 (F) Sqn ('W'). No 43 (F) Sqn ('R'). Transferred to FAA, RNAS Brawdy, 10-76.
XF516 No 19 MU. No 56 (F) Sqn ('E'). No 92 (F) Sqn ('N'). Damaged in accident, Linton, 8-2-57; pilot safe. No 229 OCU, 17-3-61. Eventually achieved the highest total of FH by a Hunter in RAF service: 5,096 FH (at 2-80).
XF517 No 19 MU. No 92 (F) Sqn ('L'). No 111 (F) Sqn. No 54 (F) Sqn. Returned to HSA, 1961. *Converted to Hunter FGA Mark 9.* No 54 (F) Sqn ('V')'
XF518 No 33 MU. No 66 (F) Sqn. No 92 (F) Sqn. Transferred to Jordanian Air Force, 6-62 to 10-62.
XF519 No 19 MU. No 66 (F) Sqn. *Converted to Hunter FGA Mark 9.* No 1 (F) Sqn ('Q').
XF520 No 5 MU. No 92 (F) Sqn ('K'). Purchased by HSA, 6-66, as G-9-208. *Converted to Jordanian Hunter FGA Mark 73 (814).* Deld 13-6-68.
XF521 No 5 MU. No 66 (F) Sqn ('E'). No 92 (F) Sqn ('X'). Purchased by HSA, 6-9-67, as G-9-243. *Converted to Indian Hunter Mark 56A (A938).* Deld 22-3-69.
XF522 No 5 MU. No 92 (F) Sqn. Crashed after abandoning take-off at Nicosia, 11-1-58; pilot safe; aircraft written off for spares.
XF523 No 5 MU. No 54 (F) Sqn ('N'). *Converted to Hunter FGA Mark 9.* No 54 (F) Sqn. Crashed and SOC, 24-6-63.
XF524 No 5 MU. No 111 (F) Sqn. No 54 (F) Sqn ('S'). Crashed into hill in Cyprus and SOC, 5-11-57; pilot killed.
XF525 No 5 MU. No 19 (F) Sqn ('O'). No 263 (F) Sqn. No 111 (F) Sqn. Crashed at North Weald during aerobatic rehearsal, 7-6-57; pilot killed and aircraft SOC.
XF526 Deld 7-9-56, No 5 MU. No 63 (F) Sqn ('C'). No 111 (F) Sqn. No 56 (F) Sqn ('C'). No 229 OCU ('9').
XF527 Deld 17-10-56, No 19 MU. No 19 (F) Sqn ('J'). No 66 (F) Sqn ('S'). No 111 (F) Sqn ('F'). AFDS ('T').

Production batch of 50 aircraft to have been built by Hawker Aircraft (Blackpool) Ltd. Contract No SP/6/13132/CB.7a dated April 22 1955. Contract cancelled by HM Government in February 1957. Aircraft were allocated as XJ945-XJ959, XK971-XK997 and XK103-XK111.

Hawker Hunter T Mark 7

Production batch of 45 new-build aircraft built by Hawker Aircraft Ltd, Kingston-upon-Thames. Contract No 6/12626/CB.9c. Original contract called for 55 aircraft, but ten were transferred to the Admiralty as Hunter T Mark 8s (*qv*).
XL563 ff 11-10-57 Frank Bullen. CA aircraft, HAL. Deld 19-12-57, A&AEE. To Bristol, 13-1-61, as chase plane for Bristol Type 188 trials.
XL564 ff 8-1-58 Frank Bullen. CA aircraft, HSA. Deld 10-3-60, A&AEE. UHF trials, A&AEE, 5-10-61.
XL565 ff 3-2-58 Frank Bullen. CA aircraft, RR. No 208 (F) Sqn. No 1417 Flt. No 8 (F) Sqn.
XL566 ff 20-2-58 Duncan Simpson. CA aircraft, HSA. Deld 4-58, A&AEE. Tropical trials, Bahrein, 20-6-58. No 43 (F) Sqn.
XL567 ff 27-2-58 Frank Bullen. Deld 30-5-58, No 229 OCU. IRS ('Z'). No 4 FTS ('84').

First production Hunter T Mark 7 with two 100-gallon drop tanks and 24 three-in rocket projectiles at Dunsfold.

XL568 ff 6-3-58 Duncan Simpson. Deld 20-10-58, No 74 (F) Sqn. *Converted to Hunter T Mark 7A*, 1963. No 74 (F) Sqn ('X').
XL569 ff 3-4-58 Frank Bullen. Deld 1-7-58, No 229 OCU (ES-85).
XL570 ff 15-3-58 Frank Bullen. Deld 30-6-58, No 229 OCU. Crashed into sea after take-off, 29-8-58; instructor and Jordanian student pilot killed; aircraft SOC.
XL571 ff 29-3-58 Hugh Merewether. Deld 22-7-58, No 229 OCU (ES-87). IRS ('X'). No 92 (F) Sqn. RNAS Brawdy, 11-76.
XL572 ff 2-4-58 Frank Bullen. Deld 1-7-58, No 229 OCU (ES-83). Aircraft entered inverted spin, 27-8-59; student pilot ejected but was killed; instructor recovered from spin and landed safely.
XL573 ff 17-4-58 Duncan Simpson. Deld 17-7-58, DFLS. AFDS. DFCS ('L'). No 229 OCU.
XL574 ff 18-4-58 Duncan Simpson. Deld 13-11-58, A&AEE. CA aircraft. HSA, windscreen rain dispersal and de-icing trials; fatigue tested to destruction, 11-61.
XL575 ff 29-4-58 Frank Bullen. Deld 7-58, No 229 OCU (ES-88). IRS ('Y').
XL576 ff 30-4-58 Duncan Simpson. Deld 25-7-58, No 229 OCU (ES-81). RNAS Brawdy, 11-76.
XL577 ff 30-4-58 Frank Bullen. Deld 15-7-58, No 229 OCU (ES-82). RNAS Brawdy, 11-76.
XL578 ff 27-5-58 David Lockspeiser. Deld 15-7-58, No 229 OCU (ES-89). RNAS Brawdy, 11-76.
XL579 ff 13-5-58 David Lockspeiser. Deld 29-7-58, No 229 OCU (ES-92). ETPS, Farnborough (fitted with nose probe), 27-9-68.

XL583 ff 28-5-58 David Lockspeiser. Deld 1-7-58, No 229 OCU (ES-84). RNAS Brawdy, 11-76.

XL586 ff 27-6-58 Duncan Simpson. Deld 6-8-58, No 229 OCU (ES-90). IRS. RNAS Brawdy, 11-76.
XL587 ff 17-7-58 Duncan Simpson. Deld 6-8-58, No 229 OCU (ES-91). RNAS Brawdy (86), 11-76.

XL591 ff 6-8-58 Duncan Simpson. Deld 18-9-58, DFLS. DFCS ('M'). AFDS. No 4 FTS (82), 1967.
XL592 ff 30-8-58 Duncan Simpson. Deld 29-9-58, No 229 OCU (ES-93). RNAS Brawdy (84), 11-76.
XL593 ff 30-8-58 Don Lucey. Deld 29-9-58, DFCS. AFDS ('N')'
XL594 ff 10-9-58 Duncan Simpson. Deld 6-10-58, IRS. No 19 (F) Sqn, 13-7-59. No 111 (F) Sqn 20-1-61.
XL595 ff 4-9-58 David Lockspeiser. Deld 9-10-58, AFDS. DFCS ('O')' RNAS Brawdy, 11-76.
XL596 ff 17-9-58 David Lockspeiser. Deld 6-8-58, No 54 (F) Sqn ('LIV'). No 4 FTS. Crashed on GCA at Valley, 11-73.
XL597 ff 22-9-58 David Lockspeiser. Deld 31-10-58, No 66 (F) Sqn. No 208 (F) Sqn ('Y').

XL600 ff 7-10-58 Duncan Simpson. Deld 14-11-58, No 65 (F) Sqn. Wattisham Stn Flt. On 10-4-63 the second pilot was ejected during a slow roll due to the seat not being locked, and was killed. No 4 FTS (83), 1967.
XL601 ff 15-10-58 David Lockspeiser. Deld 3-11-58, No 1 (F) Sqn. No 19 (F) Sqn.

XL605 ff 14-10-58 David Lockspeiser. Deld 1-12-58, No 92 (F) Sqn ('T'). No 66 (F) Sqn. Purchased by HSA, 6-4-66 as G-9-214. *Converted to Saudi Arabian Hunter T Mark 70 (70/617).* Deld 7-6-66. Returned to RAF, 7-74, and deld No 229 OCU, as XX467.

XL609 ff 1-12-58 David Lockspeiser. Deld 22-12-58, No 56 (F) Sqn. To HSA, 1-4-65, for conversion to Hunter T Mark 7A. Contract cancelled and aircraft returned to RAF. No 4 FTS (80).
XL610 ff 12-11-58 Hugh Merewether. Deld 23-1-59, No 111 (F) Sqn ('Z'). Wattisham Stn Flt. Crashed, 7-6-62; both pilots killed.
XL611 ff 11-12-58 Duncan Simpson. Deld 20-1-59, No 5 MU. No 43 (F) Sqn. *Converted to Hunter T Mark 7A,* 1963. No 43 (F) Sqn. A&AEE. Crashed on take-off at Boscombe Down, 14-5-68; both pilots killed.
XL612 ff 12-12-58 Frank Bullen. Deld 23-1-59, No 5 MU. No 402 WTS, Sylt. No 43 (F) Sqn.
XL613 ff 19-12-58 Duncan Simpson. Deld 23-1-59, No 5 MU. Khormaksar Stn Flt. No 43 (F) Sqn. No 8 (F) Sqn.
XL614 ff 1-1-59 Hugh Merewether. Deld 3-2-59, No 5 MU. *Converted to Hunter T Mark 7A.* No 402 WTS, Sylt.
XL615 ff 7-1-59 Hugh Merewether. Deld 27-1-59, No 19 MU. Khormaksar Stn Flt. No 8 (F) Sqn. Aircraft flew into high ground at night near Khormaksar, 1-6-60; both pilots killed.
XL616 ff 3-1-59 Hugh Merewether. Deld 3-2-59, No 19 MU. *Converted to Hunter T Mark 7A.* No 402 WTS, Sylt.
XL617 ff 3-1-59 Duncan Simpson. Deld 27-1-59, No 5 MU. Jever Stn Flt ('A'). No 229 OCU, 7-64.
XL618 ff 10-1-59 David Lockspeiser. Deld 4-2-59, No 5 MU. Gutersloh Stn Flt. Jever Stn Flt. No 229 OCU, 4-64. RNAS Brawdy (87), 11-76.
XL619 ff 7-1-59 David Lockspeiser. Deld 3-2-59, No 5 MU. Gutersloh Stn Flt. No 20 (F) Sqn.
XL620 ff 13-1-59 Flt Lt Gole, IAF. Deld 3-2-59, No 5 MU. No 66 (F) Sqn. No 74 (F) Sqn. Purchased by HSA, 31-3-66, as G-9-215. *Converted to Saudi Arabian Hunter T*

Appendix 2 187

Mark 70 (70/616). Deld 2-5-66. Returned to RAF, 7-74, and deld No 229 OCU as XX466.
XL621 ff 9-1-59 Duncan Simpson. Deld 4-2-59, No 5 MU. Gutersloh Stn Flt ('C'), 8-59. Jever Stn Flt, 4-61.
XL622 ff 15-1-59 Duncan Simpson. Deld 4-2-59, No 5 MU. Jever Stn Flt ('J'). No 4 FTS, 1967.
XL623 ff 17-1-59 Flt Lt Gole, IAF. Deld 4-2-59, No 5 MU. No 65 (F) Sqn. No 208 (F) Sqn. No 92 (F) Sqn. No 43 (F) Sqn. No 1 (F) Sqn. No 19 (F) Sqn. No 74 (F) Sqn. RNAS Brawdy (88), 11-76.

Conversion order for six Hunter F Mark 4s to be brought to T Mark 7 standard by Hawker Aircraft Ltd and Sir W.G. Armstrong Whitworth Aircraft Ltd during 1957-58 and delivered between February 1959 and May 1959. See under Hunter F Mark 4, WV253, WV372, WV318, WV383; XF310 and XF321.

Hawker Hunter T Mark 8

Production batch of ten new-build aircraft to be built by Hawker Aircraft Ltd, Kingston-upon-Thames. Transferred from Contract No 12626 (for Hunter T Mark 7s) to Admiralty. One Aden gun; tail parachute and aircraft arrestor hook.
XL580 ff 30-5-58 David Lockspeiser. Deld 30-7-58, FAA. No 764 Sqn, FAA. Flag Officer (Flying Training), FAA. RNAS Yeovilton, 6-62. *Converted to Hunter T Mark 8M* by BAe, Brough, 6-80, with Blue Fox equipment as trainer for Sea Harrier; reserve aircraft.
XL581 ff 30-5-58 Frank Bullen. Deld 1-5-58, FAA. RNAS Lossiemouth. Crashed on Lossiemouth airfield during low level roll, 6-8-58, and destroyed; one pilot killed.
XL582 ff 17-6-58 Frank Bullen. Deld 1-8-58, FAA. RNAS Lossiemouth. RNAS Yeovilton. No 738 Sqn, FAA. Aircraft crashed on take-off after engine failure, 26-1-68; pilots safe.

XL584 ff 8-9-58 David Lockspeiser. Deld 6-10-58, FAA. No 764 Sqn, FAA. Flag Officer (Flying Training), FAA.
XL585 ff 14-10-58 Duncan Simpson. Deld 29-10-58, RAE Bedford. RNAS Lossiemouth. No 764 Sqn, FAA. No 700 Sqn, FAA. No 738 Sqn, FAA.

XL598 ff 15-10-58 David Lockspeiser. Deld 1-12-58, FAA. No 764 Sqn, FAA. No 738 Sqn, FAA.
XL599 ff 4-11-58 David Lockspeiser. Deld 9-12-58, FAA. No 764 Sqn, FAA. Collided with WT701, 23-8-61, and SOC.

XL602 ff 18-11-58 Duncan Simpson. Deld 30-12-58, FAA. No 764 Sqn. FAA. No 759 Sqn, FAA, 8-64. *Converted to Hunter T Mark 8M* by BAe, Brough, 3-80, with Blue Fox equipment as trainer for Sea Harrier; reserve aircraft.
XL603 ff 6-12-58 David Lockspeiser. Deld 13-1-59, FAA. RNAS Lossiemouth. RNAS Yeovilton, Instrument Flt. No 759 Sqn, FAA, 8-64. Fitted with 'Turreen', 9-65. *Converted to Hunter T Mark 8M* by BAe, Brough, 4-80, with Blue Fox equipment as trainer for Sea Harrier; reserve aircraft.
XL604 ff 10-12-58 Frank Bullen. Deld 19-1-59, FAA. No 764 Sqn, FAA. *Converted to Hunter T Mark 8C*. Deld 22-11-63, No 759 Sqn, FAA. Purchased by HSA, 16-2-73, as G-9-416. 2,699.05 FH. *Converted to Kenyan Hunter T Mark 81 (802)*. Deld 24-6-74.

Conversion order for 18 Hunter F Mark 4s to be brought to T Mark 8 standard by Hawker Aircraft Ltd and Sir W.G. Armstrong Whitworth Aircraft Ltd for FAA during 1958-59. See under Hunter F Mark 4s WT701, WT702, WT722, WT745, WT755, WT772, WT799; WV319, WV322, WV363; WW661, WW664 (Prototype); XE664, XE665; XF289, XF322, XF357 and XF358.

Conversion order for four Hunter F Mark 4s and T Mark 8s to be brought to T Mark 8B standard with full TACAN equipment. See under WW664, XF967, XF978 and XF995.

Conversion order for 11 Hunter F Mark 4s and T Mark 8s to be brought to T Mark 8C standard with partial TACAN equipment. See under WV396, WV397; XF938, XF939, XF942, XF983, XF985, XF991, XF992, XF994 and XL604.

Hawker Hunter FGA Mark 9

First conversion contract to modify 40 Hunter F Mark 6s to full FGA Mark 9 standard placed with Hawker Siddeley Aviation Ltd in 1958. See under RAF Hunter F Mark 6s XE544, XE552, XE581, XE592, XE597, XE600, XE607, XE609, XE617, XE618, XE620, XE623, XE643, XE645, XE647, XE649, XE651, XE654, XE655; XF376, XF388, XF419, XF421, XF424, XF442, XF454, XF455, XF462; XG128, XG130, XG134, XG135, XG136, XG169; XJ643, XJ687; XK139, XK140, XK150 and XK151.

Second conversion contract, undertaken by the RAF and Company Working Party at Horsham St Faith in 1959, to bring 36 Hunter F Mark 6s up to Interim FGA Mark 9 standard. These aircraft initially retained their Avon 203 engines. (Later most were progressively re-engined with Avon 207 engines and achieved full FGA Mark 9 standard.) See under RAF Hunter F Mark 6s XE584, XE604, XE611, XE615, XE616, XE622, XE624, XE628, XE646, XE650; XF431, XF435, XF440, XF455, XF456, XF517, XF519, XF523; XG151, XG154, XG155, XG156, XG195, XG205, XG207, XG237, XG252, XG253, XG254, XG255, XG256, XG260, XG261, XG264, XG271 and XG273.

Third conversion contract to modify 31 Hunter F Mark 6s to full FGA Mark 9 standard placed with Hawker Siddeley Aviation Ltd in 1960. See under RAF Hunter F Mark 6s XE530, XE535, XE546, XE550, XE582, XE610, XE652; XF414, XF508; XG153 XG265, XG266, XG272, XG292, XG293, XG296, XG297, XG298; XJ632, XJ673, XJ680, XJ683, XJ684, XJ685, XJ686, XJ688, XJ692; XK136, XK137, XK138 and XK142.

Fourth conversion contract to modify six Hunter F Mark 6s to full FGA Mark 9 standard placed with Hawker Siddeley Aviation Ltd in 1964. See under RAF Hunter F Mark 6s XE532, XG291, XJ689, XJ690, XJ691 and XJ695.

Fifth conversion contract to modify six Hunter F Mark 6s to full FGA Mark 9 standard placed with Hawker Siddeley Aviation Ltd in 1965. See under RAF Hunter F Mark 6s XF430, XF446; XG251; XJ635, XJ640 and XJ674.

Sixth conversion contract, undertaken by the RAF at No 5 MU, Kemble, to modify nine Hunter F Mark 6s to full FGA Mark 9 standard in 1965. See under RAF Hunter F Mark 6s XF416, XF437, XF511; XG194, XG228; XJ642, XJ644, XJ645 and XJ646.

Hunter GA Mark 11, XE673, of the Fleet Air Arm, carrying Lossiemouth fin markings. Note the wing pylons, usually employed to carry rocket batteries.

Hawker Hunter FR Mark 10

Conversion contract to modify 33 Hunter F Mark 6s to FR Mark 10 standard placed with Hawker Siddeley Aviation in 1959, and completed during 1960-61. See under RAF Hunter F Mark 6s WW593, WW594, WW595, WW596; XE556, XE579, XE580, XE585, XE589, XE596, XE599, XE605, XE614, XE621, XE625, XE626; XF422, XF426, XF428, XF429 (prototype), XF432, XF436, XF438, XF441, XF457, XF458, XF459, XF460; XG127, XG168; XJ633, XJ694 and XJ714.

Hawker Hunter GA Mark 11

Conversion contract to modify 40 Hunter F Mark 4s to GA Mark 11 standard placed by the Admiralty with Hawker Siddeley Aviation in 1961, and completed in 1962-63. Guns removed; aircraft arrestor hook and TACAN navigation system installed. Aircraft painted in grey/white epoxy paint. See under RAF Hunter F Mark 4s WT711, WT712, WT713, WT718, WT721, WT723, WT741, WT744, WT804, WT805, WT806, WT808, WT809, WT810; WV256, WV257, WV267, WV374, WV380, WV381, WV382; WW654, WW659; XE668, XE673, XE674, XE680, XE682, XE685, XE689, XE707, XE712, XE716, XE717, XF291, XF297, XF300, XF301, XF368 and XF977.

Hawker Hunter Mark 12

One two-seat aircraft, XE531, ordered by the Ministry of Supply on behalf of the RAE, Farnborough, to be converted from F Mark 6 standard to feature two-seat cockpit with head-up display and vertical nose camera. Powered by Avon 208 engine.

3 Export and licence-built orders (new-build)

Hawker Dutch Hunter T Mark 7

Production batch of 20 aircraft built by Hawker Aircraft Ltd. First ten aircraft, numbered N-301 to N-310, ordered under Contract No HAL/55N 022; remainder, numbered N-311 to N-320, diverted from cancelled Ministry of Supply batch XM117-XM126. Avon 121A engines and single Aden gun.

N-301 ff 19-3-58 Frank Bullen. Deld 18-7-58, Twente. Purchased by HSA, 6-8-68, as G-9-289. *Converted to Abu Dhabian Hunter T Mark 77 (712).* Deld 15-5-70.

N-302 ff 30-5-58 Duncan Simpson. Deld 18-7-58, Twente.

N-303 ff 14-6-58 David Lockspeiser. Deld 9-9-58, Twente. Purchased by HSA, 27-8-68, as G-9-290. *Converted to Singaporean Hunter T Mark 75 (500).* Deld 25-7-70.

N-304 ff 24-6-58 Frank Bullen. Deld 7-8-58, Twente. Purchased by HSA, 27-8-68, as G-9-291. *Converted to Singaporean Hunter T Mark 75 (504).* Deld 25-7-70.

N-305 ff 5-9-58 David Lockspeiser. Deld 2-10-58, Twente.

N-306 ff 13-9-58 David Lockspeiser. Deld 2-10-58, Twente.

N-307 ff 20-9-58 David Lockspeiser. Deld 30-10-58, Twente.

N-308 ff 26-9-58 Bill Bedford. Deld 4-11-58, Twente.

N-309 ff 29-12-58 David Lockspeiser. Deld 23-1-59, Twente. Both Dutch pilots ejected safely, 21-7-59, after engine failure; turbine blade found four miles from aircraft's flight path.

N-310 ff 4-10-58 Hugh Merewether. Deld 4-11-58, Twente.

N-311 ff 8-11-58 David Lockspeiser. Deld 22-12-58, Twente.

N-312 ff 21-11-58 David Lockspeiser. Deld 21-1-59, Twente. Purchased by HSA, 25-7-68, as G-9-288. 1,606.26 FH. *Converted to Abu Dhabian Hunter T Mark 77 (711).* Deld 12-5-70.

N-313 ff 1-12-58 Frank Bullen. Deld 21-1-59, Twente. Purchased by HSA, 23-2-65, as G-9-212. *Converted to Swiss Hunter Mark 58A (J-4127).* Deld 1-3-73.

N-314 ff 13-12-58 Frank Bullen. Deld 23-1-59, Twente.

N-315 ff 6-12-58 David Lockspeiser. Deld 21-1-59, Twente.

N-316 ff 6-12-58 Duncan Simpson. Deld. 23-1-59, Twente. Purchased by HSA, 16-2-65, as G-9-191. *Converted to Qatari Hunter T Mark 79 (QA13).* Deld 9-12-71.

N-317 ff 12-12-58 Duncan Simpson. Deld 4-2-59, Twente. Purchased by HSA, 15-3-64, as G-9-164. Canibalised for spares.

N-318 ff 6-12-58 Duncan Simpson. Deld 23-1-59, Twente. Purchased by HSA, 9-3-65, as G-9-194. *Converted to Swiss Hunter Mark 58A (J-4128).* Deld 16-3-73.

N-319 ff 7-1-59 Duncan Simpson. Deld 3-2-59, Twente. Purchased by HSA, 2-3-65, as G-9-193. *Converted to Singaporean Hunter T Mark 75 (514).* Deld 25-9-70.

N-320 ff 1-1-59 Frank Bullen. Deld 26-1-59, Twente.

Note: Two of the above Dutch Hunter T Mark 7s were sold to Denmark where they were re-numbered ET-273 and ET-274; on the disposal of the surviving Danish Hunters, these two Mark 7s were purchased by HSA on 1-12-75 as G-9-431 and G-9-432 respectively. They were eventually disposed of to the Imperial War Museum, Duxford, and a museum at Elstree.

Hawker Swedish Hunter Mark 50

Production batch of 120 aircraft based on the Hunter F Mark 4, numbered 34001 to 34120. Aircraft 34001 to 34024 built by Hawker Aircraft Ltd, Kingston-upon-Thames; the remainder built by Hawker Aircraft (Blackpool) Ltd, Blackpool. Contract, dated June 29 1954, No HAL/54/S.016.

34001 ff 24-6-55 Frank Bullen. Deld 26-8-55 by Major Stenberg.

34002 ff 30-9-55 David Lockspeiser. Deld 27-10-55.

Right *Formation of Dutch-built Hunter F Mark 6s of No 325 Squadron, Royal Netherlands Air Force. Three of these aircraft were later purchased by Hawker for resale overseas.*

Appendix 3

34003 ff 6-10-55 David Lockspeiser. Deld 31-10-55.
34004 ff 1-11-55 David Lockspeiser. Deld 7-12-55.
34005 ff 21-11-55 David Lockspeiser. Deld 7-12-55.
34006 ff 5-12-55 Duncan Simpson. Deld 3-1-56.
34007 ff 6-12-55 Frank Bullen. Deld 3-1-56.
34008 ff 4-1-56 Duncan Simpson. Deld 7-2-56.
34009 ff 24-1-56 Hugh Merewether. Deld 22-2-56. Pilot ejected safely, 22-3-56, after explosion in rear fuselage; aircraft crashed through thick ice and was salvaged from 50 feet of water.
34010 ff 24-2-56 David Lockspeiser. Deld 9-3-56.
34011 ff 8-2-56 Duncan Simpson. Deld 22-2-56.
34012 ff 23-2-56 Hugh Merewether. Deld 9-3-56.
34013 ff 8-3-56 Hugh Merewether. Deld 28-3-56.
34014 ff 27-2-56 Hugh Merewether. Deld 21-3-56. Aircraft crashed five miles from Tullinge, 10-10-57; pilot did not eject and was killed.
34015 ff 5-3-56 Hugh Merewether. Deld 27-3-56.
34016 ff 14-3-56 David Lockspeiser. Deld 28-5-56.
34017 ff 17-3-56 David Lockspeiser. Deld 11-4-56. Purchased by HSA, 1970, as G-9-414. *Converted to Swiss Hunter T Mark 68 (J-4207).* Deld 3-6-75.
34018 ff 19-3-56 David Lockspeiser. Deld 11-4-56.
34019 ff 29-3-56 Frank Bullen. Deld 19-4-56. Pilot ejected at low level after engine trouble, 8-4-57, but was killed.
34020 ff 5-4-56 David Lockspeiser. Deld 19-4-56.
34021 ff 25-4-56 Hugh Merewether. Deld 11-5-56.
34022 ff 11-5-56 Frank Bullen. Deld 8-6-56.
34023 ff 14-5-56 David Lockspeiser. Deld 8-6-56. Aircraft dived into ground at Barkarby airfield, 29-3-57; pilot killed.
34024 ff 7-9-56 Duncan Simpson. Deld 4-10-56.
Note: Apart from the following aircraft no official information regarding the disposal of the surviving Swedish Hunters has yet been given; there are persistent reports that a number have been purchased commercially in the United States of America for refurbishing and re-sale.
34031 On 22-1-57 this aircraft failed to return from a sortie; some debris was sighted at sea, and the pilot posted Missing.
34041 On 25-4-57 the aircraft suffered engine failure on the landing approach; the pilot ejected safely.
34043 On 12-12-56 the aircraft overshot from landing at high speed and was totally destroyed.
34059 On 14-5-58 the pilot ejected safely after engine flame-out.
34072 Aircraft purchased by HSA, 1970, as G-9-413. *Converted to Swiss Hunter T Mark 68 (J-4206).* Deld 3-6-75.
34080 Aircraft purchased by HSA, 1970, as G-9-415. *Converted to Swiss Hunter T Mark 68 (J-4208).* Deld 3-6-75.
34086 Aircraft purchased by HSA, 1970, as G-9-412. *Converted to Swiss Hunter T Mark 68 (J-4205).* Deld 3-6-75.

Hawker Danish Hunter Mark 51

Production batch of 30 aircraft based on the Hunter F Mark 4, numbered 401 to 430 (later prefixed 'E-'). All aircraft built by Hawker Aircraft Ltd, Kingston-upon-Thames and Dunsfold. Contract No HAL/54/D.017 dated July 3 1954.

Appendix 3

401 ff 15-12-55 David Lockspeiser. Deld 30-1-56. Vaerløse, 1956-57.
402 ff 12-1-56 David Lockspeiser. Deld 30-1-56. Vaerløse, 1956-57. ESK-724. Purchased by HSA, 8-8-76, as G-9-433. Sold to Mr John Lee, c 1978.
403 ff 17-1-56 David Lockspeiser. Deld 9-3-56. Vaerløse, 1956-57. ESK-724. Purchased by HSA, 8-12-75, as G-9-434. Sold to Mr. Letcher, USA, 3-3-77.
404 ff 22-2-56 Duncan Simpson. Deld 9-3-56. Vaerløse, 1956-57.
405 ff 1-3-56 David Lockspeiser. Deld 19-3-56. Vaerløse, 1956. Crashed and SOC, 4-6-56.
406 ff 5-3-56 David Lockspeiser. Deld 19-3-56. Vaerløse, 1956-57.
407 ff 29-3-56 David Lockspeiser. Deld 10-9-56. Vaerløse, 1956-57. ESK-724. Purchased by HSA, 20-3-76, as G-9-435. Disposed of to Loughborough Preservation Society, 20-12-79.
408 ff 14-3-56 Frank Bullen. Deld 18-8-56. Vaerløse, 1956-57. ESK-724. Purchased by HSA, 10-4-76, as G-9-436. Disposed of to RAF/RNAS Brawdy, 28-2-78.
409 ff 21-3-56 David Lockspeiser. Deld 20-7-56. Vaerløse, 1956-57. ESK-724. Purchased by HSA, 9-12-75, as G-9-437. 3,282 FH. Disposed of to South Wales Preservation Society, Rhoos Airport.
410 ff 27-3-56 David Lockspeiser. Deld 24-8-56. Vaerløse, 1956-57. ESK-724. Purchased by HSA, 6-3-76, as G-9-438. Disposed of to Aviodrome National Aerospace Museum, Schipol, Amsterdam, 26-7-79.
411 ff 29-3-56 Hugh Merewether. Deld 10-9-56. Vaerløse, 1956-57.
412 ff 10-4-56 Hugh Merewether. Deld 24-8-56. Vaerløse, 1956-57. ESK-724. Purchased by HSA, 27-3-76, as G-9-439. 3,022 FH.
413 ff 10-4-56 Frank Bullen. Deld 24-8-56. Vaerløse, 1956-57.
414 ff 24-5-56 Frank Bullen. Deld 18-8-56. Vaerløse, 1956-57.
415 ff 27-4-56 David Lockspeiser. Deld 24-8-56. Vaerløse, 1956-57.
416 ff 25-5-56 Don Lucey. Deld 18-8-56. Vaerløse, 1956. ESK-724.
417 ff 19-4-56 Don Lucey. Deld 22-6-56. Vaerløse, 1956. ESK-724.
418 ff 19-4-56 Hugh Merewether. Deld 22-6-56. Vaerløse, 1956. ESK-724. Purchased by HSA, 20-12-75, as G-9-440. 3,574 FH (believed to be highest number of flying hours by a Hunter 4 derivative). Disposed of to Elstree Museum, 1-7-79. Became G-HUNT.
419 ff 24-4-56 Hugh Merewether. Deld 22-6-56. Vaerløse, 1956. ESK-724. Aalborg Stn Flt. Purchased by HSA, 10-4-76, as G-9-441. 3,183 FH. Disposed of to NE Vintage and Veteran Aircraft Association, Sunderland Airport, 9-2-77.
420 ff 1-5-56 David Lockspeiser. Deld 22-6-56. ESK-724. Purchased by HSA, 1-5-76, as G-9-442. 3,151 FH.
421 ff 4-5-56 David Lockspeiser. Deld 22-6-56. ESK-724. Purchased by HSA, 16-5-76, as G-9-443. Disposed of to Kingston Apprentices' School.
422 ff 4-5-56 Hugh Merewether. Deld 29-6-56. ESK-724.
423 ff 4-5-56 Hugh Merewether. Deld 6-7-56. ESK-724. Purchased by HSA, 16-5-76, as G-9-444. Disposed of to Bitteswell Apprentices' School.
424 ff 3-5-56 David Lockspeiser. Deld 29-6-56. ESK-724. Purchased by HSA, 20-2-76, as G-9-445. Disposed of to Peter Warren, Biggin Hill, 27-6-79.
425 ff 9-5-56 David Lockspeiser. Deld 9-7-56. ESK-724. Purchased by HSA, 28-2-76, as G-9-446. Disposed of to Midland Air Museum, Coventry, 28-6-79.
426 ff 11-5-56 David Lockspeiser. Deld 9-7-56. ESK-724.
427 ff 17-15-56 Frank Bullen. Deld 6-7-56. ESK-724. Purchased by HSA, 28-2-76, as G-9-447. Disposed of to Brough Apprentices' School.
428 ff 22-5-56 David Lockspeiser. Deld 20-7-56. ESK-724.
429 ff 4-6-56 Frank Bullen. Deld 29-6-56. ESK-724.

430 ff 19-6-56 Frank Bullen. Deld 18-8-56. ESK-724. Purchased by HSA, 20-3-76, as G-9-448. Disposed of to Thorpe Park Leisure Centre.

Hawker Danish Hunter T Mark 53

Production order for two aircraft based on the Hunter T Mark 7 (but without wing leading-edge extensions) built by Hawker Aircraft Ltd, Kingston-upon-Thames, in 1958. Initially numbered 35-271 and 35-272, and later EP-271 and EP-272, covered by Contract Nos HAL./56/D.026 and HAL./57/K.024 respectively.

35-271 ff 17-10-58 Frank Bullen. Deld 8-11-58, Aalborg. ESK-724. Purchased by HSA, 1-12-75, as G-9-429. 3,176 FH. Disposed of to Duxford Museum, 1976.

35-272 ff 15-11-58 Duncan Simpson. Deld 16-12-58, Aalborg. ESK-724. Purchased by HSA, 1-12-75, as G-9-430. 3,195 FH. Partly scrapped and remains given to Duxford Museum.

Hawker Indian Hunter Mark 56

Order for 160 aircraft, of which the first 32 were diverted from the cancelled Ministry of Supply Hunter F Mark 6s (see RAF Hunter F Mark 6s XK157-XK224, re-numbered BA201 to BA232), and the next 16 were ex-RAF aircraft (see under RAF Hunter F Mark 6s XE537-XE540, XE547, XE549, XE600; XF463, XF497, XF499-XF501, XF503, XF505; XG150 and XG163, re-numbered BA233 to BA248). The remainder, BA249 to BA360, were new-build aircraft manufactured by Hawker Aircraft Ltd, Kingston-upon-Thames, 1957-60, under Contract No HAL/57/I.034. All Mark 6 modifications, plus tail parachutes; aircraft later given 230-gallon drop tank facility with increased oxygen supply. The following details refer to the new-build aircraft.

BA249 ff 4-7-58 Duncan Simpson. Deld 8-8-58, No 7 Sqn, IAF.
BA250 ff 26-6-58 David Lockspeiser. Deld 18-9-58, No 27 Sqn, IAF.
BA251 ff 7-7-58 Duncan Simpson. Deld 18-9-58, No 27 Sqn, IAF. Aircraft suffered engine compressor failure, 23-9-59; pilot ejected safely.
BA252 ff 17-7-58 Frank Bullen. Deld 8-8-58, No 17 Sqn, IAF.
BA253 ff 4-7-58 Duncan Simpson. Deld 8-8-58, No 27 Sqn, IAF.
BA254 ff 1-8-58 Duncan Simpson. Deld 14-10-58, No 20 Sqn, IAF.
BA255 ff 4-9-58 David Lockspeiser. Deld 10-11-58, No 20 Sqn, IAF.
BA256 ff 30-8-58 Don Lucey. Deld 14-10-58, No 27 Sqn, IAF.
BA257 ff 3-9-58 Don Lucey. Deld 14-10-58, No 20 Sqn, IAF.
BA258 ff 10-9-58 Duncan Simpson. Deld 14-10-58, No 20 Sqn, IAF.
BA259 ff 11-9-58 Frank Bullen. Deld 14-10-58, No 20 Sqn, IAF.
BA260 ff 19-9-58 Duncan Simpson. Deld 10-11-58, No 20 Sqn, IAF.
BA261 ff 2-10-58 Frank Bullen. Deld 1-12-58, No 20 Sqn, IAF.
BA262 ff 24-9-58 Duncan Simpson. Deld 10-11-58, No 20 Sqn, IAF.
BA263 ff 3-10-58 David Lockspeiser. Deld 1-12-58, No 20 Sqn, IAF.
BA264 ff 25-9-58 Duncan Simpson. Deld 7-1-59, No 1 BRD, IAF.
BA265 ff 4-10-58 Frank Bullen. Deld 10-11-58. Crashed on take-off at Jamnagar, 24-22-58, during delivery flight; parachute streamed on take-off; RAF pilot killed and aircraft SOC.
BA266 ff 10-10-58 Duncan Simpson. Damaged at Benson, 12-58.
BA267 ff 11-10-58 Frank Bullen. Deld 11-58, No 20 Sqn, IAF.
BA268 ff 20-10-58 David Lockspeiser. Deld 12-58, No 20 Sqn, IAF.
BA269 ff 8-10-58 Frank Bullen. Deld 11-12-58, No 1 BRD, IAF.
BA270 ff 10-10-58 David Lockspeiser. Deld 1-12-58, No 20 Sqn, IAF.
BA271 ff 3-11-58 David Lockspeiser. Deld 12-58, No 20 Sqn, IAF.

Appendix 3 195

BA272 ff 31-10-58 David Lockspeiser. Deld 8-1-59, No 1 BRD, IAF.
BA273 ff 5-11-58 Hugh Merewether. Deld 19-12, No 20 Sqn, IAF.
BA274 ff 5-11-58 Hugh Merewether. Deld 11-12-58, No 20 Sqn, IAF.
BA275 ff 14-11-58 Duncan Simpson. Deld 19-12-58, No 1 BRD, IAF.
BA276 ff 5-11-58 David Lockspeiser. Deld 16-1-59, No 17 Sqn, IAF.
BA277 ff 11-11-58 Duncan Simpson. Deld 19-12-58, No 20 Sqn, IAF.
BA278 ff 11-12-58 Frank Bullen. Deld 8-1-59, No 1 BRD, IAF.
BA279 ff 21-11-58 Hugh Merewether. Deld 16-1-59.
BA280 ff 2-12-58 Duncan Simpson. Deld 27-1-59.
BA281 ff 7-12-58 Bill Bedford. Deld 4-2-59, No 1 BRD, IAF.
BA282 ff 10-12-58 Frank Bullen. Deld 23-2-59. Crashed and SOC, 1959.
BA283 ff 13-12-58 David Lockspeiser. Deld 2-2-59, No 1 BRD, IAF.
BA284 ff 1-12-58 Frank Bullen. Deld 8-1-59.
BA285 ff 13-12-58 Frank Bullen. Deld 26-2-59, No 27 Sqn, IAF.
BA286 ff 1-1-59 Frank Bullen. Deld 26-2-59, No 7 Sqn, IAF.
BA287 ff 15-1-59 Flt Lt Gole.Deld 12-3-59, No 1 BRD, IAF.
BA288 ff 21-1-59 Sqn Ldr Lowe. Deld 26-2-59, No 1 BRD, IAF.
BA289 ff 23-1-59 Duncan Simpson. Deld 23-2-59, No 1 BRD, IAF.
BA290 ff 3-2-59 David Lockspeiser. Deld 31-3-59, No 1 BRD, IAF.
BA291 ff 24-1-59 Duncan Simpson. Deld 27-2-59. Pilot crashed while landing in 'manual', at Ambala, 23-10-59; aircraft exploded, activating the ejector seat but the pilot was killed.
BA292 ff 21-1-59 Flt Lt Gole. Deld 1-4-59, No 1 BRD, IAF.
BA293 ff 3-2-59 David Lockspeiser. Deld 31-3-59, No 1 BRD, IAF.
BA294 ff 2-2-59 Sqn Ldr Lowe. Deld 2-4-59, No 1 BRD, IAF.
BA295 ff 28-1-59 Flt Lt Gole. Deld 10-4-59, No 1 BRD, IAF.
BA296 ff 31-1-59 Flt Lt Gole. Deld 7-4-59, No 1 BRD, IAF.
BA297 ff 2-2-59 David Lockspeiser. Deld 12-3-59, No 1 BRD, IAF.
BA298 ff 20-2-59 Frank Bullen. Deld 10-4-59. Crashed and SOC, 1959.
BA299 ff 23-2-59 Duncan Simpson. Deld 9-4-59, No 1 BRD, IAF.
BA300 ff 21-2-59 Duncan Simpson. Deld 9-4-59, No 1 BRD, IAF.
BA301 ff 18-2-59 Frank Bullen. Deld 10-4-59, No 1 BRD, IAF.
BA302 ff 19-2-59 Duncan Simpson. Deld 20-4-59, No 1 BRD, IAF.
BA303 ff 26-2-59 Frank Bullen. Deld 9-4-59, No 1 BRD, IAF.
BA304 ff 11-3-59 Duncan Simpson. Deld 20-4-59, No 1 BRD, IAF.
BA305 ff 19-3-59 Duncan Simpson. Deld 5-5-59, No 1 BRD, IAF.
BA306 ff 6-3-59 Frank Bullen. Deld 20-4-59, No 1 BRD, IAF.
BA307 ff 23-3-59 Frank Bullen. Deld 8-5-59, No 1 BRD, IAF.
BA308 ff 1-4-59 Duncan Simpson. Deld 6-5-59, No 1 BRD, IAF.
BA309 ff 3-4-59 David Lockspeiser. Deld 18-6-59, No 1 BRD, IAF.
BA310 ff 8-4-59 Duncan Simpson. Deld 1-6-59, No 1 BRD, IAF.
BA311 ff 14-4-59 David Lockspeiser. Deld 2-6-59, No 1 BRD, IAF.
BA312 ff 7-4-59 David Lockspeiser. Deld 3-6-59, No 1 BRD, IAF.
BA313 ff 29-4-59 David Lockspeiser. Deld 19-6-59, No 1 BRD, IAF.
BA314 ff 1-5-59 Don Lucey. Deld 19-6-59, No 1 BRD, IAF.
BA315 ff 1-5-59 Don Lucey. Deld 19-6-59, No 1 BRD, IAF.
BA316 ff 25-5-59 Don Lucey. Deld 7-7-59, No 1 BRD, IAF.
BA317 ff 4-6-59 Duncan Simpson. Deld 7-7-59, No 1 BRD, IAF.
BA318 ff 24-6-59 David Lockspeiser. Deld 9-9-59, No 1 BRD, IAF. AFSU, storage.
BA319 ff 30-6-59 Don Lucey. Deld 17-8-59, No 1 BRD, IAF.

BA320 ff 16-7-59 David Lockspeiser. Deld 9-9-59, No 1 BRD, IAF. AFSU, storage.
BA321 ff 17-8-59 Duncan Simpson. Deld 23-9-59.
BA322 ff 22-8-59 David Lockspeiser. Deld 20-10-59.
BA323 ff 2-9-59 David Lockspeiser. Deld 29-10-59.
BA324 ff 8-9-59 David Lockspeiser. Deld 28-10-59.
BA325 ff 11-9-59 Don Lucey. Deld 28-10-59.
BA326 ff 11-9-59 Don Lucey. Deld 28-10-59.
BA327 ff 24-9-59 David Lockspeiser. Deld 18-11-59.
BA328 ff 30-9-59 Duncan Simpson. Deld 18-11-59.
BA329 ff 13-10-59 Duncan Simpson. Deld 29-1-60.
BA330 ff 30-9-59 Duncan Simpson. Deld 18-11-59.
BA331 ff 13-11-59 Frank Bullen. Deld 15-12-59.
BA332 ff 19-11-59 Duncan Simpson. Deld 23-8-60.
BA333 ff 13-11-59 David Lockspeiser. Deld 29-1-60.
BA334 ff 30-11-59 Duncan Simpson. Deld 29-1-60.
BA335 ff 1-1-60 Hugh Merewether. Deld 10-3-60.
BA336 ff 6-1-60 Flt Lt Mohlah, IAF. Deld 10-3-60.
BA337 ff 4-2-60 Flt Lt Mohlah, IAF. Deld 23-5-60.
BA338 ff 3-2-60 Don Lucey. Deld 8-4-60.
BA339 ff 9-2-60 Flt Lt Mohlah, IAF. Deld 7-4-60.
BA340 ff 16-2-60 Hugh Merewether. Deld 7-4-60.
BA341 ff 7-3-60 Flt Lt Tilak, IAF. Delivery date not known.
BA342 ff 17-3-60 David Lockspeiser. Deld 24-5-60.
BA343 ff 22-3-60 Flt Lt Tilak, IAF. Deld 26-5-60.
BA344 ff 25-3-60 Duncan Simpson. Deld 23-5-60.
BA345 ff 24-1-60 Don Lucey. Deld 14-6-60.
BA346 ff 20-4-60 Don Lucey. Deld 14-6-60.
BA347 ff 27-4-60 Duncan Simpson. Deld 10-6-60.
BA348 ff 13-5-60 Duncan Simpson. Deld 14-7-60.
BA349 ff 12-5-60 David Lockspeiser. Deld 14-7-60.
BA350 ff 16-6-60 Duncan Simpson. Deld 18-8-60.
BA351 ff 28-6-60 Duncan Simpson. Delivery date not known.
BA352 ff 11-7-60 Frank Bullen. Deld 6-9-60.
BA353 ff 14-7-60 Frank Bullen. Deld 6-9-60.
BA354 ff 16-8-60 David Lockspeiser. Deld 6-10-60.
BA355 ff 18-8-60 Duncan Simpson. Deld 6-10-60.
BA356 ff 30-8-60 David Lockspeiser. Deld 11-10-60.
BA357 ff 31-8-60 David Lockspeiser. Deld 3-11-60.
BA358 ff 12-9-60 Duncan Simpson. Delivery date not known.
BA359 ff 3-10-60 Duncan Simpson. Delivery date not known.
BA360 ff 5-10-60 Don Lucey. Delivery date not known.

Hawker Swiss Hunter Mark 58

Order for 100 aircraft, of which the first 12 were ex-RAF aircraft (see under RAF Hunter F Mark 6s XE526-XE529, XE533, XE536, XE541, XE542, XE545 and XE553-XE555, re-numbered J-4001 to J-4012); remainder new-build, were numbered J-4013-J-4100 and were equipped with tail parachutes, otherwise similar to the RAF Hunter Mark 6. Built by Hawker Aircraft Ltd, Kingston-upon-Thames, during 1958-60. The following details refer only to the new-build aircraft.

J-4013 ff 7-12-58 David Lockspeiser. Deld 16-6-59, Emmen.

Appendix 3

J-4014 ff 6-12-58 Duncan Simpson. Deld 15-1-59, Dubendorf.
J-4015 ff 1-1-59 Hugh Merewether. Deld 17-2-59, Emmen.
J-4016 ff 31-12-58 David Lockspeiser. Deld 5-2-59, Emmen.
J-4017 ff 15-1-59 Duncan Simpson. Deld 16-2-59, Emmen.
J-4018 ff 28-1-59 David Lockspeiser. Deld 23-2-59, Dubendorf.
J-4019 ff 15-1-59 Frank Bullen. Deld 23-2-59, Dubendorf.
J-4020 ff 4-2-59 Duncan Simpson. Deld 9-3-59, Emmen.
J-4021 ff 19-2-59 Duncan Simpson. Deld 18-3-59, Kloten.
J-4022 ff 19-2-59 David Lockspeiser. Deld 2-4-59, Emmen.
J-4023 ff 19-2-59 Frank Bullen. Deld 10-3-59, Kloten.
J-4024 ff 18-2-59 Hugh Merewether. Deld 25-3-59.
J-4025 ff 23-2-59 Hugh Merewether. Deld 23-3-59.
J-4026 ff 4-3-59 Duncan Simpson. Deld 3-4-59, Emmen.
J-4027 ff 4-3-59 Duncan Simpson. Deld 8-4-59, Emmen.
J-4028 ff 13-3-59 Duncan Simpson. Deld 14-4-59.
J-4029 ff 4-3-59 Duncan Simpson. Deld 26-3-59.
J-4030 ff 7-3-59 Hugh Merewether. Deld 8-4-59, Emmen.
J-4031 ff 10-3-59 David Lockspeiser. Deld 17-4-59.
J-4032 ff 12-3-59 David Lockspeiser. Deld 29-4-59, Kloten.
J-4033 ff 18-3-59 David Lockspeiser. Deld 22-5-59, Kloten.
J-4034 ff 20-3-59 Duncan Simpson. Deld 21-4-59, Dubendorf.
J-4035 ff 25-3-59 Duncan Simpson. Deld 24-4-59, Dubendorf.
J-4036 ff 1-4-59 David Lockspeiser. Deld 6-5-59, Emmen.
J-4037 ff 17-4-59 David Lockspeiser. Deld 25-5-59.
J-4038 ff 13-4-59 David Lockspeiser. Deld 29-5-59, Kloten.
J-4039 ff 15-4-59 David Lockspeiser, Deld 28-5-59, Kloten.
J-4040 ff 15-4-59 Don Lucey. Deld 29-5-59, Dubendorf.
J-4041 ff 23-4-59 David Lockspeiser. Deld 2-6-59.
J-4042 ff 21-4-59 Don Lucey. Deld 27-5-59, Dubendorf.
J-4043 ff 28-4-59 Don Lucey. Deld 2-6-59, Emmen.
J-4044 ff 4-5-59 Duncan Simpson. Deld 10-6-59.
J-4045 ff 6-5-59 Don Lucey. Deld 8-59.
J-4046 ff 13-5-59 David Lockspeiser. Deld 10-6-59, Kloten.
J-4047 ff 19-5-59 Don Lucey. Deld 19-6-59, Emmen.

This early Swiss Hunter 58, displaying dayglo panels on fuselage and wings, also features modified collector tanks under the nose; these collected belt links as well as spent cases. Note also tail parachute fairing, gun-blast deflectors and practice bomb carriers on the outboard wing pylons.

J-4048 ff 14-5-59 Frank Bullen. Deld 16-6-59.
J-4049 ff 2-6-59 Duncan Simpson. Deld 2-7-59, Emmen.
J-4050 ff 2-6-59 David Lockspeiser. Deld 25-6-59, Dubendorf.
J-4051 ff 9-6-59 David Lockspeiser. Deld 8-7-59, Emmen.
J-4052 ff 10-6-59 Don Lucey. Deld 9-7-59.
J-4053 ff 10-6-59 Don Lucey. Deld 14-7-59, Kloten.
J-4054 ff 9-6-59 Duncan Simpson. Deld 17-7-59, Kloten.
J-4055 ff 12-6-59 Don Lucey. Deld 14-7-59, Kloten.
J-4056 ff 17-6-59 David Lockspeiser. Deld 7-8-59, Emmen.
J-4057 ff 19-6-59 Hugh Merewether. Deld 7-8-59.
J-4058 ff 25-6-59 Don Lucey. Deld 14-8-59, Emmen.
J-4059 ff 25-6-59 David Lockspeiser. Deld 17-8-59, Emmen.
J-4060 ff 10-7-59 Duncan Simpson. Deld 24-8-59.
J-4061 ff 3-7-59 Don Lucey. Deld 2-9-59, Dubendorf.
J-4062 ff 7-7-59 Don Lucey. Deld 31-8-59, Emmen.
J-4063 ff 16-7-59 Don Lucey. Deld 4-9-59, Dubendorf.
J-4064 ff 11-8-59 Duncan Simpson. Deld 4-9-59, Dubendorf.
J-4065 ff 13-8-59 David Lockspeiser. Deld 10-9-59, Dubendorf.
J-4066 ff 22-8-59 Duncan Simpson. Deld 23-9-59, Dubendorf.
J-4067 ff 25-8-59 Don Lucey. Deld 8-10-59, Emmen.
J-4068 ff 20-8-59 David Lockspeiser. Deld 16-10-59.
J-4069 ff 25-8-59 Don Lucey. Deld 18-9-59, Dubendorf.
J-4070 ff 3-9-59 Don Lucey. Deld 2-10-59.
J-4071 ff 28-8-59 Don Lucey. Deld 30-9-59, Dubendorf.
J-4072 ff 4-9-59 David Lockspeiser. Deld 2-10-59.
J-4073 ff 17-9-59 Don Lucey. Deld 21-10-59.
J-4074 ff 24-9-59 Don Lucey. Deld 23-10-59.
J-4075 ff 1-10-59 Frank Bullen. Deld 30-10-59.
J-4076 ff 2-10-59 Duncan Simpson. Deld 12-11-59, Dubendorf.
J-4077 ff 13-10-59 Don Lucey. Deld 12-11-59, Emmen.
J-4078 ff 15-10-59 Don Lucey. Deld 12-11-59, Emmen.
J-4079 ff 5-11-59 Duncan Simpson. Deld 11-11-59, Emmen.
J-4080 ff 7-11-59 Duncan Simpson. Deld 3-12-59, Kloten.
J-4081 ff 10-11-59 David Lockspeiser. Deld 3-12-59, Dubendorf.
J-4082 ff 11-11-59 David Lockspeiser. Deld 18-12-59, Dubendorf.
J-4083 ff 11-11-59 Duncan Simpson. Deld 21-12-59, Dubendorf.
J-4084 ff 17-11-59 David Lockspeiser. Deld 19-2-60.
J-4085 ff 18-11-59 Duncan Simpson. Deld 16-12-59, Dubendorf.
J-4086 ff 24-11-59 Bill Bedford. Deld 7-1-60.
J-4087 ff 8-12-59 Don Lucey. Deld 14-1-60.
J-4088 ff 4-12-59 Duncan Simpson. Deld 22-1-60.
J-4089 ff 8-12-59 David Lockspeiser. Deld 14-1-60.
J-4090 ff 15-12-59 Don Lucey. Deld 20-1-60, Emmen.
J-4091 ff 21-12-59 David Lockspeiser. Deld 22-1-60.
J-4092 ff 17-12-59 Duncan Simpson. Deld 27-1-60.
J-4093 ff 1-1-60 Don Lucey. Deld 6-4-60, Kloten.
J-4094 ff 31-12-59 David Lockspeiser. Deld 10-2-60, Kloten.
J-4095 ff 25-1-60 Don Lucey. Deld 10-3-60, Kloten.
J-4096 ff 7-1-60 Don Lucey. Deld 5-2-60.
J-4097 ff 8-1-60 Don Lucey. Deld 23-2-60, Dubendorf.

Appendix 3

J-4098 ff 19-1-60 Don Lucey. Deld 10-3-60, Dubendorf.
J-4099 ff 8-1-60 Duncan Simpson. Deld 19-2-60, Dubendorf.
J-4100 ff 3-3-60 David Lockspeiser. Deld 1-4-60, Kloten.

Hawker Indian Hunter T Mark 66

Production batch of 22 new-build aircraft, based on second prototype P.1101 Hunter Trainer powered by Avon 200-series engine and with twin-Aden gun armament. Built by Hawker Aircraft Ltd, Kingston-upon-Thames and Dunsfold, during 1958-59, under Contract No HAL/57/I.034. Original requirement was for 16 aircraft, numbered BS361-BS376, but this was increased by six further aircraft, BS485-BS490.

BS361 ff 6-8-58 Hugh Merewether. Deld 21-4-59, No 17 Sqn, IAF.
BS362 ff 3-2-59 David Lockspeiser. Deld 21-4-59, No 27 Sqn, IAF.
BS363 ff 18-2-59 Duncan Simpson. Deld 13-4-59, No 7 Sqn, IAF.
BS364 ff 10-4-59 David Lockspeiser. Deld 3-6-59, No 20 Sqn, IAF.
BS365 ff 7-5-59 Don Lucey. Deld 19-6-59, No 27 Sqn, IAF.
BS366 ff 21-5-59 Duncan Simpson. Paris Air Show, 6-59; Paris-to-London Air Race, 7-59. Deld 19-8-59, No 20 Sqn, IAF.
BS367 ff 9-6-59 David Lockspeiser. Deld 12-8-59, No 17 Sqn, IAF.
BS368 ff 15-6-59 Duncan Simpson. Deld 14-8-59, No 7 Sqn, IAF.
BS369 ff 3-7-59 Duncan Simpson. Deld 18-8-59.
BS370 ff 6-9-59 Duncan Simpson. Deld 9-9-59, No 14 Sqn, IAF.
BS371 ff 19-8-59 Duncan Simpson. Deld 23-9-59.
BS372 ff 18-9-59 Duncan Simpson. Deld 26-10-59.
BS373 ff 2-11-59 Duncan Simpson. Deld 15-12-59.
BS374 ff 2-11-59 Frank Bullen. Deld 15-12-59.
BS375 ff 8-12-59 David Lockspeiser. Deld 29-1-60.
BS376 ff 15-12-59 Don Lucey. Deld 8-3-60.

BS485 ff 2-6-60 Duncan Simpson. Deld 14-7-60.
BS486 ff 16-6-60 Hugh Merewether. Deld 18-8-60.
BS487 ff 15-7-60 Duncan Simpson. Deld 7-9-60.
BS488 ff 16-8-60 Duncan Simpson. Deld 28-10-60.
BS489 ff 7-9-60 Don Lucey. Deld 28-10-60.
BS490 ff 21-10-60 Don Lucey. Deld 11-60.

Hawker Jordanian Hunter T Mark 66B

One new-build aircraft, numbered 714, based on Avon 200-series powered P.1101 two-seater trainer, built by Hawker Aircraft Ltd, Kingston-upon-Thames. Two others converted from refurbished Dutch aircraft (see Dutch Hunter Mark 6s N-249 and N-283).
714 ff 24-5-60 David Lockspeiser. Deld 4-7-60, by Wg Cdr Bennett; crashed and written off, 15-8-65. Last new-build Hunter.

Hawker Hunter F Mark 4 (Licence production—Holland)

Production of 96 Hawker Hunter F Mark 4s undertaken by Fokker-Aviolanda, Amsterdam, during 1955-56. Numbered N-101 onwards. Served with the *Koninklijke Luchtmacht*, on Nos 324 and 325 Squadrons at Leeuwarden, and No 327 Squadron, Soesterberg.

Hawker Hunter F Mark 6 (Licence production—Holland)

Production of 93 Hawker Hunter F Mark 6s undertaken by Fokker-Aviolanda, Amsterdam, during 1956-58. Numbered N-201 onwards. Served with the *Koninklijke Luchtmacht* between 1957 and 1963. The following aircraft were re-purchased by Hawker Siddeley Aviation from 1963 onwards for refurbishing and resale.

N-201 Purchased by HSA, 9-8-66, as G-9-217. *Converted to Chilean Hunter FGA Mark 71 (J-708).* Deld 21-2-68.

N-202 Purchased by HSA, 18-10-66, as G-9-223. *Converted to Chilean Hunter T Mark 72 (J-720).* Deld 2-1-68.

N-203 Purchased by HSA, 15-4-64, as G-9-165. *Converted to Indian Hunter T Mark 66D (S.577).* Deld 30-11-66 (to No 5 MU).

N-204 Purchased by HSA, 22-4-64, as G-9-182. *Converted to Indian Hunter T Mark 66D (S.572).* Deld 5-5-66 (to No 5 MU).

N-205 Purchased by HSA, 25-3-64, as G-9-166. *Converted to Iraqi Hunter FGA Mark 59B (663).* Deld 8-8-66.

N-208 Purchased by HSA, 25-3-64, as G-9-167. *Converted to Indian Hunter T Mark 66D (S.571).* Deld 3-5-66 (to No 5 MU).

N-209 Purchased by HSA, 2-7-65, as G-9-188. *Converted to Indian Hunter Mark 56A (A493).* Deld 28-6-67.

N-210 Purchased by HSA, 4-10-66, as G-9-227. *Converted to Chilean Hunter FGA Mark 71 (J-704).* Deld 12-12-67.

N-212 Purchased by HSA, 22-4-64, as G-9-183. *Converted to Indian Hunter T Mark 66D (S.573).* Deld 10-5-66 (to No 5 MU).

N-213 Purchased by HSA, 6-8-68, as G-9-281. *Converted to Indian Hunter Mark 56A (A1014).* Deld 10-3-70.

N-214 Purchased by HSA, 15-4-64, as G-9-168. *Converted to Indian Hunter T Mark 66D (S.578).* Deld 27-1-67 (to No 5 MU).

N-216 Purchased by HSA, 30-7-68, as G-9-282. *Converted to Indian Hunter Mark 56A (A1015).* Deld 10-3-70.

N-218 Purchased by HSA, 22-4-64, as G-9-184. *Converted to Indian Hunter T Mark 66D (S.580).* Deld 28-2-67 (to No 5 MU).

N-219 Purchased by HSA, 30-7-68, as G-9-283. *Converted to Qatari Hunter FGA Mark 78 (QA11).* Deld 20-12-71.

N-220 Purchased by HSA, 20-9-66, as G-9-226. *Converted to Chilean Hunter FGA Mark 71 (J-705).* Deld 15-12-67.

N-221 Purchased by HSA, 1-4-64, as G-9-169. *Converted to Iraqi Hunter FGA Mark 59B (662).* Deld 16-5-66.

N-222 Purchased by HSA, 13-8-68, as G-9-284. *Converted to Qatari Hunter FGA Mark 78 (QA12).* Deld 8-12-71.

N-223 Purchased by HSA, 25-3-64, as G-9-170. *Converted to Indian Hunter T Mark 66D (S.579).* Deld 15-2-67 (to No 5 MU).

N-224 Purchased by HSA, 9-8-66, as G-9-218. *Converted to Chilean Hunter T Mark 72 (J-719).* Deld 27-11-67.

N-230 Purchased by HSA, 1-4-64, as G-9-171. *Converted to Indian Hunter T Mark 66D (S.574).* Deld 4-8-66 (to No 5 MU).

N-232 Purchased by HSA, 15-11-66, as G-9-221. *Converted to Chilean Hunter FGA Mark 71 (J-712).* Deld 24-4-68.

N-234 Purchased by HSA, 16-2-64, as G-9-172. *Converted to Iraqi Hunter FGA Mark 59 (632).* Deld 14-5-65.

Appendix 3 201

N-247 Purchased by HSA, 9-2-64, as G-9-173. *Converted to Iraqi Hunter FGA Mark 59 (633)*. Deld 14-5-65.
N-249 Purchased by HSA, 8-3-64, as G-9-174. *Converted to Jordanian Hunter T Mark 66B (716)*. Deld 7-10-66.
N-250 Purchased by HSA, 22-4-64, as G-9-185. *Converted to Indian Hunter T Mark 66D (S.581)*. Deld 21-9-67 (to No 5 MU).
N-252 Purchased by HSA, 25-7-68, as G-9-280. *Converted to Indian Hunter Mark 56A (A1013)*. Deld 10-3-70.
N-253 Purchased by HSA, 22-2-64, as G-9-175. *Converted to Iraqi Hunter FGA Mark 59A (657)*. Deld 9-11-65.
N-255 Purchased by HSA, 15-4-64, as G-9-176. *Converted to Iraqi Hunter FGA Mark 59A (658)*. Deld 9-11-65.
N-257 Purchased by HSA, 3-10-67, as G-9-266. *Converted to Kuwaiti Hunter T Mark 67 (219)*. Deld 22-5-69.
N-259 Purchased by HSA, 1-4-64, as G-9-177. *Converted to Iraqi Hunter FGA Mark 59B (664)*. Deld 8-8-66.
N-261 Purchased by HSA, 25-3-64 as G-9-178. *Converted to Indian Hunter T Mark 66D (S.575)*. Deld 3-8-66 (to No 5 MU).
N-262 Purchased by HSA, 20-9-66 as G-9-220. *Converted to Chilean Hunter FGA Mark 71 (J-707)*. Deld 24-1-68.
N-263 Purchased by HSA, 1-4-64 as G-9-179. *Converted to Iraqi Hunter FGA Mark 59B (665)*. Deld 8-9-66.
N-264 Purchased by HSA, 27-8-68 as G-9-285. *Converted to Jordanian Hunter FGA Mark 73A (840)*. Deld 14-6-71.
N-265 Purchased by HSA, 15-4-64 as G-9-180 *Converted to Indian Hunter T Mark 66B (S.576)*. Deld 30-8-66 (to No 5 MU).
N-266 Purchased by HSA, 15-11-66 as G-9-228. *Converted to Chilean Hunter FGA Mark 71 (J-709)*. Deld 27-2-68.
N-268 Purchased by HSA, 27-8-68 as G-9-286. *Converted to Qatari Hunter FGA Mark 78 (QA10)*. Deld 20-12-71.
N-269 Purchased by HSA, 25-3-64 as G-9-181. *Converted to Indian Hunter T Mark 66D (S.570)*. Deld 3-5-66 (to No 5 MU).
N-270 Purchased by HSA, 1-4-66 as G-9-219. *Converted to Chilean Hunter FGA Mark 71 (J-710)*. Deld 28-3-68.
N-271 Purchased by HSA, 18-7-68 as G-9-278. *Converted to Indian Hunter Mark 56A (A1011)*. Deld 25-11-69.
N-273 Purchased by HSA, 18-10-66 as G-9-222. *Converted to Chilean Hunter FGA Mark 71 (J-713)*. Deld 21-5-68.
N-274 Purchased by HSA, 18-7-68 as G-9-279. *Converted to Indian Hunter Mark 56A (A1012)*. Deld 25-11-69.
N-276 Purchased by HSA, 4-10-66 as G-9-224. *Converted to Chilean Hunter FGA Mark 71 (J-706)*. Deld 7-2-68.
N-277 Purchased by HSA, 1-11-66 as G-9-225. *Converted to Chilean Hunter FGA Mark 71 (J-711)*. Deld 9-4-68.
N-279 Purchased by HSA, 13-8-68 as G-9-287. *Converted to Jordanian Hunter FGA Mark 73B (841)*. Deld 14-6-71.
N-282 Purchased by HSA, 1-8-67 as G-9-236. *Converted to Kuwaiti Hunter T Mark 67 (218)*. Deld 22-5-69.
N-283 Purchased by HSA, 27-11-67 as G-9-231. *Converted to Jordanian Hunter T Mark 66B (801)*. Deld 12-2-69.

Hawker Hunter F Mark 4 (Licence Production—Belgium)

Production batch of 112 Hawker Hunter F Mark 4s undertaken by Avions Fairey, Brussels, and SABCA during 1955-56. Numbered ID-1 onwards. Served with the *Force Aérienne Belge/Belgische Luchtmacht* with Nos 1, 7 and 9 Wings at Beauvechain, Chièvres and Bierset respectively.

Hawker Hunter F Mark 6 (Licence Production—Belgium)

Production batch of 144 Hawker Hunter F Mark 6s undertaken by Avions Fairey, Brussels, and SABCA during 1956-58. Numbered IF-1 onwards. Served as above. The following aircraft were purchased by Hawker Siddeley Aviation from 1962 onwards for refurbishing and resale. Also included are a number of other aircraft whose fate is known.

IF-1 Purchased by HSA, 3-2-65, as G-9-187. *Converted to Indian Hunter Mark 56A (A482).* Deld 14-11-67.

IF-3 Purchased by HSA, 23-10-64, as G-9-107. *Converted to Indian Hunter Mark 56A (A484).* Deld 2-3-67.

IF-4 Purchased by HSA, 10-12-64, as G-9-124. *Converted to Indian Hunter Mark 56A (A460).* Deld 28-6-66.

IF-6 Purchased by HSA, 30-10-62, as G-9-70. *Converted to Iraqi Hunter FGA Mark 59 (570).* Deld 18-3-64.

IF-7 Purchased by HSA, 5-3-65, as G-9-154. *Converted to Indian Hunter Mark 56A (A474).* Deld 2-11-66.

IF-8 Purchased by HSA, 6-10-64, as G-9-127. *Converted to Iraqi Hunter FGA Mark 59A (660).* Deld 10-1-66.

IF-9 Purchased by HSA, 8-12-64, as G-9-133. *Converted to Iraqi Hunter FGA Mark 59A (661).* Deld 16-5-66.

IF-10 Purchased by HSA, 21-3-63, as G-9-71. *Converted to Iraqi Hunter FGA Mark 59 (584).* Deld 26-11-64.

IF-11 Purchased by HSA, 13-11-62, as G-9-97. *Converted to Iraqi Hunter FGA Mark 59 (631).* Deld 13-4-65.

IF-12 No 22 Sqn, *FAB/BL*. Missing at sea off Sylt, 18-4-58; believed to have collided with IF-40.

IF-13 Purchased by HSA, 10-12-64, as G-9-128. *Converted to Indian Hunter Mark 56A (A463).* Deld 17-8-66.

IF-14 Purchased by HSA, 20-11-62, as G-9-72. *Converted to Iraqi Hunter FGA Mark 59 (572).* Deld 22-4-64.

IF-16 Purchased by HSA, 23-12-64, as G-9-123. *Converted to Indian Hunter Mark 56A (A462).* Deld 28-6-66.

IF-17 Purchased by HSA, 26-1-65, as G-9-158. *Converted to Indian Hunter Mark 56A (A476).* Deld 9-12-66.

IF-18 Purchased by HSA, 5-1-65, as G-9-148. *Converted to Indian Hunter Mark 56A (A472).* Deld 2-11-66.

IF-19 Suffered forced landing in Belgian service, 21-3-58. Purchased by HSA and re-built using parts from four different aircraft to become *Hunter Mark 66A*. ff 12-8-59 Bill Bedford. HSA demonstrator; leased to Iraq, Jordan and Lebanon, 1963-65. Re-possessed by HSA, as G-9-232 on 18-12-65. *Converted to Chilean Hunter T Mark 72 (J-718).* Deld 9-8-67.

IF-20 Purchased by HSA, 24-6-63, as G-9-73. *Converted to Iraqi Hunter T Mark 69 (627).*

Appendix 3

Deld 14-1-65.
IF-21 Purchased by HSA, 2-5-63, as G-9-74. *Converted to Iraqi Hunter FGA Mark 59 (574).* Deld 14-5-64.
IF-22 Purchased by HSA, 7-10-64, as G-9-108. *Converted to Iraqi Hunter FGA Mark 59A (659).* Deld 10-1-66.
IF-24 Purchased by HSA, 22-3-63, as G-9-75. *Converted to Iraqi Hunter FGA Mark 59 (577).* Deld 24-6-64.
IF-25 Purchased by HSA, 9-2-65, as G-9-162. *Converted to Iraqi Hunter FGA Mark 59A (693).* Deld 14-11-66.
IF-26 Purchased by HSA, 12-12 62, as G-9-76. *Converted to Kuwaiti Hunter FGA Mark 57 (212).* Deld 25-2-65.
IF-27 Purchased by HSA, 19-4-63, as G-9-77. *Converted to Iraqi Hunter FGA Mark 59 (575).* Deld 14-5-64.
IF-28 Purchased by HSA, 2-4-63, as G-9-78. *Converted to Iraqi Hunter FGA Mark 59 (573).* Deld 22-4-64.
IF-31 Purchased by HSA, 13-1-65, as G-9-120. *Converted to Iraqi Hunter FGA Mark 59A (696).* Deld 8-12-66.
IF-32 Purchased by HSA, 10-12-62, as G-9-100. *Converted to Iraqi Hunter FGA Mark 59 (583).* Deld 26-11-64.
IF-33 No 26 Sqn, No 9 Wing, *FAB/BL*. Collided with IF-47 during aerobatics, 23-7-58; pilot ejected safely.
IF-34 Purchased by HSA, 16-10-62, as G-9-96. *Converted to Lebanese Hunter T Mark 66C (L.282).* Deld 27-7-66.
IF-36 Purchased by HSA, 26-1-65, as G-9-141. *Converted to Indian Hunter Mark 56A (A492).* Deld 28-6-66.
IF-37 Purchased by HSA, 12-12-63, as G-9-79. *Converted to Kuwaiti Hunter T Mark 67 (211).* Deld 25-2-65.
IF-41 Purchased by HSA, 13-11-62, as G-9-80. *Converted to Kuwaiti Hunter FGA Mark 57 (213).* Deld 6-5-65.
IF-43 Purchased by HSA, 8-12-64, as G-9-117. *Converted to Indian Hunter Mark 56A (A488).* Deld 19-4-67.
IF-44 Purchased by HSA, 12-11-64, as G-9-106. *Converted to Chilean Hunter FGA Mark 71 (J-703).* Deld 22-11-67.
IF-47 No 26 Sqn, No 9 Wing, *FAB/BL*. Collided with IF-33 during aerobatics, 23-7-58; pilot ejected safely.
IF-48 Purchased by HSA, 13-11-62, as G-9-81. *Converted to Iraqi Hunter FGA Mark 59 (571).* Deld 18-3-64.
IF-49 Purchased by HSA, 27-1-65, as G-9-159. *Converted to Iraqi Hunter FGA Mark 59A (702).* Deld 13-5-67.
IF-50 Purchased by HSA, 12-3-65, as G-9-134. *Converted to Indian Hunter Mark 56A (A465).* Deld 17-8-66.
IF-51 Purchased by HSA, 21-3-63, as G-9-82. *Converted to Iraqi Hunter FGA Mark 59 (581).* Deld 12-10-64.
IF-53 Purchased by HSA, 3-2-65, as G-9-186. Scrapped for spares.
IF-54 Purchased by HSA, 5-3-65, as G-9-116. *Converted to Iraqi Hunter FGA Mark 59A (692).* Deld 13-10-66.
IF-56 Purchased by HSA, 18-12-62, as G-9-101. *Converted to Kuwaiti Hunter T Mark 67 (210).* Deld 25-2-65.
IF-59 Purchased by HSA, 14-10-64, as G-9-125. *Converted to Iraqi Hunter FGA Mark 59A (697).* Deld 10-1-67.

IF-60 Purchased by HSA, 10-12-64, as G-9-145. *Converted to Lebanese Hunter T Mark 66C (L.280).* Deld 15-11-65.
IF-62 Purchased by HSA, 10-3-65, as G-9-146. *Converted to Indian Hunter Mark 56A (A469).* Deld 12-10-66.
IF-64 Purchased by HSA, 26-1-65, as G-9-142. *Converted to Indian Hunter Mark 56A (A479).* Deld 14-1-67.
IF-66 Purchased by HSA, 10-12-64, as G-9-138. *Converted to Indian Hunter Mark 56A (A491)* Deld 19-4-67.
IF-68 Purchased by HSA, 3-12-62, as G-9-83. *Converted to Iraqi Hunter T Mark 69 (568).* Deld 22-4-64.
IF-69 Purchased by HSA, 27-1-65, as G-9-129. *Converted to Kuwaiti Hunter FGA Mark 57 (214).* Deld 20-2-66.
IF-70 Purchased by HSA, 5-1-65, as G-9-160. *Converted to Kuwaiti Hunter FGA Mark 57 (215).* Deld 24-2-66.
IF-71 Purchased by HSA, 10-3-65, as G-9-151. *Converted to Iraqi Hunter FGA Mark 59A (668).* Deld 8-9-66.
IF-72 Purchased by HSA, 10-3-65, as G-9-150. *Converted to Iraqi Hunter FGA Mark 59A (700).* Deld 15-3-67.
IF-74 Purchased by HSA, 21-10-66, as G-9-109. *Converted to Iraqi Hunter FGA Mark 59A (695).* Deld 8-12-66.
IF-75 Purchased by HSA, 30-10-62, as G-9-84. *Converted to Iraqi Hunter FGA Mark 59 (587).* Deld 14-1-65.
IF-77 Purchased by HSA, 8-12-64, as G-9-118. *Converted to Indian Hunter Mark 56A (A461).* Deld 28-6-66.
IF-78 Purchased by HSA, 9-2-65, as G-9-163. *Converted to Indian Hunter Mark 56A (A478).* Deld 9-12-66.
IF-79 Purchased by HSA, 31-10-62, as G-9-85. *Converted to Iraqi Hunter FGA Mark 59 (628).* Deld 14-1-65.
IF-80 Purchased by HSA, 16-10-62, as G-9-86. *Converted to Iraqi Hunter FGA Mark 59 (630).* Deld 13-4-65.
IF-82 No 26 Sqn, No 9 Wing, *FAB/BL*. Aircraft crashed during high-speed run over airfield, 27-6-58; pilot killed.
IF-84 Purchased by HSA, 2-4-63, as G-9-87. *Converted to Iraqi Hunter T Mark 69 (567).* Deld 24-2-65.
IF-85 Purchased by HSA, 10-3-65, as G-9-139. *Converted to Indian Hunter Mark 56A (A467).* Deld 12-10-66.
IF-86 Purchased by HSA, 6-10-64, as G-9-110. *Converted to Lebanese Hunter FGA Mark 70 (L.176).* Deld 14-9-66.
IF-87 Purchased by HSA, 9-2-65, as G-9-149. *Converted to Iraqi Hunter FGA Mark 59A (691).* Deld 13-10-66.
IF-88 Purchased by HSA, 28-3-63, as G-9-88. *Converted to Iraqi Hunter FGA Mark 59 (578).* Deld 27-8-64.
IF-89 Purchased by HSA, 12-3-65, as G-9-161. *Converted to Indian Hunter Mark 56A (A477).* Deld 9-12-66.
IF-91 Purchased by HSA, 12-3-65, as G-9-122. *Converted to Indian Hunter Mark 56A (A459).* Deld 28-6-66.
IF-93 Purchased by HSA, 14-10-64, as G-9-126. *Converted to Iraqi Hunter FGA Mark 59A (698).* Deld 10-1-67.
IF-94 Purchased by HSA, 20-11-62, as G-9-98. *Converted to Iraqi Hunter FGA Mark 59 (629).* Deld 24-2-65.

Appendix 3 205

IF-96 Purchased by HSA, 7-10-64, as G-9-121. *Converted to Lebanese Hunter FGA Mark 70 (L.177).* Deld 14-9-65.

IF-97 Purchased by HSA, 8-5-63, as G-9-89. *Converted to Iraqi Hunter T Mark 69 (626).* Deld 17-12-64.

IF-98 Purchased by HSA, 22-12-64, as G-9-137. *Converted to Indian Hunter Mark 56A (A490).* Deld 19-4-67.

IF-99 Purchased by HSA, 5-1-65, as G-9-135. *Converted to Iraqi Hunter FGA Mark 59A (699).* Deld 15-3-67.

IF-101 Purchased by HSA, 27-10-64, as G-9-114. *Converted to Lebanese Hunter FGA Mark 70 (L.179).* Deld 15-11-65.

IF-102 No 9 Wing, *FAB/BL*. Pilot ejected after flame-out, 1958, and aircraft executed perfect wheels-up landing, killing two horses.

IF-104 Purchased by HSA, 26-1-65, as G-9-130. *Converted to Indian Hunter Mark 56A (A464).* Deld 17-8-66.

IF-106 Purchased by HSA, 12-11-64, as G-9-104. *Converted to Chilean Hunter FGA Mark 71 (J-701).* Deld 23-10-67.

IF-107 Purchased by HSA, 19-4-63, as G-9-90. *Converted to Iraqi Hunter FGA Mark 59 (580).* Deld 12-10-64.

IF-108 Purchased by HSA, 21-10-64, as G-9-105. *Converted to Chilean Hunter FGA Mark 71 (J-702).* Deld 1-11-67.

IF-110 Purchased by HSA, 11-2-65, as G-9-147. *Converted to Indian Hunter Mark 56A (A471).* Deld 2-11-66.

IF-112 Purchased by HSA, 10-12-64, as G-9-119. *Converted to Lebanese Hunter T Mark 66C (L.281).* Deld 23-12-65.

IF-113 Purchased by HSA, 23-10-64, as G-9-115. *Converted to Indian Hunter Mark 56A (A487).* Deld 19-4-67.

IF-114 Purchased by HSA, 31-10-62, as G-9-91. *Converted to Iraqi Hunter FGA Mark 59 (586).* Deld 17-12-64.

IF-115 Purchased by HSA, 13-1-65, as G-9-152. *Converted to Indian Hunter Mark 56A (A473).* Deld 2-11-66.

IF-116 Purchased by HSA, 26-1-65, as G-9-140. *Converted to Indian Hunter Mark 56A (A468).* Deld 12-10-66.

IF-117 Purchased by HSA, 26-1-65, as G-9-143. *Converted to Indian Hunter Mark 56A (A494).* Deld 28-6-67.

IF-120 Purchased by HSA, 13-1-65, as G-9-136. *Converted to Indian Hunter Mark 56A (A466).* Deld 17-8-66.

IF-122 Purchased by HSA, 3-12-62, as G-9-92. *Converted to Iraqi Hunter FGA Mark 59 (579).* Deld 27-8-64.

IF-123 Purchased by HSA, 27-1-65, as G-9-144. *Converted to Indian Hunter Mark 56A (A470).* Deld 12-10-66.

IF-124 Purchased by HSA, 27-10-64, as G-9-113. *Converted to Indian Hunter Mark 56A (A480).* Deld 14-1-67.

IF-126 Purchased by HSA, 12-11-62, as G-9-93. *Converted to Iraqi Hunter FGA Mark 59 (585).* Deld 2-12-64.

IF-127 Purchased by HSA, 11-2-65, as G-9-157. *Converted to Indian Hunter Mark 56A (A475).* Deld 9-12-66.

IF-128 Purchased by HSA, 10-12-64, as G-9-131. *Converted to Indian Hunter Mark 56A (A483).* Deld 2-3-67.

IF-129 Purchased by HSA, 10-11-64, as G-9-102. *Converted to Lebanese Hunter FGA Mark 70 (L.178).* Deld 15-11-65.

IF-131 Purchased by HSA, 10-11-64, as G-9-111. *Converted to Indian Hunter Mark 56A (A485).* Deld 2-3-67.
IF-132 Purchased by HSA, 23-1-65, as G-9-132. *Converted to Indian Hunter Mark 56A (A489).* Deld 20-7-67.
IF-135 Purchased by HSA, 11-2-65, as G-9-153. *Converted to Iraqi Hunter FGA Mark 59A (694).* Deld 14-11-66.
IF-137 Purchased by HSA, 8-12-64, as G-9-156. *Converted to Indian Hunter Mark 56A (A481).* Deld 14-1-67.
IF-138 Purchased by HSA, 22-12-64, as G-9-155. *Converted to Iraqi Hunter FGA Mark 59A (701).* Deld 13-5-67.
IF-140 Purchased by HSA, 2-5-63, as G-9-94. *Converted to Iraqi Hunter FGA Mark 59 (576).* Deld 24-6-64.
IF-141 Purchased by HSA, 23-10-64, as G-9-103. *Converted to Chilean Hunter FGA Mark 71 (J-700).* Deld 21-9-67.
IF-142 Purchased by HSA, 12-11-62, as G-9-95. *Converted to Iraqi Hunter FGA Mark 59 (582).* Deld 2-12-64.
IF-143 Purchased by HSA, 18-12-62, as G-9-99. *Converted to Iraqi Hunter T Mark 69 (569).* Deld 14-5-64.
IF-144 Purchased by HSA, 23-10-64, as G-9-112. *Converted to Indian Hunter Mark 56A (A486).* Deld 2-3-67.

4 Conversion of Hunters for export

Hawker Rhodesian Hunter FGA Mark 9
Order for 12 ex-RAF Hunter F Mark 6s to be brought up to FGA Mark 9 standard by Hawker Siddeley Aviation during 1963. See under Hunter F Mark 6s XE548, XE559, XE560, XE613, XF374, XF504, XF506, XG294, XG295, XJ638, XJ716 and XJ718.

Hawker Peruvian Hunter Mark 52
Order for 16 ex-RAF Hunter F Mark 4s to be prepared by Hawker Aircraft Ltd, for sale to Peru during 1956. See under Hunter F Mark 4s WT717, WT734, WT756, WT758, WT759, WT765, WT766, WT768, WT773, WT774, WT776, WT779, WT796, WT800, WT803 and WW662.

Hawker Indian Hunter Mark 56
Order for 160 aircraft, of which 16 were converted from Hunter F Mark 6s (BA232-BA248), by Hawker Aircraft Ltd, during 1957. See under Hunter F Mark 6s XE537, XE538, XE539, XE540, XE547, XE549, XE600 (later removed from contract), XF463, XF497, XF499, XF500, XF501, XF503, XF505, XG150 and XG163.

Hawker Indian Hunter Mark 56A
First conversion order, Contract No HSA/65/I/061, for 36 Hunter F Mark 6s to be brought to full FGA Mark 9 standard by Hawker Siddeley Aviation and delivered between June 1966 and July 1967. Conversions were of 35 ex-Belgian Mark 6s and one

Appendix 4 207

ex-Dutch Mark 6. See Belgian Mark 6s IF-1, 3, 4, 7, 13, 16, 17, 18, 36, 43, 50, 62, 64, 66, 77, 78, 85, 89, 91, 98, 104, 110, 113, 115, 116, 117, 120, 123, 124, 127, 128, 131, 132, 137 and 144, and Dutch Mark 6 N-209. Aircraft numbered A459-A494.

Second conversion order, Contract No HSA/67/I/00, first part, for eight ex-RAF Hunter F Mark 6s to be brought to full FGA Mark 9 standard by Hawker Siddeley Aviation and delivered between November 1968 and April 1969. See under RAF Hunter F Mark 6s XF521, XG129, XG170, XG186, XG189, XG190, XG201 and XG211. Aircraft numbered A936-A943.

Third conversion order, Contract No HSA/67/I/00, second part, for three ex-RAF Hunter F Mark 6s to be brought to full FGA Mark 9 standard by Hawker Siddeley Aviation and delivered between July and September 1969. See under RAF Hunter F Mark 6s XE620, XJ646 and XJ692. Aircraft numbered A967-A969.

Fourth conversion order, Contract No HSAL/68/I/077, for six Hunter F Mark 6s to be brought to full FGA Mark 9 standard by Hawker Siddeley Aviation, and delivered September 1969 and March 1970. See under RAF Hunter F Mark 6 XF446, and Dutch Mark 6s N-213, 216, 252, 271 and 274. Aircraft numbered A1010-A1015.

Hawker Kuwaiti Hunter FGA Mark 57

Conversion order for four ex-Belgian Hunter Mark 6s to be brought to full FGA Mark 9 standard by Hawker Siddeley Aviation and delivered to Kuwait between February 1965 and February 1966. See under Belgian Hunter F Mark 6s IF-26, 41, 69 and 70. Aircraft numbered 212-215.

Hawker Swiss Hunter Mark 58

Order for 100 aircraft, of which the first 12 were converted from ex-RAF Hunter F Mark 6s by Hawker Aircraft Ltd, during 1958. See under RAF Hunter F Mark 6s XE526, XE527, XE528, XE529, XE533, XE536, XE541, XE542, XE545, XE553, XE554 and XE555. Aircraft numbered J-4001 to J-4012.

Hawker Swiss Hunter Mark 58A

First conversion order for 30 aircraft to be converted from ex-RAF Hunter F Mark 4s (and GA Mark 11s) and F Mark 6s (and two Dutch Hunter T Mark 7s) to full FGA Mark 9 standard by Hawker Siddeley Aviation, for delivery to Switzerland between December 1971 and April 1973. See under RAF Hunter Mark 4/11s WT713, WT808, WV257, WV374, WV380, WV405, WV411, WW589, WW659, XE674, XE717, XF291, XF303, XF318, XF361, XF365, XF937, XF947, XF976, XF981, XF984 and XF992; RAF Hunter Mark 6s XE611, XF436, XF438, XF462, XG127 and XG272; and Dutch Hunter Mark 7s N-313 and N-318. Aircraft numbered J-4101 to J-4130.

Second conversion order for 22 aircraft to be converted from ex-RAF Hunter F Mark 4s and an F Mark 6 to full FGA Mark 9 standard by Hawker Siddeley Aviation, for delivery to Switzerland between January 1974 and April 1975. See under RAF Hunter Mark 4s WT716, WT797, WV261, WV266, WV329, WV393, WV404, WW590, XE659, XE678, XF306, XF308, XF312, XF316, XF370, XF933, XF941, XF944, XF973, XF990 and XF998; and Hunter F Mark 6 XF429. Aircraft numbered J-4131 to J-4152.

Hawker Iraqi Hunter FGA Mark 59
Conversion order for 24 aircraft to be converted from ex-Belgian and ex-Dutch Hunter F Mark 6s to full FGA Mark 9 standard by Hawker Siddeley Aviation, for delivery to Iraq between March 1964 and May 1965. See under Dutch Hunter Mark 6s N-234 and N-247, and Belgian Hunter Mark 6s IF-6, 10, 11, 14, 20, 21, 24, 27, 28, 32, 48, 75, 79, 80, 88, 94, 107, 114, 122, 126, 140 and 142. Aircraft numbered 570-587 and 628-633.

Hawker Iraqi Hunter FGA Mark 59A
Conversion order for 18 aircraft to be converted from ex-Belgian and ex-Dutch Hunter F Mark 6s to full FGA Mark 9 standard by Hawker Siddeley Aviation, under Contract Nos HSAL/65/I/060, HSAL/65/I/062 and HSAL/65/I/062A, for delivery to Iraq between November 1965 and May 1967. See under Dutch Hunter Mark 6s N-253 and N-255, and Belgian Hunter Mark 6s IF-8, 9, 22, 25, 29, 31, 54, 59, 71, 72, 74, 87, 93, 99, 135 and 138. Aircraft numbered 657-661 and 690-702.

Hawker Iraqi Hunter FGA Mark 59B
Conversion order for four aircraft to be converted from ex-Dutch Hunter F Mark 6s to full FGA Mark 9 standard by Hawker Siddeley Aviation, under Contract No HSAL/65/I/060, for delivery to Iraq between May and September 1966. See under Dutch Hunter Mark 6s N-205, 221, 259 and 263. Aircraft numbered 662-665.

Hawker Saudi Arabian Hunter F Mark 60
Conversion order for four ex-RAF Hunter F Mark 6s to be prepared for the Royal Saudi Air Force by Hawker Siddeley Aviation under Contract No HSAL/66/S/064, dated March 28 1966, for delivery to Saudi Arabia in May 1966. See under RAF Hunter F Mark 6s XE591, XF450, XJ712 and XJ715. Aircraft numbered 60/601 to 60/604. One aircraft lost in action against the Egyptian Air Force in 1967 and the remaining aircraft were presented to the Royal Jordanian Air Force the following year.

Hawker Peruvian Hunter T Mark 62
Conversion order for one ex-RAF Hunter F Mark 4, WT706, to be brought up to modified T Mark 7 standard by Hawker Aircraft Ltd, Kingston-upon-Thames, and delivered to Peru in February 1960. Numbered 681.

Hawker Hunter Mark 66A
This aircraft was originally prepared for Manufacturers' demonstration flying as a private venture, and registered as G-APUX; it was basically built from the centre and rear fuselage of ex-Belgian Hunter Mark 6 IF-19, but also included the two-seat front fuselage from a ground display unit, the wings, fin and rudder of IF-67 and the engine and gearbox from ex-RAF Mark 6 XE378. It was flown in many displays at home and abroad, was the first Hunter to carry 230-gallon drop tanks and UHF radio, and was fitted with nosewheel braking. In May 1963 it was leased to Iraq, Jordan and Lebanon for training purposes, and in 1965 was returned to HSA for conversion to Chilean Hunter T Mark 72, numbered J-718 and delivered to Chile on August 9 1967.

Hawker Jordanian Hunter T Mark 66B
Conversion orders, each for single aircraft, to be converted from ex-Dutch Hunter F Mark 6s (see N-249 and N-283) by Hawker Siddeley Aviation under Contract Nos

Appendix 4

HSAL/65/J/063 and HSAL/67/070 respectively. Full Hawker P.1101 (second prototype) two-seat trainer standard. Delivery October 1966 and February 1969, numbered 716 and 810 respectively.

Hawker Lebanese Hunter T Mark 66C

Conversion order for three ex-Belgian Hunter F Mark 6 aircraft to be converted to two-seat trainer standard (similar to that of the Indian T Mark 66) by Hawker Siddeley Aviation under Contract No HSA/64/L/059 for delivery between November 1965 and July 1966. See Belgian Hunter Mark 6s IF-34, 60 and 112. Aircraft numbered L.280 to L.282.

Hawker Indian Hunter T Mark 66D

Conversion order for 12 ex-Dutch Hunter F Mark 6s to be converted to two-seat trainers (of a standard similar to that of the Indian Hunter T Mark 66) by Hawker Siddeley Aviation under Contract No HSA/66/I/067 dated March 10 1966, for delivery between May 1966 and September 1967. See Dutch Hunter Mark 6s N-203, 204, 208, 212, 214, 218, 223, 230, 250, 261, 265 and 269. Aircraft numbered S570 to S581.

Hawker Indian Hunter T Mark 66E

Conversion order for five ex-RAF Hunter F Mark 6s to be converted to full Indian T Mark 66 standard (with further modifications) by Hawker Siddeley Aviation, for delivery between June and December 1973. See RAF Hunter F Mark 6s WW596, XE556, XE585, XF459 and XJ694. Aircraft numbered S.1389 to S.1393.

Hawker Kuwaiti Hunter T Mark 67

First conversion order for two ex-Belgian Hunter F Mark 6s to be brought to two-seat trainer standard by Hawker Siddeley Aviation under Contract No HAL/63/K/050 for delivery to Kuwait during February 1965. See Belgian Hunter F Mark 6s IF-37 and IF-56. Aircraft numbered 211 and 210.

Second conversion order for two ex-Dutch and one ex-RAF Hunter F Mark 6s to be brought to two-seat trainer standard by Hawker Siddeley Aviation under Contract No HSA/67/K/069 for delivery to Kuwait during May 1969. See Dutch Hunter F Mark 6s N-257 and N-282, and RAF Hunter F Mark 6 XE530. Aircraft numbered 218-220.

Hawker Swiss Hunter T Mark 68

Conversion order for four ex-RAF Hunter F Mark 4s and four ex-Swedish Hunter Mark 50s to be brought to two-seat trainer standard by Hawker Siddeley Aviation for delivery to Switzerland between August 1974 and June 1975. See under RAF Hunter F Mark 4s WV332, WV398, XE702 and XF951, and Swedish Hunter Mark 50s 34017, 34072, 34080 and 34086. Aircraft numbered J-4201 to J-4208.

Hawker Iraqi Hunter T Mark 69

First conversion order for three ex-Belgian Hunter F Mark 6s to be brought to two-seat trainer standard by Hawker Siddeley Aviation for delivery to Iraq during 1964. See Belgian Hunter F Mark 6s IF-68, IF-84 and IF-143. Aircraft re-numbered 567 to 569. Contract No HSA/63/I/054.

An Iraqi Hunter T Mark 69.

Second conversion order for two ex-Belgian Hunter F Mark 6s (IF-20 and IF-97) to be brought to two-seat trainer standard by Hawker Siddeley Aviation for delivery to Iraq early in 1965. Aircraft re-numbered 626 and 627. Contract No HSA/64/I/056.

Hawker Saudi Arabian Hunter T Mark 7 (unofficially T Mark 70)

Conversion order for two ex-RAF Hunter T Mark 7s to be prepared for the Royal Saudi Air Force by Hawker Siddeley Aviation under 'Magic Carpet' package air defence contract (HSAL/66/S/064), dated March 28 1966, for delivery in May 1966. See under RAF Hunter T Mark 7s XL605 and XL620. Aircraft re-numbered 70/616 and 70/617. Presented to Royal Jordanian Air Force in 1968. Returned to RAF, 7-74, as XX467 and XX466 respectively.

Hawker Lebanese Hunter FGA Mark 70

Conversion order for four ex-Belgian Hunter F Mark 6s to be refurbished and brought to full FGA Mark 9 standard by Hawker Siddeley Aviation under Contract No HSA/64/L/059, for delivery to Lebanon between September 1965 and September 1966. See Belgian Hunter F Mark 6s IF-86, 96, 101 and 128. Aircraft re-numbered L.176 to L.179.

Hawker Chilean Hunter FGA Mark 71

First conversion order for 15 aircraft (selected from refurbished Belgian and Dutch Hunter Mark 6s, and an RAF F Mark 6) to be brought up to full FGA Mark 9 standard by Hawker Siddeley Aviation under Contract No HSAL/66/C/066 dated October 26 1966 for delivery to Chile between September 1966 and June 1968. See under RAF Hunter F Mark 6 XG232, Belgian Mark 6s IF-44, 106, 108 and 141, and Dutch Mark 6s N-201, 210, 220, 232, 262, 266, 270, 273, 276 and 277. Aircraft numbered J-700 to J-714.

Second conversion order for nine aircraft to be brought up to FGA Mark 9 standard from ex-RAF Hunter F Mark 6s by Hawker Siddeley Aviation under Contract No HSAL/69/C/084 dated September 10 1969 for delivery to Chile between December 1970

Appendix 4   211

and September 1971. See under RAF Hunter F Mark 6s XE557, XE561, XE580, XE625, XE644, XF447, XF512, XG199 and XJ713. Aircraft numbered J-722 to J-730.

Third conversion order for four ex-RAF Hunter F Mark 4s to be brought up to full FGA Mark 9 standard by Hawker Siddeley Aviation for delivery to Chile between September 1973 and January 1974. See under RAF Hunter F Mark 4s WT801, WW653, XF302 and XF323. Aircraft numbered J-731, J-732, J-733 and J-737.

Hawker Chilean Hunter FR Mark 71A

First conversion order for three ex-RAF Hunter F Mark 6s (see XF453, XJ717 and XK148) to be brought up to full FR Mark 10 standard by Hawker Siddeley Aviation under Contract No HSAL/66/C/066 for delivery to Chile between July and September 1968. Aircraft numbered J-715 to J-717.

Second conversion order for three ex-RAF Hunter F Mark 4s (see WV326, XF317 and XF982) to be brought up to full FR Mark 10 standard by Hawker Siddeley Aviation for delivery to Chile during January and February 1974. Aircraft numbered J-734, J-735 and J-738.

Hawker Chilean Hunter T Mark 72

First conversion order for three aircraft to be brought up to full P.1101 two-seat trainer (second prototype) standard by Hawker Siddeley Aviation for delivery to Chile between August 1967 and January 1968. See Hunter Mark 66 (G-APUX)/Belgian Hunter Mark 6 IF-19, and Dutch Hunter Mark 6s N-202 and N-224. Aircraft re-numbered J-718 to J-720.

Second conversion order for three aircraft (extended by a fourth later) to be selected from various Hunters to be brought to full Avon 200-series two-seat trainer standard by Hawker Siddeley Aviation. Deliveries 1970-71 (fourth aircraft in February 1974). See under Hawker P.1101 second prototype, XJ627, Hunter F Mark 4 XE704, and Hunter F Mark 6s XF447 and XJ713. Aircraft numbered J-721 to J-723, and J-736.

Hawker Jordanian Hunter FGA Mark 73

Conversion order for two ex-RAF Hunter F Mark 6s (XE603 and XF520) to be brought up to full FGA Mark 9 standard by Hawker Siddeley Aviation under Contract No HSAL/68/J/075, for delivery to Jordan during June 1968. Aircraft numbered 814 and 832.

Hawker Jordanian Hunter FGA Mark 73A

First conversion order for four ex-RAF Hunter Mark 6/9s (XF389, XG234, XG237 and XJ645) to be brought to full FGA Mark 9 standard by Hawker Siddeley Aviation under Contract No HSAL/68/J/076, for delivery to Jordan between May and July 1969. Aircraft numbered 828-831.

Second conversion order for nine aircraft to be brought to full Hunter FGA Mark 9 standard by Hawker Siddeley Aviation for delivery to Jordan between June and December 1971. See under Dutch Hunter Mark 6 N-264 and RAF Hunter F Mark 4s WV325, WV407, WV408, XF364, XF936, XF952, XF968 and XF987. Aircraft numbered 840 and 842-849.

Hawker Jordanian Hunter FGA Mark 73B
Conversion order for three aircraft (see under Dutch Hunter Mark 6 N-279 and RAF Hunter F Mark 4s WV401 and XF979) to be brought up to full FGA Mark 9 standard by Hawker Siddeley Aviation for delivery to Jordan between June and November 1971. Aircraft numbered 841, 850 and 851.

Hawker Singaporean Hunter FGA Mark 74
Conversion order for 12 ex-RAF Hunter F Mark 6s to be refurbished and brought to full FGA Mark 9 standard by Hawker Siddeley Aviation under Contract No HSAL/68/SG/078 for delivery to Singapore between November 1970 and May 1971. See RAF Hunter F Mark 6s XE615 (508), XE652 (519), XG251 (507), XG260 (501), XG296 (510), XJ632 (505), XJ642 (518), XJ643 (515), XJ680 (511), XJ684 (513), XJ685 (502) and XF456 (509). Singaporean serial number given in brackets.

Hawker Singaporean Hunter FR Mark 74A
Conversion order for four ex-RAF Hunter F Mark 6s to be brought to full Mark 10 (modified) standard by Hawker Siddeley Aviation under Contract No HSAL/68/SG/078 for delivery to Singapore between June and August 1971. See RAF Hunter F Mark 6s XF437 (503), XG205 (506), XG292 (512) and XJ689 (517). Singaporean serial numbers given in brackets.

Hawker Singaporean Hunter FR Mark 74B
Conversion order for eight ex-RAF Hunter F Mark 4s and 14 ex-RAF Hunter F Mark 6s to be brought to full FR Mark 10 (modified) standard by Hawker Siddeley Aviation for delivery to Singapore between June 1972 and October 1973. See under RAF Hunter F Mark 4s WV258 (539), WV331 (543), WV364 (530), WV366 (537), XE679 (541), XF360 (542), XF369 (538) and XF969 (529), and RAF Hunter F Mark 6s XE599 (535), XE605 (523), XE614 (533), XF422 (524), XF428 (525), XF432 (526), XF441 (545), XF458 (527), XF460 (546), XG153 (520), XG266 (521), XJ633 (534), XJ714 (531), XK142 (522). Singaporean serial numbers given in brackets.

Hawker Singaporean Hunter T Mark 75
Conversion order for four Hunters to be refurbished and brought to full Hunter T Mark 7 standard by Hawker Siddeley Aviation under Contract No HSAL/68/SG/078 for delivery to Singapore between December 1969 and September 1970. See under RAF Hunter T Mark 4 WW664, Admiralty Hunter T Mark 8 XE664 and Dutch Hunter T Mark 7s N-303 and N-304. Aircraft numbered 500, 504, 514 and 516.

Hawker Singaporean Hunter T Mark 75A
Conversion order for five ex-RAF Hunter F Mark 4/11s to be brought to full two-seat T Mark 7 standard by Hawker Siddeley Aviation for delivery to Singapore between November 1972 and October 1973. See under RAF Hunter F Mark 4/11s WT741 (541), WV272 (540), WV386 (532), XF950 (536) and XF970 (528). Singaporean serials given in brackets.

Hawker Abu Dhabian Hunter FGA Mark 76
Conversion order for seven aircraft to be refurbished and brought to FGA Mark 9 standard by Hawker Siddeley Aviation under Contract No HSA/69/AD/082 dated

Appendix 4 213

February 28 1969 for delivery to Abu Dhabi between March 1970 and January 1971. See under RAF Hunter F Mark 4s WV389, WV402, XE589, XF362, XF367, XF935 and XG341. Aircraft numbered 701-707.

Hawker Abu Dhabian Hunter FR Mark 76A

Conversion order for three ex-RAF Hunters (see Hunter F Mark 4s WV400 and XF971, and Hunter F Mark 6 WW592) to be refurbished and brought to full Hunter FGA Mark 9 standard by Hawker Siddeley Aviation under Contract No HSAL/69/AD/082 for delivery during January 1971. Aircraft numbered 708-710.

Hawker Abu Dhabian Hunter T Mark 77

Conversion order for two ex-Dutch Hunter T Mark 7s to be refurbished by Hawker Siddeley Aviation under Contract No HSAL/69/AD/082 for delivery during May 1970. See Dutch Hunter T Mark 7s N-301 and N-312. Aircraft re-numbered 711 and 712.

Hawker Qatari Hunter FGA Mark 78

Conversion order for three ex-Dutch Hunter F Mark 6s to be brought to full FGA Mark 9 standard by Hawker Siddeley Aviation under Contract No HSAL/69/Q/083 for delivery to Qatar in December 1971. See Dutch Hunter F Mark 6s N-219, N-222 and N-268. Aircraft numbered QA10 to QA12.

Hawker Qatari Hunter T Mark 79

Conversion order to refurbish the ex-Dutch Hunter T Mark 7 N-316 by Hawker Siddeley Aviation for delivery to Qatar in December 1971. Re-numbered QA-13.

Hawker Kenyan Hunter FGA Mark 80

Conversion order for four ex-RAF aircraft to be brought to full Hunter FGA Mark 9 standard by Hawker Siddeley Aviation for delivery to Kenya between June 1974 and January 1975. See under RAF Hunter F Mark 4s XF309, XF972 and XF975, and RAF Hunter F Mark 6 XE626. Aircraft numbered 803 to 806.

Hawker Kenyan Hunter T Mark 81

Conversion order to two aircraft (see under RAF Hunter Mark 4/8 WT577 and Hunter T Mark 8 XL604) to be refurbished by Hawker Siddeley Aviation for delivery to Kenya during June 1974. Aircraft re-numbered 801 and 802 respectively.

Index

Abu Dhabi, Hunters supplied to, *100-101, 106, 111-112, 150, 156-159, 165, 190, 212, 213*
Aden 30 mm gun, *13, 16, 17, 20, 25, 60, 64, 70, 71, 115, 117, 124-125, 127, 135-137*
Admiralty, *11, 74, 89, 184*
Air Ministry, *9, 12;* Operational Requirements Branch, *10, 17, 25, 26, 46*
Alam, Sqdn Ldr Mohammed, PAF, *105*
Ambala, India, *98, 178, 179, 183, 195*
Anderson, George, *99*
Anderson, M., Avions Fairey, *96, 144 et seq*
Ängelholm, Sweden, *93*
Antofagasta, Chile, *110*
Armstrong Siddeley Sapphire, *10, 13, 17, 23, 24, 29, 34, 42, 50, 53, 54, 58, 125, 136, 141*
Armstrong Whitworth Aircraft, Sir W.G., *11, 19, 32, 43, 80, 141 et seq*
Australian Government, *91*
Avro Lancaster, *8*
Avro Lincoln, *8*
Aytoun, Sqdn Ldr R., *32*

BAC Jet Provost, *78, 82*
BAC TSR-2, *54, 79*
Barkarby, Sweden, *93*
Barnes, Lt-Col William F., USAF, *27*
Beamont, Wg Cdr R.P., DSO, OBE, DFC, *18*
Beasley, Sqdn Ldr C.W., *40*
Beauvechaine, Belgium, *96, 202*
Beck, Maj, USAF, *33, 38*
Bedford, A.W., OBE, *18, 44, 51, 75, 80, 138 et seq*
Belgische Luchtmacht, 96, 202
Belgium, Hunters built in, *58, 80, 92, 95, 97, 103, 104, 106, 110, 202-211*
Bierset, Belgium, *96, 202*
'Black Arrows', formation aerobatic team, *58, 64, 65, 75*
'Blue Diamonds', formation aerobatic team, *66*

Blue Fox radar, *129, 187*
Blue Jay (see de Havilland Firestreak)
Bore, Cliff, *70, 73*
Borneo, operations in, 1964, *85, 173*
Boscombe Down, Aircraft & Armament Experimental Establishment, *12, 19-22, 25, 26, 29, 31, 45, 51, 75, 86, 87, 89, 98, 135-182*
Bristol Beaufighter, *25*
Bristol Siddeley Orpheus, *79*
Bristol Type 188, *184*
Broad, Hubert, *18*
Brussels Air Shows, *22, 92*
Bullen, Frank, *36, 44, 74, 93, 94, 138 et seq*
Bulman, Gp Capt P.W.S., CBE, MC, AFC, *18*

Camm, Sir Sydney, CBE, *4, 5, 11, 12, 16-18, 28, 34, 39, 50, 69, 133*
Carver, Flt Lt N.J., *145 et seq*
Chièvres, Belgium, *96, 202*
Chile, Hunters exported to, *72, 80, 110, 111, 146, 148, 152, 154-156, 158, 164, 165, 168, 171, 172, 176, 177, 182, 183, 200-203, 205, 206, 208, 210, 211*
Chopra, Flt Lt, IAF, *98, 164 et seq*
Churchill, the Rt Hon Sir Winston, *23*

Dass, Sqdn Ldr, IAF, *97*
Dassault Super Mystère, *104*
Defence White Paper, 1957, *56, 57, 72, 74, 97*
de Havilland, Geoffrey, Jr, *14*
de Havilland Comet, *7*
de Havilland Firestreak, *24, 26, 27, 44, 50, 54, 60, 72, 136, 180*
de Havilland DH 108, *14*
de Havilland Hornet, *8, 9*
de Havilland Mosquito, *8, 10*
de Havilland Sea Venom, *87*
de Havilland Sea Vixen (DH 110), *14, 16, 23, 87*

de Havilland Vampire, *8-10, 33, 69, 75, 78, 87, 92, 130, 131*
de Havilland Venom, *9, 92*
Denmark, Hunters supplied to, *42, 53, 93-95, 100-101, 151, 190, 192-194*
Derry, John, *23*
Dey, Fg Off, IAF, *98, 164*
Dubendorf, Switzerland, *197-199*
Duke, Sqdn Ldr N.F., DSO, OBE, DFC, AFC, *4, 18-20, 22-24, 27, 28, 44, 70, 92, 138 et seq*
Dutt, Gp Capt, IAF, *97*

Eggleton, Fg Off W.D.E., *168 et seq*
Egyptian Air Force, *78, 208*
El Adem, Libya, *56, 173*
Emmen, Switzerland, *99, 112-113, 196-198*
Emmett, Sqdn Ldr R., *42*
Engineer, Air Vice-Marshal, IAF, *97*
English Electric Canberra, *9, 17, 24, 31*
English Electric Lightning, *24, 50, 53, 54, 57, 72, 78, 82*

Fairey Aviation Ltd, *44*
Fairey Fireflash, *44, 46-47, 50, 60, 74*
Fairey Gannet, *24*
Farnborough; Air Displays, *9, 20, 22, 23, 44-47, 54-55, 58, 64-65, 70, 75, 80;* Royal Aircraft Establishment, *12, 34, 50, 79, 137;* Empire Test Pilots' School, *32, 33*
Ferranti head-up display, *79*
Flack, Spencer, *94*
Fleet Air Arm Squadrons; No 736, *87;* No 738, *89;* No 739, *89;* No 759, *88;* No 764, *87-89*
Flugwaffe (Swiss Air Force), *98, 99, 105*
Flygmotor re-heat system, *93*
Fokker-Aviolanda, Amsterdam, *96, 199*
Folland Gnat, *78, 82, 92*

Index

Force Aérienne Belge, 96, 202
Fowler, Sqdn Ldr D.J., 53
Freer, Sqdn Ldr R.W.G., 42
Fuerza Aérea Peruana, 95, 96

Gick, Rear-Admiral P.D., OBE, DSC, 88-89, 90
Gloster Javelin, 14, 16, 54, 72
Gloster Meteor, 8-12, 14, 22, 23, 26, 30, 32, 33, 41, 42, 69, 75, 78, 92, 130, 131
Gole, Flt Lt, IAF, 186, 187, 195

Hawker Fury, 11
Hawker Hart, 39
Hawker Hunter prototypes, 21-27, 29, 69
Hawker Hunter F.1, 26, 28-34, 36-42, 53, 69, 92, 103, 137-141
Hawker Hunter F.2, 29, 32, 34, 35, 38, 40, 103, 141-142
Hawker Hunter 3, 27
Hawker Hunter F.4, 39-46, 48, 49, 53, 55, 71, 72, 74, 85, 87-89, 92-97, 103, 105, 112, 142-159, 187, 188, 206, 207, 210-213
Hawker Hunter F.5, 42-46, 48, 49, 53, 55, 58, 103, 159-162
Hawker Hunter F.6, 42, 44, 45, 51-53, 55, 56, 58-68, 71, 72, 80, 82, 86, 96, 99, 103, 106, 112, 127-129, 131, 162-184, 188, 189, 194, 196, 206, 207, 210-213
Hawker Hunter T.7, 69-72, 74, 75, 79-81, 87, 103, 126-127, 146, 148, 149, 154-156, 184-187, 194
Hawker Hunter T.8, 4, 74, 87-90, 103, 112, 142-145, 148-150, 152-154, 156-159, 184-188
Hawker Hunter T.8M, 129, 187
Hawker Hunter FGA.9, 45, 58, 82, 83, 85, 86, 103, 106, 115, 127-129, 163-184, 188, 206, 207
Hawker Hunter FR.10, 48-49, 58, 83, 85, 86, 103, 117, 127-129, 162-170, 174, 176, 177, 180-183, 189
Hawker Hunter GA.11, 89, 90, 103, 142-144, 146, 147, 149, 152-155, 158, 189
Hawker Hunter 12, 79, 163, 189
Hawker Hunter 66A, 79-81, 208
Hawker Hurricane, 5, 11, 39
Hawker P.1035, 11
Hawker P.1040, 7, 11, 18
Hawker P.1047, 12
Hawker P.1052, 12, 15, 18
Hawker P.1054, 10
Hawker P.1067 (Hunter at project stage), 10, 12-19, 50, 91, 135-136
Hawker P.1069, 13
Hawker P.1070, 13
Hawker P.1071, 13
Hawker P.1081, 9, 18, 91
Hawker P.1083, 25, 26, 50, 51, 136
Hawker P.1099 (Hunter 6 prototype), 137

Hawker P.1101 (Hunter two-seater prototypes), 69-72, 98, 110, 137, 199, 209
Hawker P.1109, 54, 60-61, 180
Hawker P.1114, 54
Hawker P.1115, 54
Hawker P.1120, 78
Hawker P.1121, 97
Hawker P.1127, 46, 97
Hawker P.1130, 72, 74
Hawker Sea Fury, 11, 17, 23, 39, 87, 118
Hawker Sea Hawk, 11, 17, 19, 23, 24, 87
Hawker Siddeley (BAe) Hawk T.1, 79
Hawker Siddeley (Blackburn, BAe) Buccaneer, 24, 54
Hawker Siddeley Group, 19, 50
Hawker Siddeley Harrier, 132
Hawker Siddeley Sea Harrier, 4, 129, 187
Hawker Tempest, 8, 9, 11
Hawker Typhoon, 11
Hegarty, Sqdn Ldr F.M., 42
High Flight, film, 46, 145
Hispano 20-mm gun, 9, 10, 13
Hussein, HM King of the Hashemites, 106, 110, 112

India, Hunters supplied to, 57, 72, 80, 96-98, 104, 163-167, 169-172, 175, 176, 178, 179, 182-184, 194, 199-207, 209
Indian Air Force, 98, 104-105
Indo-Pakistan Wars: 1965, 104-105; 1971, 105
Iraq, Hunters supplied to, 78, 100, 104, 112, 114, 175-178, 200-206, 208-210
Iraqi Air Force, 104

Jackson, Sqdn Ldr J.A.G., 40
Jamnagar, India, 105, 194
Jordan, Hunters supplied to, 75, 85, 100, 106, 107, 112, 114, 148, 150, 151, 156-159, 163, 164, 166, 168-170, 172-175, 179-184, 199, 201, 208, 209, 211, 212

Kalaikunda, India, 105
Karnik, Fg Off, IAF, 98, 178 et seq
Karwowski, Stefan, 94
Kenya, Hunters supplied to, 112, 144, 155, 158, 168, 187, 213
Kloten, Switzerland, 197-199
Koninklijke Luchtmacht, 96
Korean War, 23, 26, 50, 91, 94
Kuwait, Hunters supplied to, 106, 107, 163, 164, 201, 203, 204, 207, 209
Kyle, Air Commodore Wallace, 26, 50

Lebanon, Hunters supplied to the, 78, 100, 106-110, 112-113, 162, 163, 166, 175, 180, 181, 183, 203-205, 208-210

Leeuwarden, Holland, 96, 100-101, 199
Lelong, Sqdn Ldr R., 31
Limatambo, Peru, 95, 96
Lister, Sqdn Ldr F.W., 43
Lockheed F-80 (and T-33) Shooting Star, 69
Lockheed F-104 Starfighter, 96
Lockspeiser, David, 44, 93, 148 et seq
Lucas, P.G., GM, 18
Lucey, Don, 44, 138 et seq

McDonnell Douglas A-4 Skyhawk, 104, 106
McDonnell Douglas F-4 Phantom, 86, 104
Mafraq, Jordan, 106
'Magic Carpet', defence agreement with Saudi Arabia, 78, 110
Mangard, Col A., *Flygvapnet*, 93
Martin-Baker ejector seats, 13, 72, 115, 124
Martin-Baker Limited, 137
Martin-Baker MB 5, 130
Martin Bullpup, 89
Maxaret wheel brakes, 123, 132
Merewether, Hugh, 18, 36, 44, 55, 56, 93, 98, 139 et seq
Messerschmitt Me 262, 16
MiG-15, 14, 23, 91
MiG-21, 74, 104
Miles Aircraft Ltd, 137
Ministry of Supply, 9, 12, 13, 17, 44, 51, 70, 72, 79, 87, 96, 98, 99, 189; Directorate of Military Aircraft (R & D), 26, 50; Directorate of Guided Weapons, 54; Directorate of Operational Requirements, 70
Mohlah, Flt Lt, IAF, 98, 196
Molins 57-mm gun, 10
Murphy, Frank, 18, 26, 29, 40, 44, 72, 93, 137 et seq

Nationaal Lucht-en Ruintevaart-laboratorium, 96
Netherlands, Hunters built in the, 58, 74, 92, 95-96, 100-101, 103, 106, 110, 189-191, 199, 200-201, 207-213
North American (and Canadair) F-86 Sabre, 8, 14, 23, 27, 40, 42, 91, 92, 99, 105

Oman, Hunters supplied to, 86, 106, 112, 181
Osborne, Sqdn Ldr A.F., DFC, 42

Pakistan Air Force, 105
Paris Air Show, 1959, 80, 98, 199
Paris-London Air Race, 1959, 98, 199
Peckham, Cyril, 20
Peru, Hunters supplied to, 42, 94, 95, 142, 143, 145, 146, 152, 206, 208

Philco Sidewinder, *89, 93, 96, 99, 100-101*
Plessey engine starter, *125*
Poona, India, *98, 178, 179*

Qaboos, Sultan of Abu Dhabi, *106, 112*
Qatar, Hunters supplied to, *112, 190, 200, 201, 213*

Rayak, Lebanon, *180*
Republic F-84 Thunderjet, *8, 92*
Republic of Singapore Air Force, *111*
Rhodesia (Zimbabwe), Hunters supplied to, *106, 107, 164, 167, 174, 175, 177, 179, 183, 206*
Richards, Anthony, *23*
Riyadh, Saudi Arabia, *110*
Roberts, Maj R.O., USAF, *53*
Rolls-Royce Avon, *4, 13, 16, 17, 20, 24, 26, 27, 32, 34, 39, 40, 46, 50, 51, 53, 54, 70-72, 79, 80, 82, 91, 93, 97, 98, 105, 106, 115, 125, 131, 135, 136, 188, 199*
Rolls-Royce Ltd, *16, 20, 31, 34, 50, 52*
Rolls-Royce Nene, *11, 12*
Rolls-Royce Tay, *14*
Royal Air Force College, Cranwell, *75*
Royal Air Force Maintenance Units, *40, 53, 58, 78, 82, 86, 95, 138 et seq*
Royal Air Force Squadrons:
No 1, *43, 53, 75, 83, 85;* No 2, *86;* No 4, *86;* No 8, *75, 82, 85, 86;* No 14, *40, 58;* No 15, *133;* No 19, *53, 75;* No 20, *41, 85;* No 26, *40;* No 28, *75, 82, 85;* No 34, *43, 53, 58;* No 41, *31, 43;* No 43, *32, 42, 53, 75, 85;* No 45, *133;* No 54, *18, 33, 41, 58, 75, 85;* No 56, *31, 43, 75, 160;* No 58, *133;* No 63, *53;* No 65, *58, 75;* No 66, *42, 58, 75, 78;* No 67, *42;* No 74, *42, 58, 75, 78;* No 92, *42, 58, 75, 78;* No 93, *39, 42;* No 98, *40;* No 111, *41, 42, 53, 58, 64-65, 75;* No 112, *42;* No 118, *40, 58;* No 130, *42;* No 208, *59, 75, 84;* No 222, *32, 41;* No 234, *42;* No 245, *42;* No 247, *32, 40, 41, 58;* No 257, *32, 42, 43;* No 263, *32, 42, 43, 58;* No 402, *75*
Royal Air Force Stations:
Acklington, *58;* Biggin Hill, *43;* Brawdy, *79, 133;* Bruggen, *42;* Bückeberg, *42;* Chivenor, *32, 41, 74, 75, 76;* Church Fenton, *53;* Duxford, *58;* Geilenkirchen, *42;* Gutersloh, *75, 86;* Halton, *135-180;* Honington, *79, 133;* Horsham

St Faith, *42, 58, 82;* Jever, *39, 40, 42, 58, 75;* Kai Tak, *75, 85;* Kemble, *40;* Khormaksar, *75, 86;* Leconfield, *42;* Leuchars, *31, 32, 41, 42;* Linton-on-Ouse, *42, 58;* Lyneham, *40;* Manby, *41;* Marham, *32;* Melksham, *28, 135;* North Weald, *41, 42, 53, 95;* Odiham, *32, 41, 43;* Oldenburg, *41, 58;* Pembrey, *32;* Stradishall, *42;* Tangmere, *27, 43, 55, 58-59;* Valley, *78;* Waterbeach, *43, 53;* Wattisham, *32, 42, 43;* Wittering, *133*
Royal Air Force Units: Central Fighter Establishment, West Raynham, *22, 31, 32-34, 40, 44, 75, 138 et seq;* No 1 Tactical Weapons Unit, Brawdy, *79, 133;* No 4 Flying Training School, Valley, *78;* No 229 Operational Conversion Unit, *32, 74, 75;* No 233 Operational Conversion Unit, *32, 33;* No 337 Operational Conversion Unit, *79, 133;* Royal Air Force Flying College, Manby, *41*
Royal Australian Air Force, *91*
Royal Danish Air Force, *94*
Royal Jordanian Air Force, *106, 208, 210*
Royal Naval Air Stations: Ford, *40;* Lossiemouth, *87-89;* Yeovilton, *88, 89*
Royal Netherlands Air Force, *92*
Royal Saudi Air Force, *110*
Royal Swedish Air Force (*Flygvapnet*), *92, 93, 112*
Rustington, Sussex, *27*

Saab BT9K bombing computer, *105*
Saab-32 Lansen, *93*
Saab-35 Draken, *93*
Saudi Arabia, Hunters supplied to, *78, 106, 110, 111, 165, 176, 177, 182, 186-187, 208, 210*
Säve, Sweden, *93*
Sayer, P.E.G., *18*
SEPECAT Jaguar, *132*
Shamsaddine, Lt, LAF, *171*
Sharjah, Abu Dhabi, *112*
Short Bros Ltd, *89*
Silyn-Roberts, Air Commodore Glynn, *26*
Simpson, Duncan, *18, 44, 93, 140 et seq*
Singapore, Hunters exported to, *111, 146-150, 152, 153, 158, 166-169, 171-177, 180-183, 190, 212*
Six-Day War, 1967, *104, 106, 110*
Sizer, Sqdn Ldr W.M., DFC, *32*
Skrydstrup, Denmark, *94*

Smith-Carington, Sqdn Ldr J.H., *40*
Soesterberg, Holland, *96, 199*
Sonderman, Maj, R Neth AF, *96*
Sowrey, Sqdn Ldr J.A., *145 et seq*
Specifications, Air Ministry: F.43/46, *10, 14;* F.44/46, *10, 14;* F.3/48, *14, 50, 69, 135;* F.4/48, *13, 14;* FR.164D, *85, 86;* E.38/46, *12;* N.7/46, *11;* T.157D, *70, 72*
Speed Records, World, *10, 27, 28*
Stenbeck, Major D., *Flygvapnet, 93, 190*
Strong, Maj Chris, RSAF, *111*
Suez Crisis, 1956, *43, 55, 56, 57, 99*
Sukhoi Su-7, *104*
Supermarine 510, *9, 12*
Supermarine Attacker, *87*
Supermarine Scimitar, *87*
Supermarine Swift, *5, 16, 17, 24, 28, 31, 41, 43, 45, 69, 130*
Super Priority, *24*
Sweden, Hunters supplied to, *42, 53, 92-93, 112, 145, 190, 192, 209*
Switzerland, Hunters supplied to, *57, 59, 74, 82, 98-99, 100-105, 112, 133, 145-159, 163, 164, 167, 169, 173, 181-183, 190, 192, 196-199, 207, 209*
Syrian Air Force, *104*

TACAN, navigation system, *79, 88, 89, 188, 189*
Talara, Peru, *95*
Tapper, Sqdn Ldr K.F.W., *32*
Tengah, Singapore, *111*
Thumrait, Oman, *112*
Tilak, Flt Lt, IAF, *98, 196*
Topp, Sqdn Ldr R.L., AFC, *53, 58*
Tupolev Tu-16, *112, 114*
Turin, Italy, *56*
Tuttle, Air Vice-Marshal Geoffrey, *26, 50, 51, 56, 69*

Uggla, Col S., *Flygvapnet, 93*

Vaerløse, Denmark, *193*
Vietnam War, *82*
Volkers, Fg Off E.J., *165*

Wade, Sqdn Ldr T.S., DFC, AFC, *7, 9, 18*
Walker, Sqdn Ldr S., *53*
Westland Wyvern, *87*
White, Sqdn Ldr J.G., *59*

Yom Kippur War, 1973, *104, 106, 112*

Zimbabwe, see Rhodesia